Corporate Director and Officer Liability

"Discretionaries" Not Fiduciaries

MARC I. STEINBERG

*Radford Chair in Law and Professor of Law,
Southern Methodist University (SMU), USA*

Oxford University Press is a department of the University of Oxford.
It furthers the University's objective of excellence in research, scholarship,
and education by publishing worldwide. Oxford is a registered trade mark of
Oxford University Press in the UK and in certain other countries.

Published in the United States of America by Oxford University Press
198 Madison Avenue, New York, NY 10016, United States of America.

© Marc I. Steinberg 2025

All rights reserved. No part of this publication may be reproduced, stored in a retrieval system, transmitted, used for text and data mining, or used for training artificial intelligence, in any form or by any means, without the prior permission in writing of Oxford University Press, or as expressly permitted by law, by license or under terms agreed with the appropriate reprographics rights organization. Inquiries concerning reproduction outside the scope of the above should be sent to the Rights Department, Oxford University Press, at the address above.

You must not circulate this work in any other form
and you must impose this same condition on any acquirer

Library of Congress Cataloging-in-Publication Data
Names: Steinberg, Marc I., author.
Title: Corporate director and officer liability : "discretionaries" not fiduciaries / Marc I. Steinberg.
Description: New York : Oxford University Press, 2025. |
Includes bibliographical references and index.
Identifiers: LCCN 2024058402 (print) | LCCN 2024058403 (ebook) |
ISBN 9780197751503 (hardback) | ISBN 9780197751527 (updf) |
ISBN 9780197751510 (epub) | ISBN 9780197751534 (online)
Subjects: LCSH: Tort liability of corporations—United States. |
Directors of corporations—Legal status, laws, etc.—United States
Classification: LCC KF1423 .S729 2025 (print) | LCC KF1423 (ebook) |
DDC 346.73/06642—dc23/eng/20241205
LC record available at https://lccn.loc.gov/2024058402
LC ebook record available at https://lccn.loc.gov/2024058403

DOI: 10.1093/9780197751534.001.0001

The manufacturer's authorised representative in the EU for product safety is
Oxford University Press España S.A. of El Parque Empresarial San Fernando
de Henares, Avenida de Castilla, 2 – 28830 Madrid (www.oup.es/en or
product.safety@oup.com). OUP España S.A. also acts as importer into Spain
of products made by the manufacturer.

Dedication

This book is dedicated to my sons Avi (A.B.) and Phillip (Bear), my daughter Alexandra (Alex), and her husband Jesse. I also dedicate this book to the SMU School of Law. I have served on the SMU faculty for over thirty-five years at this wonderful law school. Also, this book is dedicated to those persons who have been instrumental in my career—my Mother Phyllis Steinberg, my Father Gerald Steinberg, and my Sister Nancy Burman, as well as my professional mentors, US Court of Appeals Judge Stanley Barnes, US Supreme Court Justice Arthur Goldberg, US Senator Robert Griffin, and SEC Enforcement Director and US District Court Judge Stanley Sporkin. Thank you for your encouragement, support, and love.

Contents

Table of Cases   xi
Acknowledgments   xxiii
About the Author   xxv

1. Corporate Directors and Officers Are "Discretionaries"—Not Fiduciaries   1
   - I. The Misnomer of Fiduciary Status   1
   - II. Why Does It Matter?   2
   - III. The Meaning and Responsibilities of a Corporate Fiduciary   4
   - IV. Corporate Directors Compared to Corporate Officers   5
   - V. Shareholder Primacy versus Constituency Approach   7
   - VI. Standards of Conduct versus Standards of Liability   8
   - VII. Summary of Contents   10
   - VIII. Importance of This Book   15

2. Fiduciary Duties in Business Enterprises: A Historical and Contemporary Perspective   17
   - I. Introduction   17
   - II. Select Corporate Law Cases: Lax Director and Officer Fiduciary Standards   18
   - III. Unincorporated Business Enterprises: Fiduciary Duty Standards   21
     - A. The Uniform Acts: Judicial Application   22
     - B. Delaware Law: Statutes and Case Law   26
   - IV. The Diminution of Fiduciary Duties in Unincorporated Enterprises   28

3. The Illusion of Corporate Director and Officer Fiduciary Duty: The Duty of Care, the Business Judgment Rule, and Exculpation Statutes   31
   - I. Introduction   31
   - II. The Duty of Care   33
   - III. The Business Judgment Rule   36
   - IV. Director and Officer Exculpation Statutes   42
   - V. "Discretionaries"—Not Fiduciaries   48

4. The Duty of Loyalty: Far More Bark than Bite   51
   - I. Setting the Stage   51

viii CONTENTS

    II. Waiving the Fiduciary Duty of Loyalty   53
       A. Obligations Expressly Addressed by Contract   53
       B. Fiduciary Waivers Pursuant to Stockholder Agreements   54
       C. Statutory Authorization of Waivers:
          Corporate Opportunities   57
       D. Close Corporation Shareholder Agreements   59
       E. No Longer Hallowed Ground   61
   III. State Statutes Exculpating Duty of Loyalty Breaches   61
       A. Select State Statutes: Exculpation for Duty of
          Loyalty Breaches   62
       B. The Delaware Exculpation Statute: In Reality,
          Exculpating Loyalty Breaches   64
       C. Exculpation Statutes: Corporate Directors and
          Officers Are Not Fiduciaries   66
   IV. The Duty of Good Faith   66
    V. Interested Director and Officer Transactions   70
   VI. The Corporate Opportunity Doctrine   75
  VII. Far More Bark Than Bite   80

5. Derivative Litigation: Corporate Directors
   Are "Discretionaries"   83
     I. Discretionary Rather than Fiduciary Status   83
    II. Demand Required–Demand Excused Jurisdictions   87
       A. Demand Required Cases: The Permissive Business
          Judgment Rule Applied   87
       B. Demand Excused Cases, Same Result: The Permissive
          Business Judgment Rule   89
       C. Demand Excused Cases: The Prospect of Fiduciary Standards   91
       D. Applicable Standards for Board Excusal   93
       E. The Myth of the Reasonable Doubt Standard   94
   III. Universal Demand Jurisdictions   96
       A. Applicable Standards for Dismissal of Derivative Litigation   98
       B. Minimizing the Existence of Independent Director Bias   100
       C. Absence of Fiduciary Standards   102
   IV. State Approaches That Had (But No Longer Have)
       Fiduciary Substance   103
    V. The Lack of Fiduciary Standards   106

6. Mergers, Acquisitions, and Dispositions: A Semblance of
   Fiduciary Duty   109
     I. The Presence of Differing Standards   109
    II. Business Judgment Rule Prevalence in the M&A Setting   110
   III. Tender Offers: Differing Levels of Judicial Review   115
       A. Application of the Unocal Modified Business Judgment Rule   115
       B. The Revlon Sale Standard   119

    IV. Parent–Subsidiary Relations: The Prospect of Fiduciary
        Standards   122
        A. The Implementation of Structural Safeguards:
            Business Judgment Rule Application   124
        B. Short-Form Mergers: Minority Shareholders
            Relegated to Appraisal in Delaware   125
        C. A Glimpse at Other States: Appraisal Sole Remedy in
            Merger Transactions   127
    V. "Discretionaries" Sometimes Have Fiduciary Duties   128

7. Close Corporations: The Presence (or Waiver) of
   Fiduciary Duties   129
    I. Setting the Stage   129
    II. Close Corporations (Fiduciary Duties) Likened
       to Partnerships   132
    III. The Diminution of Fiduciary Duties in Close Corporations   136
       A. Exculpation Statutes   137
       B. Taking of Corporate Opportunities   139
       C. Unanimous Shareholder Agreements   141
    IV. The Status of Fiduciary Duties in Close Corporations   143

8. Rhetoric versus Reality: The Federal Securities Laws   145
    I. Introduction   145
    II. US Supreme Court Pronouncements: Directors and
       Officers Are Fiduciaries   147
    III. The Federal Securities Laws: The Fiduciary Duty Misnomer   150
       A. Section 11 of the Securities Act: The Semblance of
          Fiduciary Standards   151
          1. Statements of Belief: The Slighting of Section 11's
             Prudent Man Standard   158
          2. Forward-Looking Statements: Abandoning the
             Prudent Man Standard   161
          3. Would a Prudent Man or Woman Act in This Manner?   162
       B. Section 10(b) of the Securities Exchange Act:
          Abandoning Fiduciary Standards   164
          1. Rejection of a Federal Fairness Standard   165
          2. Requiring Pleading and Proof of Knowing Misconduct   166
          3. Statements of Belief and Projections:
             Lacking Fiduciary Content   168
          4. Puffery: Corporate Fiduciaries as Used Car Salespersons   169
          5. Insider Trading: Misapplication of Fiduciary Standards   170
       C. Analogous Example: Investment Adviser Fees   173
    IV. Summation: "Discretionaries," Not Fiduciaries   174

9. Corporate Directors and Officers Are "Discretionaries":
    Proposed Standards of Liability   177
    I.   Setting the Stage   177
    II.   The Business Judgment Rule   178
    III. Exculpation Statutes   180
    IV.   Lack of Good Faith   182
    V.   Interested Director and Officer Transactions   183
    VI.   Derivative Litigation   186
    VII. "Independent" Director: Misapplication of Standards   190
    VIII. Conclusion   194

10. The Clear Reality: "Discretionaries" Not Fiduciaries   195
    I.   Corporate Directors and Officers Are "Discretionaries"   195
    II. A Review of the Book's Scope, Concepts, and Objectives   198
    III. The Importance of This Book   204

Index   205

Table of Cases

UNITED KINGDOM

Bristol & West Building Society v. Mathew, [1998] Ch. 1 (C.A.) 4n.17
Charitable Corporation v. Sutton, 2 Atk. 404 (1742) 2n.6

INTERNATIONAL CASES

Brazil

Brazilian Rubber Plantations & Estates, In re, 27 Times L. Rep. 109 (1910) 19n.13

United Kingdom

Bristol & West Building Society v. Mathew, [1998] Ch. 1 (C.A.) 4n.17
Charitable Corporation v. Sutton, 2 Atk. 404 (1742) 2n.6

United States

A. Teixeira & Co. v. Teixeira, 699 A.2d 1383 (R.I. 1998) 133n.24
Aaron v. Securities and Exchange Commission, 446 U.S. 680 (1980) 163–64n.91,
                164–65n.95, 167n.107, 181n.18, 202n.45
Adler v. Klawans, 267 F.2d 840 (2d Cir. 1959) 149–50n.27
Aetna, Inc. Securities Litigation, In re, 617 F.3d 272 (3d Cir. 2010) 169n.119
AgFeed USA, LLC, In re, 546 B.R. 318 (Bankr. Del. 2016) 40n.48, 47n.83
Air Products & Chemicals, Inc. v. Airgas, 16 A.3d 48 (Del. Ch. 2011) 116n.33
Akerman v. Oryx Communications, Inc., [1984 Transfer Binder]
 Fed. Sec. L. Rep. (CCH) (S.D.N.Y. 1984), aff'd, 810 F.2d 336
 (2d Cir. 1987) 151–52n.32
Alarm.com Holdings, Inc. v. ABS Capital Partners Inc., 2018 WL 3006118
 (Del. Ch. 2018) 58n.27
Albert v. Alex. Brown Management Services, Inc., 2005 WL 2130607
 (Del. Ch. 2005) 40n.47
Alford v. Shaw, 358 S.E.2d 323 (N.C. 1987) 85n.15, 103–4n.82, 189n.57, 189–90n.58
Alpert v. 28 Williams Street Corp., 473 N.E.2d 19 (N.Y. 1984) 123n.60
Amalgamated Bank v. Yahoo! Inc., 132 A.3d 752 (Del. Ch. 2016) 5n.19
Amerco v. Shoen, 907 P.2d 536 (Ariz. App. 1995) 79n.113
American Mining Corporation v. Theriault, 51 A.3d 1213 (Del. 2012) 186n.41, 186n.42
Anderson v. Magellan Health, Inc., 298 A.3d 734 (Del. Ch. 2023) 109–10n.3
Application of Topper, In re the, 433 N.Y.S.2d 359 (Sup. Ct. 1980) 134–35n.33
Aronson v. Lewis, 473 A.2d 805 (Del. 1984) 20n.18, 37n.27, 37n.30, 38n.33, 39n.42,
        72n.87, 84n.8, 87n.24, 93n.50, 95n.56, 101n.74, 192n.63, 196n.4
Asher v. Baxter International, Inc., 377 F.3d 727 (7th Cir. 2004) 14n.67, 161n.80
Atkins v. Topp Comm, Inc., 874 So.2d 626 (Fla. Ct. App. 2004) 96n.58

xii   TABLE OF CASES

Atkinson v. Marquart, 541 P.2d 556 (Ariz. 1975) 19n.10
Atlas Energy Resources, L.L.C., In re, 2010 WL 4273122 (Del. Ch. 2010) 27n.56
Attorney General v. Utica Insurance Company, 2 Johns Ch. 371 (N.Y. Ch. 1817) 2n.6
Auerbach v. Bennett, 47 N.Y.S. 2d 619, 393 N.E.2d 994
    (Ct. App. 1979) 12n.51, 38n.33, 86n.16, 90n.35, 91n.38, 188n.50, 188–89n.53
Avalon Holdings Corp. v. Gentile, 2023 WL 4744072 (S.D.N.Y. 2023)........ 149–50n.27

Baker Hughes Inc. Merger Litigation, In re, 2020 WL 6281427 (Del. Ch. 2020) ... 35n.22
Barkan v. Amsted Industries, Inc., 567 A.2d 1279 (Del. 1989)................. 120n.48
Barnes v. Andrews, 298 F. 614 (S.D.N.Y. 1924).............................. 33n.12
Barr v. Pittsburgh Plate Glass Co., 51 F. 33 (W.D. Pa. 1892)..................... 19n.11
Barth v. Barth, 659 N.E.2d 559 (Ind. 1995) 131n.10
Basic, Inc. v. Levinson, 485 U.S. 224 (1988)........................146–47n.11, 151n.29
Bay City Lumber Co. v. Anderson, 111 P.2d 771 (Wash. 1941) 4–5n.18
Bayberry Associates v. Jones, 783 S.W.2d 553 (Tenn. 1990) 121n.52
Beam ex rel. Martha Stewart Living Omnimedia v. Stewart,
    845 A.2d 1040 (Del. 2004) 95n.55, 192n.68
Benfield v. Wells, 749 S.E.2d 384 (Ga. Ct. App. 2013) 96n.58
Benihana of Tokyo, Inc. v. Benihana, Inc., 891 A.2d 150 (Del. Ch. 2005) 35n.20, 195n.2
Benihana of Tokyo, Inc. v. Benihana, Inc., 906 A.2d 114 (Del. 2006)............. 72n.86
Blasius Industries, Inc. v. Atlas Corp., 564 A.2d 651 (Del. Ch. 1988) 117n.37,
                                                                117–18n.39, 118n.43
Bliss Petroleum Co. v. McNally, 237 N.W. 53 (Mich. 1931)..................... 19n.11
Blue Chip Capital Fund II Ltd. v. Tubergen, 906 A.2d 827 (Del. Ch. 2006) 54n.10
Blue Chip Stamps v. Manor Drug Stores, 421 U.S. 723 (1975).................... 97n.61,
                                                                164–65n.95, 166n.104
Boardwalk Pipeline Partners, LP v. Bandera Master Fund LP,
    288 A.3d 1083 (Del. 2022) 10–11n.44, 17n.2, 28n.58, 131n.12, 136n.42
Boeing Company Derivative Litigation, In re, 2021 WL 4059934
    (Del. Ch. 2021)... 69n.72, 69n.76
Boland v. Boland, 31 A.3d 529 (Md. 2011)..................... 85n.12, 90n.34, 188n.50
Booth v. Robinson, 53 Md. 419 (1881).. 34n.19
Brandt v. Somerville, 692 N.W. 2d 144 (N.D. 2005) 76n.99
Brane v. Roth, 590 N.E.2d 587 (Ind. Ct. App. 1993).................... 33n.10, 46n.79
Brehm v. Eisner, 746 A.2d 244 (Del. 2000).............................. 8n.33, 40n.48
Brewster v. Brewster, 241 P.3d 357 (Utah App. 2010)....................... 99–100n.70
Bricklayers Pension Fund of Western Pennsylvania v. Brinkley,
    2024 WL 3384823 (Del. Ch. 2024) 68n.69
Burg v. Horn, 380 F.2d 897 (2d Cir. 1967) 77n.103, 77n.105
Burgess v. Patterson, 188 So.3d 537 (Miss. 2016) 99–100n.70
Burks v. Lasker, 441 U.S. 471 (1979) 90n.34

C&J Energy Services, Inc. v. City of Miami General Employees' and Sanitation
    Employees' Retirement Trust, 107 A.3d 1049 (Del. 2014)......... 120n.48, 120n.49
Calpers v. ANZ Securities, Inc., 137 S. Ct. 2042 (2017)..................... 151–52n.32
Capri v. Murphy, 856 F.2d 473 (2d Cir. 1988) 163–64n.91
Caremark International Inc. Derivative Litigation, In re, 698 A.2d 959
    (Del. Ch. 1996)...................... 11n.49, 67n.63, 67n.64, 67–68n.66, 68n.68,
                68n.69, 68n.71, 69n.73, 69n.75, 70n.78, 182n.21, 182n.24
Carvana Co. Stockholders Litigation, In re, 2024 WL 1300199
    (Del. Ch. 2024)... 91–92n.40, 92n.43

TABLE OF CASES   xiii

CCSB Financial Corp. v. Totta, 302 A.3d 387
  (Del. 2023)................................29n.68, 44n.67, 44n.69, 56n.19, 64n.52
Cede & Cede v. Technicolor, Inc., 634 A.3d 345 (Del. 1993).....................52n.5
Central Bank of Denver v. First Interstate Bank of Denver,
  511 U.S. 164 (1994)... 167n.110
Chen v. Howard-Anderson, 87 A.3d 648 (Del. Ch. 2014)............ 8n.33, 8n.34, 9n.40,
                                                  43n.61, 52–53n.9, 120n.51
Chur v. Eighth Judicial District Court, 458 P.3d 336 (Nev. 2020)......... 47n.82, 47n.83
Citigroup Shareholder Derivative Litigation, In re, 964 A.2d 106
  (Del. Ch. 2009).. 69n.73
City Capital Associates v. Interco, Inc., 551 A.2d 787 (Del. Ch. 1988)........... 116n.33
City of Coral Springs Police Officers' Pension Plan v. Dorsey, 2023 WL 3316246
  (Del. Ch. 2023).......................41n.51, 111n.9, 111n.10, 113n.18, 114n.21
City of Dearborn Heights v. Align Technology, Inc., 856 F.3d 605
  (9th Cir. 2017)... 159n.69, 159n.70, 160n.76
City of Edinburgh Council v. Pfizer, Inc., 754 F.3d 159 (3d Cir. 2014).......... 169n.119
Clark v. Lomas & Nettleton Financial Corp., 625 F.2d 49
  (5th Cir. 1980)..73–74n.92, 94n.52, 101n.75
Clovis Derivative Litigation, In re, 2019 WL 4850188 (Del. Ch. 2019)........... 69n.72
Cognizant Technology Solutions Corporation Derivative Litigation,
  In re, 101 F.4th 250 (3d Cir. 2024).. 87n.20
Cohen v. Ayers, 596 F.2d 733 (7th Cir. 1979)............................. 185–86n.40
Colon v. Bumble, Inc., 305 A.3d 352 (Del. Ch. 2023) 44n.68, 64n.52
Colorado & Utah Coal Co. v. Harris, 49 P.2d 429 (Colo. 1935).................. 19n.11
Columbia Pipeline Group, Inc., In re, 2021 WL 772562 (Del. Ch. 2021)......... 35n.22,
                         43n.65, 47n.84, 65n.53, 67n.61, 73n.88, 89n.32, 103n.80, 120n.48
Construction Industry Laborers Pension Fund v. Bingle,
  2022 WL 4102492 (Del. Ch. 2022) 69n.73
Cornerstone Therapeutics Inc. Stockholder Litigation, In re,
  115 A.3d 1173 (Del. 2015) 43n.61
Cort v. Ash, 422 U.S. 66 (1975)... 166n.104
Corwin v. KKR Financial Holdings LLC, 125 A.3d 304 (Del. 2015) 38n.34, 111n.8,
                                            112n.12, 113n.16, 121nn.53–55
Coster v. UIP Companies, Inc., 300 A.3d 656 (Del. 2023) 109n.1, 115n.28, 117n.38,
                                                  118n.41, 118n.42, 119n.44
Craftmatic Securities Litigation, In re, 890 F.2d 628 (3d Cir. 1989) 160n.74, 163–64n.91
Crosby v. Beam, 548 N.E.2d 217 (Ohio 1989)....................130nn.9–11, 133n.22
Daily Income Fund, Inc. v. Fox, 464 U.S. 523 (1984)........................... 92n.41
Davis v. The Rock Creek L. R. & M. Co., 55 Cal. 359 (1880) 70–71n.79
Demoulas v. Demoulas Super Markets, Inc., 677 N.E.2d 159 (Mass. 1997) 13n.60,
                                                        79n.113, 133n.24
Derouen v. Murray, 604 So. 2d 1086 (Miss. 1992)............................ 79n.113
Desigoudar v. Meyercord, 108 Cal. App. 4th 173, 133 Cal. Rptr. 2d 408
  (Ct. App. 2003) 12n.51, 90n.34, 188n.50
Detroit Fidelity & Surety Co. v. Wichita Falls, First National Bank,
  66 S.W.2d 406 (Tex. App. 1933) 19n.11
Dieckman v. Regency GP, L.P., 155 A.3d 358 (Del. 2017)................ 27n.56, 28n.60
Dirks v. Securities and Exchange Commission, 463 U.S. 646 (1983)...........170n.121,
                                      170n.123, 170n.125, 171n.129, 171n.130, 172n.131
Disney v. Gollan, 233 S.W.3d 591 (Tex. App. 2007) 60n.40

xiv   TABLE OF CASES

District of Columbia v. Wesby, 583 U.S. 48 (2018) 2n.8
Dodge v. Ford Motor Co., 170 N.W. 668 (Mich. 1919). 20n.16, 20n.17, 36n.25, 178n.3
Dole Food Co. Stockholder Litigation, In re, 2015 WL 5052214
    (Del. Ch. 2015) 123–24n.61
Donahue v. Davis, 68 So. 2d 163 (Fla. 1953) 21n.22
Donahue v. Rodd Electrotype Co. of New England, Inc.,
    328 N.E.2d 505 (Mass. 1975) 13n.58, 129n.1, 130n.8, 201n.35
Donoghue v. Bulldog Investors General Partnership, 696 F.3d 170
    (2d Cir. 2012). 149–50n.27
Dow Chemical Company Derivative Litigation, In re, 2010 WL 66769
    (Del. Ch. 2010) 111n.9
Drury v. Cross 74 U.S. 299 (1868) 148n.15
DSI Renal Holdings, LLC, In re, 574 B.R. 446 (D. Del. 2017) 35n.20, 195n.2
Duffy v. Piazza Construction Inc., 815 P.2d 267 (Wash. App. 1991). 22n.28

Edelman v. Fruehauf Corp., 798 F.2d 882 (6th Cir. 1986). 121n.52
Elkind v. Liggett & Myers, Inc., 635 F.2d 156 (2d Cir. 1980). 171n.129, 172n.131
Ellzey v. Fyr Pruf, Inc., 376 So. 2d 1328 (Miss. 1979). 75n.96
Emerald Partners v. Berlin, 726 A.2d 1215 (Del. 1999). 43n.61, 186n.41
Enea v. Superior Court, 132 Cal. App. 4th 1559 (Cal. App. 2005). 23n.32
Enyart v. Merrick, 34 P.2d 629 (Ore. 1934) 15n.69
Ernst & Ernst v. Hochfelder, 425 U.S. 185 (1976) 14n.66, 146n.9, 166n.104,
                                                  167n.106, 167n.108, 167n.110, 181n.18, 202n.45
Escott v. BarChris Construction Corporation, 283 F. Supp. 643
    (S.D.N.Y. 1968) 6n.24, 152n.36, 153n.38, 154n.46, 181n.18, 202n.44
European & North American Railway Co. v. Poor, 59 Me. 277 (1871) 70–71n.79

Farber v. Servan Land Co., 662 F.2d 371 (5th Cir. 1981). 75n.95, 76n.99
FDIC v. Bierman, 2 F.3d 1424 (7th Cir.1993) 33n.13
Federal Deposit Insurance Corporation v. Johnson, 2014 WL 5324057
    (D. Nev. 2014) 40n.49
Federal Deposit Insurance Corporation v. Perry, 2012 WL 589569
    (C.D. Cal. 2012) 5n.22, 38n.36, 178n.4
Feit v. Leasco Data Processing Equipment Corp., 332 F. Supp. 544
    (E.D.N.Y. 1971) 153n.43, 154n.46
Fir Tree Value Master Fund L.P. v. Jarden Corp., 236 A.3d 313 (Del. 2020) 126n.69
Firefighters' Pension System of the City of Kansas City v. Presidio, Inc.,
    251 A.3d 212 (Del. Ch. 2021). 113n.16, 121n.54
Fix v. Fix Material Co., 538 S.W.2d 351 (Mo. App. 1976). 135n.34
Flannery v. Genomic Health, Inc., 2021 WL 3615540 (Del. Ch. 2021) 35n.22
Fliegler v. Lawrence, 361 A.2d 218 (Del. 1976). 71n.82, 84n.6, 183n.29
Flood v. Synutra International Inc., 195 A.3d 754 (Del. 2018). 112n.14, 125n.64
Fought v. Morris, 543 So.2d 167 (Miss. 1989). 135n.38
Fox Corporation/Snap Inc., In re, 312 A.3d 636 (Del. 2024). 43n.60
Francis v. United Jersey Bank, 432 A.2d 814 (N.J. 1981). 33n.10, 33n.13, 34n.16
Freedman v. Adams, 58 A.3d 414 (Del. 2013) 41n.53

Gale v. Bershad, 1998 WL 118022 (Del. Ch. 1998). 54n.10
Galindo v. Stover, 2022 WL 226848 (Del. Ch. 2022) 109n.1
Ganino v. Citizens Utilities Co., 228 F.3d 154 (2d Cir. 2000) 151n.29
Gantler v. Stephens, 965 A.2d 695 (Del. 2009) 5n.21, 31n.1, 52–53n.9

TABLE OF CASES   XV

Gartenberg v. Merrill Lynch Asset Management, Inc., 694 F.2d 923
    (2d Cir. 1982)...173n.138, 173n.139
Gatz Properties, LLC v. Auriga Capital Corporation, 59 A.3d 1206 (Del. 2012)... 26n.52
General Motors Class H Shareholders Litigation, In re, 734 A.2d 611
    (Del. Ch. 1999)...111n.8
Gigax v. Repka, 615 N.E.2d 644 (Ohio App. 1992)...133n.23
Gimbal v. Signal Companies, Inc., 316 A.2d 599 (Del. Ch.), aff'd,
    316 A.2d 619 (Del. 1974)..37n.28, 111n.7
Gimpel v. Bolstein, 477 N.Y.S.2d 1014 (Sup. Ct. 1984)...135n.34
Glassman v. Unocal Exploration Corporation, 777 A.2d 242
    (Del. 2001)..12n.54, 125n.67, 126n.68, 126n.72
Globe Woolen Company v. Utica Gas and Electric Company, 121 N.E. 378
    (N.Y. 1918)...2n.6
Goldstein v. Alodex Corp., 409 F. Supp. 1201 (E.D. Pa. 1976)..................154n.46
Gordon v. Verizon Communications, Inc., 148 A.D.3d 146
    (N.Y. App. Div. 2017)...109–10n.3
Gossett v. St. Paul Fire and Marine Insurance Company, 427 So. 2d 386
    (Fla. Dist. App. 1983)..21n.22
Gotham Partners, L.P. v. Hallwood Realty Partners, L.P., 817 A.2d 160
    (Del. 2002)...27n.53
Gould v. American-Hawaiian Steamship Company, 535 F.2d 761
    (3d Cir. 1976)..163–64n.91, 181n.18
Gratz v. Claughton, 187 F.2d 46 (2d Cir. 1951)...........................149–50n.27
Green v. Santa Fe Industries, Inc., 533 F.2d 1283 (2d Cir. 1976), rev'd,
    430 U.S. 462 (1977)..........................13n.62, 145n.1, 147n.12, 165n.100,
                                                166n.101, 166n.103, 166, 202n.40
Grill v. Hoblitzell, 771 F. Supp. 709 (D. Md. 1991)............................45n.73
Grimes v. Donald, 673 A.2d 1207 (Del. 1996)...................................84n.5
Guge v. Kassel Enterprises, Inc., 962 N.W.2d 764 (Iowa 2021) 135n.35
Gustafson v. Alloyd Company, 513 U.S. 561 (1995).......................163–64n.91
Guth v. Loft, Inc., 5 A.2d 503 (Del. 1939).................51n.4, 52n.6, 75n.96, 76n.100
Guzman v. Johnson, 483 P.3d 531 (Nev. 2021) 21n.20, 47n.83

Halliburton Co. v. Erica P. John Fund, Inc., 573 U.S. 258 (2014).............164–65n.95
Hanson Trust v. ML SCM Acquisition, Inc., 781 F.2d 264 (2d Cir. 1986) 121n.52
Harcum v. Lovoi, 2022 WL 29695 (Del. Ch. 2022) 35n.22
Harden v. Eastern States Public Service Co., 122 A. 705 (Del. Ch. 1923) 2n.6
Harman International, Inc. Securities Litigation, In re, 791 F.3d 90
    (D.C. Cir. 2015)...14n.68
Harris v. Ivax Corporation, 182 F.3d 799 (11th Cir. 1999) 161n.81
Harris v. TD Ameritrade, Inc., 805 F.2d 664 (6th Cir. 2015).................146–47n.11
Harrison Metal Capital III, L.P. v. Mathe, 2024 WL 1299579 (Del. Ch. 2024).....94n.51
Harrison v. United States, 200 U.S. 662 (6th Cir. 1912).......................169n.117
Hart v. Kline, 116 P.2d 672 (Nev. 1941)..40n.49
Harvard Coll. v. Amory, 26 Mass. (9 Pick.) 446 (1830).........................152n.35
Hasan v. Clevetrust Realty Investors, 729 F.2d 372 (6th Cir. 1982)..............101n.75,
                                                                    102n.76, 189n.56
Hathaway v. Huntley, 188 N.E. 616 (Mass. 1933).....................33n.10, 34n.14
Hayes Oyster Co. v. Keypoint Oyster Co., 391 P.2d 979 (Wash. 1964)............72n.84
Hayes v. Crown Central Petroleum Corp., 78 Fed. Appx. 857 (4th Cir. 2003) 45n.73
H-B Limited Partnership v. Wimmer, 257 S.E.2d 770 (Va. 1979) 4n.17

xvi   TABLE OF CASES

Heineman v. Datapoint Corp., 611 A.2d 950 (Del. 1992)...................... 93n.48
Herman & MacLean v. Huddleston, 459 U.S. 375 (1983) 164–65n.95, 165n.96
Hoffman Steam Coal Company v. Cumberland Coal & Iron Company,
    16 Md. 456 (1860)... 4–5n.18, 70–71n.79
Holcomb v. Forsyth, 113 So. 516 (Ala. 1927).................................. 71n.80
Hollinger v. Titan Capital Corporation, 914 F.2d 1564 (9th Cir. 1990) 65n.55,
                                                                  167n.106, 181n.17
Hollis v. Hill, 232 F.3d 460 (5th Cir. 2000) 133n.24
Houle v. Low, 556 N.E.2d 51 (Mass. 1990)................................... 105n.86
Howing Co. v. Nationwide Corp., 826 F.2d 1470 (6th Cir. 1987),
    927 F.2d 263 (6th Cir. 1991), 972 F.2d 700 (6th Cir. 1992)................. 127n.77

Ikon Office Solutions, Inc. Securities Litigation, In re, 277 F.3d 658
    (3d Cir. 2002)... 65n.55, 167n.106, 181n.17
Imperial Credit Industries, Inc., In re, 2008 WL 4346785 (C.D. Cal. 2008) 71n.82
Indiana Public Retirement System v. SAIC, Inc., 818 F.3d 85 (2d Cir. 2016) 169n.119
International Brotherhood of Electrical Workers v. Tucci, 70 N.E.3d 918
    (Mass. Sup. Jud. Ct. 2017)... 96n.58

J & J Celcom v. AT&T Wireless Services, Inc., 169 P.3d 823 (Wash. 2007) 25n.46
J&R Marketing SEP v. General Motors Corp., 549 F.3d 484 (6th Cir. 2008) 146–47n.11
Jacobson v. Brooklyn Lumber Co., 76 N.E. 1075 (N.Y. 1906).................... 71n.80
Janus Capital Group, Inc. v. First Derivative Traders, 564 U.S. 135 (2011)...... 167n.110
Johnston v. Greene, 121 A.2d 919 (Del. Ch. 1956)............................ 77n.104
Jones v. Harris Associates L.P., 559 U.S. 335 (2010) 173n.137, 173n.138, 173n.139
Joy v. North, 692 F.2d 880 (2d Cir. 1982) 97n.62, 102n.76, 187n.46, 189n.56

Kahn v. Lynch Communication, Inc., 638 A.2d 1110 (Del. 1994).... 124–25n.63, 186n.41
Kahn v. M&F Worldwide Corp., 88 A.3d 634 (Del. 2014) 112n.14, 124–25n.63,
                                                                  125n.64, 201n.34
Kallick v. Sandridge Energy, Inc., 68 A.3d 242 (Del. 2013)..................... 40n.48
Kamen v. Kemper Financial Services, Inc., 500 U.S. 90 (1991) 84n.8, 87n.21,
                                                                  88n.25, 92n.41
Kaplan v. Peat, Marwick, Mitchell & Co., 540 A.2d 726 (Del. 1988) 87n.24
Kaplan v. Wyatt, 499 A.2d 1184 (Del. 1985) 92n.43
Kellner v. AIM ImmunoTech, 2024 WL 3370273 (Del. 2024).................. 118n.41
Kemp & Beatley, 473 N.E.2d 1181 .... 135n.35
Kemp & Beatley, Inc., In the Matter of, 473 N.E.2d 1173
    (N.Y. 1984)... 134n.27, 134–35n.33
Kenneth Cole Productions, Inc., Shareholder Litigation, In re, 52 N.E.3d 214
    (N.Y. 2016).. 124–25n.63
Kihm v. Mott, 2021 WL 3883875 (Del. Ch. 2023) 111n.8
Koehler v. The Black River Falls Iron Company, 67 U.S. 715 (1862)..... 4–5n.18, 147n.14
Kuznik v. Bees Ferry Associates, 538 S.E.2d 15 (S.C. App. 2000)................ 22n.28

Labovitz v. Dolan, 545 N.E.2d 304 (Ill. App. 1989) 23n.32
Lagarde v. Anniston Lime & Stone Co., 28 So. 199 (Ala. 1900) 18n.7,
                                                                  19, 75n.95, 76n.101
Lancaster Loose Leaf Tobacco Co. v. Robinson, 250 S.W. 997 (Ky. 1923) 19n.11
Larkin v. Shah, 2016 WL 4485447 (Del. Ch. 2016) 112n.12, 113n.16, 121n.55
Lear Corp. Shareholder Litigation, In re, 967 A.2d 640 (Del. Ch. 2008)... 40n.46, 88n.28

TABLE OF CASES   xvii

Lebanon County Employees' Retirement Fund v. Collis, 311 A.3d 773
  (Del. 2023).. 68n.71, 69n.73
Lenois v. Lawal, 2017 WL 5289611 (Del. Ch. 2017)..................... 87n.23, 87n.24
Level 3 Communications, Inc. Securities Litigation, In re, 667 F.3d 1331
  (10th Cir. 2012).. 169n.119
Levine v. Smith, 591 A.2d 194 (Del. 1991)..........................91–92n.40, 93n.45
Lewis v. Anderson, 615 F.2d 778 (9th Cir. 1979)............................... 12n.53
Lewis v. Graves, 701 F.2d 245 (2d Cir. 1983) 192–93n.69
Lewis v. S.L. & E., Inc., 629 F.2d 764 (2d Cir. 1980) 18n.5, 72n.84
Lincoln Stores, Inc. v. Grant, 34 N.E.2d 704 (Mass. 1941) 19n.9
Livent, Inc. Noteholders Securities Litigation, In re, 355 F. Supp. 2d 722
  (S.D.N.Y. 2005) 153n.42, 153n.43
Lloyd v. CVB Financial Corp., 811 F.3d 1200 (9th Cir. 2016) 169n.119
Lofland v. Cahall, 118 A. 1 (Del. 1922)..2n.6
Lorenzo v. Securities and Exchange Commission, 139 S. Ct. 1094 (2019) 167n.110

Madison Realty Partners 7, LLC v. AG ISA, LLC, 2001 WL 406268
  (Del. Ch. 2001).. 54n.10
Maldonado v. Flynn, 413 A.2d 1251 (Del. Ch. 1980), rev'd and remanded
  sub nom., Zapata Corp. v. Maldonado, 430 A.2d 779 (Del. 1981) 12n.51, 38n.32,
            38n.33, 73–74n.92, 84–85n.10, 85n.14, 88n.25, 90n.37,
            91–92n.40, 92n.43, 92n.44, 93n.47, 101n.75, 103, 103–4n.82,
            106n.90, 188n.50, 188n.51, 189n.57, 189–90n.58, 198n.13
Mallory v. Mallory-Wheeler Co., 23 A. 708 (Conn. 1891) 70–71n.79
Malone v. Brincat, 722 A.2d 5 (Del. 1998) 127n.77, 147n.12
Manti Holdings, LLC v. Authentix Acquisition Co., 261 A.3d 1199
  (Del. 2021)...55–56n.16, 142n.69
Manufacturers Trust Co. v. Becker, 338 U.S. 304 (1949) 148n.20
Marchand v. Barnhill, 212 A.3d 805 (Del. 2019) 68n.69, 68n.71, 69n.72, 69n.76,
            84n.6, 91n.39, 93n.48, 95n.55, 192n.66
Marciano v. Nakash, 535 A.2d 400 (Del. 1987)....................... 72n.86, 184n.31
Martin v. D.B. Martin Co., 88 A. 612 (Del. Ch. 1913) 2n.6
Martin v. Martin, Martin & Richards, Inc., 12 S.W.3d 120 (Tex. App. 1999)....... 60n.40
Match Group, Inc. Derivative Litigation, In re, 315 A.3d 446
  (Del. 2024)..............................1n.1, 37n.27, 72n.86, 88n.25, 93n.47,
            122–23n.58, 123n.60, 124–25n.63, 184n.31, 185–86n.40
Matrix Initiatives, Inc. v. Siracusano, 563 U.S. 27 (2011)....................... 151n.29
McClure v. Borne Chemical Company, Inc., 292 F.2d 824
  (3d Cir. 1961).. 147n.12, 165n.97
McConnell v. Hunt Sports Enterprises, 725 N.E.2d 1193
  (Ohio App. 1999) 17n.2, 21n.22, 26n.48, 26n.50, 136n.43
McDonald's Corporation Shareholder Derivative Litigation,
  In re, 291 A.3d 652 (Del. Ch. 2023) 37–38n.31, 40n.45, 40n.47, 40n.48,
            41n.53, 88n.30, 114n.22, 196n.5, 199n.17
McDonald's Corporation Stockholder Derivative Litigation, In re,
  289 A.3d 343 (Del. Ch. 2023)......................... 21n.20, 67–68n.66, 68n.70,
            69n.74, 69n.77, 70n.78, 91n.39, 182n.24
McKey v. Swenson, 205 N.W. 583 (Mich. 1925) 71n.80
Meinhard v. Salmon, 164 N.E. 545 (N.Y. 1928) 10n.42, 21n.21, 22–23,
            26, 76n.100, 132n.20
Meiselman v. Meiselman, 307 S.E.2d 551 (N.C. 1983) 134n.32, 134–35n.33

xviii   TABLE OF CASES

Memphis & Charleston Railroad Company v. Wood, 7 So. 108 (Ala. 1889) 70–71n.79
Metro Storage International LLC v. Harron, 275 A.3d 810
    (Del. Ch. 2022) 5n.21, 6n.28, 8n.33, 35n.21, 35n.22, 38n.36, 52n.6
Miller v. American Real Estate Partners, LP, 2001 WL 1045643 (Del. Ch. 2001). . . 28n.57
Miller v. Miller, 222 N.W. 2d 71 (Minn. 1974) 75n.97, 76n.99
Miller v. Register and Tribune Syndicate, 336 N.W. 2d 709 (Iowa 1983) 73–74n.92,
                                                                                  101n.75, 104n.84
Mills Acquisition Co. v. Macmillan, Inc., 559 A.2d 1261 (Del. 1989) 120n.47
Mills v. Electric Auto-Lite Co., 396 U.S. 375 (1970) 83n.2
Mindbody, Inc. Stockholder Litigation, In re, 2023 WL 2518149
    (Del. Ch. 2023) 120n.49, 121n.54, 127n.77
MM Companies, Inc. v. Liquid Audio, Inc., 813 A.2d 1118 (Del. 2003) 117n.37
Monty v. Leis, 123 Cal. Rptr. 3d 641 (Cal. App 2011) 117n.36
Moore Corp. v. Wallace Computer Services, Inc., 907 F. Supp. 1545 (Del. 1995) 116n.33
Moran v. Household International, Inc., 500 A.2d 1346 (Del. 1985) 117n.34
Morrison v. Berry, 191 A.3d 268 (Del. 2018) 112n.12

N.Y. Automobile Co. v. Franklin, 97 N.Y.S. 781 (1905) 19n.11
Nemec v. Shrader, 991 A.2d 1120 (Del. 2010) 54n.11
Network Technologies, Inc. Stockholder Litigation, In re, 924 A.2d 171
    (Del. Ch. 2007) 120n.51
New Enterprise Associates 14 L.P. v. Rich, 295 A.3d 520 (Del. Ch. 2023) . . . 3n.10, 28n.60,
                          29n.68, 43n.64, 47n.84, 51n.1, 51n.2, 54–55n.15,
                          55–56n.16, 56n.17, 58n.27, 58n.28, 59n.30, 65n.53,
                          67n.61, 73n.88, 80n.115, 89n.32, 103n.80, 141n.66,
                          142n.69, 142n.70, 183n.26, 184n.33, 196n.6, 197n.12
Nixon v. Blackwell, 626 A.2d 1366 (Del. 1993) 129n.3, 132n.16, 132n.17, 136n.40
Northeast Harbor Golf Club, Inc. v. Harris, 725 A.2d 1018 (Me. 1999) 79n.113
Norton v. K-Sea Transportation Partners L.P., 67 A.3d 354 (Del. 2013) 28n.60

Omnibank of Mantee v. United Southern Bank, 607 So.2d 76 (Miss. 1992) 33n.10
Omnicare, Inc. v. Laborers District Council Construction Industry
    Pension Fund, 575 U.S. 175, 135 S. Ct. 1318 (2015) 14n.67, 158n.63, 158n.65,
                          159n.67, 159n.68, 159nn.69–71, 159–60, 160n.75,
                          160n.76, 162n.84, 163–64n.91, 202n.47
Omnicare, Inc. v. NCS Healthcare, Inc., 818 A.2d 914
    (Del. 2003) 12–13n.56, 110n.4, 117n.36
Oracle Corp. Derivative Litigation, In re, 2023 WL 3408772
    (Del. Ch. 2023) 111n.9, 113n.18
Orman v. Cullman, 794 A.2d 5 (Del. Ch. 2002) 84–85n.10

Packer v. Raging Capital Management, LLC, 105 F.4th 46 (2d Cir. 2024) 149–50n.27
Paramount Communications, Inc. v. QVC Network, Inc., 637 A.2d 34
    (Del. 1993) 119n.45, 119n.46, 120n.47, 120n.50
Paramount Communications, Inc. v. Time, Inc., 571 A.2d 1140
    (Del. 1990) 111–12n.11, 112n.12, 115n.27, 116n.31, 117n.34, 119n.45
Pattern Energy Group, Inc. Shareholders Litigation, In re, 2021 WL 1812674
    (Del. Ch. 2021) 35n.22
Pearson v. Concord Railroad Commission, 62 N.H. 537 (1883) 70–71n.79
Pennsylvania Railroad Co. v. Minis, 87 A. 1062 (Md. 1913) 71n.80
Pepper v. Litton, 308 U.S. 295 (1939) 148n.19

TABLE OF CASES   xix

Pinter v. Dahl, 486 U.S. 622 (1988) 163–64n.91
Pioneer Oil & Gas Co. v. Anderson, 151 So. 161 (Miss. 1934) 19n.9, 77n.102
Plumbers & Steamfitters Loc. 773 v. Danske Bank, 11 F.4th 90
    (2d Cir. 2021)... 14n.67, 169n.119
Primedia, Inc. Shareholders Litigation, In re, 67 A.3d 455 (Del. Ch. 2023) 91–92n.40
PSE & G Shareholder Litigation, In re, 801 A.2d 295 (N.J. 2002) 106n.88, 189–90n.58

Rales v. Blasband, 634 A.2d 929 (Del. 1993) 38n.33, 93n.50, 94n.52
Reading Co., In re, 711 F.2d 509 (3d Cir. 1983)................................ 54n.13
Red Top Cab Company v. Hanchett, 48 F.2d 236 (N.D. Cal. 1931)............... 19n.10
Reed v. Robinson, 220 P. 676 (Cal. App. 1923) 4–5n.18
Reis v. Hazlett Strip-Casting Corp., 28 A.3d 442 (Del. Ch. 2011) 8n.34, 9n.40, 52–53n.9
Remillard Brick Co. v. Remillard-Dandini Co., 241 P.2d 66 (Cal. App. 1952) 1n.1
Revlon, Inc. v. MacAndrews & Forbes Holdings, Inc., 506 A.2d 173
    (Del. 1986)............... 12–13n.56, 110n.4, 112n.15, 113n.16, 116n.30, 116n.32,
                  119n.45, 119n.46, 120nn.48–50, 120n.51, 121n.52,
                                  121n.53, 121n.54, 121–22, 128
Rexford Rand Corp. v. Ancel, 58 F.3d 1215 (7th Cir. 1995) 133n.24
Ritchie v. Rupe, 443 S.W.3d 856 (Tex. 2014)...........60n.40, 132n.16, 134n.29, 142n.73
Robinson v. Watts Detective Agency, Inc., 685 F.2d 729 (1st Cir. 1982)........... 33n.10
Rosenfeld v. Metals Selling Corp., 643 A.2d 1253 (Conn. 1994).... 6n.25, 38n.37, 178n.4
Ross Holding and Management Co. v. Advance Realty Group, L.L.C.,
    2014 WL 4374261 (Del. Ch. 2014) 27n.56, 28n.60
Ryan v. Gifford, 918 A.2d 341 (Del. Ch. 2007) 93n.48

S. Peru Copper Corp. Shareholder Derivative Litigation, 52 A.3d 761
    (Del. Ch. 2011)... 112n.12
Sage v. Culver, 41 N.E. Rep. 513 (N.Y. Ct. App. 1895)...........................18n.5
Salman v. United States, 137 S. Ct. 420 (1916)............................... 170n.125
Sanders v. John Nuveen & Co., Inc., 554 F.2d 790 (7th Cir. 1977)................ 65n.55,
                                                        167n.106, 181n.17
Sanofi Securities Litigation, In re, 816 F.3d 199 (2d Cir. 2016) 160n.75
Sarasota Firefighters' Pension Fund v. Inovalon, 2024 WL 1896096
    (Del. 2024)... 124–25n.63
Schnell v. Chris-Craft Industries, Inc., 285 A.2d 437 (Del 1971).....117n.37, 117–18n.39
Schnittger v. Old Home Consolidated Mining Co., 78 P. 9 (Cal. 1904) 71n.80
Schoen v. SAC Holding Co., 137 P. 3d 1171 (Nov. 2006)....................... 94n.52
Schreiber v. Burlington Northern, Inc., 472 U.S. 1 (1985) 166n.103
Sears Hometown and Outlet Stores, Inc., In re, 309 A.3d 474
    (Del. Ch. 2024)... 123–24n.61
Securities and Exchange Commission v. Capital Gains Research Bureau,
    Inc., 375 U.S. 180 (1963) 147n.12, 173n.137
Securities and Exchange Commission v. Chenery Corporation,
    318 U.S. 80 (1943)... 149n.24
Securities and Exchange Commission v. Texas Gulf Sulphur Co.,
    401 F.2d 833 (2d Cir. 1968)...............................151n.29, 170–71n.126
Segway Inc. v. Hong, 2023 WL 8643017 (Del. Ch. 2023) 67–68n.66, 68n.68, 182n.24
Seinfeld v. Verizon Communications, Inc., 909 A.2d 117 (Del. 2006) 91–92n.40
Shenker v. Laureate Education, Inc., 964 A.2d 675 (Md. 2009)................ 121n.52
Shlensky v. Wrigley, 237 N.E.2d 776 (Ill. App. 1968) 1n.2, 37–38n.31, 84n.6
Sifferle v. Micom Corp., 384 N.W.2d 503 (Minn. App. 1986) 127n.79

xx   TABLE OF CASES

Sinclair Oil Corp. v. Levien, 280 A.2d 717 (Del. 1971) 122n.57
Singer v. Singer, 634 P.2d 766 (Okla. App. 1981)........................ 17n.2, 24n.43
Singh v. Attenborough, 137 A.3d 151 (Del. 2016)............................. 121n.55
Skierka v. Skierka Brothers, Inc., 629 P.2d 214 (Mont. 1981).................. 135n.34
Slayton v. American Express Company, 604 F.3d 758 (2d Cir. 2010) 14n.68
Smith v. Atlantic Properties, Inc., 422 N.E.2d 798 (Mass. App. 1981) 131n.10
Smith v. Pacific Pools of Washington, Inc., 530 P.2d 658 (Wash. App. 1975) 34n.14
Smith v. Van Gorkom, 488 A.2d 858 (Del. 1985) 1n.2, 32n.9, 37n.28, 39n.40,
                                          42n.55, 88n.27, 111–12n.11, 178n.4, 184n.32
Sneed v. Webre, 358 S.W.3d 322 (Tex. 2011) 84n.7
Sneed v. Webre, 465 S.W.3d 169 (Tex. 2015) 87n.20, 132n.18
Software Toolworks, Inc. Securities Litigation, In re, 38 F.3d 1078 (9th Cir. 1994) 153n.42
Sojitz America Capital Corporation v. Kaufman, 141 Conn. App. 486 (2013) 99–100n.70
Solash v. Telex Corp., 1988 WL 3587 (Del. Ch. 1988) 40n.48
Sonet v. Plum Creek Timber Co., 722 A.2d 319 (Del. Ch. 1998).................. 27n.55
Sound Infiniti, Inc. v. Snyder, 237 P.3d 241 (Wash. 2010)....................... 127n.79
Southern Pac. Co. v. Bogert, 250 U.S. 483 (1919) 148n.18, 202n.41
Spiegel v. Buntrock, 571 A.2d 767 (Del. 1990) ... 87n.23, 92n.41, 93n.45, 97n.63, 187n.47
Starr v. Fordham, 648 N.E.2d 1261 (Mass. 1995) 22n.28
Stepak v. Schey, 533 N.E.2d 1072 (Ohio 1990) 127n.79
Stone v. Ritter, 911 A.2d 362 (Del. 2006) 11n.49, 21n.20, 44n.66, 45n.74,
                      52n.7, 66n.56, 66n.57, 67n.62, 67n.64, 67n.65, 68n.67,
                      81n.119, 172n.132, 182n.21, 182n.22, 196n.8
Stoneridge Investment Partners, LLC v. Scientific-Atlanta, Inc.,
    552 U.S. 148 (2008)... 167n.110
Straight Path Communications, Inc. Stockholder Litigation, In re,
    2023 WL 6399095 (Del. Ch. 2023)........................... 109n.1, 123–24n.61
Strong v. Repide, 213 U.S. 419 (1909) 148n.21, 149n.23
Sullivan v. Easco Corporation, 656 F. Supp. 531 (D. Md. 1987) 71n.82
Superintendent of Insurance v. Bankers Life & Casualty Co., 404 U.S. 6 (1971)..... 148n.19
Sutherland v. Sutherland, 2009 WL 857468 (Del. Ch. 2009) 44n.68

Teamsters Local 443 Health Services & Insurance Plan v. Chou,
    2023 WL 7986729 (Del. Ch. 2023) 95n.55, 105n.86, 192n.67
Tellabs, Inc. v. Makor Issues & Rights, Ltd., 127 S. Ct. 2499 (2007) 168n.112
Tesla Motors, Inc. Stockholder Litigation, In re, 298 A.3d 667
    (Del. 2023)....................................113n.16, 113n.18, 124n.62, 125n.64
Texas Gulf Sulphur 50th Anniversary Symposium, 71 SMU L. Rev.
    No. 3 (2018)...170–71n.126
Theriot v. Bourg, 691 So. 2d 213 (La. App. 1997).............................. 33n.10
Thompson v. Scientific Atlanta, Inc., 621 S.E.2d 796 (Ga. Ct. App. 2005)......... 12n.52
Today Homes, Inc. v. Williams, 634 S.E. 2d 737 (Va. 2006) 76n.99
Todd v. Diamond State Iron Co., 14 A. 27 (Del. Ct. App. 1888), aff 'd,
    8 Houst. 372 (Del. Ct. Err. & App. 1889).......................................2n.6
Tomczak v. Morton Thiokol, Inc., 1990 WL 42607 (Del. Ch. 1990)....... 40n.45, 88n.29
Tooley v. Donaldson, Lufkin & Jenrette, Inc., 845 A.2d 1031
    (Del. 2004)... 83n.1, 84n.5, 109n.1
Tornetta v. Musk, 2024 WL 343699 (Del. Ch. 2024) 71n.83
Tornetta v. Musk, 310 A.3d 430 (Del. Ch. 2024)............72n.86, 185–86n.40, 192n.63
Tower Air, Inc., In re, 416 F.3d 229 (3d Cir. 2005) 11n.45, 37n.27, 40n.50
Trados Incorporated Shareholder Litigation, In re, 73 A.3d 17
    (Del. Ch. 2013) 7n.32, 8n.35, 9n.39, 32n.7, 52–53n.9

TABLE OF CASES   xxi

TransCare Corporation, In re, 81 F.4th 37 (2d Cir. 2023)...................... 72n.84
Trulia, In re, 129 A.3d 884 (Del. Ch. 2016) 109–10n.3
TSC Industries, Inc. v. Northway, Inc., 426 U.S. 438 (1976).................... 151n.29
TVI Corporation v. Gallagher, 2013 WL 5809271 (Del. Ch. 2013) 52n.6
Twin-Lick Oil Company v. Marbury, 91 U.S. 587 (1875) 18n.6, 148n.16, 148n.19

United Food and Commercial Workers Union v. Zuckerberg,
    262 A.3d 1034 (Del. 2021) 9n.40, 32n.9, 35n.22, 38n.33, 39n.42, 67n.62,
                  84n.9, 87n.20, 87n.22, 87n.24, 93nn.49–51, 95n.54, 96n.57,
                  97n.60, 178n.5, 192n.64, 193n.72, 195n.1, 198n.13, 200n.28
United Health Group, Inc. Shareholder Derivative Litigation, In re,
    754 N.W.2d 544 (Minn. 2008) 90n.34
United States v. Blaszczak, 947 F.3d 19 (2d Cir. 2019), vacated and remanded
    on other grounds, 141 S. Ct. 1040 (2021), dismissal granted on other
    grounds, 56 F.4th 230 (2d Cir. 2022)................................... 172n.135
United States v. Chiarella, 588 F.2d 1358 (2d Cir. 1978), rev'd,
    445 U.S. 222 (1980)...................... 14n.64, 147n.12, 149n.25, 149–50n.27,
                  170n.121, 170n.122, 170–71nn.126–128, 202n.43
United States v. Havens, 446 U.S. 620 (1980)......................................2n.8
United States v. Melvin, 143 F. Supp. 3d 1354 (N.D. Ga. 2015) 172n.135
United States v. O'Hagan, 521 U.S. 642 (1997) 170n.121
United States v. Ramsey, 565 F. Supp. 3d 641 (E.D. Pa. 2021)................. 172n.135
Unitrin, Inc. v. American General Corp., 651 A.2d 1361
    (Del. 1995)............................ 12–13n.56, 115n.25, 115n.28, 120n.50
Unocal Corp. v. Mesa Petroleum Co., 493 A.2d 946 (Del. 1985)...... 12–13n.56, 110n.4,
              113n.16, 115n.24, 115n.26, 115–16n.29, 116n.32, 117n.36,
              117–18n.39, 118n.42, 119n.44, 121n.53

Versata Enterprises, Inc. v. Selectica, Inc., 5 A.3d 586 (Del. 2010) 12–13n.56, 116n.30
Volcano Corp. Stockholder Litigation, In re, 143 A.3d 727
    (Del. Ch. 2016) 112n.12, 113n.16, 121n.54

W.J. Bradley Mortgage Capital, L.L.C., In re, 598 B.R. 150 (Bankr. D. Del. 2019)...... 27n.56
Walgreen Co. Stockholder Litigation, In re, 832 F.3d 718 (7th Cir. 2016) 109–10n.3
Walt Disney Company Derivative Litigation, In re, 906 A.2d 27
    (Del. 2006).............. 4–5n.18, 11n.48, 44n.66, 66n.57, 66n.59, 84n.6, 183n.25
Walta v. Gallegos Law Firm, P.C., 40 P.3d 449 (N.M. App. 2001)................ 135n.38
Wardell v. Union Pacific Railroad Company, 103 U.S. 651 (1880) 70–71n.79, 148n.17
Weinberger v. Jackson, 1990 U.S. Dist. LEXIS 18394 (N.D. Cal. 1990) 155n.49
Weinberger v. UOP, Inc., 457 A.2d 701 (Del. 1983).....................12n.54, 123n.60,
              124–25n.63, 126n.69, 127n.77, 185–86n.40, 201n.34
West Palm Beach Firefighters' Pension Fund v. Moelis & Co.,
    311 A.3d 809 (Del. Ch. 2024).. 55–56n.16
Western States Life Insurance Company v. Lockwood, 135 P. 496 (Cal. 1913).........2n.6
Wildes v. Bitconnect International PLC, 25 F.4th 1341 (11th Cir. 2022)...... 163–64n.91
Wilkes v. Springside Nursing Home, Inc., 353 N.E.2d 657
    (Mass. 1976) 13n.59, 131n.10, 133n.25, 133n.26, 134n.30, 135n.38
Willard ex rel. Moneta Building Supply, Inc. v. Moneta Building Supply, Inc.,
    515 S.E.2d 277 (Va. 1999)... 34n.18
Williams Companies Stockholder Litigation, The, 2021 WL 754593
    (Del. Ch. 2021).. 116n.33
Witchko v. Schorsch, 2016 WL 3887289 (S.D.N.Y. 2016) 45n.74

xxii TABLE OF CASES

Witmer v. Arkansas Dailies, Inc., 151 S.W.2d 971 (Ark. 1941) 19n.11
WLR Foods, Inc. v. Tyson Foods, Inc., 65 F.3d 1172 (4th Cir. 1995) 37n.29, 178n.4
Wochos v. Tesla, Inc., 985 F.3d 1180 (9th Cir. 2021).................... 14n.68, 162n.82
Wolf v. Weinstein, 372 U.S. 633 (1963) 148n.20
Worldcom, Inc. Securities Litigation, In re, 2005 WL 638268
 (S.D.N.Y. 2005) 153n.43, 154nn.45–47
Worldcom, Inc. Securities Litigation, In re, 346 F. Supp. 2d 628
 (S.D.N.Y. 2004) 153n.42, 155n.52

Yanow v. Teal Industries, Inc., 422 A.2d 311 (Conn. 1979).................... 127n.79

Acknowledgments

I am delighted that this project has come to fruition. I thank the SMU Dedman School of Law, Dean Jason Nance, and the Brian and Fay Lidji Endowment Fund for supporting this project. I also thank SMU Law Librarians Gregory Ivy, Tim Gallina, and Tom Kimbrough as well as my research assistants Ben Gerzik and Ibrahim Nasir—their research assistance is greatly appreciated.

About the Author

Marc I. Steinberg is the Rupert and Lillian Radford Chair in Law and Professor of Law at the Southern Methodist University (SMU) Dedman School of Law. He is the director of the SMU Corporate Counsel Externship Program, the former director of SMU's Corporate Directors' Institute, the former senior associate dean for academics, and the former associate dean for research at the law school. Prior to becoming the Radford Professor, Professor Steinberg taught at the University of Maryland School of Law, the Wharton School of the University of Pennsylvania, the George Washington University School of Law, and the Georgetown University Law Center. His experience includes appointments as a visiting professor, scholar, and fellow at premier universities both in and outside the United States, including at UCLA as well as universities in Argentina, Australia, China, England, Finland, France, Germany, Israel, Italy, Japan, Luxembourg, New Zealand, Scotland, South Africa, and Sweden. In addition, he has been retained as an expert witness in several significant cases, including Enron, Martha Stewart, Mark Cuban, and the National Prescription Litigation.

In addition to his university appointments, Professor Steinberg has lectured extensively both in the United States and abroad, including at Oxford University, University of Cambridge, Heidelberg University, University of Tokyo, Hong Kong University, University of Auckland, Sydney University, Peking University, UCLA, the Aresty Institute of Executive Education at the University of Pennsylvania, the American Bar Association's Annual Meeting, the Practising Law Institute (PLI) Annual Institute on Securities Regulation, the International Development Law Institute in Rome, the Hong Kong Securities and Futures Commission, the Taiwan "SEC" in Taipei, the New Zealand Securities Commission, the Australian Law Council Section on International Law in Melbourne, the David Hume Institute in Edinburgh, the German-American Lawyers' Association in Munich, the International Law Society of South Africa, the Buenos Aires Stock Exchange, the Finnish Banking Lawyers Association in Helsinki, the Swedish Banking Lawyers Association in Stockholm, and the Ministry of Internal Affairs, Economic Crimes Department of the Russian Federation in Moscow. He also has served as a member of the Financial Industry Regulatory Authority (FINRA) National Adjudicatory Council (NAC).

Professor Steinberg received his undergraduate degree at the University of Michigan and his law degrees at the University of California, Los Angeles (JD) and Yale University (LLM).

He served as the judicial law clerk for Judge Stanley N. Barnes of the US Court of Appeals for the Ninth Circuit, was an extern law clerk for Judge Anthony J. Celebrezze of the US Court of Appeals for the Sixth Circuit, was legislative counsel to US Senator Robert P. Griffin, and served as the adviser to former US Supreme Court Justice Arthur J. Goldberg for the Federal Advisory Committee Report on Tender Offers.

Professor Steinberg was an attorney in the Division of Enforcement at the US Securities and Exchange Commission (SEC), and thereafter became special projects counsel in the SEC's Office of General Counsel. In that position, he directly assisted the SEC's General Counsel in a wide variety of projects and cases and served as the General Counsel's confidential legal adviser.

Professor Steinberg is one of the most prolific authors in the United States of company law scholarship, having authored approximately 50 books and 150 law journal articles. He is editor-in-chief of *The International Lawyer* as well as *The Securities Regulation Law Journal*. Professor Steinberg is a life member of the American Law Institute (ALI). This book is Professor Steinberg's fourth book published by Oxford University Press.

1
Corporate Directors and Officers Are "Discretionaries"—Not Fiduciaries

I. The Misnomer of Fiduciary Status

The principal theme of this book is that corporate directors and officers are not in reality fiduciaries and that the use of this term should be abandoned. This is not to say that fiduciary standards never apply to these individuals. Indeed, in certain situations, fairly rigorous criteria exist. Nonetheless, with great frequency, the liability standards that apply with respect to directors and officers are so lenient that they are devoid of fiduciary status. Accordingly, to continue to identify these persons as fiduciaries perpetuates a fiction that should be corrected. Rather, a new term should be recognized that accurately portrays this situation: The corporate director or officer is a "discretionary."

Having the status of discretionary, an officer or director exercises judgment when conducting his or her responsibilities. The degree of discretion afforded before the specter of liability arises may be strict or expansive depending on the surrounding facts and circumstances. For example, a self-dealing transaction that a corporate chief executive officer orchestrates for his financial advantage may be subject to demanding standards.[1] By contrast, the business judgment rule provides substantial protection from liability. To rebut the rule's applicability, a plaintiff must prove that the defendant directors and officers had a disabling conflict of interest or acted with gross negligence.[2] Going further, exculpation provisions extend even greater insulation from monetary liability where a breach of the duty of loyalty or intentional misconduct must be shown by a plaintiff in order to recover monetary

---

[1] *See, e.g.*, Del. Gen. Corp. L. § 144; *In re Match Group, Inc. Derivative Litigation*, 315 A.3d 446 (Del. 2024); *Remillard Brick Co. v. Remillard-Dandini Co.*, 241 P.2d 66 (Cal. App. 1952); discussion in Chapter 4, notes 79–93 and accompanying text.

[2] *See, e.g.*, *Smith v. Van Gorkom*, 488 A.2d 858 (Del. 1985); *Shlensky v. Wrigley*, 237 N.E.2d 776 (Ill. App. 1968); American Law Institute, *Principles of Corporate Governance: Analysis and Recommendations* § 4.02 (1994); discussion in Chapter 3, notes 25–54 and accompanying text.

Corporate Director and Officer Liability. Marc I. Steinberg, Oxford University Press.
© Marc I. Steinberg 2025. DOI: 10.1093/9780197751534.003.0001

damages.[3] To say that a corporate director or officer acts in a manner compliant with her fiduciary duties by refraining from engaging in gross negligence is nonsensical if the meaning of fiduciary is to have realistic substance.

The correct approach is to recognize the situation for what it is: In order to avoid liability, corporate directors and officers must abide by specified standards. All too often these standards as applied lack meaningful content, thereby permitting unacceptable conduct without suitable redress. To call these individuals fiduciaries is a misnomer. Rather, corporate directors and officers should be viewed as discretionaries. While this term has not previously been used in this manner,[4] its adaptation aptly fits the contextual situation which this book addresses.

II. Why Does It Matter?

A question may be raised as to why it matters that we call corporate directors and officers fiduciaries, even assuming that, with frequency, lenient standards apply. The important point, it may be asserted, is that the liability standards are clear so that all affected persons are aware of the relevant parameters.[5] Moreover, corporate directors and officers have been identified as fiduciaries or trustees for centuries.[6] No sufficient reason exists to change this situation. And, indeed, in some situations, strict standards apply to director and officer conduct, thereby validating fiduciary status.[7]

These points have merit. Nonetheless, they underestimate the adverse impact of the present approach. First, legal principles should be truthful.[8] They

---

[3] *See, e.g.*, Del. Gen. Corp. L. § 102(b)(7). The Delaware statute excludes duty of loyalty breaches from its coverage; discussion in Chapter 3, notes 59–70 and accompanying text.

[4] Currently, the word "discretionaries" ordinarily refers to nonessential services, goods, or things that are purchased by a customer with its discretionary income. *See Your Dictionary*, https://www.yourdictionary.com.

[5] *See generally Fiduciary Obligations in Business* (Arthur B. Laby and Jacob Hall Russell eds. 2021); *The Oxford Handbook of Fiduciary Law* (Evan J. Criddle, Paul B. Miller, and Robert H. Sitkoff eds. 2019); *Philosophical Foundations of Fiduciary Law* (Andrew S. Gold and Paul B. Miller eds. 2014); *Transnational Fiduciary Law* (Seth Davis, Thilo Kuntz, and Gregory Shaffer eds. 2023).

[6] *See, e.g., Charitable Corporation v. Sutton*, 2 Atk. 404 (1742) (Lord Hardwicke); *Attorney General v. Utica Insurance Company*, 2 Johns Ch. 371 (N.Y. Ch. 1817); *Todd v. Diamond State Iron Co.*, 14 A. 27 (Del. Ct. App. 1888), *aff'd*, 8 Houst. 372 (Del. Ct. Err. & App. 1889); *Martin v. D.B. Martin Co.*, 88 A. 612 (Del. Ch. 1913); *Western States Life Insurance Company v. Lockwood*, 135 P. 496 (Cal. 1913); *Globe Woolen Company v. Utica Gas and Electric Company*, 121 N.E. 378 (N.Y. 1918); *Lofland v. Cahall*, 118 A. 1 (Del. 1922); *Harden v. Eastern States Public Service Co.*, 122 A. 705 (Del. Ch. 1923); US Supreme Court cases cited *infra* Chapter 8, notes 14–28.

[7] *See* sources cited note 1 *supra*.

[8] *See United States v. Havens*, 446 U.S. 620, 626 (1980) ("There is no gainsaying that arriving at the truth is a fundamental goal of our legal system"). *See also District of Columbia v. Wesby*, 583 U.S. 48, 63 (2018).

should be accurately applied to the situation at hand.[9] Identifying a corporate director or officer as a fiduciary yet permitting that person to engage in grossly negligent conduct (and, in certain situations, even reckless behavior) without fear of monetary liability[10] contravenes this principle.

Second, reasonable persons should be able to understand, at least in a rudimentary manner, the meaning of widely used legal terms. To an average investor or shareholder, the term fiduciary signifies that the person is obligated to act with reasonable care, good faith, and loyalty in regard to matters that are within the ambit of the relationship.[11] Applied to director and officer liability, with frequency, these concepts are not faithfully implemented. Rather, corporate director and officer conduct that is characterized by lax liability standards often prevails.[12] Therefore, investors may perceive that they have been misled and believe that corporate directors and officers enjoy preferential treatment. Although these perceptions may not unduly deter them from participating in the corporate governance process and investing in the securities markets, the disparity between the rhetoric of fiduciary duty standards and their application in litigation may reinforce the notion that the law is being applied in an uneven manner.

Third, a principle should correspond to the characteristics for which it is identified. To define a principle in a specified fashion yet have its terms mean something else underscores its incongruity. By analogy, to enter a donkey named Secretariat[13] and identify the donkey as the famous racehorse in the Kentucky Derby would engender incredulity.[14] Applied to corporate directors and officers, a similar scenario has been implemented under state company and federal securities law. Although identified as fiduciaries, the liability standards that are applied frequently lack substance. Thus, the myth of corporate fiduciary standards deviates from fact.

---

[9] *See* Sandra Day O'Connor, *Vindicating the Rule of Law: The Role of the Judiciary*, 2 Chinese J. Int'l L. 1, 1 (2003) ("Broadly speaking, the Rule of Law requires that legal rules be publicly known, consistently enforced, and even-handedly applied") (then-US Supreme Court Justice O'Connor delivering her remarks at the National Judges College, Beijing China, on Sept. 18, 2002).

[10] *See New Enterprise Associates 14 L.P. v. Rich*, 295 A.3d 520, 551 (Del. Ch. 2023) (stating that Delaware's exculpation statute § 102(b)(7) "permits exculpation for recklessness"); notes 2–3 *supra*.

[11] *See* Consumer Financial Protection Bureau, *What Is A Fiduciary?* (Aug. 5, 2016), available at <http://consumerfinance.gov>.

[12] This book addresses these concepts in depth. *See* Chapters 2–8 *infra*.

[13] "Secretariat [winner of the Triple Crown – The Kentucky Derby, The Preakness Stakes, and the Belmont Stakes] was a legendary thoroughbred racehorse whose name reigns supreme in the history of racing." *Secretariat*, History.com (April 30, 2018), available at https://www.history.com/topics/sports/secretariat. Secretariat's victory at the Belmont Stakes "where he bested his closest competitor by a mind-blowing 31 lengths, is widely considered one of the most stunning horse races of all time." *Id.*

[14] This example was used in my recent article: Marc I. Steinberg, *To Call a Donkey a Racehorse— The Fiduciary Duty Misnomer in Corporate and Securities Law*, 48 J. Corp. L. 1, 36 (2022).

Legal terms and concepts have impact. They are relied upon for what they claim to represent. In the corporate setting, fiduciary status connotes that directors and officers are to act with reasonable care, in good faith, and with loyalty—and the failure to so act gives rise to enforceable remedial measures. In actuality, this is not the situation. Rather than engage in fiction, the status of these individuals should be accurately characterized. This portrayal should define corporate directors and officers as discretionaries and thereby accurately reflect their status.

III. The Meaning and Responsibilities of a Corporate Fiduciary

Nonetheless, the law applied today provides that corporate directors and officers are fiduciaries. This status has been recognized by courts for centuries.[15] As discussed in Chapter 8, the US Supreme Court in several decisions has opined that these individuals are fiduciaries.[16]

The question arises what is the meaning of the term "fiduciary." *Black's Law Dictionary* provides a succinct definition of this term as: "Someone who is required to act for the benefit of another person on all matters within the scope of their relationship; one who owes to another the duties of good faith, loyalty, due care, and disclosure <the corporate officer is a fiduciary to the corporation>."[17] Case law and commentary confirm the accuracy of this definition.[18]

---

[15] *See* cases cited note 6 *supra*.
[16] *See* cases cited in Chapter 8 at notes 14–28 *infra*.
[17] Fiduciary, *Black's Law Dictionary* 770 (11th ed. 2019). As *Black's Law Dictionary* is viewed as the standard authority for legal definitions as well as a valuable reference source, its definition of the term "fiduciary" is used herein. I am pleased that I am on the Panel of Academic Contributors for this work. *Id.* at vi. *See H-B Limited Partnership v. Wimmer*, 257 S.E.2d 770, 773 (Va. 1979) ("A fiduciary relationship exists ... when special confidence has been reposed in one who in equity and good conscience is bound to act in good faith and with due regard for the interests of the one reposing the confidence"). *But see Bristol & West Building Society v. Mathew*, [1998] Ch. 1, 18 (C.A.) (per Millett, L.J.), *cited and quoted in* American Law Institute, *Restatement of the Law (Third) Agency* § 1.01, at 41 (2007) ("Breach of fiduciary obligation connotes disloyalty or infidelity. Mere incompetence is not enough"). For other works addressing the definition of the term fiduciary, *see, e.g.*, Deborah DeMott, *Beyond Metaphor: An Analysis of Fiduciary Obligation*, 1988 Duke L.J. 879; Tamar Frankel, *Fiduciary Law*, 71 Cal. L. Rev. 795 (1983); Austin Scott, *The Fiduciary Principle*, 37 Cal. L. Rev. 539 (1949).
[18] *See Koehler v. The Black River Falls Iron Company*, 67 U.S. 715, 719 (1862) (describing directors "as guardians of an important trust committed to their care, endeavor, [and] good faith"). For other sources, *see, e.g.*, *In re Walt Disney Company Derivative Litigation*, 906 A.2d 27 (Del. 2006); *Hoffman Steam Coal Company v. Cumberland Coal & Iron Company*, 16 Md. 456 (1860); *Bay City*

Accordingly, corporate directors and officers are identified as fiduciaries. Moreover, corporate officers are deemed fiduciaries by virtue of being agents who are entrusted with managing the enterprise for its best interests.[19] Hence, as recognized, the fiduciary duties of corporate directors and officers include acting with due care, good faith, and loyalty.[20] However, as discussed above and addressed throughout this book, the rhetoric of fiduciary duty should be distinguished from its application with respect to standards of liability.

IV. Corporate Directors Compared to Corporate Officers

It may be posited that a distinction should be made between corporate directors and officers as fiduciaries. Although they both have been held to have the same fiduciary duties, a stricter level of scrutiny may apply with respect to corporate officers as agents of the corporate enterprise.[21] For example, a number of courts hold that the business judgment rule is inapplicable to corporate officers.[22] In addition, many state exculpation statutes

---

Lumber Co. v. Anderson, 111 P.2d 771 (Wash. 1941); *Reed v. Robinson*, 220 P. 676 (Cal. App. 1923); Douglas M. Branson, *Corporate Governance* §§ 6.01–8:38 (1993); William Meade Fletcher, et al., *Fletcher Cyclopedia Corporations* § 838 et seq. (2023); Harry G. Henn and John R. Alexander, *Law of Corporations* 625 (3d ed. 1983).

[19] *See, e.g., Amalgamated Bank v. Yahoo! Inc.*, 132 A.3d 752 (Del. Ch. 2016); Deborah A. DeMott, *Corporate Officers as Agents*, 74 Wash. & Lee L. Rev. 847 (2017); William A. Gregory, *The Law of Agency and Partnership* § 66 (3d ed. 2001); Warren A. Seavey, *Handbook of the Law of Agency* § 140 (1964); Megan W. Shaner, *Restoring the Balance of Power in Corporate Management: Enforcing an Officer's Duty of Obedience*, 66 Bus. Law. 27 (2010); A. Gilchrist Sparks III and Lawrence A. Hamermesh, *Common Law Duties of Non-Director Officers*, 48 Bus. Law. 215 (1992).

[20] *See* sources cited notes 6, 17–19 *supra*.

[21] *See Gantler v. Stephens*, 965 A.2d 695, 708–09 (Del. 2009) ("In the past, we have implied that officers of Delaware corporations, like directors, owe fiduciary duties of care and loyalty, and that the fiduciary duties of officers are the same as those of directors. We now explicitly so hold"); *Metro Storage International LLC v. Harron*, 275 A.3d 810, 843 (Del. Ch. 2022) ("The officer's duty of loyalty . . . has additional dimensions, precisely because officers act as agents for the entity"); *infra* notes 22–24 and accompanying text.

[22] *See Federal Deposit Insurance Corporation v. Perry*, 2012 WL 589569, at * 4 (C.D. Cal. 2012) (applying California law and holding business judgment rule inapplicable to decisions by corporate officers). *But see* Model Business Corporation Act § 8.42 Official Comment (stating that "the business judgment rule will normally apply to decisions within an officer's discretionary authority"). *Compare* Lawrence A. Hamermesh and A. Gilchrist Sparks III, *Corporate Officers and the Business Judgment Rule: A Reply to Professor Johnson*, 60 Bus. Law. 865, 876 (2005) (asserting that "the policies that have given rise to the application of the business judgment rule to directors apply with equal force to the actions of officers within their delegated discretionary authority"), *with* Lyman P.Q. Johnson, *Corporate Officers and the Business Judgment Rule*, 60 Bus. Law. 439, 440 (2005) (arguing that "the business judgment rule—does not and should not be extended to corporate officers in the same broad manner in which it is applied to directors").

provide for the elimination of monetary liability for breach of the duty of care for corporate directors, excluding corporate officers from coverage.[23] Moreover, based on their responsibilities and greater knowledge with respect to their companies, courts may hold corporate officers to a higher level of duty than outside directors.[24] Accordingly, it may be said that fiduciary duties for corporate officers have substance, accompanied by the application of meaningful liability standards.

Nonetheless, several sources recognize the availability of the business judgment rule for corporate officers.[25] Similarly, a number of states extend their exculpation statutes to encompass corporate officers.[26] Also, significantly, similar to director liability exposure, the boundaries of alleged duty of loyalty breaches are permissibly interpreted by some courts, thereby enabling corporate officers to avert liability.[27] Thus, although corporate officers may be held to stricter liability exposure than corporate directors in certain situations, they nonetheless frequently benefit from lax liability standards.[28] Therefore, it is appropriate to treat both corporate officers and

---

[23] *See, e.g.*, Fla. Stat. § 607.0831; Ind. Bus. Corp. L. § 23-1-35-1; Mass. Gen. L. ch. 156B, § 13; Ohio Rev. Code § 1701.59; 42 Pa. Cons. Stat. Ann. § 8364; Wis. § 180.307. Delaware recently amended its statute to permit exculpation of officers in direct, but not derivative, actions. *See* Del. Gen. Corp. L. §. 102(b)(7).

[24] An example is *Escott v. BarChris Construction Corporation*, 283 F. Supp. 643 (S.D.N.Y. 1968). With respect to the due diligence defense under Section 11 of the Securities Act, the court made clear that inside directors and defendant officers who are not directors must undertake a more extensive investigation with respect to the accuracy of disclosure in a registration statement than outside directors whose sole affiliation with the company is serving as a director. For further discussion on this subject, *see infra* Chapter 8, notes 29–50 and accompanying text.

[25] *See Rosenfeld v. Metals Selling Corp.*, 643 A.2d 1253, 1261 n. 16 (Conn. 1994) ("Although the business judgment rule is usually defined in terms of the role of corporate directors, it is equally applicable to corporate officers exercising their authority"); American Law Institute, *Principles of Corporate Governance: Analysis and Recommendations* § 4.01 cmt. a ("Sound public policy points in the direction of holding officers to the same duty of care and business judgment standard as directors, as does the little case law authority that exists on the applicability of the business judgment standard to officers"); Model Business Corporation Act § 8.42 Official Comment (stating that "the business judgment rule will normally apply to decisions within an officer's discretionary authority"); Hamermesh and Sparks, *supra* note 22, at 868 n. 23 (citing court decisions stating that the business judgment rule applies to corporate officers); sources cited note 22 *supra*.

[26] *See, e.g.*, Md. Corp. Assoc. Code § 5-418; Nev. Rev. Stat. § 78.138; Va. Code Ann. § 13.1-692.1. Delaware recently amended its statute to authorize exculpation of officers in direct, but not derivative, actions. *See* Del. Gen. Corp. L. § 102(b)(7).

[27] For discussion of this subject, *see* Chapter 4 *infra*.

[28] *See Metro Storage International LLC v. Harron*, 275 A.3d 810, 845 (Del. Ch. 2022) (stating "Court of Chancery decisions have embraced gross negligence as the standard for evaluating an officer's breach of the duty of care"). Another example is that a number of state statutes authorize exculpation of corporate officers. *See* statutes cited note 26 *supra*; discussion Chapter 3 *infra*.

directors similarly for the assertion that these individuals, in actuality, are not fiduciaries. Rather, as discussed in this book, they are discretionaries.

V. Shareholder Primacy versus Constituency Approach

In recent years, there has been lively debate whether the traditional purpose of a corporation to maximize profits in a law compliant manner for the benefit of its shareholders should be "modernized" to reflect the many constituencies that are affected by its conduct.[29] The shareholder primacy focus, these proponents claim, should be abandoned in favor of an approach that seeks to serve all corporate constituencies.[30] A 2019 Statement on the Purpose of a Corporation issued by the Business Roundtable and signed by 181 chief executive officers supports this view, expressing the CEOs' commitment "to lead their companies for the benefit of all stakeholders—customers, employees, suppliers, communities, and shareholders."[31] On the other hand, a persuasive argument can be made that shareholder primacy is the law and should remain the law as this approach best promotes corporate accountability, governance, and wealth maximization.[32]

---

[29] *Compare* Stephen M. Bainbridge, *The Profit Motive—Defending Shareholder Profit Maximization* 1 (2023) (asserting that "the purpose of the corporation is to sustainably maximize shareholder value over the long term"), *with* Lynn Stout, *The Shareholder Value Myth* (2012) (advocating against shareholder value maximization from both normative and doctrinal viewpoints).

[30] *See* Stout, note 29 *supra*. In recent years, many states have enacted legislation authorizing the formation of benefit corporations. In addition to having an objective of profit maximization, these statutes allow for these corporations to employ their resources to undertake broader social objectives. *See* Mark J. Loewenstein, *Benefit Corporations: A Challenge in Corporate Governance*, 68 Bus. Law. 1007 (2013).

[31] Business Roundtable, *Statement on the Purpose of a Corporation* (Aug.19, 2019).

[32] *See In re Trados Inc. Securities Litigation*, 73 A.3d 17, 37 (Del. Ch. 2013) (stating that "stockholders' best interest must always, within legal limits, be the end [and that] [o]ther constituencies may be considered only instrumentally to advance that end"); Bainbridge, note 29 *supra* (contending shareholder profit maximization should be and is the law); Lucian A. Bebchuk and Roberto Tallarita, *The Illusory Promise of Stakeholder Governance*, 106 Cornell L. Rev. 91, 96 (2020) (asserting that "stakeholderism should be expected to be an ineffective and indeed counterproductive way to address stakeholder concerns [and that] while stakeholderism would not produce material benefits for stakeholders, it would introduce illusory hopes, misperceptions, and distractions that would have significant adverse effects on stakeholders").

Although the significance of this debate is important, it does not impact the analysis contained herein. This book focuses on the marked distinction between the rhetoric of director and officer fiduciary duty in the corporate setting and the reality of lax liability standards. Even assuming that the shareholder primacy approach becomes outdated (which at this time appears unlikely), the rhetoric as contrasted with the substance of fiduciary duty status will frequently be incompatible with one another.

VI. Standards of Conduct versus Standards of Liability

Courts and commentators have pointed to the distinction between standards of conduct versus standards of liability (also called standards of review).[33] They point out that standards of conduct represent the conduct that corporate directors and officers should adhere to while liability standards set forth the conditions that must be met in order for an officer or director to be held liable.[34] In effect, standards of conduct convey best practices or are hortatory expressions seeking to induce commendable director and officer conduct.[35] In reality, therefore, they are nothing more than recommendations lacking enforceable content. Rather than mandating the application of meaningful fiduciary conduct, these exhortations disguise the actuality that they are only tangentially relevant to a court's determination of a corporate director's or officer's liability exposure.[36] Hence, this line of reasoning reinforces the deviation between rhetoric and liability standards.

---

[33] *See, e.g., Brehm v. Eisner*, 746 A.2d 244, 255–56 (Del. 2000); *Metro Storage International LLC v. Harron*, 275 A.3d 810, 841–42 (Del. Ch. 2022); *Chen v. Howard-Anderson*, 87 A.3d 648, 666–67 (Del. Ch. 2014); William T. Allen, Jack B. Jacobs, and Leo E. Strine Jr., *Function Over Form: A Reassessment of Standards of Review in Delaware Corporation Law*, 56 Bus. Law. 1287 (2001); Melvin Aron Eisenberg, *The Divergence of Standards of Conduct and Standards of Review in Corporate Law*, 62 Fordham L. Rev. 437 (1993); E. Norman Veasey and Christine T. Di Guglielmo, *What Happened in Delaware Corporate Law and Governance From 1992–2004?*, 153 U. Pa. L. Rev. 1399 (2005).

[34] *See, e.g., Chen v. Howard-Anderson*, 87 A.3d at 666 ("When determining whether corporate fiduciaries have breached their duties, Delaware corporate law distinguishes between the standard of conduct and the standard of review"); *Reis v. Hazlett Strip-Casting Corp.*, 28 A.3d 442, 457 (Del. Ch. 2011) (stating that "the standard of review is more forgiving of [defendant fiduciaries] and more onerous for [the] plaintiffs than the standard of conduct").

[35] *See In re Trados Incorporated Shareholder Litigation*, 73 A.3d at 35 (emphasis supplied) ("The standard of conduct describes what directors are *expected* to do").

[36] *See* sources cited notes 33–35 *supra. But see* Eisenberg, *supra* note 33, at 464 ("Although under certain conditions the elements of liability under a given standard of review may differ from the elements of liability under a linked standard of conduct, under other conditions the elements of liability will be the same").

This distinction between standards of conduct and standards of review appears in the Model Business Corporation Act. Section 8.30 sets forth standards of conduct for directors,[37] while Sections 8.31 and 8.32 address standards of liability for directors. The Official Comment makes clear that the provisions contained in Section 8.30 are not liability principles, stating: "Section 8.30 addresses standards of conduct—the level of performance *expected* of directors undertaking the role and responsibilities of the office of director [but] does *not* address the liability of a director. . . ."[38] Likewise, the Delaware courts explicitly embrace this distinction, recognizing the significance of such demarcation. As stated by a fairly recent Delaware court decision: "When determining whether directors have breached their fiduciary duties, Delaware corporate law distinguishes between the standard of conduct and the standard of review [with the former standard] describ[ing] what directors are *expected* to do...."[39] And, as a subsequent Delaware decision acknowledged, "the standard of review [for determining liability exposure] is more forgiving of directors and more onerous for stockholder plaintiffs than the standard of conduct."[40]

While there exist numerous policy justifications for the divergence between these two standards,[41] the fact remains that standards of conduct exhort—without the specter of adverse consequences—corporate directors and officers to engage in exemplary conduct. By contrast, standards of liability (or standards of review as phrased by the Delaware courts) frequently apply minimal requirements. This divergence between the rhetoric of best practices and the reality of lax liability standards reinforces the validity of the

---

[37] *See* § 8.30 (Standards of Conduct for Directors); § 8.31 (Standards of Liability for Directors); § 8.32 (Directors' Liability for Unlawful Distributions).
[38] Section 8.30 of the Model Business Corporation Act (Official Comment) (emphasis supplied).
[39] *See In re Trados Incorporated Shareholder Litigation*, 73 A.3d at 35 (emphasis supplied).
[40] *Chen v. Howard-Anderson*, 87 A.3d at 666, *quoting Reis*, 28 A.3d at 457. Indeed, in a recent decision, the Delaware Supreme Court set forth the standard of conduct and the standard of liability in the same sentence. *See United Food and Commercial Workers Union v. Zuckerberg*, 262 A.3d 1034, 1049–50 (Del. 2021) (emphasis supplied) ("Predicated upon concepts of *gross negligence*, the *duty of care requires* that [corporate] fiduciaries *inform themselves of material information* before making a business decision and act *prudently* in carrying out their duties").
[41] *See* Allen, Jacobs, and Strine, *supra* note 33 at 1296:

> In most areas of law, standards of conduct and standards of review tend to conflate and become one and the same, but in corporate law the two standards often diverge. The reasons are rooted in policy reasons. First, directors must make decisions in an environment of imperfect information. Second, given the limited investment in publicly held firms that typical corporate directors are able or willing to make, any risk of liability would likely dwarf the incentives for assuming the role. Third, courts are ill-equipped to determine after-the-fact whether a particular business decision was reasonable in the circumstances confronting the corporation.

proposition that corporate directors and officers in fact are not fiduciaries. Rather, they are "discretionaries" whose legal obligations fluctuate from minimal to substantial depending on the pertinent facts and circumstances.

With the preceding discussion in focus, the following section briefly describes the book's contents.

VII. Summary of Contents

In asserting that corporate directors and officers in actuality are not fiduciaries, this book covers a broad range of situations that impact their liability exposure. The subjects that are addressed include the duties of care and loyalty, derivative litigation, controlling shareholder duties, fiduciary obligations in closely held corporations, fiduciary duties in mergers and acquisitions, and the presence of fiduciary duty principles in the context of the federal securities laws. In addition, a chapter proffers a recommended approach that recognizes the actual status of corporate directors and officers as "discretionaries," opting for a framework that implements liability standards that are congruent with sound corporate governance practices. Adoption of this framework would be consistent with the proposition that corporate directors and officers are discretionaries rather than fiduciaries.

From a historical perspective, the second chapter addresses liability standards that were applied to defendant fiduciaries in business enterprises many decades ago. Justice Cardozo's famous opinion in *Meinhard v. Salmon* is a marked example.[42] Much of this chapter focuses on unincorporated business enterprises (including partnerships and limited liability companies). While strict fiduciary standards traditionally were embraced, these standards today are significantly more relaxed.[43] Impacting this analysis is the use of contractual provisions that have been judicially enforced that enable participants in these unincorporated enterprises to greatly reduce their fiduciary and other obligations.[44] With contractual agreements

---

[42] 164 N.E. 545 (N.Y. 1928).

[43] For example, a partner's duty of care under the Uniform Partnership Act is not a fiduciary duty. Under the Act, a partner's duty is minimal in this regard, namely, "to refrain from engaging in grossly negligent or reckless conduct, willful or intentional misconduct, or a knowing violation of law." Uniform Partnership Act § 409(c). For further discussion, *see* Chapter 2 *infra*.

[44] *See, e.g., Boardwalk Pipeline Partners, LP v. Bandera Master Fund LP*, 288 A.3d 1083 (Del. 2022) (holding fiduciary duties, that otherwise would have applied, were contractually waived in case at bar). *See generally* J. Dennis Hynes, *Freedom of Contract, Fiduciary Duties, and Partnerships: The Bargain Principle and the Law of Agency*, 54 Wash. & Lee L. Rev. 439 (1997); Mark J. Loewenstein,

being given primacy by statutes and courts, fiduciary duties in this context frequently are displaced.

The third chapter addresses important issues impacting corporate director and officer liability in duty of care cases not implicating alleged breaches of the duty of loyalty. As discussed, the business judgment rule having a gross negligence culpability standard provides an impressive shield from liability for these individuals.[45] Providing further insulation from monetary liability exposure, the state exculpation statutes require that greater culpability be proven,[46] with Delaware adopting a knowing misconduct approach.[47] It may be posited that identifying corporate directors and officers as fiduciaries when they benefit from these lax standards is a misnomer.

The fourth chapter examines director and officer liability in duty of loyalty cases. Topics covered include interested director transactions and corporate opportunity takings. In addition, the duty of good faith—a duty that comes within the duty of loyalty—is addressed,[48] with attention focused on the law compliance *Caremark* obligations to which directors and officers must adhere.[49] This chapter also discusses state statutes that address conflict of interest transactions impacting directors and officers.[50] As will be seen by the analysis in this chapter, the liability standards that apply in the duty of loyalty setting often are unduly permissive. Indeed, laxity frequently prevails to the extent that the applicable standards lack meaningful substance, thereby supporting the position that corporate directors and officers in actuality are not fiduciaries.

Fiduciary Duties and Unincorporated Business Entities: In Defense of the "Manifestly Unreasonable" Standard, 41 Tulsa L. Rev. 411 (2006).

[45] *See, e.g., In re Tower Air, Inc.*, 416 F.2d 229, 238 (3d Cir. 2005) (applying Delaware law) ("Overcoming the presumption of the business judgment rule on the merits is a near-Herculean task").

[46] *See* sources cited notes 10, 23, 26 *supra*.

[47] Del. Gen. Corp. L. § 102(b)(7) (permitting a provision in the subject corporation's articles of incorporation limiting or eliminating monetary liability of directors and officers (except for officers, not in derivative actions) other than in situations involving a breach of the duty of loyalty, knowing improper declaration of a distribution, receipt of an improper personal benefit, or acts or omissions not in good faith or involving a knowing violation of law or intentional misconduct).

[48] *See, e.g., In re Walt Disney Co. Derivative Litigation*, 906 A.2d 27, 67 (Del. 2006).

[49] *See, e.g., Stone v. Ritter*, 911 A.2d 362, 370 (Del. 2006) (ruling that "because a showing of bad faith conduct... is essential to establish director oversight liability, the fiduciary duty violated by that conduct is the duty of loyalty"): *In re Caremark International Inc. Derivative Litigation*, 698 A.2d 959, 970 (Del. Ch. 1996) (opining that directors have an obligation to oversee the corporation's law compliance as part of their oversight function).

[50] *See, e.g.,* Del. Gen. Corp. L. § 144; Texas Bus. Orgs. Code § 21.418; Model Bus. Corp. Act §§ 8.60–8.63.

The fifth chapter addresses derivative litigation, focusing on the myriad ways that corporate directors are authorized to terminate this type of litigation. Both statutes and case law are discussed.[51] Applying lax standards, supposed independent and disinterested directors are given great deference to cause the termination of even meritorious claims.[52] The effect of this permissive framework is to prevent the substance of a plaintiff's claims from being adjudicated. Hence, the underlying conflict of interest transaction or other allegedly improper conduct never sees the light of day.[53] There may exist sound public policy to support this approach. But it cannot be reconciled with the fiduciary standards to which corporate directors and officers are said to be held accountable. Thus, once again, there exists a glaring gap between laudatory corporate governance rhetoric and the application of liability standards.

The sixth chapter addresses corporate director and officer liability standards in the merger and acquisition contexts. In addition to such transactions as sales of substantially all assets and long-form mergers, the chapter also focuses on parent–subsidiary mergers. In this respect, the duties of controlling shareholders are discussed with emphasis on state statutes and court decisions in going-private transactions.[54] Another important focus of the chapter is on tender offers.[55] The director and officer liability standards that apply in the tender offer setting are examined. What becomes clear is that although supposedly stricter standards apply in this setting when evaluating the propriety of director and officer conduct, these more rigorous standards frequently apply only in actions for injunctive relief.[56] For actions seeking damages against corporate directors, the applicable exculpation provision

---

[51] *See, e.g.*, Texas Bus. Orgs. Code § 21.558; *Zapata Corp. v. Maldonado*, 430 A.2d 779 (Del. 1981); *Auerbach v. Bennett*, 47 N.Y.S. 2d 619 (Ct. App. 1979); *Desigoudar v. Meyercord*, 133 Cal. Rptr. 2d 408 (Ct. App. 2003).

[52] *See, e.g.*, *Thompson v. Scientific Atlanta, Inc.*, 621 S.E.2d 796 (Ga. Ct. App. 2005); sources cited note 51 *supra*.

[53] *See, e.g.*, *Lewis v. Anderson*, 615 F.2d 778 (9th Cir. 1979) (applying California law); sources cited notes 51–52 *supra*.

[54] *See, e.g.*, Minn. Stat. Ann. § 302A.601 (allowing corporations to merge "with or without a business purpose"); *Glassman v. Unocal Exploration Corporation*, 777 A.2d 242 (Del. 2001) (in short-form mergers, absent fraud or illegality, appraisal is the sole remedy); *Weinberger v. UOP, Inc.*, 457 A.2d 701 (Del. 1983) (in long-form mergers, appraisal ordinarily exclusive remedy unless specified exceptions apply). A going-private transaction occurs when the minority shareholders of the subject company exchange their securities for cash, thereby resulting in the company attaining privately held status. SEC Rules 13e-3 and 13e-4, 17 C.F.R. §§ 240.13e-3, .13e-4, regulate going private-private transactions on the federal level.

[55] The focus of Chapter 6 is on state, rather than federal, law. Pursuant to federal law, Sections 14(d) and 14(e) of the Securities Exchange Act, 15 U.S.C. §§ 78m, n, and SEC rules and regulations promulgated thereunder, regulate tender offers.

[56] *See, e.g.*, *Versata Enterprises, Inc. v. Selectica, Inc.*, 5 A.3d 586 (Del. 2010); *Omnicare, Inc. v. NCS Healthcare, Inc.*, 818 A.2d 914 (Del. 2003); *Unitrin, Inc. v. American General Corp.*, 651 A.2d 1361

will provide exoneration from monetary liability unless there exists a loyalty breach or knowing misconduct is perpetrated.[57] Once again, the divide between the rhetoric of fiduciary standards and their application to director and officer monetary liability exposure is evident.

The seventh chapter focuses on corporate director and officer liability standards in closely held corporations.[58] In this setting, liability exposure also exists when these individuals are found to engage in misconduct acting as shareholders.[59] Many courts liken the duties that shareholders owe one another in the closely held corporation context to that of general partners where the utmost duties of care and loyalty have been recognized.[60] However, as discussed in the chapter, this analogy no longer is accurate. Partnership law today is largely based on contractual agreement whereby fiduciary duties may be drastically reduced. Indeed, the duty of care no longer is defined as a fiduciary duty under the current version of the Uniform Partnership Act.[61]

The eighth chapter addresses concepts of fiduciary duty under the federal securities laws. Given that the federal securities laws are premised fundamentally on disclosure rather than substantive fairness,[62] fiduciary duty analysis nonetheless remains pertinent. For example, under US Supreme Court precedent, the law of insider trading under the key antifraud provision, Section 10(b) of the Securities Exchange Act,[63] is premised on fiduciary

---

(Del. 1995); *MacAndrews & Forbes Holdings v. Revlon*, 506 A.2d 173 (Del. 1986); *Unocal Corp. v. Mesa Petroleum Co.*, 493 A.2d 946 (Del. 1985).

[57] *See, e.g.*, Del. Gen. Corp. L. § 102(b)(7); notes 10, 47 *supra*.

[58] Generally, a closely held corporation (1) is a validly formed corporation under the applicable state law; (2) has few shareholders (often less than ten); (3) has its shareholders frequently derive their livelihood from working for the corporation drawing salaries; and (4) has no public market for the trading of its stock. *See, e.g., Donahue v. Rodd Electrotype Co. of New England, Inc.*, 328 N.E.2d 505 (Mass. 1975).

[59] *See, e.g., Wilkes v. Springside Nursing Home, Inc.*, 353 N.E.2d 657 (Mass. 1976).

[60] *See, e.g., Demoulas v. Demoulas Super Markets, Inc.*, 677 N.E.2d 159, 179 (Mass. 1997) (stating, that with respect to closely held corporations, "duties of loyalty extend to shareholders, who owe one another substantially the same duty of utmost good faith and loyalty in the operation of the enterprise that partners owe to one another"). Fletcher, *supra* note 18, at § 844.20 ("Close corporation shareholders . . . stand in a fiduciary relationship to each other").

[61] *See* discussion *supra* notes 42–44 and accompanying text.

[62] *See, e.g., Santa Fe Industries, Inc. v. Green*, 430 U.S. 462, 477–78 (1977) (stating that the US Supreme Court "repeatedly has described the fundamental purpose of the [Securities Exchange] Act as implementing a philosophy of full disclosure"). *See generally* Ralph C. Ferrara and Marc I. Steinberg, *A Reappraisal of Santa Fe: Rule 10b-5 and the New Federalism*, 129 U. Pa. L. Rev. 263 (1980).

[63] 15 U.S.C. § 78j(b). Rule 10b-5, 17 C.F.R. § 240.10b-5, is the SEC's broad antifraud rule adopted pursuant to its Section 10(b) rulemaking authority. *See generally* Alan R. Bromberg, et al., *Bromberg and Lowenfels on Securities Fraud* (2023).

duty analysis.[64] Moreover, although the Supreme Court has recognized on many occasions that corporate directors and officers are fiduciaries,[65] liability frequently is imposed against these persons only if a claimant can prove knowing or intentional misconduct.[66] Related thereto, forward-looking statements, statements of belief, and puffery are rarely actionable against corporate directors and officers.[67] This approach is seen in federal statutes as well as court decisions, including the safe harbor for forward-looking statements provided by the Private Securities Litigation Reform Act (PSLRA).[68] Hence, although the US Supreme Court calls corporate directors and officers fiduciaries, the liability standards applied frequently contradict this status.

The ninth chapter posits that permissive standards often are adopted that enable corporate directors and officers to avert liability unless they act with gross negligence or greater culpability. Nonetheless, sound policy justifications exist for the implementation of permissive standards in certain situations—including the public policy of attracting competent independent directors to serve on corporate boards and granting broad discretion to directors under the business judgment rule when they undertake challenging entrepreneurial or operational decisions, such as the development of a new line of products. In practical effect, however, exhortations for corporate directors and officers to implement sound corporate governance practices are frequently empty gestures unless adverse consequences flow to these individuals when they engage in improper conduct. Accordingly, the approach that is recommended seeks to establish meaningful director and officer liability standards within the contours of a sensible remedial framework.

---

[64] *See, e.g., Chiarella v. United States*, 445 U.S. 222 (1980). *See generally* Marc I. Steinberg and William K. S. Wang, *Insider Trading* (Oxford Univ. Press 3d ed. 2010).

[65] *See* discussion in Chapter 8 *infra* at notes 14–28 and accompanying text.

[66] *See, e.g., Ernst & Ernst v. Hochfelder*, 425 U.S. 185 (1976) (holding that scienter is required to be proven in § 10(b) private actions).

[67] *See, e.g., Omnicare, Inc. v. Laborers Dist. Council Constr. Indus. Pension Fund*, 575 U.S. 175 (2015) (statements of belief); *Plumbers & Steamfitters Loc. 773 v. Danske Bank*, 11 F.4th 90 (2d Cir. 2021) (puffery); *Asher v. Baxter International, Inc.*, 377 F.3d 727 (7th Cir. 2004) (forward-looking statements).

[68] Pub. L. No. 104-67, 109 Stat. 737 (1995). The protections for forward-looking statements in private litigation are contained in Section 27A of the Securities Act, 15 U.S.C. § 77z-2, and Section 21E of the Securities Exchange Act, 15 U.S.C. § 78u-5. For cases interpreting the safe harbor for forward-looking information, *see, e.g., Wochos v. Tesla, Inc.*, 985 F.3d 1180 (9th Cir. 2021); *In re Harman International, Inc. Securities Litigation*, 791 F.3d 90 (D.C. Cir. 2015); *Slayton v. American Express Company*, 604 F.3d 758 (2d Cir. 2010).

Chapter 10 is the book's concluding chapter. It summarizes many of the key points made earlier in the book. Based on the prevailing liability standards, the chapter asserts that the label of fiduciary should be removed from corporate director and officer status. In its stead, directors and officers should be deemed discretionaries. By adopting this approach, director and officer liability standards would reflect reality.

VIII. Importance of This Book

Although admittedly viewed from the author's perspective, this is an important book. Insofar as I am aware, this is the first source to call for the removal of corporate director and officer fiduciary status in favor of the adoption of a new term that provides an accurate and neutral portrayal: corporate directors and officers are "discretionaries."

A number of commentators have recognized the dilution of director and officer fiduciary standards.[69] The description is accurate. This book seeks significantly to build on that perception. Through research, analysis, and insight, the book explains why directors and officers in actuality are not fiduciaries and that the use of that term in this context is inaccurate.

The adverse impact of the continued utilization of the term "fiduciary" is that it mischaracterizes its meaning as applied in practice. Legal principles and terms should be truthful, should be faithfully interpreted, and should be applied to accurately implement these principles and terms. Moreover, identifying corporate directors and officers as fiduciaries yet adhering to lax liability standards presents a false portrayal. Investors, particularly those who are uninitiated, reasonably believe that these individuals owe meaningful duties and that their failure to comply with these duties (namely, the

---

[69] *See, e.g.*, David Kershaw, *The Foundations of Anglo-American Corporate Fiduciary Law* (2018); Jacob Hale Russell and Arthur B. Laby, *The Decline and Rise of Fiduciary Obligations in Business* at 1, in *Fiduciary Obligations in Business* (Arthur B. Laby and Jacob Hale Russell eds. 2021); Julian Velasco, *Fiduciary Principles in Corporate Law* at 61, in *Oxford Handbook of Fiduciary Law* (Evan J. Criddle, Paul B. Miller, and Robert H. Sitkoff eds. 2019).

Some sources have opined that the relation of director and corporation is *sui generis*. *See, e.g.*, *Enyart v. Merrick*, 34 P.2d 629, 632 (Ore. 1934) ("The truth is that the status of director and corporation is a distinct legal relationship"); Lyman Johnson, *The Three Fiduciaries of Delaware Corporate Law—and Eisenberg's Error*, in *Fiduciary Obligations in Business*, at 57 ("Directors are not agents of the corporation or shareholders, and, after decades of fretful and inconclusive theorizing, owe duties to both of them in a *sui generis* capacity"); Note, *Fiduciary Duty of Officers and Directors Not to Compete with the Corporation*, 54 Harv. L. Rev. 1191 (1941) (stating that "courts have recognized that the relation of director and corporation is to some extent *sui generis*").

duties of care, good faith, and loyalty) will incur liability. This false portrayal is detrimental to the rule of law,[70] contravenes reasonable investor expectations, and impairs the integrity of the financial markets.[71]

Thus, corporate directors and officers no longer should be deemed fiduciaries. Rather, their status is accurately characterized by defining them as "discretionaries." The following chapters seek to provide compelling support for this position. As this is my fourth book with Oxford University Press, with the most recent being awarded winner best law book of 2021 by American Book Fest, I am hopeful that this work will provide a meaningful contribution to advancing the sound development of the law.[72]

---

[70] See Lord Hacking, *Preface—The Rule of Law Papers*, 43 Int'l Law. 3 (2009) ("The law itself has to be fair. It has to be certain. . . .") (I am pleased to be the editor-in-chief of *The International Lawyer* from 2001 to the present, the longest serving EIC in the Journal's history); sources cited notes 8–9 *supra*.

[71] In an article published nearly fifty years ago, Stanley A. Kaplan recognized this situation, stating: "The concept of a fiduciary may serve as a useful legal fiction to stimulate development of new or expanding obligations by analogy to the seminal concept of the trustee [but] clarity of description and precision in defining duties might at this stage better be achieved through abandonment of so amorphous a term. . . ." Stanley A. Kaplan, *Fiduciary Responsibility in the Management of the Corporation*, 31 Bus. Law. 883, 887 (1976). See also, Kelli Alces Williams, *Self-Interested Fiduciaries and Invulnerable Beneficiaries: When Fiduciary Duties Do Not Fit*, in *Fiduciary Obligations in Business*, *supra* note 69, at 334, 337 (arguing that "the officers and directors of large, public corporations do not act as fiduciaries of the corporation or its shareholders, with limited exceptions").

[72] See Marc I. Steinberg, *Rethinking Securities Law* (2021); Marc I. Steinberg, *The Federalization of Corporate Governance* (2018); Marc I. Steinberg and William K. S. Wang, *Insider Trading* (3d ed. 2010).

2
Fiduciary Duties in Business Enterprises: A Historical and Contemporary Perspective

I. Introduction

This chapter principally addresses fiduciary duties in unincorporated business enterprises, including partnerships and limited liability companies (LLCs). To some extent, these duties in the corporate law setting, primarily from a historical perspective, are also examined. The chapter's objective is to highlight that the existence of fiduciary principles in partnerships and LLCs, namely, unincorporated business enterprises, have been substantially diminished. This diminution largely is due to the presence of enabling statutes that permit partners and LLC members, pursuant to the contractual provisions of the governing agreement, to decrease and, at times, eliminate fiduciary duties that otherwise would apply.[1] This approach has received judicial approbation.[2]

The following discussion also posits that the supposed strict fiduciary duties in the corporation setting that were enunciated several decades ago may have been overstated. While several commentators point to the current diminishing application of fiduciary duties with respect to corporate directors and officers,[3] case law evidences that at least in a number of jurisdictions, lax standards were applied in days of yesteryear.[4] This chapter next turns to some older corporate law cases to illustrate this point.

---

[1] See discussion *infra* notes 23–31, 52–53 and accompanying text.
[2] See, e.g., Boardwalk Pipeline Partners, L.P. v. Bandera Master Fund LP, 288 A.3d 1083 (Del. 2022); McConnell v. Hunt Sports Enterprises, 725 N.E.2d 1193 (Ohio App. 1999); Singer v. Singer, 634 P.2d 766 (Okla. App. 1981); discussion *infra* notes 32–61 and accompanying text.
[3] See, e.g., Reza Dibadj, *Delayering Corporate Law*, 34 Hofstra L. Rev. 469 (2005); Jacob Hale Russell and Arthur B. Laby, *The Decline and Rise of Fiduciary Obligations in Business* at 1, in *Fiduciary Obligations in Business* (Arthur B. Laby and Jacob Hale Russell eds. 2021); Julian Velasco, *Fiduciary Principles in Corporate Law* at 61, *in* Oxford Handbook of Fiduciary Law (Even J. Criddle, Paul B. Miller, and Robert H. Sitkoff eds. 2019).
[4] See *infra* notes 7–18 and accompanying text.

Thereafter, the discussion focuses on the lessening of fiduciary duties with respect to unincorporated business enterprises.

II. Select Corporate Law Cases: Lax Director and Officer Fiduciary Standards

Traditionally, corporate directors and officers were held to demanding standards of conduct—particularly when these fiduciaries engaged in alleged breaches of the duty of loyalty, such as interested director transactions.[5] As the US Supreme Court stated in several cases, corporate directors and officers are fiduciaries and are held to rigorous standards.[6]

Nonetheless, several cases serve as examples to illustrate that, with some frequency, laxity prevailed. For instance, in *Lagarde v. Anniston Lime & Stone Co.*, decided in 1900, the Alabama Supreme Court narrowly defined a corporate opportunity as "property wherein the corporation has an interest already existing or in which it has an expectancy growing out of an existing right."[7] There, the subject company owned one-third of a gravel pit, had a contract to purchase one-third, and had expressed interest in acquiring the remaining one-third. As to the one-third of the gravel pit that the company had expressed interest in acquiring but neither owned nor had a contract to acquire, the Alabama Supreme Court held that no corporate opportunity

---

[5] *See, e.g.*, Harold Marsh Jr., *Are Directors Trustees?*, 22 Bus. Law. 35, 36 (1966) ("In 1880 it could have been stated with confidence that in the United States the general rule was that any contract between a director and his corporation was voidable at the instance of the corporation or its shareholders, without regard to the fairness or unfairness of the transaction"). *But see* Norwood P. Beveridge Jr., *The Corporate Director's Fiduciary Duty of Loyalty: Understanding the Self-Interested Director Transaction*, 41 DePaul L. Rev. 655, 660 (1992) (disagreeing with Marsh's characterization and stating that interested director transactions "were never thought to be voidable without regard to fairness"). For cases supporting Beveridge's position, at least from the 1890s, *see, e.g., Lewis v. S.L. & E, Inc.*, 629 F.2d 764, 769 (2d Cir. 1980) (citing cases and applying New York law) ("At common law [an interested director] transaction was voidable unless shown by its proponent to be fair, and reasonable to the corporation"); *Sage v. Culver*, 41 N.E. Rep. 513, 514 (N.Y. Ct. App. 1895) (stating that when a corporate director or officer engages in a transaction with the corporation, he "is bound to explain the transaction, and show that the same was fair...."). *See also* Robert S. Saunders, et al., *Folk on the Delaware General Corporation Law* § 144.01 (7th ed. 2022) ("The principle of voidability for interested transactions, which was sometimes characterized as the common law rule, was significantly ameliorated by the 1967 enactment of section 144 of the Delaware General Corporation Law"); Velasco, *supra* note 3, at 1051–52. For cases supporting Marsh's position, *see* Chapter 4, note 79.

[6] *See, e.g., Twin-Lick Oil Company v. Marbury*, 91 U.S. 587, 588 (1875) ("That a director of a joint-stock corporation occupies one of those fiduciary relations where his dealings with the subject matter of his trust . . . and with the beneficiary or party whose interest is confided to his care, is viewed with jealousy by the courts...."); discussion and cases cited Chapter 8 *infra*, notes 14–28 and accompanying text; discussion Chapter 4 *infra*.

[7] 28 So. 199, 201 (Ala. 1900).

existed, thereby entitling the subject officer to purchase the remaining one-third interest.[8]

A similar result followed in *Pioneer Oil & Gas Co. v. Anderson*, decided by the Mississippi Supreme Court in 1933. In that case, the court held that a corporate director's purchase of property that the corporation was seeking to acquire was not the usurpation of a corporate opportunity. Relying on *Lagarde* for the proposition that "the mere fact that a plaintiff corporation was negotiating for the purchase of certain property did not give it such an interest or expectancy therein as would render a purchase thereof by the president and secretary a breach of fiduciary obligation...," the Mississippi court held that the subject director had properly acted.[9] With respect to a director or officer competing with her corporation, a number of older cases likewise have permissive language. For example, one appellate court opined: "The directors or officers of a corporation are not, by reason of the fiduciary relationship they bear toward the corporation, precluded from entering into an independent business *in competition with* the corporation."[10] Citing more than a dozen cases to support his proposition, one commentator stated in a law journal article published in 1943: "In the absence of special circumstances, courts have refused to compel the director to act for the corporation or not at all on the ground that this would place an unwarranted restriction upon personal business activity [and that this] rule has been applied even in fields in which the corporation is directly interested."[11]

With respect to the duty of care, a 1910 English case serves as an example. This case was discussed in an insightful law review article authored by Victor Brudney.[12] In *In re Brazilian Rubber Plantations and Estates*,[13] a number of the directors were "absolutely ignorant of business" and accepted

---

[8] *Id.* at 201–02.

[9] 151 So. 161, 164 (Miss. 1934). *See Lincoln Stores, Inc. v. Grant*, 34 N.E.2d 704 (Mass. 1941) (ruling no breach of the duty of loyalty when two directors, making use of information they learned from the company, purchased a competitor's stock rather than enabling the company to make the acquisition).

[10] *Red Top Cab Company v. Hanchett*, 48 F.2d 236, 238 (N.D. Cal. 1931) (applying California law) (emphasis supplied). *See Atkinson v. Marquart*, 541 P.2d 556, 558 (Ariz. 1975) (stating that "it is not the fact of [the director's] engaging in a competing business that gives rise to liability").

[11] Richard M. Ramsey, *Director's Power to Compete with His Corporation*, 18 Ind. L.J. 293, 302 (1943), *citing, inter alia, Barr v. Pittsburgh Plate Glass Co.*, 51 F. 33 (W.D. Pa. 1892); *Witmer v. Arkansas Dailies, Inc.*, 151 S.W.2d 971 (Ark. 1941); *Colorado & Utah Coal Co. v. Harris*, 49 P.2d 429 (Colo. 1935); *Lancaster Loose Leaf Tobacco Co. v. Robinson*, 250 S.W. 997 (Ky. 1923); *Bliss Petroleum Co. v. McNally*, 237 N.W. 53 (Mich. 1931); *N.Y. Automobile Co. v. Franklin*, 97 N.Y.S. 781 (1905); *Detroit Fidelity & Surety Co. v. Wichita Falls, First National Bank*, 66 S.W.2d 406 (Tex. App. 1933).

[12] Victor Brudney, *The Role of the Board of Directors: The ALI and Its Critics*, 37 U. Miami L. Rev. 223, 223–24 (1983).

[13] *In re Brazilian Rubber Plantations & Estates*, 27 Times L. Rep. 109 (1910).

their positions with the understanding that little was expected of them.[14] They were sued for allegedly failing to make any inquiry into the veracity of representations that they relied upon in authorizing the company to purchase rubber plantations despite the presence of warnings that these representations were false. The investments proved disastrous. In holding that the defendant directors were not liable for the losses sustained by the company, Justice Neville opined that a director "may undertake the management of a rubber company in complete ignorance of everything connected with rubber, without incurring responsibility for the mistakes which may result from such ignorance...."[15]

Another example that may be overlooked from this perspective is *Dodge v. Ford Motor Co.*, decided by the Michigan Supreme Court in 1919. The case frequently is viewed today for the proposition that "a corporation is organized and carried on primarily for the profit of the stockholders [and the] powers of the directors are to be employed for that end."[16] For purposes here, another key holding was the recognition of the business judgment rule whereby the court declined to scrutinize decisions made by the company's board of directors, reasoning that "judges are not business experts."[17] Hence, the *Ford Motor* decision may be viewed as a foundational decision for the eventual broad application and expansion of the business judgment rule that exists today—a standard that has been extended to a myriad of situations and insulates directors from liability exposure unless they act with gross negligence.[18]

Moreover, during the last three decades, efforts have been undertaken to avoid describing a corporate director as a fiduciary. For example, in revising the Model Business Corporation Act in 1984, the American Bar Association's Committee on Corporate Laws took the position that the

---

[14] *Id.* at 110.
[15] *Id.* at 111.
[16] 170 N.W. 668, 684 (Mich. 1919). Whether shareholder primacy—whereby a board of directors principal role is to maximize profits in a law compliant manner—should be abandoned in favor of an approach that seeks to serve all corporate constituencies currently is being debated. *See* discussion, *supra* Chapter 1, at notes 30–32 and accompanying text.
[17] 170 N.W. at 684 (also stating that "[t]here is committed to the discretion of directors, a discretion to be exercised in good faith, the infinite details of business....").
[18] The business judgment rule is applied by courts in many settings to protect directors from liability exposure. For example, this standard is invoked with respect to director decisions concerning the subject company's business operations, executive compensation, corporate acquisitions, and derivative litigation. The culpability standard required to be shown to overcome the presumption of the business judgment rule is gross negligence. *See, e.g., Aronson v. Lewis*, 473 A.2d 805, 812 (Del. 1984) (opining that "under the business judgment rule director liability is predicated upon concepts of gross negligence"). The business judgment rule is addressed in Chapters 3, 5, and 6 of this book.

applicable statute should avoid using the term fiduciary when referring to a director. As a Comment to the Act provided: "Section 8.30 [of the Model Business Corporation Act] does not use the term 'fiduciary' in the standard for directors' conduct, because that term could be confused with the unique attributes and obligations of a fiduciary imposed by the law of trusts, some of which are not appropriate for directors of a corporation."[19] However, as both case law and legal commentary evidence, corporate directors and officers continue to be deemed fiduciaries.[20]

The thrust of the foregoing discussion is that, with some frequency, director and officer fiduciary duties were interpreted with laxity in cases decided many decades ago. Certainly, during that time period, there existed much case law that held directors and officers to meaningful fiduciary standards. Nonetheless, the point made here is that the presence of laxity today with respect to corporate director and officer liability is not a novel phenomenon.

III. Unincorporated Business Enterprises: Fiduciary Duty Standards

From a traditional perspective, Justice Cardozo's language in *Meinhard v. Salmon* provides a clear holding that partners owe to one another "the duty of the finest loyalty": "Not honesty alone, but the punctilio of an honor the most sensitive, is then the standard of behavior."[21] Subsequent to this decision, recognizing that general partners are agents and thus subject to fiduciary duties, this strict standard has been restated by courts.[22] However, its

---

[19] Model Business Corporation Act § 8.30, Comment (1984). Likewise, the American Law Institute's *Principles of Corporate Governance: Analysis and Recommendations* (1994) declines to use the term "fiduciary" with respect to a director in its provisions. *See, e.g.,* § 4.01.

[20] *See, e.g., Stone v. Ritter,* 911 A.2 362 (Del. 2006); *Guzman v. Johnson,* 483 P.3d 531 (Nev. 2021); *In re McDonald's Corporation Derivative Litigation,* 289 A.3d 343 (Del. Ch. 2023); Douglas M. Branson, *Corporate Governance* §§ 6.01–8.38 (1993); William Meade Fletcher, et al., *Fletcher Cyclopedia Corporations* §§ 837.50 et seq. (2023); Harry G. Henn and John R. Alexander, *Law of Corporations* § 235, at 625 (1983).

[21] 164 N.E. 545, 546 (N.Y. 1928). To be precise, *Meinhard* involved a joint venture. This principle is applicable to partnerships.

[22] *See, e.g., Donahue v. Davis,* 68 So. 2d 163, 171 (Fla. 1953); *Gossett v. St. Paul Fire and Marine Insurance Company,* 427 So. 2d 386, 387 (Fla. Dist. App. 1983); *McConnell v. Hunt Sports Enterprises,* 725 N.E.2d 1193, 1216 (Ohio App. 1999). *See generally* Deborah A. DeMott, *Fiduciary Principles in Agency Law* in *The Oxford Handbook of Fiduciary Law, supra* note 3, at 23, 30–31, *quoting* American Law Institute, *Restatement (Third) of Agency* § 8.01 (2006) (discussing "an overarching fiduciary principle [that] the agent's 'duty [is] to act loyally for the principal's benefit in all matters connected with the agency relationship' ").

continued embracement today conflicts with the modern day reality that fiduciary duties in the partnership setting have been drastically reduced.

A. The Uniform Acts: Judicial Application

Pursuant to the Revised Uniform Partnership Act (RUPA), which has been adopted by the majority of states,[23] the duties of care and loyalty are diluted. Indeed, pursuant to the 2013 version of RUPA, a partner's duty of care is no longer recognized as a fiduciary obligation.[24] A partner need only "refrain from engaging in grossly negligent or reckless conduct, willful or intentional misconduct, or a knowing violation of law."[25] The 2001 Uniform Limited Partnership Act (ULPA) contains similar language,[26] as does the Uniform Limited Liability Company Act (ULLCA).[27] Nonetheless, these provisions arguably are not a significant departure from prior law as a number of courts had applied a gross negligence standard in determining a partner's liability for breach of the duty of care.[28]

It is with respect to the duty of loyalty that RUPA departs markedly from Justice Cardozo's language in *Meinhard*. Pursuant to RUPA, a partner's fiduciary duty of loyalty arises only in specified situations. The 1997 version of RUPA provides that the duty of loyalty "is limited" to specified obligations while the 2013 version of RUPA states that the duty of loyalty "includes" these obligations. Generally, pursuant to both versions, a partner is precluded from usurping a partnership opportunity, competing with the partnership, acting on a person's behalf whose interest is adverse to the partnership, and misappropriating partnership assets.[29] ULPA has similar language with

---

[23] *See State Law Governing Partnerships*, U.S. Legal, available at https://partnerships.uslegal.com.
[24] *See* Comments to RUPA § 409(c): "The Act no longer refers to the duty of care as a fiduciary duty."
[25] *Id.* § 409(c).
[26] *See* ULPA § 409(c).
[27] *See* ULLCA § 409(c).
[28] *See, e.g., Kuznik v. Bees Ferry Associates*, 538 S.E.2d 15, 27 (S.C. App. 2000); *Starr v. Fordham*, 648 N.E.2d 1261, 1265–66 (Mass. 1995); *Duffy v. Piazza Construction Inc.*, 815 P.2d 267, 269 (Wash. App. 1991). Hence, as observed by one source: "Courts typically apply the business judgment rule to decisions made by partners." J. Dennis Hynes and Mark J. Loewenstein, *Agency, Partnership, and the LLC* 598 (10th ed. 2019). *See* Christine Hurt, et al., *Bromberg & Ribstein on Partnership* § 6.07(f) (2023).
[29] *See* both the 1997 and 2013 versions of RUPA § 409(b). *See also* J. Dennis Hynes, *Freedom of Contract, Fiduciary Duties, and Partnerships: The Bargain Principle and the Law of Agency*, 54 Wash. & Lee L. Rev. 439, 452 (1997) ("The partnership relationship is viewed most appropriately as contractual in nature [and] surely reflects the expectations of most people who enter into a partnership—that they will be able to agree on the parameters of their internal relationship").

respect to a general partner's duty of loyalty to the limited partnership and the limited partners[30] as does ULLCA with respect to a manager's duty of loyalty in a manager-managed LLC and to a member's duty of loyalty in a member-managed LLC.[31] Notably, a number of courts, focusing on the applicable statute's language that the fiduciary duty of loyalty "includes" specified obligations, have deemed actionable other inappropriate conduct by a general partner even though such conduct is not enumerated in the governing statute.[32] Nonetheless, from a historical perspective, this treatment of partner conduct is not characteristic of the traditional standards that were applied. RUPA recognizes this development, stating in a Comment that "[a]rguably, the term 'fiduciary' is inappropriate when used to describe the duties of a partner because a partner may legitimately pursue self-interest ... [but] partners have long been characterized as fiduciaries."[33]

This diminution in duties owed is magnified by statutory authorization that significantly reduces these duties pursuant to a governing agreement entered into by the participants. Thus, in general partnerships, limited liability partnerships, limited partnerships, and LLCs, the parties may enter into an agreement that drastically reduces these already diminished obligations. For example, under RUPA, a general partnership agreement, "if not manifestly unreasonable," may alter both the duty of care and the duty of loyalty.[34] With respect to the duty of care, the agreement may reduce the duty of care but it "may not authorize conduct involving bad faith, willful or intentional misconduct, or knowing violation of law."[35] Similarly, a general partnership agreement may "alter or eliminate the aspects of the duty of loyalty" that are set forth in RUPA and may also "identify specific types or categories of activities that do not violate the duty of loyalty."[36] ULPA has identical language,

---

[30] *See* ULPA § 409(b).
[31] *See* ULLCA § 409(b), (i).
[32] *See Enea v. Superior Court*, 132 Cal. App. 4th 1559 (Cal. App. 2005); *Labovitz v. Dolan*, 545 N.E.2d 304 (Ill. App. 1989). As discussed in the text, the 1997 version of RUPA, rather than stating that the duty of loyalty "includes" specified obligations, provides that a partner's "duty of loyalty to the partnership and the other partners *is limited*" to these specified obligations. *See* RUPA § 404(b) (1997) (emphasis supplied).
[33] RUPA § 409 Comment. *See id.* § 409(e): "A partner does not violate a duty or obligation under this [Act] or under the partnership agreement solely because the partner's conduct furthers the partner's own interest."
[34] *See id.* § 105(d)(3). With respect to the meaning of the term "manifestly unreasonable," *see* Mark J. Loewenstein, *Fiduciary Duties and Unincorporated Business Entities: In Defense of the "Manifestly Unreasonable" Standard*, 41 Tulsa L. Rev. 411, 431 (2006) (citing cases interpreting the meaning of the term "manifestly unreasonable" under RUPA).
[35] RUPA § 105(d)(3)(C).
[36] *Id.* §105(d)(3)(A)–(B). *See* Larry E. Ribstein, *The Revised Uniform Partnership Act: Not Ready for Prime Time*, 49 Bus. Law. 45, 57 (1993) (stating that "courts ... have enforced partnership

enabling a general partner pursuant to the limited partnership agreement to significantly reduce the duties that otherwise would be owed to the limited partnership and the limited partners.[37] Likewise, ULLCA authorizes an LLC's operating agreement to diminish the duties of care and loyalty that would otherwise be owed to the LLC and its members.[38]

Pursuant to the foregoing statutes, the partnership agreement (or operating agreement) may significantly reduce but may not eliminate the duties of care and loyalty.[39] Any diminution of these duties set forth in the governing agreement must be "stated clearly and with particularity."[40] When sufficient disclosure is made in the applicable agreement and the limitation is not deemed "manifestly unreasonable,"[41] courts ordinarily uphold the limitation.[42] A number of illustrative examples follow.

In *Singer v. Singer*, the general partnership agreement permitted each partner to engage in business and other endeavors for his or her individual benefit even though such conduct would conflict or be in competition with the partnership.[43] Suit was initiated after two partners purchased a parcel of property which had been discussed as a possible purchase by the partnership at a meeting attended by several members of the general partnership. Basing its decision on the permissive language of the partnership agreement, the court ruled for the defendant partners, stating that the pertinent provision

---

agreements permitting partners to compete with the partnership and to engage in self-dealing"). *See also* RUPA § 409(d): "A partner shall discharge the duties and obligations under this [Act] or under the partnership agreement and exercise any rights consistently with the contractual obligation of good faith and fair dealing." The Comment to this provision states that contract law implies this obligation of good faith and fair dealing in every contract. Importantly, "[t]he partnership agreement cannot eliminate this obligation, neither in whole (i.e., generally) nor in part (i.e., as applicable to specified situations)." *Id.*

[37] *See* ULPA § 105(d).
[38] *See* ULLCA § 105(d).
[39] *See* RUPA § 105(b)(5), (d)(3). Hence, RUPA "rejects the notion that a contract can completely transform an inherently fiduciary relationship into a merely arm's length association." *Id.* § 105 Comment.
[40] *Id.* (citing cases holding that "displacement of fiduciary duties is effective only to the extent that the displacement is stated clearly and with particularity"). *See* Douglas K. Moll, *Contracting Out of Partnership*, 47 J. Corp. L. 753, 769 (2022) (asserting that "there is logic to authorizing limitations while prohibiting eliminations [as] [l]imitations convey specific information about foreseeable conflicts that parties without legal backgrounds can understand [while] [e]liminations convey no information about the problem envisioned by the proposer, and they require parties to have a legal understanding of what 'no fiduciary duty of loyalty' means").
[41] *See* Loewenstein, *supra* note 34, at 431 (citing cases and stating, "While there are relatively few cases that specifically address the meaning of manifestly unreasonable as it appears in various statutes, case law does shed some light on the term").
[42] *See* cases discussed *infra* notes 43–61 and accompanying text.
[43] 634 P.2d 766 (Okla. App. 1981).

"legitimize[d] and extend[ed] free competition between the partners to partnership prospects and opportunities. . . ."[44] Indeed, the court construed the provision to be "uniquely drafted to promote spirited, if not outright predatory competition between the partners."[45]

Similarly, in *J & J Celcom v. AT&T Wireless Services, Inc.*, the Washington Supreme Court upheld a general partner's sale of all of the partnership's assets at a fair price to an affiliated party where the transaction was disclosed to the remaining partners.[46] The terms of the partnership agreement expressly authorized the sale of partnership assets pursuant to majority vote. Using its controlling interest, the defendant general partner sold all of the partnership's assets to an affiliated entity, thereby engaging in self-dealing. Interpreting the waiver provision of the general partnership agreement in a broad manner, the court held that the language of the agreement was adequately specific to contract around the controlling general partner's duty to refrain from self-dealing.[47]

The Ohio appellate court's decision in *McConnell v. Hunt Sports Enterprises* provides a striking example of broadly interpreting a waiver provision in the LLC setting. There, members formed an LLC with the objective of acquiring ownership of a National Hockey League team to be located in Columbus Ohio. The applicable provision in the LLC agreement provided: "Members shall not in any way be prohibited from or restricted in engaging or owning an interest in any other business venture of any nature, including any venture which might be competitive with the business

---

[44] *Id.* at 772. The pertinent provision provided that each partner "shall be free to enter into business and other transactions for his or her own separate individual account even though such business or other transactions may be in conflict with and/or in competition with the business of [the partnership] . . . [and] it being the intention and agreement that . . . any individual partner of the partnership . . . shall be free to deal on his or her own account to the same extent and with the same force and effect as if he or she were not and never had been members of said partnership." *Id.* at 768.

[45] *Id.* at 772 (also stating that the provision's "strong wording leaves no doubt in our minds that its drafters intended to effect such a result").

[46] 169 P.3d 823 (Wash. 2007).

[47] *Id.* at 824–25. *See id.* at 826 (Madsen, J., concurring):

RUPA represents a major overhaul in the nature of the fiduciary duties imposed on partners. There are two general views of the partnership relation: one emphasizes the fiduciary nature of the partnership and the other emphasizes the contractual nature of the partnership. The common law and UPA are based on the fiduciary view, the fundamental principle of which is that partners must subordinate their own interests to the collective interest, absent consent of all the partners. . . . RUPA represents a major shift away from the fiduciary view and toward the "libertarian" or "contractarian" view, by (a) expressly limiting fiduciary duties, (b) sanctioning a partner's pursuit of self-interest, and (c) allowing partners to waive most fiduciary duties by contract. RUPA was intended to bring the law of partnership into the "modern age," to make partnerships more rational, efficient, and stable business entities.

of the Company."[48] Subsequently, one of the LLC members formed a separate group that successfully purchased the franchise, the validity of which was challenged. Looking at the composition of the LLC members, a number of whom had ownership interests in other professional sports franchises,[49] a logical reading of the provision was that the members were free to have ownership interests in other sports and entertainment business endeavors regardless whether these franchises were competitive with the Columbus hockey franchise. It may be argued that it would be nonsensical for the LLC agreement to allow the members to compete with the LLC for the same Columbus hockey franchise.

In its decision, the Ohio court invoked Justice Cardozo's language in *Meinhard*, stating that LLC members "owe one another the duty of utmost trust and loyalty."[50] Nonetheless, this duty must be considered in the context of the LLC's operating agreement which limited the fiduciary duties that otherwise would have applied. Reviewing the plain language of the operating agreement, the court held that the applicable provision specifically authorized its members to compete with the LLC. Accordingly, no breach of fiduciary duty was committed by a LLC member's formation of a separate investment group that successfully purchased the Columbus hockey franchise.[51]

B. Delaware Law: Statutes and Case Law

Given its prominence, Delaware law must be addressed. The default rule in Delaware is that fiduciary duties apply in LLCs and partnerships.[52]

---

[48] 725 N.E.2d 1193, 1206 (Ohio App. 1999). In the LLC's operating agreement, the title of this provision was "Members May Compete."

[49] For example, an affiliated enterprise of the Hunt family owns the National Football League's (NFL) Kansas City Chiefs. *See, e.g.*, Chase Peterson-Withorn, *After 50 Years, The $15.3 Billion Hunt Family Just Won The Super Bowl*, Forbes (Feb. 2, 2020).

[50] 725 N.E.2d at 1216. *See id.* at 1214 ("In the case at bar, a limited liability company is involved which, like a partnership, involves a fiduciary relationship").

[51] *Id.* at 1216 (stating that the general duty of loyalty that was owed in the case at bar "must be considered in the context of [the LLC] members' ability, pursuant to [the] operating agreement, to compete with the company").

[52] *See, e.g.*, Delaware General Partnership Act § 15-4-4(a)-(b); Delaware Limited Liability Company Act § 18-1104 ("In any case not provided for in this chapter, the rules of law and equity, including the rules of law and equity relating to fiduciary duties and the law merchant, shall govern"). Prior to this 2018 amendment to the Delaware Limited Liability Company Act, the law was unclear whether default fiduciary duties applied in the LLC context. *See Gatz Properties, LLC v. Auriga Capital Corporation*, 59 A.3d 1206, 1219 (Del. 2012) (stating that "the merits of the issue whether the LLC statute does—or does not—impose default fiduciary duties is one about which reasonable minds could differ").

Significantly, Delaware expands upon the Uniform Acts by authorizing not only the reduction of fiduciary duties but also their elimination by the terms of the governing agreement. Thus, in general and limited partnerships as well as in LLCs, the governing agreement may eliminate fiduciary duties that otherwise would apply.[53] The Delaware courts dutifully have applied these waiver provisions.[54]

As stated by one Delaware court, "principles of contract preempt fiduciary principles where the parties to a limited partnership have made their intentions to do so plain."[55] As elaborated upon by subsequent decisions, absent contractual modification, fiduciary duties apply to general partners and LLC managers but these duties may be eliminated pursuant to the terms of the governing agreement.[56] As the Delaware Chancery Court strikingly admonished the plaintiff limited partners: "This court has made clear that it will not [be] tempted by the piteous pleas of limited partners who are seeking to escape the consequences of their own decisions to become investors in a partnership whose general partner has clearly exempted itself [pursuant

---

[53] *See* Del. Code Ann. tit. 6, § 15-103(f) (general partnerships); *id.* § 17-1101(d) (limited partnerships); *id.* § 18-1101(c) (limited liability companies). For example, the LLC statute provides, "To the extent that, at law or in equity, a member or manager or other person has duties (including fiduciary duties) to a limited liability company or to another member or manager or to another person that is a party to or is otherwise bound by a limited liability company agreement, the member's or manager's or other person's duties may be expanded or restricted or eliminated by provisions in the limited liability company agreement; provided, that the limited liability company agreement may not eliminate the implied contractual covenant of good faith and fair dealing." Thus, a policy underlying Delaware unincorporated business enterprises is to give "maximum effect to the principle of freedom of contract and to the enforceability" of governing agreements." *Gotham Partners, L.P. v. Hallwood Realty Partners, L.P.*, 817 A.2d 160, 167 (Del. 2002). With respect to the duty of good faith and fair dealing, *see* note 36 *supra*.

[54] *See, e.g.*, cases cited *infra* notes 55–61 and accompanying text.

[55] *Sonet v. Plum Creek Timber Co.*, 722 A.2d 319, 322 (Del. Ch. 1998).

[56] *See, e.g., Dieckman v. Regency GP, L.P.*, 155 A.3d 358. 366 (Del. 2017) (stating that "investors can no longer hold the general partner to fiduciary standards of conduct, but instead must rely on the express language of the partnership agreement to sort out the rights and obligations among the general partner, the partnership, and the limited partner investors"); *In re W.J. Bradley Mortgage Capital, L.L.C.*, 598 B.R. 150, 165 (Bankr. D. Del. 2019) (stating that "courts recognize contractual agreements where the fiduciary duties have been limited"); *Ross Holding and Management Co. v. Advance Realty Group, L.L.C.*, 2014 WL 4374261, at *12 (Del. Ch. 2014) ("By default, the traditional fiduciary duties applicable to corporations apply to limited liability companies [but,] where such default rules have been clearly supplanted or modified, those contractual choices will be respected"); *In re Atlas Energy Resources, L.L.C.*, 2010 WL 4273122, at *12 (Del. Ch. 2010) (stating that the LLC agreement "unambiguously eliminates the traditional fiduciary duties" of [the LLC's] governing persons so that "the only duties owed ... are those set forth elsewhere in the LLC Agreement"); Myron T. Steele, *Judicial Scrutiny of Fiduciary Duties in Delaware Limited Partnerships and Limited Liability Companies*, 32 Del. J. Corp. L. 1, 4 (2007) (authored by then Chief Justice of the Delaware Supreme Court) (opining that "parties to contractual entities such as limited liability partnerships and limited liability companies, should be free—given a full, clear disclosure paradigm—to adopt or reject any fiduciary duty obligation by contract").

to the limited partnership agreement] from traditional fiduciary duties ... [and that, accordingly,] investors should be careful to read partnership agreements before buying units."[57] As a last example, in a 2022 decision, the Delaware Supreme Court emphasized the maximum flexibility permitted in partnership agreements under Delaware law. In *Boardwalk Pipeline Partners L.P.*, the court held that the limited partnership agreement's elimination of fiduciary duties, coupled with full disclosure to investors, authorized the general partner to legally engage in the challenged conduct.[58] As the court opined, "[t]he Partnership Agreement allowed [the general partner] to exercise the call right to its advantage—and to the disadvantage of the minority unitholders—free from fiduciary duties."[59] Accordingly, with respect to unincorporated enterprises under Delaware law, maximum effect is given to effectuating freedom of contract and the enforceability of governing agreements.[60] Thus, under Delaware law, by contractual agreement pursuant to a partnership or LLC agreement, fiduciary duties may be eliminated in their entirety.[61]

IV. The Diminution of Fiduciary Duties in Unincorporated Enterprises

The preceding discussion aptly demonstrates that fiduciary duties have been drastically curtailed in unincorporated enterprises. By means of a governing contractual agreement, fiduciary obligations that otherwise would apply are significantly limited. Indeed, in Delaware, fiduciary duties may be eliminated pursuant to agreement among the participants. No longer in the vast majority of states do traditional fiduciary duties apply if a governing agreement exists that reduces those obligations. Consequently, the fiduciary

---

[57] *Miller v. American Real Estate Partners, LP,* 2001 WL 1045643, at *8 (Del. Ch. 2001) (stating that the Delaware limited partnership act "puts investors on notice that fiduciary duties may be altered by partnership agreements" and that, in large measure, the Act "reflects the doctrine of *caveat emptor*").

[58] *Boardwalk Pipeline Partners LP v. Bandera Master Fund LP,* 288 A.3d 1083 (Del. 2022).

[59] *Id.* at 1099. The defendants in the case at bar "took full advantage of the flexibility permitted under Delaware law." *Id.* at 1087.

[60] *See id.* at 1108 ("Delaware courts respect the terms of a partnership's governing agreements to preserve the maximum flexibility of contract"). *Accord, Dieckman v. Regency GP LP,* 155 A.3d 358, 366 (Del. 2017); *Norton v. K-Sea Transportation Partners L.P.,* 67 A.3d 354 (Del. 2013); *New Enterprise Associates 14 L.P. v. Rich,* 295 A.3d 520 (Del. Ch. 2023); *Ross Holding and Management Co. v. Advance Realty Group, L.L.C.,* 2014 WL 4374261 (Del. Ch. 2014).

[61] *See* discussion *supra* notes 52–60 and accompanying text.

nature of the partnership and LLC relationship has been greatly diminished. In its stead, a contractarian approach is the dominant force.[62]

Whether contractarian primacy is the appropriate approach for unincorporated enterprises is disputed.[63] Much of this dispute in many states, however, is no longer pertinent as the contractarian approach has emerged as the victor.[64] This consequence particularly is evidenced in Delaware where major limited partnerships and LLCs are established.[65] In Delaware, provided that sufficient disclosure is made, general partners of limited partnerships and managers of LLCs may entirely eliminate their fiduciary duties by means of a definitive governing agreement.[66]

Compare the unincorporated enterprise contractarian primacy approach with that of corporate law. With specified exceptions,[67] fiduciary duties cannot be waived in the corporate context.[68] However, as this book

---

[62] See Alan W. Vestal, *Fundamental Contractarian Error in the Revised Uniform Limited Partnership Act of 1992*, 73 B.U. L. Rev. 523, 535 (1993) (criticizing "the drafters' rejection of the fiduciary essence of the partnership relationship in favor of the contractarian premise" and contending that "the drafters have made the partners adversaries, whereas before they were bound by 'the duty of finest loyalty'").

[63] *Compare* Claire Moore Dickerson, *Is It Appropriate to Appropriate Corporate Concepts: Fiduciary Duties and the Revised Uniform Partnership Act*, 64 U. Colo. L. Rev. 111, 155–56 (1993) (disagreeing with "contractarian commentators who maintain that the traditional fiduciary duties are so vague and aspirational as to be meaningless" and opining that the application of fiduciary duties "serve to guide the parties to a standard of behavior that reduces the need to monitor"), *with* Ribstein, *supra* note 36, at 45 (asserting that contractarian primacy is the correct approach).

[64] *See* discussion *supra* notes 34–61 and accompanying text.

[65] *See* Steele, *supra* note 56, at 32 ("There is as much a premium on the Delaware courts focusing clearly on the contractual relationship of parties to unincorporated business entities as there is on the parties bargaining for and negotiating clear, precise terms that define that relationship"); discussion *supra* notes 52–61 and accompanying text.

[66] *See supra* note 53 and accompanying text.

[67] Examples in the corporate context include waiver of corporate opportunities, director exculpation statutes eliminating monetary liability for breach of the duty of care, and shareholder agreements in closely held corporations whereby specified fiduciary obligations are waived. These issues are discussed in Chapters 3, 4, and 7 of the book.

[68] *See, e.g., New Enterprise Associates 14, L.P. v. Rich*, 295 A.3d 520, 549 (Del. Ch. 2023):

> Delaware corporate law is popularly understood to impose mandatory fiduciary duties that cannot be modified. Although monetary liability for the duty of care can be eliminated, the underlying duty cannot be altered, and the duty of loyalty stands inviolate. That view gains currency from contrasting Delaware corporations with alternative entities, where the governing statutes authorize the full elimination of fiduciary duties.

Likewise, the Delaware Supreme Court in *CCSB Financial Corp. v. Totta*, 302 A.3d 387 (Del. 2023), invalidated a charter provision that stated that any "good faith" board of director decision applying a shareholder voting limitation would be binding. Holding that this provision was inconsistent with Section 102(b)(7) because it limited "director liability for breaches of the duty of loyalty" and was "prohibited by Delaware statute and public policy," the court ruled that the charter provision was invalid. *Id.* at 398–400. Notably, the court concluded that such a provision permissibly may be included in a limited partnership or LLC agreement. *Id.* at 402 (stating that "the option to alter or eliminate fiduciary duties, if desired, resides in the land of alternative entities, not through a Delaware corporation").

addresses, in actuality, the fiduciary duties of corporate directors and officers have been greatly diminished. Indeed, these duties have been reduced to the degree that no longer should directors and officers be deemed fiduciaries.

Returning to unincorporated enterprises, in those states where fiduciary duties can be drastically reduced (if not eliminated) pursuant to the terms of the applicable governing agreement, it is clear that the nature of the relationship has changed. No longer should general partners and LLC managers be deemed fiduciaries. To a significant degree, the Uniform Acts recognize this transition with respect to the duties of care and loyalty.[69] In view of reality, like corporate directors and officers, general partners and LLC managers should be recognized as "discretionaries." In this manner, the duties that these persons owe are dependent on the applicable statutory provisions, judicial interpretation, the terms of the governing agreement, and the underlying facts and circumstances of the situation at issue.

---

[69] *See* discussion *supra* notes 23–61 and accompanying text. *See generally* Richard A. Booth, *Fiduciary Duty, Contract, and Waiver in Partnerships and Limited Liability Companies*, 1 J. Small & Emerging Bus. L. 55 (1997); Rutherford B. Campbell, *Bumping Along the Bottom: Abandoned Principles and Failed Fiduciary Standards in Uniform Partnership and LLC Statutes*, 96 Ky. L.J. 163 (2008); Melvin Aron Eisenberg, *The Limits of Cognition and the Limits of Contract*, 47 Stan. L. Rev. 211 (1995); J. Dennis Hynes, *Fiduciary Duties and RUPA: An Inquiry Into Freedom of Contract*, 58 Law & Cont. Prob. 29 (1995); Mohsen Manesh, *Creatures of Contract: A Half-Truth About LLCs*, 42 Del. J. Corp. L. 391 (2018); Leo E. Strine Jr. and J. Travis Laster, *The Siren Song of Unlimited Contractual Freedom*, in *Research Handbook on Partnerships, LLCs, and Alternative Forms of Business Organizations* at 11 (Robert W. Hillman & Mark J. Loewenstein eds. 2014); Donald J. Weidner, *RUPA and Fiduciary Duty: The Texture of Relationship*, 58 Law & Contem. Prob. 82 (1995); sources cited notes 22, 28, 29, 34, 36, 40, 56, 62, 63 *supra*.

3

The Illusion of Corporate Director and Officer Fiduciary Duty: The Duty of Care, the Business Judgment Rule, and Exculpation Statutes

I. Introduction

This chapter focuses on directors' and officers' liability exposure in situations where the duty of loyalty is *not* implicated. Among the obligations that directors and officers owe are the duty of care and the duty of loyalty. As the Delaware Supreme Court has made clear, both officers and directors owe these obligations.[1] As will be illustrated in this chapter, directors and officers are rarely held liable for breach of the duty of care in either direct or derivative actions initiated by shareholders.

For several decades, this has been the situation. As Yale law professor Joseph Bishop commented over fifty years ago: "The search for cases in which directors of industrial corporations have been held liable ... for negligence uncomplicated by self-dealing is a very small number of needles in a very large haystack ..."[2] Similarly, as phrased by Harper, James and Gray, "honest stupidity has been no excuse in negligence law ... except perhaps for business executives."[3] Other legal commentators likewise have viewed the duty of care as "moribund"[4] and in a state of "demise."[5]

---

[1] *See, e.g., Gantler v. Stephens*, 965 A.2d 695, 708–09 (Del. 2009) ("In the past, we have implied that officers of Delaware corporations, like directors, owe fiduciary duties of care and loyalty, and that the fiduciary duties of officers are the same as those of directors. We now explicitly so hold").

[2] Joseph Bishop, *Sitting Ducks and Decoy Ducks: New Trends in the Indemnification of Corporate Directors and Officers*, 77 Yale L.J. 1078, 1099 (1968).

[3] Fowler V. Harper, Fleming James Jr., and Oscar S. Gray, *Harper, James and Gray on Torts* § 16.11 (3d ed. 2023).

[4] George W. Dent Jr., *The Revolution in Corporate Governance, the Monitoring Board, and the Director's Duty of Care*, 61 B.U. L. Rev. 623, 646 (1981).

[5] Stuart R. Cohn, *Demise of the Director's Duty of Care: Judicial Avoidance of Standards and Sanctions Through the Business Judgment Rule*, 62 Tex. L. Rev. 591 (1983). *See* Krishnan Chittur, *The Corporate Director's Standard of Care: Past, Present, and Future*, 10 Del. J. Corp. L. 505 (1985);

Corporate Director and Officer Liability. Marc I. Steinberg, Oxford University Press.
© Marc I. Steinberg 2025. DOI: 10.1093/9780197751534.003.0003

Nonetheless, the standard of conduct, as reflected in the Model Business Corporation Act, enunciates that standard as conduct that a reasonable person would engage in under similar circumstances.[6] As discussed in Chapter 1 of this book, however, standards of conduct are to be distinguished from standards of review (or standards of liability).[7] As stated by one authority: "A standard of conduct states how an actor should conduct a given activity or play a given role [while a] standard of review states the test a court should apply when it reviews an actor's conduct to determine whether to impose liability or grant injunctive relief."[8] That is not to say that liability is never imposed against corporate fiduciaries for breach of the duty of care, as the well-known *Van Gorkom* decision demonstrates.[9]

It should be emphasized that the objective of this chapter is not to criticize application of the business judgment rule or adoption of exculpation statutes. Particularly, with respect to the business judgment rule, there are sound reasons for the implementation of this principle in certain situations. This point is discussed elsewhere in the book, including in this chapter as well as Chapter 9.

The fact remains that rarely is monetary liability imposed against a corporate director or officer for breach of fiduciary duty *unaccompanied* by loyalty considerations—even when such individual's conduct constitutes gross negligence or even more culpable behavior. The focus of this chapter is to provide ample support for this statement, thereby evidencing the misnomer

---

Henry Ridgeley Horsey (former Justice, Delaware Supreme Court), *The Duty of Care Component of the Delaware Business Judgment Rule*, 19 Del. J. Corp. L. 971 (1994).

[6] *See* § 8.30 of the Model Business Corporation Act (Standards of Conduct for Directors). Note, however, as a Comment to that provision states: "Section 8.30 addresses standards of conduct—the level of performance expected of directors undertaking the rule and responsibilities of the office of director [but] does not address the liability of a director...."

[7] *See* Chapter 1, notes 33–41 and accompanying text. As stated by the Delaware Court of Chancery: "When determining whether directors have breached their fiduciary duties, Delaware corporate law distinguishes between the standard of conduct and the standard of review [with the former standard] describ[ing] what directors are expected to do. . . ." *In re Trados Incorporated Shareholder Litigation*, 73 A.3d 17, 35 (Del. Ch. 2013).

[8] Melvin Aron Eisenberg, *The Divergence of Standards of Conduct and Standards of Review in Corporate Law*, 62 Fordham L. Rev. 437, 437 (1993), *quoted in*, William T. Allen, Jack B. Jacobs and Leo E. Strine Jr., *Function Over Form: A Reassessment of Standards of Review in Delaware Corporation Law*, 56 Bus. Law. 1287, 1295 (2001).

[9] *See Smith v. Van Gorkom*, 488 A.2d 858 (Del. 1985); discussion *infra* notes 55–58 and accompanying text. In a recent decision, the Delaware Supreme Court conflated the standard of conduct and the standard of liability in a single sentence. *See United Food and Commercial Workers Union v. Zuckerberg*, 262 A.3d 1034, 1049–50 (Del. 2021) (emphasis supplied) ("Predicated upon concepts of *gross negligence*, the *duty of care* requires that [corporate] fiduciaries *inform themselves of material information* before making a business decision and act *prudently* in carrying out their duties").

of identifying corporate directors and officers as fiduciaries. Accordingly, the chapter examines the duty of care, the business judgment rule, and director and officer exculpation statutes to validate this assertion.

II. The Duty of Care

With respect to the duty of care, a number of courts adhere to an ordinary negligence standard. Applying this standard, courts ascertain whether the defendant director or officer exercised the degree of care that an "ordinarily prudent person in a like position would use in similar circumstances."[10] Nonetheless, monetary liability premised on a corporate director's or officer's breach of the duty of care has been rarely imposed.[11]

One explanation is the proximate cause requirement that a plaintiff must satisfy before liability is imposed. Judge Learned Hand made this point in *Barnes v. Andrews* where he opined that "the plaintiff must accept the burden of showing that the performance of the [director] defendant's duties would have avoided the loss, and what loss it would have avoided."[12] Expanding, Judge Hand explained, "when a business fails from general mismanagement, business incapacity, or bad judgment, how is it possible to say that a single director could have made the company successful?" Rather, "the plaintiff must show that, had [the defendant director] done [his] duty, he could have made the company prosper, or at least broken its fall ... [and also] must show what sum [such director] could have saved the company."[13] In another case, although finding that the defendant director's conduct was wrongful, no liability was imposed as her negligence "in failing to perform

---

[10] *Brane v. Roth*, 590 N.E.2d 587, 590 (Ind. Ct. App. 1993). The Indiana statute that the court construed had been repealed and replaced by a statute that provided greater protection from liability for directors. *See* Ind. Code § 23-1-35-1. The court declined to give that statute retroactive effect. *See* 590 N.E.2d at 590. For other cases applying a reasonable care standard, *see, e.g., Robinson v. Watts Detective Agency, Inc.*, 685 F.2d 729, 737 (1st Cir. 1982) (applying Massachusetts law and citing *Hathaway v. Huntley*, 188 N.E. 616, 618 (Mass. 1933)); *Omnibank of Mantee v. United Southern Bank*, 607 So.2d 76, 89 (Miss. 1992); *Francis v. United Jersey Bank*, 432 A.2d 814, 822 (N.J. 1981); *Theriot v. Bourg*, 691 So. 2d 213, 222 (La. App. 1997).

[11] *See* sources cited *supra* notes 2–5 and accompanying text.

[12] 298 F. 614 (S.D.N.Y. 1924) (applying New York law).

[13] *Id.* at 617. When the defendant director's alleged misconduct involves failing to object to an improper loan or other concrete transaction, courts more readily find that proximate causation has been shown. *See, e.g., FDIC v. Bierman*, 2 F.3d 1424 (7th Cir. 1993) (finding liability with respect to those directors who failed to object to a loan); *Francis v. United Jersey Bank*, 432 A.2d 814 (N.J. 1981) (holding proximate causation requirement shown where defendant director failed to object to patently improper loans authorized by her sons to themselves who were fellow directors).

her duties as director was not a cause contributing to the bankruptcy of the corporation."[14]

Another key reason is that many courts apply a lax version of what constitutes negligent misconduct even if the business judgment rule is not invoked.[15] In a number of cases, permissive language is used when ascertaining what constitutes negligence. For example, the New Jersey Supreme Court opined that "a director should acquire at least rudimentary understanding of the business of the corporation."[16] Synonyms for "rudimentary" include "simple," "crude," "primitive," and "basic,"[17] evidencing that the standard adopted is lenient.

Another approach embraces a pure heart empty head rationale. As the Virginia Supreme Court stated, "a director's discharge of duties is not measured by what a reasonable person would do in similar circumstances or by the rationality of the ultimate decision [but rather by] a director act[ing] in accordance with his/her good faith business judgment of what is in the best interests of the corporation."[18]

Providing further insulation, several courts have applied a gross negligence standard in determining whether a corporate director or officer breached the duty of care. A number of these cases were decided over a century ago. Citing case authority, the Maryland high court opined in 1881 that "directors are personally liable for the consequences of their frauds or malfeasance, or for such gross negligence as may amount to a breach of trust, to the damage of the corporation or its stockholders."[19] In Delaware, gross negligence is the applicable culpability standard for duty of care claims. As stated by one court: "When analyzing a claim for breach of the duty of care, Delaware courts apply a standard of gross negligence, which has been

---

[14] *See Hathaway v. Huntley*, 188 N.E. 616, 618 (Mass. 1933). *See also Smith v. Pacific Pools of Washington, Inc.*, 530 P.2d 658 (Wash. App. 1975) (holding that adverse economic conditions, rather than corporate president's alleged alcoholism, were responsible for severe downturn in the company's financial condition).

[15] *See* sources cited notes 2–5 *supra*.

[16] *Francis v. United Jersey Bank*, 452 A.2d 814, 821 (N.J. 1981). *See id.* at 820 ("Generally, directors are accorded broad immunity...").

[17] "Rudimentary," Merriam-Webster.com Thesaurus, Merriam-Webster, https://www.merriam-webster.com/thesaurus/rudimentary (accessed Aug. 4, 2023).

[18] *Willard ex rel. Moneta Building Supply, Inc. v. Moneta Building Supply, Inc.*, 515 S.E.2d 277, 284 (Va. 1999).

[19] *Booth v. Robinson*, 53 Md. 419, 438 (1881). *See* Cleaveland D. Miller, *The Fiduciary Duties of a Corporate Director*, 4 U. Balt. L. Rev. 259, 270 (1975) (stating that case law indicates that "Maryland holds a director liable [for duty of care breach] only for gross negligence").

defined as 'reckless indifference to or a deliberate disregard of the whole body of stockholders or actions which are without the bounds of reason.'"[20]

Because a corporate officer is an agent and owes the corporate principal specified obligations, it may be posited that, consistent with agency principles, that individual owes a duty to act with reasonable care, competence, and diligence.[21] Nonetheless, at least in Delaware, that position has been rejected. As the Delaware Court of Chancery observed, Delaware court decisions "have embraced gross negligence as the standard for evaluating an officer's breach of the duty of care."[22] Hence, like directors, officer liability for breach of the duty of care is measured by standards of gross negligence.[23] Thus, corporate director and officer compliance with the duty of care is evaluated pursuant to lax liability standards. Indeed, the duty of care in the corporate context has been described as "moribund."[24] Whether this

---

[20] *In re DSI Renal Holdings, LLC*, 574 B.R. 446, 470 (D. Del. 2017), *quoting Benihana of Tokyo, Inc. v. Benihana, Inc.*, 891 A.2d 150, 192 (Del. Ch. 2005). For further discussion with respect to the meaning of gross negligence, *see infra* notes 22, 43–53 and accompanying text.

[21] *See Metro Storage International LLC v. Harron*, 275 A.3d 810, 844 & n. 16 (Del. Ch. 2022), *quoting* American Law Institute, *Restatement of Agency (Third)* § 8.08 (2006) (quoting the *Restatement of Agency*, acknowledging that an officer's duty as agent encompasses the duty of care, and stating that an agent "has a duty to use reasonable care, competence, and diligence..."). In that decision, Vice Chancellor Laster framed the issue as follows:

> Because of the different standards that govern the duty of care, a debate has long existed over whether an officer's duty of care would resemble the agency regime or the director regime. If the former applied, then an officer could be liable for simple negligence, like agents generally, and the analysis would take into account the officer's special knowledge or expertise. If the latter applied, then a more deferential standard, such as gross negligence, would apply, and the analysis would not take into account the officer's special knowledge or expertise.

275 A.3d at 845. *See also* Deborah A. DeMott, *Fiduciary Principles in Agency Law* in *The Oxford Handbook of Fiduciary Law* at 23 (Evan J. Criddle, Paul B. Miller, and Robert H. Sitkoff eds. 2019).

[22] *Metro Storage International*, 275 A.3d at 845, *citing and quoting Harcum v. Lovoi*, 2022 WL 29695, at * 27 (Del. Ch. 2022) (applying gross negligence standard with respect to officer liability for allegedly misleading proxy disclosures). *See United Food and Commercial Workers Union v. Zuckerberg*, 262 A.3d 1034, 1049 (Del. 2021) (stating that the duty of care is "predicated upon concepts of gross negligence"); *Flannery v. Genomic Health, Inc.*, 2021 WL 3615540, at * 1 (Del. Ch. 2021) (with respect to duty of care claim against corporate officer, applying gross negligence standard); *In re Pattern Energy Group, Inc. Shareholders Litigation*, 2021 WL 1812674, at * 66 (Del. Ch. 2021) ("An officer's compliance with the duty of care is evaluated for gross negligence"); *In re Baker Hughes Inc. Merger Litigation*, 2020 WL 6281427, at * 15 (Del. Ch. 2020) ("Under Delaware law, the standard of care applicable to the fiduciary duty of care of an officer is gross negligence"). Indeed, there is authority in Delaware that breach of the duty of care requires proof of reckless misconduct. *See In re Columbia Pipeline Group, Inc.*, 2021 WL 772562, at * 50 n. 22 (Del. Ch. 2021) ("In the corporate context, a breach of the duty of care requires recklessness").

[23] *See* cases cited note 22 *supra*.

[24] *See* Dent, *supra* note 4, at 646. Similarly, another authority opined that the duty of care has a "twilight existence." John C. Coffee, *Litigation and Corporate Governance: An Essay on Steering Between Scylla and Charybdis*, 52 Geo. Wash. L. Rev. 789, 796 (1984). *See* Cohn, *supra* note 5, at 591.

description is an overstatement is not central to the foregoing discussion. Rather, the point here is that the standards frequently applied in this setting are devoid of fiduciary status. When the liability of a corporate director or officer is measured by a pure heart empty head approach or by the application of gross negligence principles, the viability of fiduciary obligation dissipates.

III. The Business Judgment Rule

The business judgment rule is one of the bedrock principles of corporate law. The rule is lauded for its attributes of: enabling corporate fiduciaries to engage in risk-taking business decisions without these decisions being adjudicated with hindsight; recognizing that judges are not business experts and therefore are ill-suited to assess the merits of business decisions; and rejecting the application of onerous liability standards that would deter corporate fiduciaries, particularly independent directors, from serving in their positions.[25] When applied in an appropriate setting, the business judgment rule may be viewed as a commendable legal principle in that it promotes entrepreneurship, limits undue liability exposure for corporate directors, and deters meritless shareholder litigation. Nonetheless, the rule is not consonant with fiduciary duty standards for the simple reason that it is premised on concepts of gross negligence.[26] To say that corporate directors and officers may avoid liability to the subject corporation and shareholders to whom they owe meaningful obligations if they act without gross negligence in a context

---

[25] *See* William T. Allen, Jack B. Jacobs, and Leo E. Strine Jr., *Realigning the Standard of Review of Director Due Care With Delaware Public Policy: A Critique of Van Gorkom and Its Progeny as a Standard of Review Problem*, 96 Nw. U. L. Rev. 449, 449 (2002):

> [Delaware's] deference ["to business decisions made by well-motivated fiduciaries"] furthers important public policy values and underscores the social utility of encouraging corporate directors to make decisions that may create corporate wealth but that are also risky. If law-trained judges are permitted to make after-the-fact judgments that businesspersons have made "unreasonable" or "negligent" business decisions for which they must respond in monetary damages, directors may, in the future, avoid committing their companies to potentially valuable corporate opportunities that have some risk of failure. Highly qualified directors may also avoid service if they face liability risks that are disproportionate to the benefits of service.

The well-known case of *Dodge v. Ford Motor Co.* recognized the business judgment rule, reasoning that "judges are not business experts." 170 N.W. 668, 684 (Mich. 1919), *discussed in* Chapter 2, notes 16–18 and accompanying text.

[26] *See* Allen, Jacobs, and Strine, *supra* note 25, at 449 ("The gross negligence standard is consistent with Delaware's long-standing policy of deferring to business decisions made by well-motivated fiduciaries"); discussion *infra* notes 27–54 and accompanying text.

THE DUTY OF CARE AND RELATED SUBJECTS 37

not implicating the duty of loyalty belies the substantive meaning of fiduciary status.

Generally, the business judgment rule "is a presumption that directors [or officers] act in good faith, on an informed basis, honestly believing that their action is in the best interests of the company."[27] Hence, the rule insulates a board of director's or officer's conduct from successful challenge provided that a deliberative decision was made by the decisionmaker, who is not subject to a disabling conflict of interest, after being adequately informed and having a rational basis for such decision.[28] Notably, in their recognition of the business judgment rule, several courts do not require that the decision reached be rational. Rather, for these courts, adequacy of process and absence of disabling conflicts are the sole criteria—namely, that the decisionmaker makes a deliberative decision to act or not to act after being adequately informed and that no disabling conflict of interest (such as bad faith or self-dealing) exists.[29]

The scope of the business judgment rule to shield corporate directors and officers from liability is a steady theme in company law. Courts apply the rule to insulate these individuals from liability for deliberative decisions made with respect to a broad range of activities—even if these decisions were negligent.[30] From a traditional perspective, the business judgment rule focuses on managerial or entrepreneurial decisions by boards of directors, such as determinations whether the subject corporation should enter into a contract with a prospective vendor, launch a new product, make capital improvements, or terminate its chief executive officer.[31] In this setting, the rule acts as a shield to deflect shareholder allegations that the defendant

---

[27] *In re Tower Air, Inc.*, 416 F.3d 229, 238 (3d Cir. 2005) (interpreting Delaware law), *citing Aronson v. Lewis*, 473 A.2d 805, 812 (Del. 1984) (The business judgment rule "is a presumption that in making a business decision the directors of a corporation acted on an informed basis, in good faith and in the honest belief that the action taken was in the best interests of the company"). *See In re Match Group, Inc. Derivative Litigation*, 315 A.3d 446, 459 (Del. 2024) ("If the plaintiff rebuts the business judgment rule, the court will review the challenged act by applying the entire fairness standard of review").

[28] *See Smith v. Van Gorkom*, 488 A.2d 858 (Del. 1985); *Gimbal v. Signal Companies*, 316 A.2d 619 (Del. 1974); American Law Institute, *Principles of Corporate Governance: Analysis and Recommendations* § 4.01 (1992) (requiring that the subject director or officer "rationally believes that the business judgment is in the best interests of the corporation").

[29] *See, e.g., WLR Foods, Inc. v. Tyson Foods, Inc.*, 65 F.3d 1172, 1182–83 (4th Cir. 1995) (interpreting Virginia law).

[30] *Aronson v. Lewis*, 473 A.2d at 812 (stating that "under the business judgment rule director liability is predicated upon concepts of gross negligence").

[31] The Illinois decision of *Shlensky v. Wrigley*, 237 N.E.2d 776 (Ill. App. 1968), provides a classic example. There, the business judgment rule was applied in upholding a board of directors' decision not to install lights in Wrigley Field, the home baseball stadium of the Chicago Cubs, as well as its decision not to schedule night games. For a recent application of the business judgment rule, *see, e.g., In re McDonald's Corporation Shareholder Derivative Litigation*, 291 A.3d 652, 688–90 (Del.

directors or officers committed actionable misconduct.[32] More recently, the rule has been used as a sword to terminate shareholder derivative litigation, thereby enabling independent and disinterested directors to cause the dismissal of lawsuits that are determined by these directors not to be in the company's best interests.[33] The business judgment rule also is applied in the context of corporate mergers and acquisitions.[34] The protective umbrella of the rule thus provides broad insulation from liability for corporate directors and officers when they engage in negligent conduct.[35]

As discussed in Chapter 1, a number of courts take the position that a stricter level of scrutiny should apply to corporate officers because they are agents of the subject corporation and earn their livelihood from their employment with that company. Accordingly, these courts hold that the business judgment rule is inapplicable to corporate officers.[36] Nonetheless, reputable sources, including several cases, take a contrary view and conclude that corporate officers may invoke the business judgment rule.[37] In Delaware, irrespective whether the business judgment rule technically applies to officers, a gross negligence culpability standard is employed for assessing an officer's breach of the duty of care.[38] Hence, directors and officers of Delaware corporations are liable only if they act with gross negligence or more culpable misconduct for breach of fiduciary duty unaccompanied by loyalty

---

Ch. 2023) (holding that decision by board of directors to hire company's CEO was protected by the business judgment rule).

[32] *See Zapata Corp. v. Maldonado*, 430 A.2d 779, 782 (Del. 1981) (stating that the business judgment rule "is generally used as a defense to an attack on the decision's soundness").

[33] *See, e.g., United Food & Commercial Workers Union v. Zuckerberg*, 262 A.2d 1034 (Del. 2021); *Rales v. Blasband*, 634 A.2d 929 (Del. 1993); *Aronson v. Lewis*, 473 A.2d 805 (Del.1984); *Zapata Corp. v. Maldonado*, 430 A.2d 779 (Del. 1981); *Auerbach v. Bennett*, 393 N.E.2d 994 (N.Y. Ct. App. 1979); discussion in Chapter 5.

[34] *See, e.g., Corwin v. KKR Financial Holdings LLC*, 125 A.3d 804 (Del. 2015) (and cases cited therein); discussion in Chapter 6.

[35] *See* discussion *infra* notes 36–53 and accompanying text.

[36] *See, e.g., Federal Deposit Insurance Corporation v. Perry*, 2012 WL 589569, at * 4 (C.D. Cal. 2012) (applying California law and holding that the business judgment rule does not apply to decisions made by corporate officers). *See also Metro Storage International LLC v. Harron*, 275 A.3d 810, 843 (Del. Ch. 2022) ("The officer's duty of loyalty . . . has additional dimensions, precisely because officers act as agents for the entity").

[37] *See, e.g., Rosenfeld v. Metals Selling Corp.*, 643 A.2d 1253, 1261 n. 16 (Conn. 1994) ("Although the business judgment rule is usually defined in terms of the role of corporate directors, it is equally applicable to corporate officers exercising their authority"); Model Business Corporation Act § 8.42 Official Comment (stating that "the business judgment rule will normally apply to decisions within an officer's discretionary authority"); American Law Institute, *Principles of Corporate Governance: Analysis and Recommendations* § 4.01(c) (1992) (applying the business judgment rule both to officers and directors); discussion in Chapter 1, notes 21–28 and accompanying text.

[38] *See supra* notes 21–23 and accompanying text.

considerations. Thus, in breach of the duty of care claims against directors and officers in Delaware, gross negligence or more culpable misconduct must be proven.[39]

The fallacy of corporate directors and officers being deemed fiduciaries is striking in this setting. In one decision, the Delaware Supreme Court stated that directors have "an unyielding fiduciary duty," yet held that this obligation is measured pursuant to the business judgment rule by "concepts of gross negligence."[40] Elaborating on this unyielding fiduciary duty, the court loftily stated that "[r]epresentation of the financial interests of others imposes on a director an affirmative duty to protect those interests and to proceed with a critical eye in assessing information of the type and under the circumstances present."[41] Yet two paragraphs thereafter, the court held that gross negligence is the governing standard in determining under the business judgment rule whether a defendant director is subject to liability for breach of the duty of care.[42] The marked distinction between the court's rhetoric (or standard of conduct) and the applicable legal standard for imposing liability (or standard of review) is crystal clear. To state that corporate directors and officers act in a law compliant manner unless they engage in grossly negligent conduct calls into question whether these individuals, in actuality, are fiduciaries.

This point is buttressed by the meaning of gross negligence—the level of misconduct that must be proven in order to rebut the business judgment rule. *Black's Law Dictionary* defines gross negligence as "the omission of even such diligence as habitually careless and inattentive people do actually exercise in avoiding danger to their own person or property."[43]

In other contexts, a defendant's gross negligence constitutes a culpability level that warrants the imposition of exemplary damages.[44]

---

[39] *See* supra notes 21–23, *infra* notes 40–53 and accompanying text.
[40] *Smith v. Van Gorkom*, 488 A.2d at 873.
[41] *Id.* at 872.
[42] *Id.* at 873 (*quoting Aronson*, 473 A.2d at 812). A more recent example is the Delaware Supreme Court's decision in *United Food and Commercial Workers Union v. Zuckerberg*, 262 A.3d 1034, 1049–50 (Del. 2021) (emphasis supplied), where the court conflated the standard of conduct and the standard of liability in a single sentence: "Predicated upon concepts of *gross negligence*, the *duty of care* requires that [corporate] fiduciaries *inform themselves of material information* before making a business decision and act *prudently* in carrying out their duties."
[43] Gross Negligence, *Black's Law Dictionary* 1246 (11th ed. 2019).
[44] *Id.* (also defining gross negligence as "a conscious, voluntary act or omission in reckless disregard of a legal duty and of the consequences to another party, who may typically recover exemplary damages").

Similarly, pursuant to case law, gross negligence in the corporate setting may be categorized as aberrant or egregious misconduct. For example, the Delaware courts have defined gross negligence in the following ways:

(1) "In the corporate context, gross negligence means reckless indifference to or a deliberate disregard of the whole body of stockholders or actions which are without the bounds of reason."[45]
(2) "[T]he definition [of gross negligence in corporate law] is so strict that it imports the concept of recklessness into the gross negligence standard..."[46]
(3) "Gross negligence has a stringent meaning under Delaware corporate (and partnership) law, one which involves a devil-may-care attitude or indifference to duty amounting to recklessness."[47]
(4) To be grossly negligent under Delaware law, a board of director decision "has to be so grossly off-the-mark as to amount to reckless indifference or a gross abuse of discretion."[48]

In Nevada, gross negligence is similarly defined as constituting conduct that "is substantially and appreciably higher in magnitude and more culpable than ordinary negligence [and] is equivalent to the failure to exercise even a slight degree of care."[49] As stated by the US Court of Appeals: "Overcoming the presumptions of the business judgment rule on the merits is a near-Herculean task."[50] This point is illustrated by a recent Delaware Court of Chancery decision where the court observed that a transaction approved by

---

[45] *Tomczak v. Morton Thiokol, Inc.*, 1990 WL 42607, at *12 (Del. Ch. 1990), *quoted in, In re McDonald's Corporation Stockholder Derivative Litigation*, 291 A.3d 652, 689 n. 21 (Del. Ch. 2023) ("cleaned up").

[46] *In re Lear Corp. Shareholder Litigation*, 967 A.2d 640, 652 n. 45 (Del. Ch. 2008).

[47] *Albert v. Alex. Brown Management Services, Inc.*, 2005 WL 2130607, at * 4 (Del. Ch. 2005), *quoted in, In re McDonald's Corporation Stockholder Derivative Litigation*, 291 A.3d at 689 n. 21 ("cleaned up").

[48] *Solash v. Telex Corp.*, 1988 WL 3587, at * 9 (Del. Ch. 1988), *quoted in, In re McDonald's Corporation Stockholder Derivative Litigation*, 291 A.3d at 689 n. 21 ("cleaned up"). *See In re AgFeed USA, LLC*, 546 B.R. 318, 330 (Bankr. Del. 2016) (stating that, to overcome the business judgment rule, "the complaint must allege facts establishing a decision that is so unreasonable that it seems essentially inexplicable on any ground other than bad faith"); *Kallick v. Sandridge Energy, Inc.*, 68 A.3d 242, 257 (Del. 2013) (stating that the business judgment rule provides "something so close to non-review as our law contemplates"); *Brehm v. Eisner*, 746 A.2d 244, 264 (Del. 2000) ("irrationality is the outer limit of the business judgment rule").

[49] *Federal Deposit Insurance Corporation v. Johnson*, 2014 WL 5324057, at *3 (D. Nev. 2014), *citing Hart v. Kline*, 116 P.2d 672, 673–74 (Nev. 1941).

[50] *In re Tower Air, Inc.*, 416 F.3d 229, 238 (3d Cir. 2005) (interpreting Delaware law).

a board committee "seemed, by all accounts, a terrible business decision."[51] Nonetheless, as Chancellor McCormick opined, under Delaware law, "a board comprised of a majority of disinterested and independent directors is free to make a terrible business decision without any meaningful threat of liability, so long as the directors approve the action in good faith."[52]

Hence, the business judgment rule is a protective standard for corporate directors and officers. This expansive standard is further evidenced by a recent Delaware court of chancery decision where Vice Chancellor Laster opined: "To hold a director liable for gross negligence requires conduct more serious than what is necessary to secure a conviction for criminal negligence."[53] Thus, at least in Delaware, it is easier to convict and incarcerate an individual than it is for a shareholder to rebut the presumption of the business judgment rule.

With this backdrop, it borders on incredulity to identify corporate directors and officers as fiduciaries. To say that an individual is a fiduciary, who is held to a legal standard of acting with only a slight degree of care so long as such conduct is unaccompanied by a disabling conflict of interest and does not amount to utter indifference, is nonsensical. Indeed, an individual can go to prison more readily than can a corporate director or officer lose the protection of the business judgment rule. As illogical as this characterization

---

[51] *City of Coral Springs Police Officers' Pension Plan v. Dorsey*, 2023 WL 3316246, at *1 (Del. Ch. 2023).

[52] *Id.* For commentary on the business judgment rule, *see, e.g.*, Stephen A. Raden, et al., *The Business Judgment Rule: Fiduciary Duties for Corporate Directors* (6th ed. 2009); Stephen M. Bainbridge, *The Business Judgment Rule as Abstention Doctrine*, 57 Vand. L. Rev. 83 (2004); Bernard S. Sharfman, *The Importance of the Business Judgment Rule*, 14 NYU J. L. & Bus. 27 (2017).

[53] *In re McDonald's Corporation Stockholder Derivative Litigation*, 291 A.3d 652, 690 n. 21 (Del. Ch. 2023). Under Delaware law, criminal negligence is defined as follows:

> A person acts with criminal negligence with respect to an element of an offense when the person fails to perceive a risk that the element exists or will result from the conduct. The risk must be of such a nature and degree that failure to perceive it constitutes a gross deviation from the standard of conduct that a reasonable person would observe in the situation.

11 Del. Code § 231(a).

Note that at least theoretically, a claim for waste may also be brought by a plaintiff shareholder. Such claims rarely are successful. In *Freedman v. Adams*, 58 A.3d 414, 417 (Del. 2013) (quotations and citations omitted), the Delaware Supreme Court described a claim for waste as follows:

> To recover on a claim for corporate waste, the plaintiffs must shoulder the burden of proving that the exchange was so one sided that no business person of ordinary, sound judgment would conclude that the corporation has received adequate consideration. A claim of waste will arise only in the rare, unconscionable case where directors irrationally squander or give away corporate assets. This onerous standard for waste is a corollary of the proposition that where business judgment presumptions are applicable, the board's decision will be upheld unless it cannot be attributed to any rational purpose.

is, it is exacerbated by the enactment of director and officer exculpation statutes that provide even greater insulation from monetary liability exposure for these so-called fiduciaries.[54] These statutes magnify the illusion of fiduciary duty status for corporate directors and officers. The following section of the chapter addresses this subject.

IV. Director and Officer Exculpation Statutes

In *Smith v. Van Gorkom*, the Delaware Supreme Court shocked the corporate world by holding directors monetarily liable for breach of the duty of care.[55] The court's rationale was that, having clearly inadequate information before them, the directors had acted with gross negligence when they approved a merger transaction. The directors thereby incurred monetary liability.[56] Shocked at the Delaware Supreme Court's audacity in holding highly respected directors financially liable where no self-dealing or other duty of loyalty breach occurred, corporate fiduciaries and company counsel clamored for action.[57] Their position was buttressed by the specter of qualified independent directors declining to serve on corporate boards because of the liability risks posed by *Van Gorkom* as well as the concern that director liability insurance would become more difficult to obtain, with drastically reduced coverage and significantly increased premiums.[58]

Desiring to retain its preeminent position as the favored state of incorporation for publicly traded companies,[59] Delaware swiftly responded by enacting Section 102(b)(7). The statute is not self-enabling. The exculpation

---

[54] *See* discussion *infra* notes 55–85 and accompanying text.

[55] 488 A.2d 858 (Del. 1985).

[56] *Id.* at 874–93 (*id.* at 893—holding that the Trans Union board of directors was "grossly negligent" and "breached their fiduciary duty to their stockholders . . . for their failure to inform themselves of all information reasonably available to them and relevant to their decision to recommend the Pritzger merger..."). The decision was extensively criticized. *See, e.g.*, Daniel Fischel, *The Business Judgment Rule and the Trans Union Case*, 40 Bus. Law. 1437, 1455 (1985) (describing the case as "one of the worst decisions in the history of corporate law"); Bayless Manning, *Reflections and Practical Tips on Life in the Boardroom after Van Gorkom*, 41 Bus. Law. 1, 1 (1985) (asserting that "the corporate bar generally views the decision as atrocious").

[57] Gilchrist Sparks, *Delaware's D&O Liability Law: Other States Should Follow Suit*, Legal Times, Aug. 18, 1986, at 10.

[58] *See, e.g.*, Dennis J. Block, et al., *Advising Directors on the D&O Insurance Crisis*, 14 Sec. Reg. L.J. 130 (1986); Leo Katz, et al., *Next-to-Last Word on Endangered Directors*, Harv. Bus. Rev. at 38 (Jan.-Feb. 1987); Marc I. Steinberg, *The Evisceration of the Duty of Care*, 42 Sw. L.J. 919 (1988).

[59] *See, e.g., Delaware Incorporation: Everything You Need to Know*, available at https://www.upcounsel.com/delaware-corporation (2020) ("Over 50 percent of publicly traded companies in the US and 65 percent of Fortune 500 companies are incorporated in Delaware").

provision must be included in a subject company's articles of incorporation. Provided that this is done, a subject company may eliminate monetary liability for its directors for breach of the duty of care.[60] The exculpation provision, however, may not eliminate liability for a director's: breach of the duty of loyalty; intentional misconduct; knowing violation of law; knowing authorization of an illegal distribution; or receipt of an improper personal benefit.[61] In 2022, Section 102(b)(7) was amended to permit exculpation for specified high-level officers in direct (but not derivative) actions.[62] Hence, provided that a company adopts an exculpation provision in its articles of incorporation, monetary liability in Delaware for "mere" *gross* negligence is a relic of the past for directors (and, in direct actions, for specified senior officers as well).

Shortly after the enactment of Section 102(b)(7) in 1986, many other states followed Delaware's lead adopting similar, if not identical, statutes.[63] The Delaware courts have construed the statute broadly, opining that Section 102(b)(7) "permits exculpation for recklessness"[64] and that "[t]he real function of exculpation is to eliminate liability for recklessness."[65] Hence,

---

[60] *See* §102(b)(7) of the Delaware General Corporation Law. Like the majority of state exculpation statutes, Section 102(b)(7) does not apply to actions for injunctive relief or other actions against corporate directors and officers seeking nonmonetary relief. *See also In re Fox Corporation/Snap Inc.*, 312 A.3d 636 (Del. 2024) (holding that subject corporation's exculpation provision did not require the approval of nonvoting common stockholders who owned a separate class of stock).

[61] *Id. See, e.g., In re Cornerstone Therapeutics Inc. Stockholder Litigation*, 115 A.3d 1173, 1176 (Del. 2015) (holding that "[w]hen the independent directors are protected by an exculpatory charter provision and the plaintiffs are unable to plead a non-exculpatory claim against them, those directors are entitled to have the claims against them dismissed"); *Emerald Partners v. Berlin*, 726 A.2d 1215, 1224 (Del. 1999) (ruling that, for an exculpatory provision to apply, there must be a finding that "the factual basis for [the] claim solely implicates a violation of the duty of care"); *Chen v. Howard-Anderson*, 87 A.3d 648, 676 (Del. Ch. 2014) ("An exculpatory provision shields the directors from personal liability for monetary damages for a breach of fiduciary duty, except liability for the four categories listed in Section 102(b)(7)").

[62] *See* § 102(b)(7). These senior corporate officers include "a company's president, chief executive officer, chief operating officer, chief legal officer, controller, treasurer or chief accounting officer, as well as other individuals identified in public filings as the company's most highly compensated officers." Jones Day, *Delaware Authorizes 102(b)(7) Exculpation of Senior Officers* (Aug. 16, 2022).

[63] *See* Stephen A. Radin, *The Director's Duty of Care Three Years After Smith v. Van Gorkom*, 39 Hastings L.J. 707, 747–48 (1988) ("As of the end of 1987, legislation modeled upon the Delaware statute has been enacted in Arizona, Arkansas, California, Colorado, Georgia, Idaho, Iowa, Kansas, Louisiana, Massachusetts, Michigan, Minnesota, Montana, New Jersey, New Mexico, New York, North Carolina, Oklahoma, Oregon, Pennsylvania, Rhode Island, South Dakota, Texas, Utah, Washington, and Wyoming"). *See generally* Harvey Gelb, *Director Due Care Liability: An Assessment of the New Statutes*, 61 Temple L. Rev. 13 (1988); Frances S. Fendler, *Director-Exculpation Clauses Under the Arkansas Business Corporation Act of 1987*, 15 U. Ark. L.R. L. Rev. 337 (1993); E. Norman Veasey, et al., *Delaware Supports Directors With a Three-Legged Stool of Limited Liability, Indemnification, and Insurance*, 42 Bus. Law. 399 (1987).

[64] *New Enterprise Associates 14 L.P. v. Rich*, 295 A.3d 520, 551 (Del. Ch. 2023).

[65] *In re Columbia Pipeline Group, Inc.*, 2021 WL 772562, at * 50 n. 22 (Del. Ch. 2021).

pursuant to this rationale, an exculpation provision's impact in Delaware is to insulate corporate directors (and senior officers in direct actions) from monetary liability for breaches of the duty of care unless the subject fiduciary acts with intentional misconduct. If that in fact is the law in Delaware, then the duty of care rarely, if ever, exists in actions for money damages where there is an exculpation provision. Indeed, when a director or officer intentionally acts with an objective other than that of advancing the corporation's best interests or intentionally violates applicable law, he or she fails to act in good faith and thereby violates the duty of loyalty.[66]

Nonetheless, the Delaware Supreme Court has held that an exculpation provision cannot limit a director's liability for violation of the duty of loyalty. In a 2023 decision, the court addressed the validity of a corporate charter provision that stated that a determination made by the subject company's board of directors with respect to a shareholder voting limitation, "if made in good faith and on information reasonably available," would be deemed binding and conclusive on the corporation and its shareholders.[67] Finding that this provision was inconsistent with Section 102(b)(7), the court held that the statute "specifically prohibits a charter provision that directly or indirectly limits director liability for breaches of the duty of loyalty."[68] The court thereby declared the provision invalid because it was contrary to Delaware law and its public policy.[69] By contrast, the court suggested that if this provision had been included in a limited partnership or limited liability company agreement, it would have been enforceable.[70]

Seeking to attract or retain corporations within their borders, many other states have enacted exculpation provisions that provide even greater insulation from monetary liability for directors and officers than the Delaware

---

[66] *In re Walt Disney Co. Derivative Litigation*, 906 A.2d 27, 67 (Del. 2006). *See Stone v. Ritter*, 911 A.2d 362, 369 (Del. 2006) (stating that "a failure to act in good faith requires conduct that is quantitatively different from, and more culpable than, the conduct giving rise to a violation of the fiduciary duty of care (i.e., gross negligence)"). *See* discussion in Chapter 4, notes 52–55 and accompanying text.

[67] *CCSB Financial Corp. v. Totta*, 302 A.3d 387, 390 (Del. 2023).

[68] *Id.* at 400. *See Colon v. Bumble, Inc.*, 305 A.3d 352, 359 (Del. Ch. 2023) ("Some default rights are so significant that the charter cannot eliminate them [including] [t]he right to sue for breach of the fiduciary duty of loyalty. . . ."); *Sutherland v. Sutherland*, 2009 WL 857468, at * 4 (Del. Ch. 2009) (voiding charter provision that eviscerate[d] the duty of loyalty for corporate directors," reasoning that the provision was not authorized under § 102(b)(7)).

[69] *CCSB Financial Corp.*, 302 A.3d at 398–402.

[70] *Id.* at 402 (stating that "the option to alter or eliminate fiduciary duties, if desired, resides in the land of alternative entities, not through a Delaware corporation. . ."). Statutes and courts have given their approbation to contractual agreements that limit or eliminate fiduciary duties in the partnership and limited liability company settings. This subject is discussed in Chapter 2.

statute. Several of these statutes are self-enabling, being effective without requiring that the exculpatory provision be contained in a subject company's articles of incorporation.[71] A number of the statutes apply to both directors and officers.[72] A review of several of these statutes follows.

The Maryland statute applies to both directors and officers. The statute authorizes a Maryland corporation to include an exculpatory provision in its charter that bars money damages from being recovered by the corporation or its stockholders from its directors and officers unless it is proved that the defendant fiduciary received "an improper benefit or profit" or there is a finding that such fiduciary's conduct "was the result of active and deliberate dishonesty and was material to the cause of action adjudicated in the proceeding."[73] This statute clearly is more protective than the Delaware version as it provides insulation from monetary liability for certain breaches of the duty of loyalty, including a director's oversight obligations, that depending on the circumstances, may implicate the duty of good faith.[74]

The Ohio statute, applying to directors, is self-executing. Unlike Delaware and many other state exculpation statutes, the Ohio statute eliminates liability for breach of the duty of care both for suits for injunctive relief and for actions for monetary damages. The statute insulates directors from liability unless it is proved "by clear and convincing evidence" that the defendant director deliberately intended "to cause injury to the corporation" or undertook the conduct at issue "with reckless disregard for the best interests of the corporation."[75] By raising the standard of proof from preponderance to clear and convincing evidence and its vague language that may insulate from

---

[71] *See, e.g.*, Ind. Stat. § 23-1-35-1(e); Nev. Rev. Stat. § 78.138(7); Ohio Rev. Code § 701.59(D)-(E);

[72] *See, e.g.*, Md. Code § 5-418(a); Nev. Rev. Stat. § 78.138(7); Va. Code § 13.1692.1(A)-(B).

[73] Md. Code §§ 2-405.2, 5-418(a). The statute does not apply to "an action brought by or on behalf of a State governmental entity, receiver, conservator, or depositor against a director or officer of: (1) A banking institution . . . ; (2) A credit union . . . ; (3) A savings and loan association . . . ; or (4) A subsidiary of a banking institution, credit union, or savings and loan association described in this subsection." *Id.* § 5-418(b). *See Hayes v. Crown Central Petroleum Corp.*, 78 Fed. Appx. 857, 865 (4th Cir. 2003) (applying Maryland law and stating that, provided that an exculpation provision is validly adopted, plaintiffs "must allege an improper benefit or active and deliberate dishonesty in order to state a claim"); *Grill v. Hoblitzell*, 771 F. Supp. 709, 712 (D. Md. 1991) (corporation had adopted charter provision pursuant to Maryland statute that "restrict[ed] director monetary liability to situations involving 'active and deliberate dishonesty' or the actual receipt of an improper benefit").

[74] *See, e.g., Witchko v. Schorsch*, 2016 WL 3887289, at * 8 (S.D.N.Y. 2016) (construing the Maryland statute and stating: "With respect to 'active and deliberate dishonesty,' Maryland courts have held that the term 'dishonesty' involves lying or the intent to commit fraud. . ."). With respect to the director's duty of oversight, *see, e.g., Stone v. Ritter*, 911 A.2d 362 (Del. 2006). The duty of oversight is addressed in Chapter 4.

[75] Ohio Rev. Code § 1701.59(D)-(E). Corporations may opt out of this exculpation protection for their directors.

monetary liability certain breaches of the duty of loyalty, the Ohio statute may be viewed as more protective for defendant directors than the Delaware statute.[76]

The Virginia statute authorizes the inclusion of an exculpatory provision in a subject corporation's articles of incorporation (or a company's bylaws if approved by such company's shareholders) that reduces or eliminates monetary liability of an officer or director. The exclusion is narrow, providing that no such limitation is permitted if the director or officer "engaged in willful misconduct or a knowing violation of the criminal law or of any federal or state securities law. . . ."[77] The statute's language may be construed to encompass certain breaches of the duty of loyalty, including situations where a director or officer benefits at the expense of the corporation so long as there is no willful misconduct or a knowing violation of specified law. The Virginia statute thus is more protective for defendant directors and officers than the Delaware statute.

The Indiana statute clearly provides protection from liability for directors for certain breaches of the duty of loyalty. The statute is self-executing and, by its language, includes "alleged breaches of the duty of care, the duty of loyalty, and the duty of good faith."[78] The exception occurs when a director fails to comply with his or her duties as specified (such as acting in good faith or with adequate care) *and* such "breach or failure to perform constitutes willful misconduct or recklessness."[79] By exculpating breaches of the duty of loyalty unless a director engages in willful or reckless misconduct, the statute insulates defendant directors to a greater degree than the Delaware provision.

---

[76] As set forth in the Comment to the statute by the Ohio State Bar Association Corporation Law Committee: The Ohio exculpation statute "is designed to relieve the director of responsibility for money damages except when it is proven by clear and convincing evidence that the director has breached or failed to perform his duties and that his act or omission in so doing was consciously undertaken with deliberate intent to cause injury to the corporation or with reckless disregard for the interests of the corporation. . . ." The Committee "believed that it is important for corporations to be able to attract and retain 'outside' (non-management) directors who are in a position to provide independent judgment."

[77] Va. Code § 13.1692.1(A)-(B). With respect to the application of the business judgment rule, Virginia has the following standard: "A director shall discharge his duties as a director, including his duties as a member of a committee, in accordance with his good faith business judgment of the best interests of the corporation." *Id.* § 13.1-690(A). *See* discussion in Dennis R. Honabach, *All That Glitters: A Critique of the Revised Virginia Stock Corporation Act*, 12 J. Corp. L. 433 (1987).

[78] Ind. Code § 23-1-35-1(e).

[79] *Id.* (using the word "and" between subsection (1) and subsection (2), thereby making clear that the director's breach of fiduciary duty must constitute "willful misconduct or recklessness"). *See Brane v. Roth*, 590 N.E.2d 587, 590 (Ind. Ct. App. 1993) (making reference to this statute but not giving it retroactive effect in the case at bar).

THE DUTY OF CARE AND RELATED SUBJECTS 47

The last example is Nevada, viewed as the Delaware of the West.[80] The Nevada statute is self-executing and expansive, covering both directors and officers. Under the statute, an officer or director is not liable to the corporation, shareholders, or creditors unless it is proved that such officer or director breached a fiduciary duty *and* "such breach involved intentional misconduct, fraud, or a knowing violation of law."[81] The Nevada Supreme Court has held that this statute is the "sole avenue to hold directors and officers individually liable for damages arising from official conduct."[82] Construing the language "intentional" misconduct and "knowing" violation of law, the court ruled that this terminology requires knowledge of wrongdoing on the part of the defendant director or officer.[83] The Nevada exculpatory statute thus extends to duty of loyalty breaches so long as such breach does not involve fraud, intentional misconduct, or a knowing violation of law. It accordingly provides significantly greater insulation from liability for directors and officers than the Delaware statute.

Irrespective whether an exculpation statute is the version adopted in Delaware or provides even greater protection from monetary liability for corporate directors and officers (such as the Nevada statute), it is clear that these statutes contravene the principle that these individuals are fiduciaries. Even under the Delaware statute, an exculpation provision may eliminate monetary liability for recklessness, thereby requiring that intentional misconduct must be proven in duty of care cases.[84] Identifying a corporate director or officer as a fiduciary, while entitling that person to be insulated from monetary liability for reckless misconduct, is nonsensical.

It may be asserted that the majority of the exculpation statutes, including the Delaware statute, require the inclusion of a provision in a subject corporation's articles of incorporation to be effective. By shareholders opting to vote in favor of an exculpation provision, it may be posited that principles

---

[80] *See* Lydia Moynihan, *Why CEOs Are Rolling the Dice on a Move to Delaware*, New York Post (April 27, 2023) (reporting on Twitter electing to move from Delaware and incorporate in Nevada as greater insulation from liability is provided under Nevada law).

[81] Nev. Rev. Stat. § 78.138(7). "This section applies to all cases, circumstances, and matters, including, without limitation, any change or potential change in control of the corporation unless otherwise provided in the articles of incorporation or an amendment thereto." *Id.* § 78.138(8).

[82] *Chur v. Eighth Judicial District Court*, 458 P.3d 336, 340 (Nev. 2020).

[83] *Id.* at 342. *See Guzman v. Johnson*, 483 P.3d 531, 535–37 (Nev. 2021) (applying principles set forth in *Chur* to case at bar); *In re Agfeed USA, LLC*, 546 B.R. 318, 329–30 (D. Del. 2016) (construing language of the Nevada exculpation statute).

[84] *See New Enterprise Associates 14 L.P. v. Rich*, 295 A.3d 520, 551 (Del. Ch. 2023); *In re Columbia Pipeline Group, Inc.*, 2021 WL 772562, at * 50 n. 22 (Del. Ch. 2021); *supra* notes 64–65 and accompanying text.

of corporate governance are enhanced. Opponents may assert, however, that this position lacks meaningful substance due to management's influence over the proxy machinery process, the inclination of at least some institutional investors to vote with management, and the lack of financial sophistication by many individual shareholders in regard to corporate charter provisions.[85] While these divergent positions appeal to their respective proponents, the objective of this chapter and book is not to assess whether these exculpation statutes make good or bad policy. Rather, the point to be made here is that the state exculpation statutes are antithetical to the established principle that corporate directors and officers are fiduciaries.

V. "Discretionaries"—Not Fiduciaries

The analysis contained in this chapter demonstrates that corporate directors and officers are not fiduciaries. First, in a number of jurisdictions, including Delaware, breach of the duty of care by a director or officer requires proof of gross negligence.[86] In other contexts, this level of culpability results in the levying of exemplary damages.[87] With respect to the business judgment rule, it is more difficult for a complainant to rebut the presumption of that rule than it is for a prosecutor to procure a conviction for criminal negligence. Hence, a corporate officer or director can be sent to the slammer with greater ease than being denied business judgment rule protection in a shareholder lawsuit.[88] As a last example, the state exculpation statutes enable corporate directors (as well as officers under a number of statutes) to avoid monetary liability for duty of care breaches unless intentional misconduct is perpetrated. Pursuant to these statutes, the duty of care, in actuality, transforms to a duty not to engage in blatantly wrongful conduct.[89]

Clearly, corporate directors and officers are not fiduciaries. Rather, different standards of liability exposure apply depending upon the underlying setting and the applicable jurisdiction. In this chapter, the analysis focused on director and officer liability in situations that are unaccompanied by duty of loyalty considerations. Rather than fiduciary principles being applied,

---

[85] See discussion in Gelb, *supra* note 63, at 30; Steinberg, *supra* note 58, at 927.
[86] See discussion *supra* notes 19–24 and accompanying text.
[87] See discussion *supra* notes 43–44 and accompanying text.
[88] See discussion *supra* note 53 and accompanying text.
[89] See discussion *supra* notes 55–85 and accompanying text.

legislatures and courts evaluate legal concepts and public policy to determine appropriate standards to implement. By establishing this framework, in the duty of care context, corporate directors and officers are treated as "discretionaries"—being held accountable for specified obligations and subject to varying degrees of lax monetary liability exposure.

4
The Duty of Loyalty: Far More Bark than Bite

I. Setting the Stage

The fiduciary duty of loyalty is the core obligation that corporate directors and officers owe to their respective corporations. Historically, the duty of loyalty has been understood as imposing mandatory duties that are not subject to diminution.[1] As stated by the Delaware Court of Chancery in a recent decision, "the duty of loyalty stands inviolate."[2] Today, irrespective of such rhetoric, the duty of loyalty has been significantly diluted. Although perhaps overstated, it has been said that the current likelihood of a corporate director or officer incurring liability for engaging in a breach of the duty of loyalty "is very low."[3]

The scope of the fiduciary duty of loyalty for corporate directors and officers was deemed all-encompassing by the Delaware Supreme Court in its famous decision *Guth v. Loft*. This extensive duty "demands of a corporate officer or director, peremptorily and inexorably, the most scrupulous observance of his [or her] duty, not only affirmatively to protect the interests of the corporation committed to his [or her] charge, but also to refrain from doing anything that would work injury to the corporation . . ."[4] Pursuant to this duty, corporate and shareholder best interests generally must take

---

[1] *See, e.g., New Enterprise Associates 14, L.P. v. Rich*, 295 A.3d 520, 549 (Del. Ch. 2023) ("Delaware corporate law is popularly understood to impose mandatory fiduciary duties that cannot be modified"). Nonetheless, the court recognized that Delaware "has not rejected the traditional methods of fiduciary tailoring." *Id. See* John C. Coffee Jr., *The Mandatory/Enabling Balance in Corporate Law: An Essay on the Judicial Role*, 89 Colum. L. Rev. 1618, 1650 (1989) (stating that "the duty of loyalty is at the core of fiduciary duties"); Julian Velasco, *Fiduciary Principles in Corporate Law* at 61 in *Oxford Handbook of Fiduciary Law* (Evan J. Criddle, Paul B. Miller, and Robert H. Sitkoff eds. 2019) (stating that "fiduciary duty is the very heart of corporate law").

[2] *New Enterprise Associates*, 295 A.3d at 549 ("Although monetary liability for the duty of care can be eliminated, the underlying duty cannot be altered, and the duty of loyalty stands inviolate").

[3] Jacob Hale Russell and Arthur B. Laby, *The Decline and Rise of Fiduciary Obligations in Business*, at 1, 2, in *Fiduciary Obligations in Business* (Arthur B. Laby and Jacob Hale Russell eds. 2021) ("All told, the likelihood of financial liability for a director stemming from a fiduciary breach is very low").

[4] *Guth v. Loft*, 5 A.2d 503, 510 (Del. 1939).

Corporate Director and Officer Liability. Marc I. Steinberg, Oxford University Press.
© Marc I. Steinberg 2025. DOI: 10.1093/9780197751534.003.0004

precedence over those held of a subject director or officer.[5] Accordingly, directors and officers are not allowed to use their respective position(s) to enhance their personal interests.[6]

With frequency, the foregoing language today is mere rhetoric, lacking substantive application. This chapter illustrates this point by examining several contexts where the breadth of the duty of loyalty has been significantly diluted. First, the chapter addresses principles of waiver impacting the duty of loyalty, followed by an examination of the state exculpation statutes. Thereafter, the duty of good faith, held in Delaware to be an obligation within the ambit of the duty of loyalty,[7] is discussed. The next part of the chapter examines interested director and officer transactions. The chapter then focuses on the propriety of these individuals taking corporate opportunities. The concluding section of the chapter provides insights into the substantial dilution of the duty of loyalty with respect to director and officer liability.

As discussed earlier in this book, there exists a sharp distinction between standards of conduct and standards of review for corporate directors and officers.[8] In effect, standards of conduct represent best practices with respect to which corporate fiduciaries should adhere. In reality, they are only recommendations that lack enforcement. Standards of review, on the other hand, focus on the liability of directors and officers. Hence, while standards of conduct exhort these individuals to engage in exemplary conduct, standards of review (or standards of liability) frequently are interpreted with laxity. As the Delaware courts have acknowledged, "the standard of review [for assessing liability exposure] is more forgiving of directors [and officers] and more onerous for stockholder plaintiffs than the standard of conduct."[9]

---

[5] *See, e.g., Cede & Cede v. Technicolor, Inc.*, 634 A.3d 345, 361 (Del. 1993). A corporate director's or officer's best interests permissibly may coincide with the corporation's and stockholders' best interests when the applicable benefit is "shared by the stockholders generally." *Id.*

[6] *See Metro Storage International LLC v. Harron*, 275 A.3d 810, 842 (Del. Ch. 2022), *quoting Guth v. Loft, Inc.*, 5 A.3d at 510. Like directors, officers must "place the interests of the corporation and shareholders that they serve before their own." *TVI Corporation v. Gallagher*, 2013 WL 5809271, at * 25 (Del. Ch. 2013).

[7] *See, e.g., Stone v. Ritter*, 911 A.2d 362, 370 (Del. 2006) (holding that "because a showing of bad faith conduct ... is essential to establish director oversight liability, the fiduciary duty violated by that conduct is the duty of loyalty").

[8] *See, e.g.*, discussion in Chapter 1, notes 33–41 and accompanying text.

[9] *Chen v. Howard-Anderson*, 87 A.3d 648, 666 (Del. Ch. 2014), *quoting Reis v. Hazlett Strip-Casting Corp.*, 28 A.3d 442, 457 (Del. Ch. 2011). *See Gantler v. Stephens*, 965 A.2d 695, 708-09 (Del. 2009) (holding that "officers of Delaware corporations, like directors, owe fiduciary duties of care and loyalty, and that the fiduciary duties of officers are the same as those of directors"); *In re Trados Incorporated Securities Litigation*, 73 A.3d 17, 35 (Del. Ch. 2013) ("The standard of conduct describes what directors are expected to do...."); William T. Allen, Jack B. Jacobs, and Leo E. Strine Jr., *Function Over Form: A Reassessment of Standards of Review in Delaware Corporation Law*, 56 Bus. Law. 1287, 1296 (2001) ("In most areas of law, standards of conduct and standards of review

Thus, the rhetoric of best practices, when contrasted with the reality of lax liability standards, evidences that, in actuality, corporate directors and officers are not fiduciaries. The analysis contained in this chapter supports this proposition.

This chapter declines to address all situations where the duty of loyalty is implicated for corporate directors and officers. Rather, the objective at hand is to provide an ample showing that, even in the duty of loyalty context, corporate directors and officers should not be deemed fiduciaries. Although it is true that in certain defined duty of loyalty situations fiduciary standards are applicable and meaningful, nonetheless, in many other situations implicating the duty of loyalty, fiduciary standards are absent. Thus, an accurate portrayal conveys that corporate directors and officers are "discretionaries" rather than fiduciaries.

II. Waiving the Fiduciary Duty of Loyalty

In a number of jurisdictions, including Delaware, key aspects of the duty of loyalty can be validly waived. When such waiver occurs, fiduciary obligations no longer apply to director and officer conduct that would otherwise be judged pursuant to those standards. The applicability of a given waiver provision effectively relieves corporate directors and officers of certain fiduciary obligations, thereby giving these individuals far greater leeway to engage in self-interested transactions. In such instances, corporate directors and officers should not be deemed fiduciaries.

A. Obligations Expressly Addressed by Contract

Provided certain conditions are met, one such example occurs where a plaintiff stockholder alleges against corporate directors and/or officers breach of both fiduciary and contractual duties. Generally, where the claims brought arise from obligations that expressly are addressed by contract, the case will be dealt with as a breach of contract matter. For example, in *Gale v. Bershad*, the Delaware Court of Chancery precluded a preferred stockholder from

---

tend to conflate and become one and the same, but in corporate law the two standards often diverge...").

bringing a claim for breach of fiduciary duty against the corporation and its directors, reasoning that (1) the same facts that formed the basis for his contract claim also underlaid the fiduciary duty claim; and (2) the obligation that allegedly was breached arose out of the parties' contractual (rather than fiduciary) relationship.[10] As the Delaware Supreme Court has held: "It is a well-settled principle that where a dispute arises from obligations that are expressly addressed by contract, that dispute will be treated as a breach of contract claim [and that, accordingly,] any fiduciary claims arising out of the same facts that underlie the contract obligations would be foreclosed as superfluous."[11]

B. Fiduciary Waivers Pursuant to Stockholder Agreements

Similarly, even where there is not an alleged contractual breach, an agreement between or among a corporation and certain (or all) of its stockholders may be held to validly waive specified fiduciary duties. To be distinguished from corporate charter exculpatory provisions that are discussed in Chapter 3 and later in this chapter,[12] stockholder agreements are on a different footing. As stated by a federal appellate court construing Delaware law over four decades ago: "Under Delaware law, the rights of stockholders are contractual, and may be altered by binding agreements between the stockholders and the corporation."[13] In such case, the fiduciary duties that otherwise would have been owed to the affected stockholder(s) are altered.[14] Hence, under Delaware law, "stockholders can agree to greater constraints on their rights in a stockholders' agreement than a corporation can impose in its charter or bylaws."[15]

---

[10] 1998 WL 118022, at * 5 (Del. Ch. 1998). *Accord Blue Chip Capital Fund II Ltd. v. Tubergen*, 906 A.2d 827, 832–34 (Del. Ch. 2006); *Madison Realty Partners 7, LLC v. AG ISA, LLC*, 2001 WL 406268, at * 6 (Del. Ch. 2001).

[11] *Nemec v. Shrader*, 991 A.2d 1120, 1129 (Del. 2010) (affirming the Chancellor's finding that "the Stock Plan created contract duties that superseded and negated any distinct fiduciary duties arising out of the same conduct that constituted the contractual breach" and stating that, in that specific situation, "any fiduciary claims arising out of the same facts that underlie the contract obligations would be foreclosed as superfluous").

[12] *See* discussion in Chapter 3, notes 55–85 and accompanying text and, in this chapter, *infra* notes 43–55 and accompanying text.

[13] *In re Reading Co.*, 711 F.2d 509, 519 (3d Cir. 1983) (citations omitted).

[14] *Id. See* Coffee, *supra* note 1, at 1669 (stating that "the Third Circuit [interpreting Delaware law] explicitly recognized that contractual provisions could overcome fiduciary duties").

[15] *New Enterprise Associates 14, L.P. v. Rich*, 295 A.3d 520, 570 (Del. Ch. 2023). *See id.* at 571 ("To state the obvious, a stockholders agreement is not a charter or bylaw provision, so restrictions on

This broad principle, however, is not as expansive as the above language suggests. Generally, in order for a shareholder to waive an aspect of the duty of loyalty, it has been held that the waiver provision (provision) (1) must appear in a stockholder agreement; (2) must be clear and unambiguous; (3) must be narrow and targeted, thereby identifying the specific type of conduct or transaction that otherwise would be regarded as a breach of the duty of loyalty; and (4) must pass close judicial scrutiny for reasonableness, with relevant criteria including: "(i) a written contract formed through actual consent, (ii) a clear provision, (iii) knowledgeable stockholders who understood the provision's implications, (iv) the [affected stockholders'] ability to reject the provision, and (v) the presence of bargained-for consideration."[16] In addition, the waiver provision must not violate public policy.

---

charter or bylaw provisions do not govern stockholders agreements"). Note, however, that notwithstanding the court's statement of law, a board of directors under Delaware law may amend corporate bylaws or adopt a board resolution whereby business opportunities are renounced, thereby enabling the subject company's directors and officers to seize such opportunities. *See* Del. Gen. Corp. L. § 122(17); discussion *infra* notes 21–32, 107–109 and accompanying text.

[16] *New Enterprise Associates*, 295 A.3d at 589–90, *relying on Manti Holdings, LLC v. Authentix Acquisition Co.*, 261 A.3d 1199 (Del. 2021). Moreover, the applicable waiver provision must not conflict with the corporation's charter or bylaws or the Delaware corporate code. In *New Enterprise Associates*, the chancery court identified several waiver provisions that "would face deep skepticism and a steep uphill slog" in their quest to be upheld, including "an agreement binding a retail stockholder, an employee stock grant, a dividend reinvestment plan, an employee stock compensation plan, [and] a stock transmittal letter...." 295 A.3d at 591 (cleaned up). In that case, Vice Chancellor Laster disagreed with the view of two Delaware practitioners who asserted that "Delaware offers a corporate product that comes with commonly understood attributes, including mandatory and generally immutable fiduciary duties [and that] to permit a stockholder to waive a mandatory feature of Delaware law would undermine the common understanding of a Delaware corporation." *Id.* at 576, citing Edward P. Welch and Robert S. Saunders, *Freedom and Its Limits in the Delaware General Corporation Law*, 33 Del. J. Corp. L. 845, 846–47 (2008). Another recent development that may impact the roles and obligations of directors and officers under Delaware law is the 2024 enactment of Del. Gen. Corp. L. § 122(18).

Although this provision does not address fiduciary duties, it authorizes a Delaware corporation to enter into a stockholder agreement that requires a particular stockholder's consent in order for the subject corporation to take (or not to take) specified actions as set forth in such stockholder agreement. This new statute thus provides a nonexclusive list of measures that may be included in such stockholder agreements, including:

[1] Restricting or prohibiting a corporation from taking actions specified in a contract, regardless of whether the taking of such action would require approval of the board under the Delaware General Corporation Law.

[2] Requiring the approval or consent of one or more persons or bodies before the corporation may take actions specified in the contract (including directors, stockholders or beneficial owners).

[3] Requiring the corporation or one or more persons or bodies to take or refrain from taking, actions specified in the contract (including directors, stockholders or beneficial owners).

For example, a provision whereby shareholders agree to waive their entitlement to bring a claim for intentional breach of fiduciary duty would be invalid.[17] On the other hand, a waiver provision may validly foreclose specified breach of duty of loyalty claims where directors and officers engage in "self-dealing transactions with reckless disregard for the best interests of the company."[18]

Hence, even though the Delaware Supreme Court has held that a charter exculpatory provision may not immunize directors and officers from liability for breaches of the duty of loyalty,[19] this consequence may occur if specified conditions are met by means of a shareholder agreement.[20] Where such a valid waiver exists, corporate directors and officers may engage in reckless self-dealing conduct that otherwise would violate the duty of loyalty. Clearly, in this situation, fiduciary status is illusory.

Jonathan Doigin and Emily J. Yukich, *Closure on Moelis: Delaware Takes Action*, Fox Rothschild LLP (June 26, 2024). The effect of this statute nullifies the Delaware chancery court's decision in *West Palm Beach Firefighters' Pension Fund v. Moelis & Co.*, 311 A.3d 809 (Del. Ch. 2024). In that case, citing extensive Delaware precedent, the chancery court invalidated provisions in a stockholder agreement because they materially impinged on the board of directors' authority to oversee the corporation's business and affairs. Not surprisingly, the statute has generated severe criticism. *See, e.g.*, Marcel Kahan and Edward B. Rock, *Proposed DGCL § 122(18), Long-Term Investors, and the Hollowing Out of DGCL § 141(a)*, Harvard Law School Forum on Corporate Governance (May 21, 2024) ("If the proposed DGCL § 122(18) is adopted by the Delaware legislature, § 141(a) will no longer impose meaningful limits on a board's ability to delegate key governance functions and responsibilities").

[17] *New Enterprise Associates*, 295 A.3d at 593 ("To the extent the [waiver provision] seeks to prevent the [stockholders] from asserting a claim for an intentional breach of fiduciary duty, then [such provision] is invalid—not as an impermissible form of fiduciary tailoring, but because of policy limitations on contracting").

[18] *Id.*

[19] *See CCSB Financial Corp. v. Totta*, 302 A.3d 387, 400 (Del. 2023) (holding that § 102(b)(7) "specifically prohibits a charter provision that directly or indirectly limits director liability for breaches of the duty of loyalty"); discussion in Chapter 3, notes 67–70 and accompanying text.

[20] *See* discussion *supra* notes 12–18 and accompanying text. *See generally* Jill E. Fisch, *Stealth Governance: Shareholder Agreements and Private Ordering*, 99 Wash. U. L. Rev. 913, 913–14 (2021) (asserting that the use of shareholder agreements for corporate governance objectives (which her article calls "stealth governance"), "sacrifices critical corporate law values" and, in its stead, there should be adopted "a uniform structural approach to corporate law that would limit private ordering to the charter and bylaws").

C. Statutory Authorization of Waivers: Corporate Opportunities

Going further, by statute in Delaware and several other states as well as pursuant to the Model Business Corporation Act, the fiduciary duty of loyalty with respect to corporate directors and officers taking corporate opportunities may be waived in advance of any such opportunity arising.[21] Pursuant to the Delaware statute, a Delaware corporation has the power to "[r]enounce, in its certificate of incorporation or by action of its board of directors, any interest or expectancy of the corporation in, or in being offered an opportunity to participate in, specified business opportunities or specified classes or categories of business opportunities that are presented to the corporation or one or more of its officers, directors or stockholders."[22] This statute is a significant expansion of Delaware's exculpation statute that insulates directors (and officers in direct actions) from monetary liability for breaches of the duty of care and that requires that the elimination of monetary liability provision be contained in the subject company's certificate of incorporation.[23] By contrast, the corporate opportunity provision waives an obligation central to the duty of loyalty and may be adopted by a board of directors by such means as a board resolution or a board-promulgated bylaw amendment (provided that the board has such authority pursuant to the corporation's charter).[24]

Pursuant to the legislative synopsis accompanying the Delaware statute, such advance corporate opportunity waivers are subject to the same level of

---

[21] *See* Del. Gen. Corp. L. § 122(17). For other states that have enacted similar statutes allowing corporate opportunity waivers, *see, e.g.,* Kan. Stat. Ann. § 17-6102(17); Md. Code Ann. Corps. & Ass'ns § 2-103(15); Mo. Rev. Stat. § 351.385(16); N.J. Stat. Ann. § 14A:3-1(q); Okla. Stat. tit. 18, § 1016(17); Tex. Bus. Org. Code § 2.101(21); Wash. Rev. Code § 23B.02.020(5)(k). The Model Business Corporation Act provision (§ 2.02(b)(6)) is discussed in note 22 *infra* and in Chapter 7, notes 58–64 and accompanying text. Unlike the director exculpation statutes, the corporate opportunity waiver statutes have been enacted by fewer states. From a more general perspective, the corporate opportunity doctrine is further discussed later in this chapter. *See infra* notes 94–114 and accompanying text; Chapter 7, notes 55–74 and accompanying text.

[22] Del. Gen. Corp. L. § 122(17). Section 2.02 (b)(6) of the Model Business Corporation Act likewise authorizes the inclusion of a provision in a subject corporation's articles of incorporation "limiting or eliminating" the obligation of its directors and officers to offer corporate opportunities to such corporation. "The limitation or elimination may be blanket in nature and apply to any business opportunities...." *Id.* Official Comment. In addition, for officers to take business opportunities, qualified directors must give their approval. For further discussion of this statute, *see* Chapter 7 at notes 58–64 and accompanying text.

[23] *See* Del. Gen. Corp. L. § 102(b)(7); discussion in Chapter 3, notes 59–70 and accompanying text.

[24] *See* Del. Corp. L. § 122(17); Gabriel Rauterberg and Eric Talley, *Contracting Out of the Fiduciary Duty of Loyalty: An Empirical Analysis of Corporate Opportunity Waivers,* 117 Colum. L. Rev. 1075, 1097 (2017). *See generally* Martha M. Effinger, *A New Corporate Statute: Adding Explicit Procedures to Maryland's Corporate Opportunity Waiver Provision,* 48 U. Balt. L. Rev. 293 (2019).

judicial scrutiny that applies "to the renunciation of an interest or expectancy of the corporation in a business opportunity, which will be determined based on the common law of fiduciary duty, including the duty of loyalty."[25] There exists sparse case law interpreting corporate opportunity statutory waivers. Whether broad and general renunciations of corporate opportunities will be upheld remain unresolved.[26] Focusing on the statute's specificity language, the Delaware Court of Chancery opined that any such corporate opportunity waiver "must be narrowly tailored to 'specified business opportunities or specified classes or categories of business opportunities.'"[27] The bill's legislative synopsis supports this position, providing that "categories of business opportunities may be specified by any manner of defining or delineating business opportunities . . . , including, without limitation, by line or type of business, identity of the originator of the business opportunity, identity of the party or parties to or having an interest in the business opportunity, identity of the recipient of the business opportunity, periods of time or geographical location."[28] Nonetheless, the Delaware Chancery Court has upheld a corporation's broadly worded waiver provision that entitled an outside director to take any corporate opportunity so long as such opportunity was not presented to or acquired by such director or otherwise did not come into his or her possession "expressly and solely" in such individual's capacity as a corporate director.[29]

Thus, by means of a corporate opportunity waiver, a subject company, through its board of directors, may preclude the company and its shareholders from bringing breach of duty of loyalty claims against corporate directors

---

[25] *Senate Bill 363: Original Synopsis*, Delaware General Assembly., 72 Del. Laws 619 (2000).
[26] *See* discussion in Rauterberg and Talley, *supra* note 24, at 1089–1104.
[27] *New Enterprise Associates 14, L.P. v. Rich*, 295 A.3d 520, 552–53 (Del. Ch. 2023), *quoting* Del. Gen. Corp. L. § 122(17), and *citing Alarm.com Holdings, Inc. v. ABS Capital Partners Inc.*, 2018 WL 3006118, at * 8–9 & n. 46 (Del. Ch. 2018).
[28] Senate Bill 363, 72 Del. Laws 619 (2000), *quoted in, New Enterprise Associates*, 295 A.3d at 553.
[29] *See* Nate Emeritz and Brian Currie, *Corporate Opportunity Doctrine: Litigation Continues Into 2020*, Harv. Law Sch. Forum on Corp. Gov. (Feb. 27, 2020). As contained in that post, the *Outlaw Beverage* corporate opportunity waiver provision that was upheld provided:

> [The corporation] renounces any interest or expectancy . . . in, or in being offered an opportunity to participate in an Excluded Opportunity. . . . [The term Excluded Opportunity means] any matter, transaction or interest that is presented to, or acquired, created or developed by, or which otherwise comes into the possession of (i) any director of the corporation who is not an employee of this corporation . . . unless such matter, transaction or interest is presented to, or acquired, created or developed by, or otherwise comes into the possession of [such director] expressly and solely in such [individual's] capacity as a director of the corporation.

For a definition of outside director, *see* note 110 *infra*.

and officers if their conduct comes within the applicable waiver's specified parameters. Functioning like a covenant not to sue, a corporate opportunity waiver enhances the likelihood that corporate directors and officers may engage in specified self-interested transactions without being held liable for breach of the duty of loyalty.[30] Whatever merits or demerits that these waiver provisions have,[31] they are antithetical to historically accepted principles of corporate governance that focus on a corporate director's and officer's duty of loyalty to the company and collectively to its shareholders.[32]

D. Close Corporation Shareholder Agreements

In closely held corporations, unanimous shareholder agreements are entered into with regularity.[33] These agreements may modify governance norms that otherwise would apply. For example, pursuant to a unanimous shareholder agreement, the board of directors may be eliminated, with the corporation being managed by designated shareholders who are identified in the agreement.[34] The question arises to what extent may a unanimous shareholder agreement waive aspects of the fiduciary duty of loyalty.

Pursuant to Section 7.32(a)(8) of the Model Business Corporation Act, a unanimous shareholder agreement may modify fiduciary duties that otherwise would be owed so long as "not contrary to public policy."[35] The Official Comment to the section states that a provision that exculpates directors from

---

[30] *See New Enterprise Associates*, 295 A.3d at 552.

[31] For example, these corporate opportunity waivers provide greater certainty that these types of transactions will not be subject to successful judicial challenge, thereby providing an inducement for independent directors (who have extensive and varied business interests) to serve on corporate boards.

[32] *See generally* Marc I. Steinberg, *The Federalization of Corporate Governance* (2018).

[33] This discussion does not address statutory close corporations as few business enterprises avail themselves of this option. The subject of fiduciary duties in closely held corporations is discussed further in Chapter 7.

[34] *See, e.g.*, Del. Gen. Corp. L. § 141 (stating that, if provided in the subject company's certificate of incorporation, "the powers and duties conferred or imposed upon the board of directors by this chapter shall be exercised or performed to such extent and by such person or persons as shall be provided in the certificate of incorporation").

[35] Section 7.32(a)(8) provides: "An agreement among the shareholders of a corporation that complies with this section is effective among the shareholders and the corporation even though it is inconsistent with one or more other provisions of this Act in that it: . . . (8) otherwise governs the exercise of the corporate powers or the management of the business and affairs of the corporation or the relationship among the shareholders, the directors and the corporation, or among any of them, and is not contrary to public policy." Section 7.32(a)(8) has been enacted by numerous states. *See, e.g.*, Ala. Code § 10A-2A-7.32(a)(8); Ariz. Rev. Stat. § 10-732(A)(11); Fla. Stat. § 607.0732(1)(j); Ga. Stat. § 14-2-732(a)(8); Utah Stat. § 16-10a-732(1)(h).

liability more expansively than allowed by Section 2.02(b)(4) of that Act may not be valid.[36] Section 2.02(b)(4), the exculpatory provision, authorizes a corporation to eliminate or limit the monetary liability of a director to the company or its shareholders except for liability based on the improper receipt of a financial benefit, intentional infliction of injury to the company or its shareholders, improper authorization of an unlawful distribution, or an intentional violation of criminal law.[37] Under this provision, specified director conduct that otherwise would violate the duty of loyalty may be engaged in without monetary liability exposure provided that the unanimous shareholder agreement at issue did not contravene the parameters of Section 2.02(b)(4).

Some statutes are more expansive than the Model Business Corporation Act. For example, pursuant to a unanimous shareholder agreement, the Texas statute provides that the relationship among the corporation and its directors and shareholders may be treated as if such corporation were a partnership, with the condition that any such provision must not be contrary to public policy.[38] As discussed in Chapter 2, pursuant to applicable partnership law, a partner may not misappropriate partnership assets, deal or compete with the partnership in a manner that is adverse to its interests, or act on a person's behalf whose interests are adverse to the partnership.[39] However, these mandates may be diminished if the partnership agreement identifies "specific types of activities or categories of activities that do not violate the duty of loyalty [so long as] the types or categories are not manifestly unreasonable."[40] Hence, under the Texas statute, specified director or officer conduct that otherwise would constitute a breach of the duty of loyalty may be permitted if authorized in a unanimous shareholder agreement and not

---

[36] Section 7.32 Official Comment (stating that "a provision that exculpates directors from liability more broadly than permitted by section 2.02(b)(4) ... might not be validated under section 7.32 because of strong public policy reasons for the statutory limitations on the right to exculpate directors from liability...").

[37] By its language, Section 2.02(b)(4)'s exculpation provision extends to certain breaches of the duty of loyalty. An example would be a director's breach of the duty of good faith in situations where adequate law compliance policies were neither adopted nor implemented. See discussion *infra* notes 43–51 and accompanying text; Chapter 7, notes 46–75 and accompanying text.

[38] See Texas Bus. Org. Code § 21.101(a)(12).

[39] See discussion in Chapter 2, notes 29–33 and accompanying text; Texas Bus. Org. Code § 152.205.

[40] Texas Bus. Org. Code § 152.002(b)(2). See discussion in Chapter 2, notes 34–47 and accompanying text. For Texas cases discussing shareholder agreements in closely held corporations, see *Ritchie v. Rupe*, 443 S.W.3d 856 (Tex. 2014); *Disney v. Gollan*, 233 S.W.3d 591 (Tex. App. 2007); *Martin v. Martin, Martin & Richards, Inc.*, 12 S.W.3d 120 (Tex. App. 1999). This subject is addressed further in Chapter 7.

deemed manifestly unreasonable. The extent of this exoneration from liability in this setting remains to be determined.

Although the degree of flexibility is unresolved, unanimous shareholder agreements in the close corporation context provide a further illustration that the duty of loyalty may be waived. Depending on the provisions contained in a unanimous shareholder agreement and the underlying facts and circumstances, corporate directors and officers may engage in conduct that otherwise would contravene the duty of loyalty.

E. No Longer Hallowed Ground

Traditionally, the duty of loyalty comprised the hallowed centerpiece of corporate director and officer fiduciary duties and was viewed as a foundational directive of corporate law.[41] This perspective no longer is accurate. Pursuant to statutory and judicial approbation, the fiduciary duty of loyalty may be waived in several situations. The discussion in this section provides four contextual illustrations. The following section of this chapter focuses on yet another setting where corporate directors and officers may avoid monetary liability exposure for their duty of loyalty breaches—namely, state exculpation statutes.

III. State Statutes Exculpating Duty of Loyalty Breaches

In Chapter 3, state exculpation statutes are addressed. That discussion focuses mainly on statutes that authorize exculpation for breach of the duty of care.[42] Significantly, a number of state statutes also exculpate certain breaches of the duty of loyalty. These statutes are the subject of this section.

---

[41] *See* Ruterberg and Talley, *supra* note 24, at 1075. From a historical perspective, the authors reflected: "The duty of loyalty is . . . notable because of its historically inveterate and unyielding nature: While much of corporate law consists of 'default rules' that parties may freely alter, the duty of loyalty is widely perceived as 'immutable'—immune to private efforts to dilute, tailor, or eliminate it." *Id.* at 1077, *citing among others*, Lucian Ayre Bebchuk and Assaf Hamdani, *Optimal Defaults for Corporate Law Evolution*, 96 Nw. U. L. Rev. 489 (2002); Melvin Aron Eisenberg, *The Structure of Corporation Law*, 89 Colum. L. Rev. 1461 (1989).

[42] *See* Chapter 3, notes 55–85 and accompanying text.

A. Select State Statutes: Exculpation for Duty of Loyalty Breaches

A perception exists that state exculpation statutes insulate directors (and, in a number of statutes, officers) from monetary liability for breach of the duty of care, excluding duty of loyalty breaches from exculpation. That perception is mistaken as several state statutes also exculpate directors and officers from monetary liability for certain breaches of the duty of loyalty. For example, the following statutes provide ample support for this assertion:

(1) The Maryland statute applies to both directors and officers, authorizing a Maryland corporation to have an exculpation provision in its charter that encompasses duty of loyalty breaches. The statute requires proof that the defendant director or officer received "an improper benefit or profit" or that his or her conduct "was the result of active and deliberate dishonesty [that] was material to the cause of action adjudicated in the proceeding" in order for money damages to be recovered from such individual in an action brought by the subject corporation or its stockholders.[43] The statute thus insulates directors and officers who, for example, passively are dominated by a controlling shareholder or who cavalierly ignore their oversight obligations—misconduct that should constitute a lack of good faith and a breach of the duty of loyalty.

(2) The Ohio statute insulates directors from monetary liability unless it is proved by "clear and convincing evidence" that the subject director either deliberately intended to harm the company or engaged in conduct recklessly disregarding such corporation's best interests.[44] Under the language of this statute, for instance, a director acting with gross negligence could usurp a corporate opportunity that properly belonged to the corporation without being subject to liability.

(3) Provided that an exculpatory provision is contained in a subject corporation's articles of incorporation, the Virginia statute absolves

---

[43] Md. Code §§ 2-405.2, 5-418(a). The statute does not apply to "an action brought by or on behalf of a State governmental entity, receiver, conservator, or depositor against a director or officer of: (1) A banking institution...; (2) A credit union...; (3) A savings and loan association...; or (4) A subsidiary of a banking institution, credit union, or savings and loan association described in this subsection." Id. § 5-418(b). For further discussion and case law interpreting the Maryland statutes, see Chapter 3, notes 72–74 and accompanying text.

[44] Ohio Rev. Code § 1701.59(D)-(E). Corporations may opt out of this exculpation protection for their directors. See discussion in Chapter 3, notes 75–76 and accompanying text.

directors and officers from monetary liability unless it is shown that such persons "engaged in willful misconduct or a knowing violation of the criminal law or of any federal or state securities law."[45] Pursuant to this statute, for example, a director or officer acting with gross negligence may engage in a self-dealing transaction.

(4) Under the Nevada exculpation statute, directors and officers are insulated from liability unless it is proven that the subject defendant engaged in a breach of fiduciary duty *and* "such breach involved intentional misconduct, fraud, or a knowing violation of law."[46] By requiring intentional misconduct, fraud, or a knowing violation of law, this statute absolves directors and officers of certain duty of loyalty breaches, such as when a subject director or officer engages in self-dealing transactions, usurps corporate opportunities, or is controlled by a dominating director or officer when voting or taking other action with respect to a transaction that financially benefits the dominating director or officer—so long as such person does not intentionally or knowingly engage in this misconduct.

(5) The Model Business Corporation Act exculpation provision, adopted by a number of states, likewise insulates directors from certain duty of loyalty breaches.[47] Provided that the exculpation provision is contained in the subject corporation's articles of incorporation, a defendant director is insulated from monetary liability unless he or she receives an improper financial benefit, intentionally inflicts harm on the company or its stockholders, votes for or assents to an unlawful distribution, or engages in an intentional violation of criminal law.[48] Like the Maryland statute, this provision precludes the levying

---

[45] Va. Code § 13.1692.1(A)-(B). *See* discussion in Chapter 3, note 77 and accompanying text.
[46] Nev. Rev. Stat. § 78.138(7). *See* discussion and cases cited in Chapter 3, notes 80–83 and accompanying text.
[47] *See* MBCA § 2.02(b)(4) (stating that a corporation's articles of incorporation may include "a provision eliminating or limiting the liability of a director to the corporation or its shareholders for money damages for any action, or any failure to take action, as a director, except liability for (i) the amount of a financial benefit received by a director to which the director was not entitled; (ii) an intentional infliction of harm on the corporation or the shareholders; (iii) a violation of section 8.32 [addressing director liability for unlawful distributions]; or (iv) an intentional violation of criminal law").
Several states have enacted Section 2.02(b)(4) of the Model Business Corporation Act. *See, e.g.*, Ala. Stat. § 10A-2A-2.02(b)(4); Ariz. Stat. § 10-202(B)(1); Colo. Stat. § 7-102-102(2)(d); Idaho Stat. § 30-29-202(b)(4); Miss. Stat. § 79-4-2.02(b)(4); Neb. § 21-220(b)(4); Wyo. Stat. § 17-16-202(b)(iv).
[48] Model Business Corporation Act § 2.02(b)(4). This MBCA provision recently has been amended to encompass officer exculpation in direct (but not derivative) actions. *See* Corporate Laws Committee, *Changes in the Model Business Corporation Act—Proposed Amendments to Section 2.02 Relating to Officer Exculpation*, 79 Bus. Law. 125, 127 (2023–2024).

of money damages against passive directors who are dominated by a controlling shareholder or who cavalierly ignore their oversight obligations—misconduct that evidences a lack of good faith and a breach of the duty of loyalty.[49]

(6) The Indiana exculpation statute serves as the last example and is as clear as day. That is because the statute is self-executing and, by its language, exonerates a defendant director for "alleged breaches of the duty of care, the duty of loyalty, and the duty of good faith."[50] By the terms of the statute, duty of loyalty breaches are exonerated unless a defendant director fails to adhere to his or her duties *and* such "breach or failure to perform constitutes willful misconduct or recklessness."[51] Hence, a director's breach of the duty of loyalty committed with a mental culpability of gross negligence is not actionable under the statute. An example would be that, with gross negligence, a director usurped a corporate opportunity properly belonging to the corporation.

B. The Delaware Exculpation Statute: In Reality, Exculpating Loyalty Breaches

By contrast, the Delaware statute projects that it is focused solely on exculpation for duty of care breaches.[52] But in actuality, is that accurate? Pursuant to Section 102(b)(7), if a defendant director's or officer's behavior constitutes

---

[49] The Official Comment to Section 2.02(b)(4) makes clear that intentional, rather than reckless, conduct is required with respect to the infliction of harm upon the corporation:

> There may be situations in which a director intentionally causes harm to the corporation even though the director does not receive any improper benefit. The use of the word "intentional," rather than a less precise term such as "knowing," is meant to refer to the specific intent to perform, or fail to perform, the acts with actual knowledge that the director's action, or failure to act, will cause harm, rather than a general intent to perform the acts which cause the harm.

[50] Ind. Code § 23-1-35-1(e).
[51] *Id. See* discussion in Chapter 3, notes 78–79 and accompanying text.
[52] *See CCSB Financial Corp. v. Totta*, 302 A.3d 387, 398–402 (Del. 2023) (invalidating charter provision that limited director liability for breach of the duty of loyalty); *Colon v. Bumble, Inc.*, 305 A.3d 352, 359 (Del. Ch. 2023) ("Some default rights are so significant that the charter cannot eliminate them [including] [t]he right to sue for breach of the fiduciary duty of loyalty...."); discussion in Chapter 3, notes 55–70 and accompanying text.

intentional misconduct, breach of the duty of loyalty, knowing violation of law, knowing authorization of an unlawful distribution, or receipt of an improper personal benefit, exculpation is prohibited. As construed by a number of Delaware courts, when a corporation's charter contains such an exculpation provision, directors (and officers in direct actions) can be insulated from monetary liability for their reckless conduct (unless one of the foregoing exceptions applies).[53]

But query whether reckless conduct by a corporate director or officer, by its culpability level alone, should be more than sufficient to constitute a loyalty breach. Black's Law Dictionary defines recklessness as "[t]he state of mind in which a person does not care about the consequences of his or her actions."[54] Under the federal securities laws, reckless conduct represents "an extreme departure from the standards of ordinary care to the extent that the danger was either known to the defendant or [was] so obvious that the defendant must have been aware of it."[55] Under such circumstances, how can a corporate director or officer behave with this degree of culpability yet be deemed to act with the motivation of acting in the subject corporation's best interests? Logically, a director or officer who acts without caring about the consequences of his or her actions upon the corporation and its stockholders violates the duty of loyalty. Yet under Delaware law and many other state statutes, such conduct is deemed a duty of care breach which may be insulated from monetary liability by means of an exculpation provision contained in the corporation's certificate of incorporation. By treating a loyalty breach as a duty of care breach, Delaware engages in a misdirected approach that ill serves its preeminent stature in corporation law.

---

[53] Del. Gen. Corp. Law § 102(b)(7). *See New Enterprise Associates 14 L.P. v. Rich*, 295 A.3d 520, 551 (Del. Ch. 2023) (stating that § 102(b)(7) "permits exculpation for recklessness"); *In re Columbia Pipeline Group, Inc.*, 2021 WL 772562, at * 50 n. 22 (Del. Ch. 2021) (stating that "[t]he real function of exculpation is to eliminate liability for recklessness").

[54] *Black's Law Dictionary* 1524 (11th 2019). Another definition provided in this source is: "Conduct whereby the actor does not desire harmful consequences but nonetheless foresees the possibility and consciously takes the risk." *Id.*

[55] This definition of recklessness is commonly used by the federal courts in securities law cases. *See, e.g., In re Ikon Office Solution, Inc. Securities Litigation*, 277 F.3d 658, 667 (3d Cir. 2002); *Hollinger v. Titan Capital Corporation*, 914 F.2d 1564, 1569 (9th Cir. 1990) (en banc); *Sanders v. John Nuveen & Co., Inc.*, 554 F.2d 790, 793 (7th Cir. 1977).

C. Exculpation Statutes: Corporate Directors and Officers Are Not Fiduciaries

The foregoing discussion aptly demonstrates that several state exculpation statutes insulate corporate directors (and, in some states, also officers) from monetary liability for breaches of the duty of loyalty. By engaging in this conduct, these individuals frequently act for their own financial interests rather than for the benefit of the corporation and its stockholders. Insulating this conduct from monetary liability exposure, these statutes reinforce the reality that corporate directors and officers are not fiduciaries.

IV. The Duty of Good Faith

The following discussion addresses the duty of good faith which in Delaware is a component of the duty of loyalty.[56] A director's or officer's failure to act in good faith may be shown, for example, by such individual (1) intentionally taking action with an objective other than that of advancing the company's best interests; (2) engaging in conduct with the motive of violating applicable positive law; or (3) failing to take appropriate action where there is a known duty to act, thereby manifesting a conscious disregard for adhering to his or her fiduciary obligations.[57] By confining the defendant director's or officer's breach of good faith to the commission of intentional misconduct, the duty of good faith is substantially limited.[58]

Pursuant to this liability standard, as embraced by the Delaware Supreme Court, a director who, for example, recklessly engages in conduct that is detrimental to the company's best interests (unaccompanied by other duty of loyalty considerations) does not breach the duty of good faith.[59] Indeed, as

---

[56] *See, e.g., Stone v. Ritter*, 911 A.2d 362, 369 (Del. 2006).

[57] *In re Walt Disney Company Derivative Litigation*, 906 A.2d 27, 67 (Del. 2006). *See Stone v. Ritter*, 911 A.2d at 369 (quoting *Disney* with approbation and opining that "a failure to act in good faith requires conduct that is quantitatively different from, and more culpable than, the conduct giving rise to a violation of the fiduciary duty of care (i.e., gross negligence").

[58] *See* Mercer Bullard, *Caremark's Irrelevance*, 10 U. Cal. Berk. Bus. L.J. 15, 44 (2013); Megan W. Shaner, *The (Un)Enforcement of Corporate Officers' Duties*, 48 U.C. Davis L. Rev. 271, 307 (2014). *See generally* Mark J. Loewenstein, *The Diverging Meaning of Good Faith*, 34 Del. J. Corp. L. 433 (2009).

[59] *See, e.g., Disney*, 906 A.2d at 67 (stating that a director breaches the duty of good faith "where the fiduciary intentionally acts with a purpose other than that of advancing the best interests of the corporation").

discussed in Chapter 3 and earlier in this chapter,[60] a number of Delaware cases have stated that such reckless conduct is within the scope of a suitably drafted exculpation provision, thereby insulating a defendant director or officer (in direct actions) from monetary liability for this misconduct.[61] Under this rationale, recklessly slighting the corporation's best interests by a director or officer, unadorned by self-dealing or other duty of loyalty breach, does not give rise to money damages. Hence, in this setting, the duty of good faith, comprising a component of the duty of loyalty, resonates with noise yet with hardly a bang.

The glaring gap between standards of conduct and standards of review is highlighted by the Delaware Supreme Court's decision in *Stone v. Ritter*.[62] There, quoting from the well-known *Caremark* decision decided by Chancellor Allen,[63] the court opined that "it is important that the board exercise its good faith judgment that the corporation's information and reporting system is in concept and design adequate to assure the board that appropriate information will come to its attention in a timely manner as a matter of ordinary operations, so that it may satisfy its responsibility."[64] Making clear that this exhortation did not represent applicable liability standards, the court adopted far more narrow parameters. Hence, in order for directors to incur liability for their failure to act in good faith in regard to their oversight functions, it must be established that "(a) the directors *utterly failed* to implement *any* reporting or information system or controls; or (b) having implemented such a system or controls, *consciously failed* to monitor or oversee its operations, thus disabling themselves from being informed of risks or problems requiring their attention."[65] Subsequently, this standard (the *Caremark* standard), defining the standard of liability in this setting, has been applied to corporate officers.[66] Accordingly, directors and officers

---

[60] *See* discussion in Chapter 3, notes 64–66 and accompanying text; *supra* notes 52–55 and accompanying text in this chapter.

[61] *See, e.g., New Enterprise Associates 14 L.P. v. Rich*, 295 A.3d 520, 551 (Del. Ch. 2023); *In re Columbia Pipeline Group, Inc.*, 2021 WL 772562, at * 50 n. 22 (Del. Ch. 2021).

[62] 911 A.2d 362 (Del. 2006). For a more recent example, *see United Food and Commercial Workers Union v. Zuckerberg*, 262 A.3d 1034, 1049–50 (Del. 2021) (emphasis supplied), where the Delaware Supreme Court conflated the standard of conduct and the standard of liability in a single sentence: "Predicated upon concepts of *gross negligence*, the *duty of care* requires that [corporate] fiduciaries *inform themselves of material information* before making a business decision and act *prudently* in carrying out their duties."

[63] *In re Caremark Int'l Inc. Derivative Litigation*, 698 A.2d 959 (Del. Ch. 1996).

[64] 911 A.2d at 368, *quoting Caremark*, 698 A.2d at 970.

[65] 911 A.2d at 370 (emphasis supplied). *See id.* (opining that either of these prongs mandates "a showing that the directors knew that they were not discharging their fiduciary obligations").

[66] *See In re McDonald's Corporation Stockholder Derivative Litigation*, 289 A.3d 343 (Del. Ch. 2023). To plead a *Caremark* claim, the same standard applies for directors and officers. *See, e.g.*,

breach their duty to act in good faith when they "utterly" or "consciously fail" to adhere to their oversight obligations. The levying of liability thus requires proof that the defendant directors and officers "knew" that they were not adequately performing their law compliance oversight obligations.[67] The gap between the Delaware Supreme Court's rhetoric and the substance of its holding is glaring.

Consistent with this approach, the Delaware courts have been demanding of shareholder-plaintiffs who seek to recover on this basis.[68] As the Delaware Supreme Court has recognized, "*Caremark* claims are difficult to plead and ultimately to prove out. . . ."[69] Indeed, to successfully pursue a *Caremark* claim, plaintiffs must adequately plead either that: (1) the defendant director(s) or officer(s) undertook *no actions* to implement a needed reporting or information system or controls; or (2) if such action was taken, they *consciously disregarded* their ongoing obligation to oversee its effectiveness.[70] While the Delaware Supreme Court has opined that "to satisfy their duty of loyalty, directors must make a good faith effort to implement an oversight system and monitor it,"[71] it is clear that a violation of the duty of good faith requires that a director or officer engage in intentional misconduct.

Applying this standard, a number of recent Delaware decisions have held that *Caremark* claims were adequately pled. These cases alleged that the

---

Segway Inc. v. Hong, 2023 WL 8643017, at * 1 (Del. Ch. 2023) (rejecting the assertion that "the high bar to plead a *Caremark* claim is lowered when the claim is brought against an officer").

[67] See *Ritter v. Stone*, 911 A.2d at 370.
[68] See *Segway Inc. v. Hong*, 2023 WL 8643017, at * 5 (stating that the *Caremark* doctrine "is intended to address the extraordinary case where fiduciaries' 'utter failure' to implement an effective compliance system or 'conscious disregard' of the law gives rise to a corporate trauma"); Paul E. McGreal, *Corporate Compliance Survey*, 78 Bus. Law. 475, 488–89 (2023) (citing Delaware cases).
[69] *Marchand v. Barnhill*, 212 A.3d 805, 820 (Del. 2019). The *Caremark* decision itself recognized the difficulty for plaintiffs to prove a breach of loyalty claim premised on deficient board of director oversight. *See* 698 A.2d at 971. For a recent decision, *see Bricklayers Pension Fund of Western Pennsylvania v. Brinkley*, 2024 WL 3384823, at * 15 (Del. Ch. 2024) (dismissing *Caremark* claims as the plaintiff has "not painted the extreme picture" required for such claims).
[70] *See, e.g., In re McDonald's Corporation Stockholder Derivative Litigation*, 289 A.3d at 359–60.
[71] *Marchand v. Barnhill*, 212 A.3d at 822: "*Caremark* does have a bottom-line requirement that is important: the board must make a good faith effort—i.e., try—to put in place a reasonable board-level system of monitoring and reporting." Holding that the allegations in the complaint were sufficient to state a *Caremark* claim, the Delaware Supreme Court stated:

> [T]he complaint supports an inference that no system of board-level compliance monitoring and reporting existed at Blue Bell. Although *Caremark* is a tough standard for plaintiffs to meet, the plaintiff has met it here. When a plaintiff can plead an inference that a board has undertaken no efforts to make sure it is informed of a compliance issue intrinsically critical to the company's business operation, then that supports an inference that the board has not made the good faith effort that *Caremark* requires.

Id. Accord Lebanon County Employees' Retirement Fund v. Collis, 311 A.3d 773 (Del. 2023).

subject company's board of directors either (1) made no effort to implement a board-level compliance system that sought to address the area(s) of risk;[72] or (2) once such a compliance system was implemented, defendant directors consciously failed to oversee its effectiveness.[73] Plaintiffs typically plead this second prong by alleging that the subject "board's information systems generated red flags indicating wrongdoing and that the directors failed to respond."[74] These *Caremark* allegations likewise have been successfully pled against corporate officers.[75] Although a number of these cases resulted in substantial settlements,[76] the fact remains that most of these decisions have ruled on motions to dismiss. As *Caremark* claims are derivative, they face obstacles with the demand on the board of directors requirement and the dismissal of the subject case in accordance with the recommendation made by a special litigation committee comprised of independent and disinterested directors.[77] The subject of derivative litigation is addressed in Chapter 5.

---

[72] A number of these cases involved failure by the subject board of directors to adopt a monitoring and reporting system where there existed a "mission critical" regulatory compliance risk for the company. *See Marchand v. Barnhill*, 212 A.3d at 824; *In re Boeing Company Derivative Litigation*, 2021 WL 4059934, at * 26 (Del. Ch. 2021); *In re Clovis Derivative Litigation*, 2019 WL 4850188, at * 12 (Del. Ch. 2019).

[73] *See Lebanon County Employees' Retirement Fund v. Collis* 311 A.3d at 804–05 (holding that the complaint adequately alleged that the company's directors knew of and consciously failed to take any action with respect to their law compliance oversight duties); *Construction Industry Laborers Pension Fund v. Bingle*, 2022 WL 4102492, at * 1 (Del. Ch. 2022) ("Historically, only utter failures by directors to impose a system for reporting risk, or failure to act in the face of 'red flags' disclosed to them so vibrant that lack of action implicates bad faith . . . have led to viable claims under *Caremark*"). *See also In re Citigroup Shareholder Derivative Litigation*, 964 A.2d 106, 125 (Del. Ch. 2009) ("The presumption of the business judgment rule, the protection of an exculpatory Section 102(b)(7) provision, and the difficulty of proving a *Caremark* claim together function to place an extremely high burden on a plaintiff to state a claim for personal director liability for a failure to see the extent of a company's business risk").

[74] *In re McDonald's Corporation Stockholder Derivative Litigation*, 289 A.3d at 360.

[75] *Id.* at 369 (citations omitted):

[O]fficers owe duties of oversight comparable to those of directors. But this does not mean that the situational application of those duties will be the same. Most notably, directors are charged with plenary authority over the business and affairs of the corporation. It also means that the board has oversight duties regarding the corporation as a whole. Although the CEO and Chief Compliance Officer likely will have company-wide oversight portfolios, other officers generally have a more constrained area of authority. With a more constrained area of responsibility comes a constrained version of the duty that supports a [*Caremark*] claim. . . .

[76] For example, the *Boeing* derivative action settled for approximately $238 million and *Marchand* for approximately $60 million. *See* Linda Chiem, *Boeing Board Inks $238M Deal to End 737 Max Derivative Suit*, Law360 (Nov. 5, 2021); Roy Shapira, *Max Oversight Duties: How Boeing Signifies a Shift in Corporate Law*, 48 J. Corp. L. 121, 133 (2022) (stating that *Marchand* was settled for $60 million). *See also* Roy Shapira, *A New Caremark Era: Causes and Consequences*, 98 Wash. U. L. Rev. 1857 (2021).

[77] *See In re McDonald's Corporation Derivative Litigation*, 289 A.3d at 367 (stating that "oversight claims are derivative, so the board controls the claim unless a stockholder can plead demand futility or show wrongful refusal"); discussion in Chapter 5.

For purposes of this discussion, the duty of good faith is based on a director's or officer's intentional dereliction of his or her obligations. By "consciously" and "utterly failing" to adhere to their obligations, including their oversight functions, duty of loyalty breaches may ensue.[78] Although plaintiff-shareholders have enjoyed some success, this onerous standard reflects the high bar that exists. Equating good faith with conduct that falls short of intentional or conscious wrongdoing reflects poorly on the application of fiduciary duty principles. Once again, there is a marked contrast between rhetoric and substance. In actuality, the liability standards that are applied in this context are largely devoid of meaningful fiduciary concepts.

V. Interested Director and Officer Transactions

Although subject to vigorous judicial scrutiny many decades ago, interested director and officer transactions today frequently enjoy lenient review. Indeed, approximately 150 years ago, interested director and officer transactions were deemed voidable. As Harold Marsh stated in a 1966 law journal article: "In 1880 it could have been stated with confidence that in the United States the general rule was that any contract between a director and his corporation was voidable at the instance of the corporation or its shareholders, without regard to the fairness or unfairness of the transaction."[79] Three decades thereafter, in 1910, the general rule had been modified

---

[78] *See* discussion *supra* notes 56–77 and accompanying text. Significantly, corporate directors and officers may incur liability under federal and state law for the failure by their companies to comply with regulatory directives. *See* American Bar Association, Section of Business Law (Committee on Corporate Laws), *Corporate Director's Guidebook* 37–43 (7th ed. 2020). Also, the Organizational Sentencing Guidelines promulgated by the United States Sentencing Commission address corporate compliance programs. *See* § 8B2.1 (Effective Compliance and Ethics Program); United States Sentencing Commission, *The Organizational Sentencing Guidelines: Thirty Years of Innovation and Influence* 10–11 (2022). Effective compliance programs must be implemented in order for a corporation to receive credit pursuant to the Sentencing Guidelines. The Guidelines provide: "High-level personnel of the organization shall ensure that the organization has an effective compliance and ethics program...." Sentencing Guidelines § 882.1(b)(2)(B), *discussed in Caremark*, 698 A.2d at 970, and *McDonald's Stockholder Derivative Litigation*, 289 A.3d at 361. *See generally* Carliss Chatman and Tammi S. Etheridge, *Federalizing Caremark*, 70 UCLA L. Rev. 908 (2023).

[79] Harold Marsh Jr., *Are Directors Trustees?*, 22 Bus. Law., 35, 36 (1966), *citing Wardell v. Union Pacific Railroad Company*, 103 U.S. 651 (1880); *Memphis & Charleston Railroad Company v. Wood*, 7 So. 108 (Ala. 1889); *Davis v. The Rock Creek L. R. & M. Co.*, 55 Cal. 359 (1880); *Mallory v. Mallory-Wheeler Co.*, 23 A. 708 (Conn. 1891); *European & North American Railway Co. v. Poor*, 59 Me. 277 (1871); *Hoffman Steam Coal Co. v. Cumberland Coal and Iron Co.*, 16 Md. 456 (1860); *Pearson v. Concord Railroad Commission*, 62 N.H. 537 (1883). Beveridge disputes this characterization, asserting that interested director transactions "were never thought to be voidable without regard to fairness." Norwood P. Berveridge Jr., *The Corporate Director's Fiduciary Duty of*

THE DUTY OF LOYALTY 71

whereby "a contract between a director and his corporation was valid if it was approved by a disinterested majority of his fellow directors and was not found to be unfair or fraudulent by the court if challenged"; but a contract where a majority of the directors was interested was deemed voidable at the option of the subject company or its shareholders without regard to whether such transaction was fair or unfair.[80] By 1960, according to Marsh, the general rule had been relaxed so that no interested director or officer transaction would be automatically voidable if challenged in a properly brought action. Rather, any such transaction would be subject to careful scrutiny and would be invalidated if held to be unfair to the corporation.[81]

Absent independent director or shareholder approval, this rule prevails today[82] and is consistent with fiduciary principles. Requiring that the defendant prove that the subject transaction is both procedurally and substantively fair to the corporation places an appropriate burden on the director or officer to justify his or her conduct.[83] Indeed, with some frequency, such self-dealing transactions may benefit the subject company. If such director or officer cannot establish the transaction's fairness, resulting in a breach of the duty of loyalty, meaningful relief may be ordered whereby the wrongdoer

---

Loyalty: Understanding the Self-Interested Director Transaction, 41 DePaul L. Rev. 655, 660 (1992). *See* additional sources cited in Chapter 2, note 5.

Generally, an interested director or officer transaction is "a contract or transaction between a corporation and 1 or more of its directors or officers, or between a corporation and any other corporation, partnership, association, or other organization in which 1 or more of its directors or officers, are directors or officers, or have a financial interest...." Del. Gen. Corp. L. § 144(a).

[80] Marsh, *supra* note 79, at 39–40, citing, *inter alia*, *Holcomb v. Forsyth*, 113 So. 516 (Ala. 1927); *Schnittger v. Old Home Consolidated Mining Co.*, 78 P. 9 (Cal. 1904); *Pennsylvania Railroad Co. v. Minis*, 87 A. 1062 (Md. 1913); *McKey v. Swenson*, 205 N.W. 583 (Mich. 1925); *Jacobson v. Brooklyn Lumber Co.*, 76 N.E. 1075 (N.Y. 1906).

[81] Marsh, *supra* note 79, at 43.

[82] *See, e.g.,* Del. Gen. Corp. L. § 144(a); *In re Imperial Credit Industries, Inc.*, 2008 WL 4346785 (C.D. Cal. 2008) (interpreting California law); *Sullivan v. Easco Corporation*, 656 F. Supp. 531 (D. Md. 1987) (interpreting Maryland law); *Fliegler v. Lawrence*, 361 A.2d 218 (Del. 1976).

[83] *See* Official Comment to Model Business Corporation Act § 8.60:

In considering the "fairness" of the transaction, the court will be required to consider not only the market fairness of the terms of the deal . . . but also . . . whether the transaction was one that was reasonably likely to yield favorable results. . . . Thus, if a manufacturing company that lacks sufficient working capital allocates some of its scarce funds to purchase at a market price a sailing yacht owned by one of its directors, it will not be easy to persuade the court that the transaction was "fair" in the sense that it was reasonably made to further the business interests of the corporation . . . [irrespective that] the full measure of disclosures made by the director is beyond challenge. . . .

See also Tornetta v. Musk, 2024 WL 343699 (Del. Ch. 2024) (voiding Elon Musk's compensation plan of $55 billion as excessive under the entire fairness standard whereby the defendants failed to satisfy this standard of review).

may be held financially accountable to the corporation, including forfeiting all ill-gotten gains.[84] If faithfully enforced by the courts, this standard incentivizes corporate directors and officers to act fairly when engaging in self-dealing transactions with the corporation to whom they serve.

Today, this rigorous standard is regularly avoided by having disinterested directors approve the subject self-dealing transaction.[85] As recognized by the Delaware Supreme Court, approval by disinterested and adequately informed directors often signifies that the interested director transaction is reviewed under the business judgment rule.[86] As discussed in Chapter 3, the business judgment rule places the burden on the plaintiff to prove that the directors who approved the subject transaction were themselves conflicted or acted with gross negligence.[87] Moreover, when the directors who approve the conflicted transaction are deemed to be independent and disinterested, the applicable violation alleged would be a duty of care breach. With the customary presence of an exculpation provision, such directors

---

[84] *See, e.g.*, *In re TransCare Corporation*, 81 F.4th 37 (2d Cir. 2023) (applying Delaware law); *Lewis v. S. L. & E., Inc.*, 629 F.2d 764 (2d Cir. 1980) (applying New York law); *Hayes Oyster Co. v. Keypoint Oyster Co.*, 391 P.2d 979 (Wash. 1964). *See generally* Lawrence E. Mitchell, *Fairness and Trust in Corporate Law*, 43 Duke L.J. 425 (1993); Andrew F. Tuch, *Reassessing Self-Dealing: Between No Conflict and Fairness*, 88 Fordham L. Rev. 939 (2019).

[85] *See, e.g.*, Del Gen. Corp. L. § 144(a)(1) ("The material facts as to the director's or officer's relationship or interest and as to the contract or transaction are disclosed or are known to the board of directors or the committee, and the board or committee in good faith authorizes the contract or transaction by the affirmative votes of a majority of the disinterested directors, even though the disinterested directors be less than a quorum").

[86] *See, e.g.*, *Benihana of Tokyo, Inc. v. Benihana, Inc.*, 906 A.2d 114, 120 (Del. 2006) ("After approval by disinterested directors, courts review the interested transaction under the business judgement rule. . . ."); *Marciano v. Nakash*, 535 A.2d 400, 405 n. 3 (Del. 1987) (stating that "approval by fully informed disinterested directors . . . permits invocation of the business judgment rule"). Note that in conflicted-controller transactions under Delaware law, including outside of the M&A setting, approval by informed disinterested directors shifts the burden of proof to the plaintiff-shareholder to proof unfairness. *See In re Match Group, Inc. Derivative Litigation*, 315 A.3d 446, 461 (Del. 2024) (describing this standard); *Tornetta v. Musk*, 310 A.3d 430, 497–510 (Del. Ch. 2024) (adhering to this standard with respect to controller's (Elon Musk's) compensation plan). As stated by the Delaware Supreme Court in *In re Match Group*:

> [W]e conclude, based on long-standing [Delaware] Supreme Court precedent, that in a suit claiming that a controlling stockholder stood on both sides of a transaction with the controlled corporation and received a non-ratable benefit, entire fairness is the presumptive standard of review. The controlling stockholder can shift the burden of proof to the plaintiff by properly employing a special committee or an unaffiliated stockholder vote. But the use of just one of these procedural devices does not change the standard of review. If the controlling stockholder wants to secure the benefits of business judgment review, it must [employ both a special committee and an unaffiliated stockholder vote.]

315 A.3d at 451.

[87] *See, e.g.*, *Aronson v. Lewis*, 473 A.2d 805, 812 (Del. 1984) (stating that "under the business judgment rule director liability is predicated upon concepts of gross negligence"); Chapter 3, notes 25–54 and accompanying text.

would be monetarily liable only if they acted with intentional misconduct when authorizing the subject self-dealing transaction.[88] With this forgiving standard, interested director and officer transactions are far less likely to be successfully challenged. The application of lenient culpability levels marks a drastic departure from how these transactions were historically scrutinized and tellingly conveys that meaningful fiduciary standards have been diminished in this setting.

This permissive approach has been expanded by the Model Business Corporation Act (MBCA) and several states in favor of an even more lax standard. Pursuant to this standard, judicial scrutiny of an interested director transaction is foreclosed once disinterested and independent directors, being adequately informed, approve the transaction.[89] Hence, as stated in the Official MBCA Comment, once such director approval is procured, "then a director's conflicting interest transaction is immune from attack by a shareholder or the corporation on the ground of an interest of the director."[90] Likewise, the Texas statute precludes the subject corporation or its shareholders from successfully bringing an action alleging breach of fiduciary duty with respect to a transaction involving an interested director or officer—provided that a majority of adequately informed disinterested directors (or a majority of the disinterested directors comprising a committee) in good faith authorized the subject contract or transaction.[91] Pursuant to this approach, judicial review of an interested director or officer transaction is foreclosed so long as the disinterested directors who authorized the transaction acted in good faith and were adequately informed. This approach slights the structural bias concerns that prevail on corporate boards.[92] Through their laxity of facilitating interested director and officer

---

[88] *See, e.g., New Enterprise Associates 14 L.P. v. Rich*, 295 A.3d 520, 551 (Del. Ch. 2023); *In re Columbia Pipeline Group, Inc.*, 2021 WL 772562, at * 50, n. 22 (Del. Ch. 2021); discussion Chapter 3, notes 64–66 and accompanying text.

[89] *See, e.g.*, Model Business Corporation Act § 8.61 Official Comment (providing that, if the requisite procedures are complied with and disinterested director approval is obtained, "then a director's conflicting interest transaction is immune from attack by a shareholder or the corporation on the ground of an interest of the director"). The same result follows if the requisite shareholder approval is procured. *Id.* § 8.61 (Official Comment), § 8.63.

[90] Model Business Corporation Act § 8.61 (Official Comment). For states adopting the MBCA approach, *see, e.g.*, Ariz. Rev. Stat. §§ 10-860-863; Conn. Gen. Stat. §§ 33-781-784; Ga. Code §§ 14-2-860-863; Iowa Code § 490.860-.863; Neb. Rev. Stat. §§ 21-2.120-.123; Tenn. Code §§ 48-18-701-704; Utah Code §§ 16-10a-850-853; Wash. Code §§ 23B.08.700-.730.

[91] *See* Texas Bus. Org. Code § 21.418.

[92] A number of courts have recognized the presence of structural bias with respect to outside directors. *See, e.g., Clark v. Lomas & Nettleton Financial Corp.*, 625 F.2d 49, 53–54 (5th Cir. 1980); *Zapata Corporation v. Maldonado*, 430 A.2d 779, 787 (Del. 1981); *Miller v. Register and Tribune Syndicate*, 336 N.W. 2d 709, 716–18 (Iowa 1983). Structural bias may be defined as "inherent

transactions and deterring challenges to such transactions, these statutes are antithetical to the concept of corporate directors and officers being fiduciaries.

In sum, the approaches currently adopted with respect to the validity of corporate director and officer transactions belittle fiduciary principles. As commonly implemented, particularly in publicly traded companies, conflicted self-dealing transactions are routinely approved by adequately informed disinterested directors. Under Delaware law and the majority of US states, such approval signifies that the expansive business judgment rule is applied to the decision of such disinterested directors to authorize the disputed transaction. With the presence of charter exculpation provisions, defendant disinterested directors who authorized such transactions ordinarily face monetary liability only if they acted with intentional misconduct. In other jurisdictions, such as Texas, the law is even more protective of defendant self-dealing insiders. Pursuant to these statutes, judicial review of a conflicted director or officer transaction is precluded if a majority of the disinterested directors (either as members of the board or a board committee) authorize such transaction in good faith having adequate information. Again, with the presence of charter exculpation provisions, these disinterested directors normally may incur liability only if they engage in intentional misconduct. These approaches drastically modify the traditional principle mandating that an interested director or officer transaction may be upheld only if the conflicted director or officer establishes the transaction's fairness. The adherence to these lax approaches evidences that even in the contextual setting where structural bias reigns and selfish insiders are motivated to benefit at their company's expense, fiduciary standards have been drastically reduced.[93]

---

prejudice . . . resulting from the composition and character of the board of directors." Note, *The Business Judgement Rule in Derivative Suits Against Directors*, 65 Cornell L. Rev. 600, 601 n. 14 (1980). *See* James D. Cox and Harry L. Munsinger, *Bias in the Boardroom: Psychological Foundations and Legal Implications of Corporate Cohesion*, 48 Law & Contemp. Probs. 79 (1985) (addressing bias among directors on corporate boards); Note, *The Propriety of Judicial Deference to Corporate Boards of Directors*, 96 Harv. L. Rev. 1894, 1901 (1983) ("Given cohesiveness and informational dependence in the boardroom, directors are likely to conform to the expectations of both management and of their fellow board members").

[93] *See generally* William W. Bratton, *Reconsidering the Evolutionary Erosion Account of Corporate Fiduciary Law*, 76 Bus. Law. 1157, 1159 (2021) (asserting that the "erosion of the standards that courts apply to management self-dealing has continued unabated since Marsh published in 1966 and even though there is no reason to think that management self-dealing benefits the shareholder interest"), *referring to* Harold Marsh Jr., *Are Directors Trustees?*, 22 Bus. Law. 35 (1966). The subject of structural bias also is examined in the context of derivative litigation where independent directors

VI. The Corporate Opportunity Doctrine

Another situation where fiduciary duties have been minimized is with respect to the corporate opportunity doctrine. Although much of this erosion has occurred recently, courts have long recognized the delicate assessments that must be made in this setting. On the one hand, sound principles should be adopted to deter corporate directors and officers from usurping opportunities that properly belong to their corporation. On the other hand, recognizing that successful businesspersons may be engaged in a wide array of financial endeavors, unduly strict standards would dissuade competent independent directors from accepting director positions. Courts thus tend to balance these competing objectives, weighing their sense of sound business ethics with the practicalities of facilitating independent director board service.[94] In the process, director and officer fiduciary duties are minimized.

Various tests are employed to ascertain whether an endeavor constitutes a corporate opportunity. These tests include the interest or expectancy test,[95] the line (and foreseeable line) of business test,[96] the fairness test,[97]

(or a special litigation committee comprised of independent directors) recommend the termination of the lawsuit. *See* discussion in Chapter 5 of this book.

[94] *See* American Law Institute, *Principles of Corporate Governance: Analysis and Recommendations* § 5.05; *id.* § 5.05(b) comment (1994). Generally, a corporate opportunity may be taken by a director or officer only after making adequate disclosure and the disinterested directors (or disinterested shareholders) reject the opportunity. *See, e.g.*, Model Business Corporation Act § 8.70(a).

[95] Generally, this test examines whether the subject corporation has a cognizable interest in the pertinent opportunity that the director or officer takes for himself. *See, e.g., Farber v. Servan Land Co.*, 662 F.2d 371 (5th Cir. 1981) (applying Florida law). The traditional approach to this standard defines a corporate opportunity as "property wherein the corporation has an interest already existing or in which it has an expectancy growing out of an existing right." *Lagarde v. American Lime & Stone Co.*, 28 So. 199, 201 (Ala. 1900).

[96] This test focuses on business opportunities that are in the same line of business. *See, e.g., Guth v. Loft, Inc.*, 5 A.2d 503, 511 (Del. 1939) (holding that a corporate opportunity exists "if there is presented to a corporate officer or director a business opportunity which the corporation is financially able to undertake [and which] is in the line of the corporation's business, and is of practical advantage to it"). A flexible approach encompasses opportunities that are "logically related to the corporation's existing or prospective activities." *Ellzey v. Fyr Pruf, Inc.*, 376 So. 2d 1328, 1335 (Miss. 1979).

[97] "This test looks to see if the transaction was a corporate opportunity, either by the line of business test or the expectancy test, and, if so, then the court applies a fairness test [which] looks to factors such as whether the fiduciary learned of the opportunity in her personal or official capacity, whether the fiduciary is an inside or outside director, whether the corporation had the financial ability to exploit and profit from the opportunity, and whether the fiduciary used any corporate resources to gain the opportunity." Marc I. Steinberg, *Developments in Business Law and Policy* 191 (2012). For an application of the fairness test, *see Miller v. Miller*, 222 N.W. 2d 71 (Minn. 1974).

and the American Law Institute (ALI) test.[98] Many courts have rigorously applied the applicable standard to hold corporate directors and officers accountable,[99] with an available remedy being the ordering of a constructive trust.[100] On other occasions, even in older cases, lax standards have been applied. For example, in a decision handed down well over 100 years ago, the Alabama Supreme Court restrictively defined a corporate opportunity. There, the corporation owned one-third of a gravel pit, had a contract to purchase one-third, and had expressed its interest in acquiring the remaining one-third. As to the one-third interest that the corporation had expressed interest in purchasing but neither owned nor had a contractual agreement to acquire, the court held that no corporate opportunity existed. The corporate officer thereby was entitled to purchase that one-third interest.[101]

---

[98] Under the ALI test, a corporate opportunity is defined as:

1. any opportunity to engage in a business activity of which a director or senior executive officer becomes aware, either:
   (A) in connection with the performance of [his or her] functions as a director or senior executive, or under circumstances that should reasonably lead the director or senior executive to believe that the person offering the opportunity expects it to be offered to the corporation; or
   (B) through the use of corporate information or property, if the resulting opportunity is one that the director or senior executive should reasonably be expected to believe would be of interest to the corporation; or
2. any opportunity to engage in a business activity of which a senior executive becomes aware and knows is closely related to a business in which the corporation is engaged or expects to engage.

ALI, *Principles of Corporate Governance, supra* note 94, at § 5.05(b).

[99] *See, e.g., Today Homes, Inc. v. Williams*, 634 S.E. 2d 737 (Va. 2006); *Brandt v. Somerville*, 692 N.W. 2d 144 (N.D. 2005); *Farber v. Servan Land Co.*, 662 F.2d 371 (5th Cir. 1981) (interpreting Florida law). *See also Miller v. Miller*, 222 N.W. 2d 71, 78 (Minn. 1974) (stating that "the doctrine of corporate opportunity is derived essentially from fundamental rules of agency concerning the duty of utmost good faith and loyalty owed by a fiduciary to his principal").

[100] *See, e.g., Guth v. Loft, Inc.*, 5 A.2d 503, 510 (Del. 1939) ("If an officer or director of a corporation, in violation of his duty as such, acquires gain or advantage for himself, the law charges the interest so acquired with a trust for the benefit of the corporation, at its election, while it denies to the betrayal all benefit and profit"). The court's language in *Guth* reminds one of Justice Cardozo's opinion in *Meinhard v. Salmon*, 164 N.E. 545 (N.Y. Ct. App. 1928) (see Chapter 2, notes 21–22 and accompanying text). In *Guth*, Chief Justice Layton, delivering the Delaware Supreme Court's decision, stated:

> Corporate officers and directors are not permitted to use their position of trust and confidence to further their private interests. While technically not trustees, they stand in a fiduciary relation to the corporation and its stockholders.... The rule that requires an undivided and unselfish loyalty to the corporation demands that there shall be no conflict between duty and self-interest. The occasions for the determination of honesty, good faith and loyal conduct are many and varied, and no hard and fast rule can be formulated. The standard of loyalty is measured by no fixed scale.

5 A.2d at 510.

[101] *Lagarde v. Anniston Lime & Stone Co.*, 20 So. 199, 201–02 (Ala. 1900).

As a subsequent decision handed down in 1934 by the Mississippi Supreme Court opined: "The mere fact that a plaintiff corporation was negotiating for the purchase of certain property did not give it such an interest or expectancy therein as would render a purchase thereof by the president and secretary [of that same corporation] a breach of fiduciary obligation...."[102] Thus, in decisions handed down scores of years ago, numerous courts applied lenient standards with respect to the corporate opportunity doctrine.

This leniency also is evidenced by a decision rendered by the Second Circuit in *Burg v. Horn*, a 1967 decision interpreting New York law.[103] In that case, the defendants were directors and majority stockholders in a corporation that owned and operated apartment buildings. Being invested in other business enterprises that engaged in the same business, the defendants offered apartment properties they uncovered to these other companies. The Second Circuit rejected the plaintiff minority stockholder's assertion that the defendants had usurped corporate opportunities that belonged to the subject corporation. Although the properties that were not offered to such corporation were clearly within its line of business, the court held that fact by itself was insufficient. Rather, a court must consider in each case "the relationship between the director and the corporation [and] whether a duty to offer the corporation all opportunities within its line of business is fairly to be implied."[104] Because the defendants held substantial interests in other business enterprises holding similar properties and the plaintiff was aware of these investments, the defendants therefore had no duty to offer to the subject corporation the real estate opportunities which were presented absent persuasive evidence that they had agreed to do so.[105] The decision arguably makes good sense, taking into account the underlying facts and circumstances. Nonetheless, as corporate directors of the subject corporation, the defendants had a duty of loyalty to act in such corporation's best interests. By taking business opportunities that were directly in that corporation's line of business and thereby preventing it from realizing reasonably attainable profits that were foreseeably available, the defendants' actions were detrimental to the corporation's interests. Viewed from this

---

[102] *Pioneer Oil & Gas Co. v. Anderson*, 151 So. 161, 164 (Miss. 1934).
[103] 380 F.2d 897 (2d Cir. 1967) (interpreting New York law).
[104] *Id.* at 900, *citing Johnston v. Greene*, 121 A.2d 919 (Del. Ch. 1956).
[105] 380 A.2d at 900–02.

perspective, the defendants' conduct cannot be reconciled with the fiduciary duties that they owed to the corporation that was denied the business opportunities.[106]

As discussed earlier in this chapter, Delaware as well as several other states have enacted statutes authorizing advance corporate opportunity waivers.[107] Pursuant to these statutes, a corporation may renounce in its articles of incorporation or by means of a board-promulgated bylaw provision or a board resolution "any interest or expectancy of the corporation in, or in being offered an opportunity to participate in, specified business opportunities or specified classes or categories of business opportunities that are presented to the corporation or one or more of its officers, directors or stockholders."[108] Although there exists sparse case law interpreting corporate opportunity statutory waivers, these provisions significantly increase the likelihood that corporate directors and officers will lawfully seize attractive opportunities that would have been financially beneficial to the subject corporation. By authorizing waivers of this aspect of the duty of loyalty, these statutes evidence the diminution, if not the elimination, of fiduciary duty in this contextual situation.[109]

Even the American Law Institute has come on board with its minimization of fiduciary duties in this setting. Under the ALI standards, provided that an outside director[110] is not carrying out her functions as a director, employing

---

[106] The view is supporting by the dissent of Judge Hays, opining that "in the absence of a contrary agreement or understanding between the parties, the Horns, who were majority stockholders and managing officers of the Darand Corporation and whose primary function was to locate suitable properties for the company, were under a fiduciary obligation to offer such properties to Darand before buying the properties for themselves." Id. at 902 (Hays, J., dissenting).

[107] See discussion supra notes 21–32 and accompanying text.

[108] Del. Gen. Corp. L. § 122(17). Several states have enacted similar statutes authorizing corporate opportunity waivers. See statutes cited note 21 supra.

[109] See discussion in Rauterberg and Talley, supra note 24, at 1089–1104; supra notes 21–32 and accompanying text.

[110] Generally, an outside director does not have an employment or other significant relationship with the company. In this regard, the New York Stock Exchange defines a director as not being independent when he or she is or has been: "an employee or executive of the listed company within the past three years"; "directly compensated (other than the receipt of director and committee fees or payment of deferred compensation based on prior service) more than $120,000 by the listed company within any twelve-month period during the last three years"; "a current employee or partner of the listed company's internal or external auditor"; "an executive officer within the past three years of another company where any of the listed company's current executive officers serves or served on such other company's compensation committee"; and "a current employee of an enterprise that within any of the past three fiscal years has made payments to, or received payments from the listed company for property or services, provided such amount exceeds the greater of $1 million or 2% of such other [enterprise's] consolidated gross revenues." Marc I. Steinberg, The Federalization of Corporate Governance 235 (Oxford Univ. Press 2018), citing New York Stock Exchange Manual § 303A.02(b). These rules also are applicable to the immediate family members of the subject director. Id. § 303A.02.

corporate resources to avail herself of the opportunity, and is not offered the opportunity with the understanding that such opportunity is to be offered to the corporation, she may properly take the opportunity even if it is in the corporation's line of business or closely related thereto.[111] The ALI approach is premised on the practical reality of inducing outside directors to serve on corporate boards. It is posited that a rigorous approach would deter competent businesspersons from board service as they frequently are investors or are significantly involved in other ventures. At least theoretically, the relaxed standard adhered to by the ALI facilitates the recruitment by companies of sought-after prospective outside directors.[112] Irrespective of the validity of this rationale, the fact remains that the ALI standard authorizes outside directors to seize attractive business opportunities that would have financially benefitted the corporations to whom they owe the duty of loyalty.[113] With these opportunities being in the subject corporation's line of business, the consequence of corporate harm and outside director benefit contravenes fiduciary duty concepts. Indeed, provided that the conditions of the ALI provision are met, the fiduciary duty of loyalty is inapplicable in this setting.

The corporate opportunity doctrine thus provides another example where, with some frequency, fiduciary duties of directors and officers have been minimized, if not eliminated. It may well be that sound policy reasons exist for this laxity, particularly with respect to outside directors. Nonetheless, the pertinent analysis for purposes here is that application of the corporate opportunity doctrine at times has resulted in holdings and consequences contrary to the perceived fiduciary status of corporate directors and officers, providing a vivid illustration of the distinction between rhetoric and reality in this setting.[114]

---

[111] See ALI, *Principles of Corporate Governance, supra* note 98, at § 5.05(b)(2).
[112] See id. § 5.05(b) cmt.
[113] Numerous courts have cited the ALI standard addressing the corporate opportunity doctrine in their decisions. *See, e.g., Northeast Harbor Golf Club, Inc. v. Harris*, 725 A.2d 1018, 1021–22 (Me. 1999); *Demoulas v. Demoulas Super Markets, Inc.*, 677 N.E. 2d 159, 180 (Mass. 1997); *Derouen v. Murray*, 604 So. 2d 1086, 1092–93 (Miss. 1992); *Amerco v. Shoen*, 907 P.2d 536, 545 (Ariz. App. 1995).
[114] Although not otherwise addressed in this book, the subject of permissive indemnification of directors and officers is raised at this point. *See* E. Norman Veasey, et al., *Delaware Supports Directors with a Three-Legged Stool of Limited Liability, Indemnification, and Insurance*, 42 Bus. Law. 399, 413 (1987) (stating that, pursuant to Del. Gen. Corp. Law § 145(f), "statutory rights and procedures regarding indemnification are not exclusive, thus permitting a corporation to indemnify a litigant [such as a defendant director or officer] pursuant to intracorporate polices under circumstances not defined in the statute"). The issue of indemnification frequently arises when directors and officers are sued in direct and derivative actions alleging breaches of the duty of loyalty. Insurance coverage often is available to cover the bulk of the litigation expenses (such as attorneys' fees) and amounts

VII. Far More Bark Than Bite

The duty of loyalty is the principal fiduciary duty. A recent Delaware court decision asserts that "the duty of loyalty stands inviolate."[115] As this chapter has shown, this rhetoric does not reflect the situation that exists. Although the duty of loyalty continues to be meaningfully applied in some situations, severe dents have been administered to drastically diminish its stature and effectiveness. Today, corporate directors and officers may engage in a myriad of conflicted self-dealing situations without violating the duty of loyalty. To support the veracity of this proposition, this chapter provides several pertinent examples.

First, key aspects of the duty of loyalty validly may be waived. For instance, fiduciary duties may be waived pursuant to shareholder agreements. Indeed, provided that specified conditions are met, a waiver provision contained in a shareholder agreement may authorize corporate directors and officers to engage in conduct that otherwise would violate the duty of loyalty.[116]

Second, Delaware and several other states by statute authorize waivers of corporate opportunities. These statutes allow, pursuant to a provision in the subject company's articles, a bylaw amendment, or a board of director resolution, corporate directors and officers to take corporate opportunities that would otherwise belong to the corporation. By means of a valid corporate opportunity waiver, breach of loyalty claims are precluded from being brought if the corporate director's or officer's conduct comes within the applicable waiver's specified parameters. Functioning like a covenant not to sue, a valid corporate opportunity waiver increases the probability that corporate directors and officers may seize corporate opportunities without violating their duty of loyalty.[117]

---

paid in settlement. Nonetheless, if fiduciary duties are to have substantive meaning, those fiduciaries who engage in misconduct that is not covered by insurance should be held financially responsible. As has been observed by others, current indemnification practices generally are lax, thereby providing comfort to wrongdoing directors and officers that they are unlikely to incur personal financial responsibility for their actions. *See, e.g.*, Susan Beck, *Summary Judgment: Until Directors and Officers Start Paying Some of Their Legal Fees, Corporate Accountability Is a Myth*, The Amer. Law. (Feb. 3, 2010) ("There's a moral hazard in corporate boardrooms and executive suits, [namely,] . . . ridiculously cushy indemnification contracts that insulate directors and officers from responsibility for their own actions").

[115] *New Enterprise Associates, 14 L.P. v. Rich*, 295 A.3d 520, 549 (Del. Ch. 2023).
[116] *See* discussion *supra* notes 10–20 and accompanying text.
[117] *See* discussion *supra* notes 21–32 and accompanying text.

Third, several state statutes, in addition to the duty of care, also exculpate directors (and some statutes, officers as well) from certain duty of loyalty breaches. These statutes, for example, permit wrongdoing directors to avoid monetary liability when they engage in self-dealing transactions for their personal financial benefit acting with gross negligence. The broad exculpatory language contained in these statutes conflicts with the long-held perception that this type of conduct is at the core of the fiduciary duty of loyalty.[118]

Fourth, the duty of good faith, at least in Delaware, requires intentional or conscious misconduct by a director or officer in order to constitute a breach of the duty of loyalty. With respect to director and officer oversight functions, it must be shown that: "(a) the directors utterly failed to implement any reporting or information system or controls; or (b) having implemented such a system or controls, consciously failed to monitor or oversee its operations, thus disabling themselves from being informed of risks or problems requiring their attention."[119] Provided that the subject corporation has an exculpation provision, this lenient standard permits corporate directors to avoid monetary liability for their reckless misconduct. Acting with reckless culpability, whereby the corporation's interests are disregarded by the subject director or officer, should constitute a duty of loyalty breach.[120]

Fifth, standards addressing interested director and officer transactions have been significantly diluted. Rather than these transactions being scrutinized for fairness (with the corporate director or officer bearing the burden of proof), they are subject to the business judgment rule if approval is obtained from disinterested and informed directors. With gross negligence being the standard to rebut the business judgment rule and with the presence of exculpation statutes, these transactions are far more difficult to successfully challenge. Further, several states adhere to an even more lenient standard whereby judicial scrutiny of an interested director or officer transaction is foreclosed once disinterested and independent directors, being adequately informed, approve the transaction. Hence, through their laxity of facilitating such transactions, these statutes significantly minimize the historical judicial skepticism that existed with respect to the propriety of

---

[118] *See* discussion *supra* notes 42–51 and accompanying text.
[119] *Stone v. Ritter*, 911 A.2d 362, 370 (Del. 2006). *See id.* (opining that either of these prongs mandates "a showing that the directors knew that they were not discharging their fiduciary obligations").
[120] *See* discussion *supra* notes 56–78 and accompanying text.

director and officer self-dealing practices. As a consequence, the duty of loyalty in this context has been greatly diminished.[121]

Sixth, although many courts have held corporate directors and officers liable for usurping corporate opportunities, laxity all too frequently prevails. Lenient applications, for example, of the expectancy or interest test, line of business test, and the ALI standard reflect the making of accommodations to permit corporate directors and officers to have more leeway in their self-interested investment decisions. While there may exist sound policy reasons for this approach, particularly with respect to outside directors, its effect is to diminish the duty of loyalty. Permitting corporate directors and officers to personally benefit at the expense of the subject corporation is incompatible with their obligations to act in such corporation's best interests.[122] By means of these examples, this chapter vividly illustrates that the duty of loyalty has been drastically curtailed. Although judicial rhetoric continues to emphasize the importance and vitality of the duty of loyalty, reality strikes a markedly different note. Indeed, the duty of loyalty has been diminished to such a degree that no longer should corporate directors and officers be deemed fiduciaries. More fittingly, they should be viewed as "discretionaries" whose obligations are defined by the applicable situation's facts and circumstances. In this fashion, the duty of loyalty, as seen in its myriad contexts, will reflect an accurate portrayal.

---

[121] *See* discussion *supra* notes 79–93 and accompanying text.
[122] *See* discussion *supra* notes 94–114 and accompanying text.

5
Derivative Litigation: Corporate Directors Are "Discretionaries"

I. Discretionary Rather than Fiduciary Status

The focus of this chapter is to provide another important contextual situation—namely, that of derivative litigation[1]—where, although identified as fiduciaries, corporate directors, in reality, act as "discretionaries." Whether derivative litigation ill serves its objectives of effectuating the implementation of sound corporate governance practices and meaningful corporate redress is not a subject explored herein.[2] Rather, irrespective of the ultimate value of derivative actions, applicable legal principles—with certain exceptions—fail to adhere to fiduciary principles with respect to director conduct in the derivative suit setting.[3]

In Chapters 3 and 4 of this book, the duties of care and loyalty are addressed. Tellingly, exculpation statutes play a major role in reducing the

---

[1] *See* American Law Institute, *Principles of Corporate Governance: Analysis and Recommendations*, vol. 2, at 4 (1994) ("Since at least the middle of the 19th century, it has been accepted in this country that the law should permit shareholders to sue derivatively on their corporation's behalf under appropriate conditions"). In derivative actions, monetary amounts awarded (less attorney fees and costs) go to the corporation. The prospect of improper settlements whereby a minimal corporate recovery occurs with a high award of attorneys' fees remains a concern. *Id.* By contrast, with respect to an individual action, "the recovery or other relief flows directly to the stockholders, not to the corporation." *Tooley v. Donaldson, Lufkin & Jenrette, Inc.*, 845 A.2d 1031, 1036 (Del. 2004).

[2] The derivative suit's principal objectives are compensation and deterrence. By providing a means by which an allegedly aggrieved shareholder may sue on the corporation's behalf and thereby vindicate its rights, the derivative action plays a positive role in seeking to effectuate enhanced corporate governance norms. *Cf. Mills v. Electric Auto-Lite Co.*, 396 U.S. 375, 396 (1970) (recognizing that shareholder litigation has a key role "in vindicating statutory policy" and "render[s] a substantial service to the corporation and its shareholders"). On the other hand, many derivative actions have been criticized as nuisance suits, non-meritorious actions brought solely to procure a settlement. Even with respect to derivative actions that may be viewed as meritorious, the costs of such litigation may far exceed its benefits. Undue rigorous enforcement also may deter competent independent directors from serving on corporate boards, particularly with respect to companies that are financially troubled or are perceived to lack adequate insurance or indemnification coverage. *See* ALI *Principles of Corporate Governance*, *supra* note 1, vol. 2, at 6–14; Joan MacLeod Heminway, Mark J. Loewenstein, Marc I. Steinberg, and Manning Gilbert Warren III, *Business Enterprises—Legal Structures, Governance, and Policy* 679–81 (5th ed. 2024).

[3] *See* discussion *infra* notes 25–91 and accompanying text.

monetary liability exposure of corporate directors and officers.[4] Significantly, the vast majority of shareholder lawsuits that allege duty of care and loyalty breaches must be brought as derivative, rather than direct, actions.[5] Hence, proceedings instituted against corporate directors and officers alleging misconduct for interested director transactions, usurpation of corporate opportunities, excessive management compensation, failure to implement adequate law compliance policies, improperly competing against their companies, and the making of irrational business decisions (e.g., with respect to developing a new line of products) ordinarily are derivative suits.[6] Thus, as a generality, much of the litigation that ensues as a consequence of such corporate director and officer conduct (see discussion in Chapters 3 and 4) must be pursued derivatively on behalf of the subject corporation.[7]

This consequence has significant substantive impact. Unlike a direct action, a shareholder instituting a derivative action must make a demand on the board of directors.[8] In some jurisdictions, including Delaware, such demand may be excused if deemed futile.[9] Even in these situations, the subject board of directors may appoint a special litigation committee (SLC) comprised of independent directors who ordinarily will seek dismissal of the action.

For purposes of this chapter, the term "independent" encompasses both the terms "independent" and "disinterested."[10] As set forth in a Comment

---

[4] For discussion of state exculpation statutes, *see* Chapter 3, notes 55–85 and accompanying text; Chapter 4, notes 42–55 and accompanying text.

[5] As the Delaware Supreme Court stated in determining whether an action may be brought directly by an allegedly aggrieved shareholder or must be instituted as a derivative action: "The analysis must be based solely on the following questions: Who suffered the alleged harm—the corporation or the suing stockholder individually—and who would receive the benefit of the recovery or other remedy?" *Tooley v. Donaldson, Lufkin & Jenrette, Inc.*, 845 A.2d 1031, 1035 (Del. 2004), citing *Grimes v. Donald*, 673 A.2d 1207 (Del. 1996). *See infra* notes 6–7 and accompanying text.

[6] *See, e.g., Marchand v. Barnhill*, 212 A.3d 805 (Del. 2019) (alleging director and officer failure to adopt and implement procedures with respect to consumer safety); *In re Walt Disney Company Derivative Litigation*, 906 A.2d 27 (Del. 2006) (alleging excessive executive compensation); *Fliegler v. Lawrence*, 361 A.2d 218 (Del. 1976) (alleging wrongful usurpation of corporate opportunity); *Shlensky v. Wrigley*, 237 N.E.2d 776 (Ill. App. 1968) (alleging breach of duty of care for directors' decision not to install lighting in Wrigley Field for Chicago Cubs' games).

[7] Note that in closely held corporations, many of these actions may be brought as direct actions. *See, e.g., Sneed v. Webre*, 358 S.W.3d 322 (Tex. 2011). For further discussion, *see* Chapter 7.

[8] *See, e.g.*, Model Business Corp. Act § 7.42; *Aronson v. Lewis*, 473 A.2d 805 (Del. 1984); discussion *infra* notes 23–33, 58–80 and accompanying text. *See also* Rule 23.1(b)(3) of the Federal Rules of Civil Procedure (setting forth that a complaint must state with particularity the reasons for not making a demand); *Kamen v. Kemper Financial Services, Inc.*, 500 U.S. 90 (1991) (holding that a court in determining whether demand on the board of directors is required with respect to a claim under the Investment Company Act is to apply the demand-futility exception as interpreted by the law of the subject corporation's state of incorporation).

[9] *See, e.g., United Food and Commercial Workers Union v. Zuckerberg*, 262 A.3d 1034 (Del. 2021); discussion *infra* notes 34–57 and accompanying text.

[10] *See, e.g., Zapata Corporation v. Maldonado*, 430 A.2d 779 (Del. 1981); discussion *infra* note 11 and accompanying text. With respect to the distinction between independence and disinterestedness,

to a statute on this subject: Although "decisions that have examined the qualifications of special litigation committees have required that they be both 'disinterested' in the sense of not having a personal interest in the transaction being challenged as opposed to a benefit which devolves upon the corporation or all shareholders generally and 'independent' in the sense of not being influenced in favor of the defendants by reason of personal or other relationships," the governing statute uses "only the word 'independent' ... because this word necessarily also includes the requirement that a person have no interest in the transaction."[11] The chapter follows this approach.

Stated succinctly, as will be discussed in this chapter, pursuant to many statutes and court decisions, dismissal must be granted if adequately informed independent directors determine in good faith that the derivative suit is not in the corporation's best interests.[12] This approach tellingly signifies that judicial evaluation of the underlying breach of duty allegedly committed by the defendant directors and officers does not occur. The singular inquiry is whether the adequately informed independent directors' or independent SLC's determination is within the parameters of the business judgment rule or other applicable standard.[13] If so, dismissal is granted, thereby precluding review of the propriety of the underlying alleged director or officer misconduct.[14]

In view of this consequence—precluding judicial review of the underlying alleged breach—one reasonably may conclude that meaningful standards would apply with respect to this determination.[15] With certain exceptions,

---

see Orman v. Cullman, 794 A.2d 5 (Del. Ch. 2002). A director may be disinterested if she does not "receive a personal financial benefit from a transaction that is not shared equally by the stockholders." A director lacks independence if "the director's decision resulted from that director being controlled by another." *Id.* at 29.

For ease of reference, this chapter frequently uses the term independent to encompass both independence and disinterestedness. Moreover, frequently, as used by case law and commentators, the term independence signifies that a director or officer has not personally benefited (in a manner not shared equally with the other shareholders) from the challenged transaction, is not controlled or dominated by another corporate director, officer, or other subject person, and does not otherwise have a disabling conflict of interest. *See infra* note 11 and accompanying text.

[11] Georgia Code Ann. § 14-2-744 Comment. *See* discussion *supra* note 10 and accompanying text.
[12] *See, e.g., Boland v. Boland*, 31 A.3d 529 (Md. 2011); discussion *infra* notes 25-91 and accompanying text.
[13] *See, e.g.*, George Dent, *The Power of Directors to Terminate Shareholder Litigation: The Death of the Derivative Suit?*, 75 Nw. U. L. Rev. 96 (1980); discussion *infra* notes 25-33, 58-80 and accompanying text.
[14] *See, e.g., Zapata Corporation v. Maldonado*, 430 A.2d 779 (Del. 1981); discussion *infra* notes 25-33, 58-80 and accompanying text.
[15] In the past, some courts applied meaningful standards. *See, e.g., Alford v. Shaw*, 358 S.E.2d 323 (N.C. 1987); discussion *infra* notes 81-89 and accompanying text.

the contrary prevails. Lenient standards ordinarily apply, thereby enabling directors to cause the dismissal of derivative actions alleging that their colleagues engaged in actionable misconduct.[16] This chapter analyzes the standards applied, positing that their laxity shows in this context as well that corporate directors are not fiduciaries. It may well be that these lenient standards at times may be appropriate, enabling the subject corporation to rid itself of time-consuming and costly litigation which lacks meaningful benefits to the corporation and its shareholders.[17] Irrespective of the veracity of this position, the fact remains that the legal principles applied in this setting normally do not resemble standards that are fiduciary in character. Hence, although the costs incurred by derivative litigation at times may outweigh the benefits and dismissal at an early stage of the litigation may be appropriate,[18] the applicable standards lack fiduciary content.[19]

This assertion is aptly supported by the analysis contained in this chapter. The chapter focuses on jurisdictions, including Delaware, that adhere to requiring that a demand be made on the subject corporation's board of directors unless deemed futile as well as the impact of the increasing number of states that mandate universal demand on the board of directors. Upon analysis, the widespread application of standards that lack fiduciary content in the derivative action setting becomes evident. Pursuant to the adoption and implementation of these lenient standards, fiduciary standards all too frequently are nonexistent. The significance of this analysis is that identical to other settings where corporate directors and officers ostensibly act as fiduciaries, the reality is that—with respect to their prospective liability exposure—the governing principles frequently are devoid of fiduciary substance. Thus, the overriding point emphasized in this chapter is that in the derivative suit setting corporate directors act as "discretionaries" rather than fiduciaries.

---

[16] *See, e.g.*, Model Business Corporation Act § 7.44; *Auerbach v. Bennett*, 393 N.E.2d 994 (N.Y. 1979); discussion *infra* notes 25–33, 58–80 and accompanying text.

[17] *See, e.g.*, *ALI Principles of Corporate Governance, supra* note 1, vol. 2, at 6 (stating that "in both class and derivative litigation, incentives exist for a private enforcer to bring a non-meritorious action for its nuisance or settlement value").

[18] *See* Heminway, et al., *supra* note 2, at 680 ("Derivative litigation presents problems other species of litigation do not present: multiple lawsuits, as there may be hundreds or thousands of shareholders who may be aggrieved; unfaithful champions—that is, lawyers—intent on reaping a large fee from a corporate fisc rather than ensuring that justice is done; and strike suits in which plaintiff shareholders know little of the suit's merits and attorneys are the true parties in interest").

[19] *See* discussion *infra* notes 20–91 and accompanying text.

II. Demand Required–Demand Excused Jurisdictions

In many jurisdictions, including Delaware, a shareholder seeking to bring a derivative suit must make a demand on the subject corporation's board of directors unless such demand is deemed futile.[20] The objective of the demand requirement, as stated by the United States Supreme Court, "is to protect the directors' prerogative to take over the litigation or to oppose it."[21] In this regard, a corporate board's authority to govern the company's affairs encompasses decisions regarding the remedial measures that should be taken after the company has been harmed, including whether litigation should be pursued against the alleged wrongdoers.[22] Because litigation decisions (like most other corporate decisions) are within the province of the board of directors, a demand on the board must be made unless deemed futile.[23] The demand requirement, as stated by the Delaware Supreme Court, thus "is a substantive requirement that ensures that a stockholder exhausts his intracorporate remedies, provides a safeguard against strike suits, and assures that the stockholder affords the corporation the opportunity to address an alleged wrong without litigation and to control any litigation which does occur."[24]

A. Demand Required Cases: The Permissive Business Judgment Rule Applied

In a number of the jurisdictions that require an aggrieved shareholder to make a demand on the board of directors unless such demand is deemed futile, this mandate has a huge substantive impact. As the US Supreme Court has

---

[20] *See, e.g., United Food and Commercial Workers Union v. Zuckerberg*, 262 A.3d 1034 (Del. 2021); Delaware Court of Chancery Rule 23.1. Rule 23.1 of the Federal Rules of Civil Procedure (FRCP) also has a futility exception to the demand requirement. *See* FRCP Rule 23.1(b)(3)(B); *In re Cognizant Technology Solutions Corporation Derivative Litigation*, 101 F.4th 250 (3d Cir. 2024). Note that in closely held corporations, demand on the board of directors or shareholders is often excused. *See, e.g., Sneed v. Webre*, 465 S.W.3d 169 (Tex. 2015); discussion in Chapter 7.

[21] *Kamen v. Kemper Financial Services, Inc.*, 500 U.S. 90, 101 (1991). *See* Deborah DeMott, *Shareholder Derivative Actions* § 5.03 (2023–2024).

[22] *See Zuckerberg*, 262 A.3d at 1047.

[23] *See Spiegel v. Buntrock*, 571 A.2d 767, 772–73 (Del. 1990); *Lenois v. Lawal*, 2017 WL 5289611, at *9 (Del. Ch. 2017).

[24] *Zuckerberg*, 262 A.3d at 1047, *quoting Kaplan v. Peat, Marwick, Mitchell & Co.*, 540 A.2d 726, 730 (Del. 1988); *Aronson v. Lewis*, 473 A.2d 805, 811–12 (Del. 1984*); Lenois v. Lewal*, 2017 WL 5289611, at *9 (Del. Ch. 2017).

observed in situations where demand is required, the independent directors' determination to seek dismissal on the basis that the prospective lawsuit is not in the corporation's best interests "is subject only to the deferential business judgment rule standard of review."[25] As discussed in Chapter 3, to rebut the presumption of the business judgment rule, the plaintiff-shareholder must establish, for example, that a disabling conflict of interest existed (e.g., that the directors who made the determination that the lawsuit would not be in the company's best interests were interested or dominated by a person who benefitted from the transaction).[26] Alternatively, application of the business judgment rule under Delaware law may be rebutted if the plaintiff shows that the independent directors' determination lacked good faith, was not adequately informed, or was irrational—with gross negligence being the standard of review.[27]

To rebut this presumption and establish gross negligence is a monumental task. As the Delaware courts have opined, the definition of gross negligence in the corporate law setting "is so strict that it imports the concept of recklessness into the gross negligence standard . . ."[28] Stated in somewhat different terms by the Delaware Chancery Court: "In the corporate context, gross negligence means reckless indifference to or deliberate disregard of the whole body of stockholders or actions which are without the bounds of reason."[29] And, as Vice Chancellor Laster has opined: "To hold a director liable for gross negligence requires conduct more serious than what is necessary to secure a conviction for criminal negligence."[30] Thus, in Delaware, it is an easier task for a prosecutor to procure a criminal conviction than it is for an aggrieved shareholder to rebut the presumption of the business judgment rule.

---

[25] *Kamen*, 500 U.S. at 101, *citing Zapata Corp. v. Maldonado*, 430 A.2d 779, 784 n. 10 (Del. 1981). Under Delaware law, the demand rule applies with full vigor when controllers are sued in derivative actions. *See In re Match Group, Inc. Derivative Litigation*, 315 A.3d 446, 451–52 (Del. 2024) ("Of course, derivative claims against controlling stockholders . . . are subject to Court of Chancery Rule 23.1 and our demand review precedent").
[26] *See* discussion in Chapter 3, notes 25–53 and accompanying text.
[27] *See, e.g., Smith v. Van Gorkom*, 488 A.2d 858, 873 (Del. 1985).
[28] *See, e.g., In re Lear Corporation Shareholder Litigation*, 967 A.2d 640, 652 n. 45 (Del. Ch. 2008).
[29] *Tomczak v. Morton Thiokol, Inc.*, 1990 WL 42607, at * 12 (Del. Ch. 1990).
[30] *In re McDonald's Corporation Stockholder Derivative Litigation*, 291 A.3d 652, 690 n. 21 (Del. Ch. 2023). *See id.* at 689–90 n. 21 (citing Delaware cases defining gross negligence in the business judgment rule context to mean reckless indifference); discussion in Chapter 3, notes 45–49 (citing Delaware and Nevada cases defining the meaning of grossly negligent conduct in the corporate law context.)

Importantly, the business judgment rule in this setting is not being applied to a board of director's decision with respect to an entrepreneurial or operational decision. Rather, its application here extends to a determination by independent directors that the prospective lawsuit is not in the company's best interests. The effect of this permissive approach is to prevent the substance of a plaintiff's claims focusing on director and officer alleged misconduct from being adjudicated. Thus, the underlying alleged duty of loyalty breach or other allegedly improper conduct never sees the light of day. While there may be sound policy reasons to support this approach, the application of a gross negligence standard in procuring the dismissal of otherwise meritorious actions against corporate directors and officers does not comport with fiduciary standards.[31]

This lenient approach is exacerbated by the fact that, if the subject corporation has adopted an exculpation provision, independent directors making the determination that the prospective lawsuit is contrary to the corporation's best interests can be held monetarily liable for making an improper decision only if they act with intentional misconduct.[32] Engaging in "merely" reckless misconduct absolves an independent director in this setting from monetary liability.[33] To say that independent directors are held to fiduciary standards in this setting ignores reality.

B. Demand Excused Cases, Same Result: The Permissive Business Judgment Rule

In several jurisdictions which permit demand to be excused on a corporation's board of directors, the broad parameters of the business judgment rule are applied to a special litigation committee's determination that the subject shareholder derivative action is not in the corporation's best

---

[31] I authored one of the first articles addressing the propriety of independent directors (or special litigation committees comprised of independent directors) to terminate shareholder derivative actions. *See* Marc I. Steinberg, *The Use of Special Litigation Committees to Terminate Shareholder Derivative Suits*, 35 U. Miami L. Rev. 1 (1980).

[32] *See, e.g.*, New Enterprise Associates 14 L.P. v. Rich, 295 A.3d 520, 551 (Del. Ch. 2023) ("The real function of exculpation is to eliminate liability for recklessness"); *In re Columbia Pipeline Group, Inc.*, 2021 WL 772562, at * 50 n. 22 (Del. Ch. 2021) (opining that § 102(b)(7) of the Delaware Corporation Law "permits exculpation for recklessness"); discussion in Chapter 3, notes 63–84 and accompanying text.

[33] *See* sources cited note 32 *supra*.

interests.[34] In other words, the business judgment rule in these jurisdictions applies in both demand required and demand excused cases. For example, In *Auerbach v. Bennett*, the New York high court, invoking the business judgment rule's applicability in this setting, recognized the propriety of a special litigation committee comprised of independent directors to terminate a shareholder derivative suit that sought damages against their fellow directors.[35] In its ruling, the court held that a reviewing tribunal's inquiry is limited to assessing the SLC members' independence and good faith and the adequacy and appropriateness of the committee's investigation. Applying an expansive version of the business judgment rule, the court held that a SLC's substantive decision to terminate a plaintiff shareholder's derivative suit "is beyond judicial inquiry...."[36]

As applied in New York as well as other jurisdictions, this version of the business judgment rule is even more protective of defendant corporate directors and officers than the Delaware prescription. In Delaware, the decision reached by the special litigation committee to terminate a shareholder derivative suit must be rational or made without gross negligence or greater culpability.[37] By contrast, in New York and a number of other jurisdictions, the SLC's determination is to be upheld, irrespective that it may be irrational

---

[34] *See, e.g., Boland v. Boland*, 31 A.3d 529 (Md. 2011); *In re United Health Group, Inc. Shareholder Derivative Litigation*, 754 N.W.2d 544 (Minn. 2008); *Desigoudar v. Meyercord*, 108 Cal. App. 4th 173 (2003). Unlike the traditional business judgment rule which presumes that the subject directors acted in a manner that entitled them to invoke the rule, a number of these decisions require a special litigation committee to come forward with evidence to establish that the applicable criteria were met. *See, e.g., Boland*, 31 A.3d at 556 (holding that "the court should not grant summary judgment on the basis of an SLC's decision unless the directors have stated how they chose the SLC members and come forward with some evidence that the SLC followed reasonable procedures and that no substantial business or personal relationships impugned the SLC's independence and good faith"). With respect to federal law, *see Burks v. Lasker*, 441 U.S. 471, 486 (1979) (holding that a federal court's recognition whether the determination by disinterested directors that a derivative action instituted against company directors for alleged violation of the Investment Company Act should be terminated is subject to two inquiries: whether the applicable state law authorizes disinterested directors to terminate such an action and whether the state law is consistent with the policies of the federal securities laws).

[35] 393 N.E.2d 994 (N.Y. 1979). The court opined:

[C]ourts are ill equipped and infrequently called on to evaluate what are and must be essentially business judgments. The authority and responsibilities vested in corporate directors both by statute and decisional law proceed on the assumption that inescapably there can be no available objective standard by which the correctness of every corporate decision may be measured, by the courts or otherwise...

Id. at 1000.

[36] *Id.* at 1002. *See id.* at 1001 (requiring the defendants to submit proof on the matter of the SLC's "disinterested independence").

[37] *See Zapata*, 430 A.2d at 784 n. 10 ("[W]hen stockholders, after making demand and having their suit rejected, attack the board's decision as improper, the board's decision falls under the business judgment rule and will be respected if the requirements of the rule are met"). For the requirements of invoking the business judgment rule, *see* Chapter 3, notes 27–39 and accompanying text.

or grossly negligent.[38] This standard further illustrates the lack of fiduciary standards that prevail in this context. So long as the SLC members are independent, act in good faith, and utilize proper investigative procedures, their grossly negligent misconduct with respect to the determination reached is irrelevant. Succinctly put, the application of culpability standards that constitute or exceed gross negligence—whereby independent directors are authorized to preclude aggrieved shareholders from pursuing otherwise meritorious litigation on their corporation's behalf—are devoid of fiduciary status.[39]

C. Demand Excused Cases: The Prospect of Fiduciary Standards

When a shareholder's demand on the board of directors is excused, Delaware applies a far more rigorous approach. In such cases, first, the defendants *must* show that the independent directors conducted a thorough investigation, acted in good faith, and had reasonable bases supporting their conclusion that the litigation is not in the corporation's best interests. Second, the court *may* apply its own independent business judgment in seeking to strike an appropriate balance between legitimate corporate claims as alleged by a plaintiff-shareholder in a derivative action and the independent directors' decision (as ordinarily determined by a special litigation committee) that the action is not in the corporation's best interests. Phrased somewhat differently by a number of Delaware courts, the tribunal's "task in the [discretionary] second step is to determine whether the SLC's recommended result falls within a range of reasonable outcomes that a disinterested and independent decision maker for the corporation, not acting under any compulsion and with the benefit of the information then available, *could* reasonably accept."[40]

---

[38] *See Auerbach*, 393 N.E.2d at 1000-03. Note that unlike the traditional business judgment rule, a somewhat stricter standard is applied in this context with respect to requiring that the defendants submit proof of the SLC's independence. *Id.* at 1002.

[39] In Delaware, a showing of bad faith requires that a defendant director or officer act with conscious or intentional misconduct. Recklessness is not sufficient. *See, e.g., Marchand v. Barnhill*, 212 A.3d 805 (Del. 2019); *In re McDonald's Corporation Stockholder Derivative Litigation*, 289 A.3d 343 (Del. 2023). *See generally* Marc I. Steinberg, *Securities Regulation: Liabilities and Remedies* §§ 14.01–14.05 (2023); John C. Coffee and Daniel E. Schwartz, *The Survival of the Derivative Suit: An Evaluation and a Proposal for Legislative Reform*, 81 Colum. L. Rev. 261 (1981); Charles W. Murdoch, *Corporate Governance—The Role of Special Litigation Committees*, 68 Wash. L. Rev. 79 (1993).

[40] *In re Carvana Co. Stockholders Litigation*, 2024 WL 1300199, at *15 (Del. Ch. 2024) (emphasis supplied), *quoting In re Primedia, Inc. Shareholders Litigation*, 67 A.3d 455, 468 (Del. Ch. 2023).

In theory, this approach may be viewed as faithfully applying a fiduciary standard. Because litigation decisions are business decisions generally within the discretion of the board of directors, qualified directors (i.e., those individuals who are independent and disinterested) should play a vital role in determining whether the subject derivative action should go forward as being consistent with corporate interests.[41] Nonetheless, its practical application deviates from the legal standard enunciated for a number of reasons. First, as discussed later in this chapter, due to the presence of structural bias and other factors, independent directors making this assessment almost always recommend that the shareholder derivative action be dismissed.[42] Second, courts rarely apply their own independent business judgment in their rulings, signifying that this discretionary evaluation largely has become a nonfactor.[43] Third, this standard applies only if demand on the board of directors is excused.[44] As discussed below, with respect to demand excusal, the Delaware courts have adopted stringent requirements that a shareholder plaintiff must satisfy.

See Zapata, 430 A.2d at 789 ("If the Court determines either that the committee is not independent or has not shown reasonable bases for its conclusions, or, if the Court is not satisfied for other reasons relating to the process, including but not limited to the good faith of the committee, the Court shall deny the corporation's motion"). With respect to these inquiries, the court may afford the shareholder-plaintiff limited discovery. By contrast, in a demand-required case, no discovery is permitted. *See Levine v. Smith*, 591 A.2d 194, 209 (Del. 1991). Nonetheless, a shareholder can obtain some relevant information by means of inspecting the corporation's books and records, provided that such shareholder has a proper purpose and presents a credible basis to infer director or officer wrongdoing, *See, e.g., Seinfeld v. Verizon Communications, Inc.*, 909 A.2d 117 (Del. 2006).

[41] *See Kamen v. Kemper Financial Services, Inc.*, 500 U.S. 90, 101 (1991) ("The purpose of requiring a precomplaint demand is to protect the directors' prerogative to take over the litigation or to oppose it"), citing *Spiegel v. Buntrock*, 571 A.2d 767, 773 (Del. 1990). Hence, the demand requirement effectuates "the basic principle of corporate governance that the decisions of a corporation—including the decision to initiate litigation—should be made by the board of directors or the majority of shareholders." *Daily Income Fund, Inc. v. Fox*, 464 U.S. 523, 530 (1984).

[42] *See* discussion *infra* notes 54–57, 66–76 and accompanying text.

[43] In *Zapata*, the Delaware Supreme Court stated that a reviewing court, applying its own business judgment to the SLC's determination, provides "the essential key in striking the balance between legitimate corporate claims as expressed in a derivative stockholder suit and a corporation's best interests as expressed by an independent investigating committee." 430 A.2d at 789. Yet subsequently in *Kaplan v. Wyatt*, 499 A.2d 1184, 1192 (Del. 1985), the Delaware Supreme Court held that "proceeding to the second step [where the reviewing court applies its own business judgment] ... is wholly within the discretion of the [chancery] court." For a recent decision where the chancery court applied *Zapata*'s second step in its determination to dismiss a shareholder derivative action, *see In re Carvana Co. Stockholder Litigation*, 2024 WL 1300199 (Del. Ch. 2024).

[44] In cases where demand on the board of directors is required in Delaware, the business judgment rule applies. *See Zapata*, 430 A.2d at 784 n. 10.

D. Applicable Standards for Board Excusal

In Delaware—whether demand on the board of directors is required or excused—frequently is determinative of whether the derivative action has a realistic possibility of moving forward. If demand is required, then the permissive business judgment rule is applied to the independent directors' decision that the derivative suit is not in the company's best interests and accordingly should be dismissed.[45] With the undertaking of an adequately thorough inquiry or investigation that nearly always concludes that the action should be dismissed, it is a rare situation where a shareholder plaintiff prevails in a demand required situation.[46] On the other hand, where demand is excused, the reviewing court must examine, among other issues, whether the special litigation committee's recommendation of dismissal has a reasonable basis.[47] In this circumstance, a derivative plaintiff has a significantly better chance of fending off the corporation's motion to dismiss.[48]

In the 2021 *Zuckerberg* decision,[49] the Delaware Supreme Court reformulated the applicable test for ascertaining whether demand should be excused as futile. This test is applied on a director-by-director basis.[50] As set forth by the court, demand is excused when the derivative plaintiff's complaint raises a reasonable doubt that at least half of the members of the subject company's board of directors (1) "received a material personal benefit from the alleged misconduct that is the subject of the litigation demand";

---

[45] *Id. See Levine v. Smith*, 591 A.2d 194, 209 (Del. 1991) (holding that the plaintiff-shareholder is not entitled to discovery where demand is made and refused by the board of directors or committee thereof); *Spiegel v. Buntrock*, 571 A.2d 767, 776 (Del. 1990) ("A shareholder who makes a demand [on the subject corporation's board of directors] can no longer argue that demand is excused").

[46] *See, e.g.*, court decisions cited in Steinberg, *supra* note 39, at § 14.03[2].

[47] *See Zapata*, 430 A.2d at 789 (requiring the chancery court, among other inquiries, to determine whether the special litigation committee has "shown reasonable bases for its conclusions"). In *In re Match Group, Inc. Derivative Litigation*, 315 A.3d 446 (Del. 2024), the court held that all members of the SLC must be independent; a majority of independent members is not sufficient. *Id.* at 472–73 (opining that "all" committee "members must be independent").

[48] *See, e.g.*, *Marchand v. Barnhill*, 212 A.3d 805 (Del. 2019); *Heineman v. Datapoint Corp.*, 611 A.2d 950 (Del. 1992); *Ryan v. Gifford*, 918 A.2d 341 (Del. Ch. 2007).

[49] *United Food and Commercial Workers Union v. Zuckerberg*, 262 A.3d 1034 (Del. 2021). In *Zuckerberg*, the Delaware Supreme Court conflated the standard of conduct and the standard of liability in a single sentence, stating: "Predicated upon concepts of *gross negligence*, the *duty of care* requires that [corporate] fiduciaries *inform themselves of material information* before making a business decision and act *prudently* in carrying out their duties." *Id.* at 1049–50 (emphasis supplied).

[50] *Id.* at 1059. Note that the Delaware Supreme Court in *Zuckerberg* did not overrule *Rales v. Blasband*, 634 A.2d 927 (Del. 1993), and *Aronson v. Lewis*, 473 A.2d 805 (Del. 1984), stating: "[B]ecause the three-part test [adopting herein] is consistent with and enhances *Aronson, Rales*, and their progeny, the Court need not overrule *Aronson* to adopt this refined test, and cases properly construing *Aronson, Rales*, and their progeny remain good law." 262 A.3d at 1059.

(2) "would face a substantial likelihood of liability on any of the claims that are the subject of the litigation demand"; or (3) "whether the director lacks independence from someone who received a material personal benefit from the alleged misconduct that is the subject of the litigation demand or who would face a substantial likelihood of liability on any of the claims that are the subject of the litigation demand."[51] On its face, this test seems protective of corporate and shareholder interests. Its application, however, tellingly conveys that this test is burdensome for plaintiff-shareholders to meet unless at least half of the board directors received an allegedly improper material personal benefit that is the subject of the litigation demand or are dependent upon the defendant director(s) or officer(s) for their employment or other material financial benefit.[52] As addressed in the following discussion, the application of the reasonable doubt standard by the Delaware courts is illusory.

E. The Myth of the Reasonable Doubt Standard

Because the Delaware Supreme Court opined that a derivative plaintiff's complaint need only raise a reasonable doubt as to a director's independence, it would seem to follow that this task would not be overly burdensome. After all, as two eminent federal judges—Judges Jon O. Newman and Jack Weinstein—maintain, reasonable doubt in the criminal setting generally signifies that there exists at least a 95 percent likelihood that the defendant committed the charged offense. In other words, the probability of guilt must be at least 95 percent.[53] Applied to the derivative suit setting, a reasonable

---

[51] See 262 A.3d at 1059 ("If the answer to any of the [three] questions is 'yes' for at least half of the members of the demand board, then demand is excused as futile"). Significantly, under the second prong above, exculpated duty of care violations do not excuse demand. Rather, where a subject corporation has adopted an exculpation provision—in order to excuse demand on the board of directors—the complaint must set forth "particularized allegations raising a reasonable doubt that a majority of the demand board is subject to a sterilizing influence because directors face a substantial likelihood of liability for engaging in the conduct that the derivative claim challenges." Id. at 1057. For a recent application of this test, see, e.g., Harrison Metal Capital III, L.P. v. Mathe, 2024 WL 1299579 (Del. Ch. 2024).

[52] For example, corporate employees who may be terminated by the defendant CEO and major suppliers whose relationship with the corporation likewise may be ended by the defendant CEO should not be deemed independent directors in the derivative suit setting. See Rales v. Blasband, 634 A.2d 927 (Del. 1993). Other examples include close family relationships and lucrative consultantships. See Clark v. Lomas & Nettleton Financial Corporation, 625 F.2d 49 (5th Cir. 1980); Schoen v. SAC Holding Co., 137 P. 3d 1171 (Nov. 2006). See also discussion infra notes 53–57 and accompanying text.

[53] See Jon O. Newman, Taking "Beyond a Reasonable Doubt" Seriously, 103 Judicature 33, 36 (2019) (published by the Bolch Judicial Institute at the Duke University School of Law); Jack B. Weinstein and Ian Dewsbury, Comment on the Meaning of "Proof Beyond a Reasonable Doubt,"

doubt exists with respect to a director's independence for ascertaining whether a demand on the board is required if there accordingly exists a five percent or greater likelihood that such director is not independent.

Clearly, this reasonable doubt standard has not been accurately applied. Numerous situations have arisen where the Delaware courts, despite the clear specter of director bias, have held that a reasonable doubt as to such director bias was lacking. For example, a complaint failed to raise a reasonable doubt about an outside director's independence when (1) an outside director was alleged to be the mentor of the defendant founder and CEO of the subject company;[54] (2) an outside director was alleged to be a friend of the defendant director;[55] and (3) the outside directors were dependent on the defendant who owned 47 percent of the company's common stock for their continued positions and, in all practicality, were subject to removal from their board positions at the behest of this defendant.[56]

In the above situations, to hold that a reasonable doubt did not exist (namely, no more than five percent) that the subject outside directors were not independent belies reality. In real life, friends, mentors, and those who can undeniably be removed from their worthwhile positions have incentives to side with their benefactors, friends, and individuals who have championed their careers. To hold that such outside directors do not have greater than a five percent possibility of being biased in view of these meaningful

---

5 Law Probability & Risk 167, 167–73 (2006), *quoted in*, Newman, 103 Judicature at 35. At the time of authoring their articles, Judge Newman was a judge on the US Court of Appeals for the Second Circuit and Judge Weinstein was a US district judge for the Eastern District of New York. Judge Weinstein was a premier expert in the law of evidence. *See, e.g.*, Jack B. Weinstein, et al., *Weinstein's Federal Evidence: Commentary on Rules of Evidence for the United States Courts* (1997).

[54] *See Zuckerberg*, 262 A.3d at 1063 (alleging that director Thiel is Zuckerberg's mentor).

[55] *See id.* ("alleging that Thiel is a personal friend of Zuckerberg is insufficient to establish a lack of independence"); *Beam ex rel. Martha Stewart Living Omnimedia v. Stewart*, 845 A.2d 1040, 1051–52 (Del. 2004) (allegations of "mere personal friendship or a mere outside business relationship, standing alone, are insufficient" to excuse demand); *Teamsters Local 443 Health Services & Insurance Plan v. Chou*, 2023 WL 7986729, at * 31 (Del. Ch. 2023) (holding that sole member of SLC who was a member of the same golf club as former chairman of company's board of directors was "not disabling or suspicious"). *See also Marchand v. Barnhill*, 212 A.3d 805, 820 (Del. 2019) ("Although the fact that fellow directors are social acquaintances who occasionally have dinner or go to common events does not, in itself, raise a fair inference of non-independence, our law has recognized that deep and longstanding friendships are meaningful to human beings and that any realistic consideration of the question of independence must give weight to these important relationships and their natural effect on the ability of the parties to act impartially toward each other").

[56] *See Aronson v. Lewis*, 473 A.2d 805, 815 (Del. 1984). Among the plaintiff-shareholder's assertions in *Aronson* was that defendant Fink dominated and controlled the corporation's board of directors because he owned 47 percent of the company's outstanding stock and that he personally selected each director of the company. In response, the Delaware Supreme Court stated: "Such contentions do not support any claim under Delaware law that these directors lack independence." *Id.*

relationships and willing to subject their benefactors, friends, and mentees to contentious shareholder litigation is fantasy. Thus, the consequence of Delaware's framework is that frequently demand is excused only when at least half of the directors financially benefit from the challenged transaction or when those directors considering the shareholder demand are dependent upon the defendant director(s) or officer(s) for their livelihood or the receipt of other material financial benefit(s).[57] This chapter next examines the growing number of jurisdictions that have embraced universal demand. As will be seen, the lenient standards applied in that setting tellingly convey that corporate directors are not fiduciaries.

III. Universal Demand Jurisdictions

An increasing number of jurisdictions today adhere to universal demand.[58] Pursuant to this approach, generally unless irreparable harm will be incurred, a shareholder seeking to bring a derivative action must make a demand on the company's board of directors in all instances. In other words, the making of a demand is a necessary prerequisite that a plaintiff-shareholder must satisfy prior to initiating a derivative action.[59]

---

[57] See, e.g., Zuckerberg, 262 A.3d at 1061 (quotation marks omitted):

> A variety of motivations, including friendship, may influence the demand futility inquiry. But, to render a director unable to consider demand, a relationship must be of a bias-producing nature. Alleging that a director had a personal friendship with someone else, or that a director had an outside business relationship are insufficient to raise a reasonable doubt that the director lacked independence. Consistent with [the] predicate materiality requirement, the existence of some financial ties between the interested party and the director, without more, is not disqualifying.

See supra note 52 and accompanying text.

[58] Approximately 20 states adhere to universal demand based on the Model Business Corporation Act. See, e.g., Arizona Rev. Stat. Ann. §§ 10-740 et seq.; Connecticut Gen. Stat. Ann. §§ 33-720 et seq.; Florida Stat. Ann. §§ 607.0741 et seq.; Nebraska Rev. Stat. Ann. §§ 21-275 et seq.; North Carolina Gen. Stat. Ann. §§ 55-7-40 et seq.; Texas Bus. Org. Code §§ 21.551 et seq.; Virginia Code Ann. §§ 13.1-672.1 et seq. For case law interpreting these statutes, see, e.g., International Brotherhood of Electrical Workers v. Tucci, 70 N.E.3d 918 (Mass. Sup. Jud. Ct. 2017); Benfield v. Wells, 749 S.E.2d 384 (Ga. Ct. App. 2013); Atkins v. Topp Comm, Inc., 874 So.2d 626 (Fla. Ct. App. 2004); cases cited note 70 infra.

[59] Many states have enacted § 7.42 of the Model Business Corporation Act which provides:

> No shareholder may commence a derivative proceeding until: (i) a written demand has been made upon the corporation to take suitable action and (ii) 90 days have expired from the date delivery of the demand was made unless the shareholder has earlier been notified that the demand has been rejected by the corporation or unless irreparable injury to the corporation would result by waiting for the expiration of the 90-day period.

Mandating that demand must be made on the subject board of directors makes good sense and is consistent with fiduciary standards. Litigation decisions, like many other corporate decisions, are ordinarily within the province of the board of directors.[60] Absent director lack of independence or failure to adhere to meaningful standards, these decisions merit due deference. With some frequency, meritless shareholder suits are sought to be instituted for their perceived settlement value.[61] It also may be that the benefits of a prospective recovery are significantly outweighed by the costs that will be incurred by the corporation in connection with that litigation.[62] Even when a prospective derivative suit raises creditable claims, internal corporate sources should be provided the opportunity to inquire into the alleged misconduct and undertake corrective measures to remediate the problematic situation.[63] In this manner, the best interests of the subject corporation and its shareholders collectively are served.

The disconnect occurs when the independent directors' decision or the processes that are employed to make the determination to terminate the litigation are given undue deference. In this setting, independent directors foreclose aggrieved shareholders from pursuing causes of action that strike at the heart of sound corporate governance practices, such as allegedly improper self-dealing or interested director transactions. As discussed earlier in this chapter, validating the authority of independent directors to preclude the bringing of derivative suits signifies that the underlying alleged director or officer misconduct never is adjudicated. Absent persuasive

---

[60] *See, e.g., Zuckerberg*, 262 A.3d at 1047 ("The board's authority to govern corporate affairs extends to decisions about what remedial actions a corporation should take after being harmed, including whether the corporation should file a lawsuit against its directors, its officers, its controller, or an outsider").

[61] *See ALI Principles of Corporate Governance*, supra note 1, vol. 2, at 6 (stating that "in both class and derivative litigation, incentives exist for a private enforcer to bring a non-meritorious action for its nuisance or settlement value"). The concern with the costs of "vexatious" shareholder litigation has been raised in US Supreme Court decisions that restrict the scope of Section 10(b) of the Securities Exchange Act. *See, e.g., Blue Chip Stamps v. Manor Drug Stores*, 421 U.S. 723, 740 (1975) (referring to the danger of vexatious litigation in holding that a plaintiff must be a purchaser or seller of the subject securities in connection with alleged deceptive or manipulative conduct in order to have standing to bring a private action for damages under § 10(b)); discussion Chapter 8.

[62] *See Joy v. North*, 692 F.2d 880, 892 (2d Cir. 1982) (applying Connecticut law) (stating that "judicial scrutiny of special litigation committee recommendations should be limited to a comparison of the direct costs imposed upon the corporation by the litigation with the potential benefits" and also observing that "other less direct costs may be incurred, such as negative impact on morale and upon the corporate image").

[63] *See, e.g., Spiegel v. Buntrock*, 571 A.2d 767, 773 (Del. 1990) ("The purpose of pre-suit demand is to assure that the stockholder affords the corporation the opportunity to address an alleged wrong without litigation, to decide whether to invest the resources of the corporation in litigation, and to control any litigation which does occur").

justification supporting the independent directors' (or SLC's) determination, shareholders should be permitted the opportunity to pursue meritorious derivative litigation against corporate directors and officers.[64]

Accordingly, the determination by independent directors to terminate shareholder derivative actions should be consistent with fiduciary standards. The universal demand standards, as reflected by the Model Business Corporation Act (MBCA) and the many states that have enacted this statute,[65] provide far too lenient judicial scrutiny. As will be discussed below, the nearly unfettered discretion given to independent directors in this context is contrary to holding these directors to a standard by which fiduciary conduct should be assessed.

A. Applicable Standards for Dismissal of Derivative Litigation

In the many universal demand jurisdictions that have enacted the MBCA version of the statute, undue permissiveness is applied to the decision by independent directors to terminate shareholder derivative litigation. Pursuant to this statute, once a majority of independent directors recommend that a subject derivative action should be dismissed, a court is required to grant such dismissal if it finds that the independent directors (or independent special litigation committee) have "determined in good faith, after conducting a reasonable inquiry upon which its conclusions are based, that the maintenance of the derivative proceeding is not in the best interests of the corporation."[66] Significantly, an independent director may be appointed to a subject board of directors by inside directors or outside directors who are not independent.[67] Subsequently, if a special litigation committee comprised solely of

---

[64] See discussion *supra* notes 12–59 and accompanying text.
[65] *See, e.g.*, Georgia Code Ann. § 14-2-742 Comment (stating that the Georgia statute "requires a written demand on the corporation in all cases [and that such] demand must be made at least 90 days before commencement of suit unless irreparable injury to the corporation would result, in which case the period may be shortened"); statutes cited notes 58–59 *supra*.
[66] Section 7.44(a) of the Model Business Corporation Act and as adopted in many states. For an example of states, *see* note 58 *supra*. Note that the MBCA uses the term "qualified" director in this context. Nonetheless, several of the state statutes adopting this provision use the term "independent" director. *See, e.g.*, Hawaii Rev. Stat. Ann. § 414-175; North Carolina Gen. Stat. § 55-7-44; South Dakota Bus. Corp. Act § 47-1A-744.1; Utah Code Ann. § 16-10a-740.
[67] *See* MBCA § 1.43(c)(1) (stating that a director "shall not automatically" be deemed precluded from serving as a qualified (or independent) director due to that individual's "nomination or election of [such] director to the current board by any director who is not a qualified [*e.g.*, independent] director with respect to the matter (or any person that has a material relationship with that director), acting alone or participating with others"). As set forth in MBCA § 1.43(a), a "qualified" director in this setting is a director "who, at the time action is to be taken, ... does not have (i) a material

independent directors is formed, the members of that committee must themselves be appointed by independent directors.[68]

The standard for dismissal pursuant to the recommendation by the independent directors (or special litigation committee) is lax. Under the statute, a court's review is limited to assessing the subject directors' independence, their exercise of good faith, and the reasonableness of the inquiry made with respect to the conclusions reached.[69] This standard constitutes an expansive application of the business judgment rule. Generally, only the directors' independence, exercise of good faith, and procedures utilized are evaluated. The substance of the determination—namely, that the derivative action is not in the company's best interests is beyond judicial scrutiny, even if such determination lacks an adequate basis or is irrational. As stated by one court, the statute "authorizes courts to conduct a limited inquiry into the process of the board's decision, but not to review the reasonableness of the board's determination to reject a demand or seek dismissal of a derivative action."[70]

---

interest in the outcome of the proceeding, or (ii) a material relationship with a person who has such an interest." Section 1.43(b) defines the term "material relationship" to mean "a familial, financial, professional, employment or other relationship that would reasonably be expected to impair the objectivity of the director's judgment when participating in the action to be taken" and defines the term "material interest" to mean "an actual or potential benefit or detriment (other than one which would devolve on the corporation or the shareholders generally) that would reasonably be expected to impair the objectivity of the director's judgment when participating in the action to be taken."

[68] See MBCA § 7.44(b)(2). Note that the burden of proving that the independent (i.e., "qualified") directors' determination to dismiss the derivative action is to be ordered by a court turns on whether a majority of the board of directors consisted of independent (i.e. "qualified") directors. See MBCA § 7.44(d) (stating that if a majority of the board of directors were independent (i.e., "qualified") directors at the time that the decision was made, the burden would be on the plaintiff-shareholder and, if not, the burden would be on the corporation).

[69] See MBCA § 7.44(a); discussion *supra* notes 58, 66 and accompanying text.

[70] *Sojitz America Capital Corporation v. Kaufman*, 141 Conn. App. 486, 491 n. 4 (2013), citing MBCA § 7.44 Official Comment. See MBCA § 7.44 Official Comment (stating that the statute "does not authorize the court to review the reasonableness of the determination to reject a demand or seek a dismissal" and that the phrase "upon which its conclusions are based" requires that "the conclusions follow logically from the inquiry"). For case law interpreting this statute, as enacted by the applicable state, *see, e.g., Burgess v. Patterson*, 188 So.3d 537, 560 (Miss. 2016) (dismissing derivative action on the ground that the plaintiff-shareholder "failed to demonstrate that the Special Committee's decision was not made in good faith after it had conducted a reasonable inquiry"); *Sojitz America Capital Corporation*, 141 Conn. App. at 509 (2013) (in dismissing shareholder derivative action, stating "the court may conduct a limited review into the board's conclusions to determine that they follow logically from the inquiry, but may not scrutinize the reasonableness of its determination"); *Brewster v. Brewster*, 241 P.3d 357, 361 (Utah App. 2010) (stating that "the plain language of the [statute] prohibit[s] the trial court from inquiring into the reasonableness of [the SLC's] recommendation").

Note that if a majority of the directors are not independent, then the corporation has the burden of proving that the independent directors' or SLC's determination in fact was made by independent directors, who acted in good faith and concluded, after conducting a reasonable inquiry, that the shareholder derivative action is not in the corporation's best interests. In this respect, by shifting the burden of proof to the corporation, this statute modifies the presumption of the business judgment

100 CORPORATE DIRECTOR AND OFFICER LIABILITY

This approach is not consonant with holding directors to fiduciary standards. An individual who is a fiduciary (and who is independent, acts in good faith, and makes a reasonable inquiry) should be held accountable for the substance of the applicable decision that is made. By contrast, under the MBCA approach, as adopted by many states, the determination rendered by independent directors that the derivative action is not in the corporation's best interests is beyond judicial purview.[71] Hence, the independent directors' or independent special litigation committee's decision may be irrational and grossly negligent yet evade examination by a court. Enabling independent directors to act in such an arbitrary manner that may preclude meritorious shareholder derivative actions from proceeding contravenes fiduciary principles.[72] The status of these directors as discretionaries—rather than fiduciaries—is crystal clear.

Accordingly, the MBCA approach, as enacted by about two dozen states, does not treat independent directors as fiduciaries. The impact of this approach is magnified by its failure to recognize the importance of an independent director's personal liability exposure, relationships with fellow directors, and structural bias. The following discussion focuses on the slighting of these substantial concerns.

B. Minimizing the Existence of Independent Director Bias

Similar to the Delaware courts, states that have enacted the MBCA statute minimize or ignore the presence of several indicia of independent director bias with respect to the determination to terminate shareholder derivative

---

rule and requires that the requisite showing be made by the corporation. *See* MBCA § 7.44(a), (d). Nonetheless, the reasonableness of the independent directors' or SLC's determination that the derivative suit is not in the corporation's best interests and therefore should be dismissed is not a matter for judicial review. Moreover, because publicly traded companies must have a majority of independent directors on their boards of directors as a condition of listing (*e.g.*, New York Stock Exchange Listed Company Manual § 303A.01, Rule 5605(b)(1) of the Nasdaq Listing Rules), in the vast majority of situations, the expansive business judgment rule will be applied in this setting—thereby limiting a court's review to the SLC's independence, good faith, and the making of a reasonable inquiry, *with the burden of proof placed on the plaintiff-shareholder. See, e.g.*, North Carolina Gen. Stat. Ann. § 55-7-44(e), at note 83 *infra*.

[71] *See* discussion *supra* notes 58, 66, 69–70 and accompanying text.
[72] *See ALI, Principles of Corporate Governance, supra* note 1, vol. 2, at 6 ("Experience suggests that the social costs associated with intracorporate litigation can sometimes outweigh the benefits... and that, "[i]n light of [the] problems associated with private enforcement, this Chapter assigns only a limited role to the derivative action as a mechanism of corporate accountability").

actions. For example, the following circumstances do not by themselves disqualify a director from being deemed independent: (1) as a board member, such director approved the conduct or transaction that is the subject of the lawsuit; (2) as a result of such approval, such director is a named defendant in the derivative action; (3) such director was nominated or elected to the board of directors by a defendant director who engaged in a self-dealing transaction that is the subject of the derivative action; and (4) such director serves as a director on another corporation's board of directors on which a defendant director who engaged in the self-dealing transaction also is a board member.[73] To deem a director as independent who approved the challenged transaction and, as a consequence thereof, is a named defendant to impartially determine whether a derivative suit seeking to recover damages against such director should be dismissed ignores the conflicts of interest that permeate throughout this process.[74]

As discussed in Chapter 4, this approach also ignores the presence of structural bias.[75] With many directors having similar backgrounds and work experiences as well as sharing a common bond of being colleagues on the same board of directors, it is not surprising that nearly all of these situations

---

[73] *See* MBCA § 1.43(c). For state statutes enacting this provision, *see, e.g.*, Hawaii Rev. Stat. Ann. § 414-175(c); North Carolina Gen. Stat. Ann. § 55-7-44(c); Rhode Island Bus. Corp. Act § 7-1.2-711(e)(3); South Dakota Bus. Corp. Act § 47-1A-744.2; Utah Code Ann. § 16-10a-740(4)(c); Wisconsin Stat. Ann. § 180.0744(3).

[74] The reply to this assertion is that, by simply naming the requisite number of directors as defendants, plaintiff-shareholders could avoid making a demand in all situations. *See, e.g., Aronson v. Lewis*, 473 A.2d 805 (Del. 1984). Nonetheless, if a director approves or otherwise authorizes the transaction or other action being challenged, it is perplexing how that individual could objectively evaluate the allegations at issue, particularly if damages or other sanctions are sought by the plaintiff-shareholders against such director. Moreover, if the allegations are frivolous or do not state a cause of action, a motion to dismiss should follow.

[75] *See, e.g.*, Douglas M. Branson, *Corporate Governance* § 11.30 (1993) (addressing structural bias with respect to independent directors in the derivative suit setting); Note, *The Business Judgment Rule in Derivative Suits Against Directors*, 65 Cornell L. Rev. 600, 601 n. 14 (1980) (defining structural bias as "inherent prejudice . . . resulting from the composition and character of the board of directors"); Note, *The Propriety of Judicial Deference to Corporate Boards of Directors*, 96 Harv. L. Rev. 1894, 1901 (1983) ("Given cohesiveness and informational dependence in the boardroom, directors are likely to conform to the expectations of both management and their fellow members"). *See also* Michael P. Dooley and E. Norman Veasey, *The Role of the Board in Derivative Litigation: Delaware Law and the Current ALI Proposals Compared*, 44 Bus. Law. 503, 534 (1989) ("As we understand the argument, it is that no professional colleague can be expected to be as neutral on questions of management behavior as a court when the alleged malefactor is a stranger"). A number of courts have recognized the presence of structural bias with respect to outside directors. As stated by the US Court of Appeals for the Sixth Circuit in *Hasan v. Clevetrust Realty Investors*, 729 F.2d 372, 376 (6th Cir. 1982): "The delegation of corporate power to a special committee, the members of which are hand-picked by defendant directors, carries with it inherent structural biases." *See Clark v. Lomas & Nettleton Financial Corp.*, 625 F.2d 49, 53–54 (5th Cir. 1980); *Zapata Corp. v. Maldonado*, 430 A.2d 778, 787 (Del. 1981); *Miller v. Register and Tribune Syndicate*, 336 N.W.2d 709, 716–18 (Iowa 1981) (*infra* note 84 and accompanying text).

result in the independent directors determining that the subject shareholder derivative suit is inimical to the corporation's best interests.[76] Clearly, to effectuate a more even-handed approach, the criteria for determining director independence should be changed to better reflect corporate director biases and conflicts.[77]

C. Absence of Fiduciary Standards

Irrespective of whether the universal demand statutes are good policy in their mission to eliminate meritless derivative suits, they decline to hold independent directors to a fiduciary standard. Similar to Delaware's approach, directors are deemed independent even though they may have biases and conflicts that materially impede objective decision-making. Even if directors who are truly independent make a determination that a derivative action should be dismissed as not in the corporation's best interests, the permissive standards applied to uphold this determination lack fiduciary substance. Applying a broad business judgment rule standard, independent directors may engage in grossly negligent and perhaps even reckless conduct in their decision to terminate a derivative suit[78] as such determination is not an issue

---

[76] *See Joy v. North*, 619 F.2d 880, 888 (2d Cir. 1982), where Judge Winter opined:

> As a practical matter, new board members are selected by incumbents. The reality is, therefore, that special litigation committees created to evaluate the merits of certain litigation are appointed by the defendants to that litigation. It is not cynical to expect that such committees will tend to view derivative actions against the other directors with skepticism. Indeed, if the involved directors expected any result other than a recommendation of termination at least as to them, they would probably never establish the committee. The conflict of interest which renders the business judgment rule inapplicable in the case of directors who are defendants is hardly eliminated by the creation of a special litigation committee.

Similarly, as stated by another federal appellate court:

> The delegation of corporate power to a special committee, the members of which are hand-picked by defendant directors, carries with it inherent structural biases....
> The problems of peer pressure and group loyalty exist a fortiori where the members of a special litigation committee are ... carefully selected by the majority of directors for their advice. Far from supporting a presumption of good faith, the pressures placed upon such a committee may be so great as to justify a presumption against independence.

Hasan v. Clevetrust Realty Investors, 729 F.2d 372, 376–77 (6th Cir. 1982). *See* discussion note 86 *infra*.

[77] *See, e.g.*, Richard Mansouri, *How Independent Are the Independent Directors of Public Companies?*, Forbes (May 18, 2023) ("Clearly, the standard of what defines an 'independent' director has to change given the importance of ensuring that decisions made at the board level be impartial and free from bias").

[78] *See, e.g.*, discussion *supra* notes 31–39, 64–72 and accompanying texts.

for judicial review under the universal demand statutes.[79] Moreover, the application of director exculpation statutes signifies that independent directors in this context ordinarily would incur monetary liability exposure only if they acted with intentional misconduct.[80] Clearly, these standards illustrate that independent directors in the derivative suit termination setting are not fiduciaries. Rather, they are discretionaries who must satisfy specified conditions in order for their determinations to be enforced.

The following discussion addresses a similar development. Several decades ago a number of state court decisions adopted approaches in this setting that had fiduciary substance. These decisions, however, no longer retain validity due to the enactment by these states of the MBCA's universal demand statute with its permissive standards that apply to the dismissal of shareholder derivative actions.

IV. State Approaches That Had (But No Longer Have) Fiduciary Substance

In the aftermath of the Delaware Supreme Court's decision in *Zapata*, a relatively small number of states adhered to fiduciary-like standards with respect to upholding and enforcing a recommendation by independent directors (or a special litigation committee) to terminate a shareholder derivative action. Generally, these decisions are largely irrelevant today due to the enactment by those states of the MBCA's universal demand statute.[81] Several examples follow:

(1) In *Alford v. Shaw*, the North Carolina Supreme Court held that, irrespective of whether demand on the board of directors is required or excused, a reviewing court would be required to assess the merits of the special litigation committee's recommendation that the derivative lawsuit should be dismissed.[82] In view of North Carolina's

---

[79] See discussion *supra* notes 58–77 and accompanying text.
[80] See, e.g., *New Enterprise Associates 14 L.P. v. Rich*, 295 A.3d 520, 551 (Del. Ch. 2023) (stating that § 102(b)(7) "permits exculpation for recklessness); *In re Columbia Pipeline Group, Inc.*, 2021 WL 772562, at * 50 n. 22 (Del. Ch. 2021) (stating that "[t]he real function of exculpation is to eliminate liability for recklessness"). For discussion of exculpation statutes that insulate directors (and, with respect to a number of statutes, officers as well) from monetary liability under specified conditions, *see* Chapter 3, notes 55–85 and accompanying text; Chapter 4, notes 42–55 and accompanying text.
[81] See *supra* notes 58–77 and accompanying text; *infra* notes 81–89 and accompanying text.
[82] 358 S.E.2d 323, 326 (N.C. 1987) ("We conclude from the pertinent statutes that a modified *Zapata* [430 A.2d 779 (Del. 1981)] rule, requiring judicial scrutiny of the merits of the litigation

enactment of the MBCA statute, this decision no longer is good law. In its stead, as discussed above, is the expansive application of the business judgment rule. Pursuant to the North Carolina statute, the reviewing court must dismiss a derivative proceeding if the independent directors at a board meeting or as the sole members of the SLC "determine in good faith after conducting a reasonable inquiry upon which its conclusions are based that the maintenance of the derivative proceeding is not in the best interests of the corporation."[83]

(2) Four decades ago, the Iowa Supreme Court recognized the presence of structural bias with respect to the composition of special litigation committees. There, the court held that, at least in demand-excused situations, defendant directors did not have the authority to confer upon a special litigation committee the power to determine the corporation's position with respect to a shareholder derivative action. Instead, the subject corporation could apply to an Iowa court "for appointment of a 'special panel' to make an investigation and report on the pursuit or dismissal of a stockholder derivative action."[84] Because Iowa subsequently enacted the MBCA statute, this decision likewise no longer retains validity.[85]

(3) Over three decades ago, the Massachusetts high court ruled that, in evaluating a SLC's decision that a derivative suit should be dismissed,

---

committee's recommendation, is most consistent with the intent of our legislature and is therefore the appropriate rule to be applied in our courts"); *id.* at 327 (While "the *Zapata* Court limited its two-step judicial inquiry to cases in which demand upon the corporation was futile and therefore excused ... we find no justification for such limitation in our statutes [and therefore we draw] no distinctions between demand-excused and other types of cases").

[83] North Carolina Gen. Stat. Ann. § 55-7-44(a). *See id.* § 55-7-44(e) ("If a majority of the board of directors does not consist of independent directors at the time the determination is made, the corporation shall have the burden of proving the requirements of subsection (a) of this section have been met. If a majority of the board of directors consists of independent directors at the time the determination is made, the plaintiff shall have the burden of proving that the requirements of subsection (a) of this section have not been met").

[84] *Miller v. Register and Tribune Syndicate, Inc.*, 393 N.W.2d 709, 716 (Iowa 1983). That decision addressed a demand-excused situation, although the court's opinion can be read to encompass both demand-required and demand-excused cases. *See id.* at 716 (holding that "directors of Iowa corporations ... who are parties to a derivative action may not confer upon a special committee ... the power to bind the corporation as to its conduct of the litigation"). In its decision, the court focused on structural bias concerns. *See id.* (expressing concerns with respect to structural bias that "it is unrealistic to assume that the members of independent committees are free from personal, financial, or moral influences which flow from the directors who appoint them [and] all the more so where, as in the present derivative action, the members of the special committee are fellow directors"). The presence of structural bias is addressed elsewhere herein, including earlier in this chapter. *See, e.g., supra* note 75 and accompanying text; note 86 *infra*.

[85] *See* Iowa Code Ann. § 490.744.

a reviewing court was to assess the merits of the lawsuit in making its determination. In conducting this review, pertinent factors included "the likelihood of a judgment in the plaintiff's favor, the expected recovery as compared to out-of-pocket costs, whether the corporation itself took corrective action, whether the balance of corporate interests warrants dismissal, and whether dismissal would allow any defendant who has control of the corporation to retain a significant improper benefit."[86] In view of Massachusetts subsequently enacting the MBCA statute, this decision no longer is good law.[87]

(4) Likewise, over three decades ago, the New Jersey Supreme Court held that in determining whether to grant a corporation's motion to dismiss a shareholder derivative suit, the subject corporation had the initial burden to show that its board members or SLC making the decision to seek termination were independent and disinterested, acted in good faith, exercised due care in the investigation that was

---

[86] *Houle v. Low*, 556 N.E.2d 51, 59 (Mass. 1990) (also stating that "this inquiry will allow the special litigation committee to point out to the judge on what factors it relied and why those factors support its decision [while] the test will also allow the derivative plaintiff to point out factors not considered by the committee or why those relied upon by the committee do not support its conclusions"). While supporting the use of the special litigation committee device to terminate shareholder derivative actions when warranted, the court also recognized the risk of structural bias. *Id.* at 54, quoting James D. Cox and Harry L. Munsinger, *Bias in the Boardroom: Psychological Foundations and Legal Implications of Corporate Cohesion*, 48 Law & Contemp. Probs. 83, 84–85 (1984) (authors "examin[ing] several social-psychological mechanisms that can generate bias in the directors' assessment of the suit, including biases established by appointment of members to the board or a special litigation committee, control of pecuniary or nonpecuniary rewards made available to the independent directors by the defendant members of the board of directors, the independent directors' prior associations with the defendants, and their common cultural and social heritages . . . [which] in combination . . . can be expected to generate subtle, but powerful, biases which result in the independent directors reaching a decision insulating colleagues on the board from legal sanctions"). More recently, the Delaware Court of Chancery reasoned:

> That recommendation [that the derivative action should be dismissed in a case where demand on the board of directors has been excused] is entitled to some credit but not to the full deference of the application of the business judgment rule. There is a tension in review by any special litigation committee, which this Court recognizes is faced with the rather daunting task of evaluating publicly the behavior of fellow board members. That tension is not a conflict sufficient to sterilize the business judgment of the SLC, but it is sufficient to cause the Court, in evaluating a determination that a derivative action should be dismissed, to review the Committee's work and the bases for its conclusion, for reasonableness. The pressure on a sole-member SLC is especially evident, and causes a need for close review by the Court.

Teamsters Local 443 Health Services & Insurance Plan v. Chou, 2023 WL 7986729, at * 27 (Del. Ch. 2023).

[87] *See* Massachusetts Gen. Laws Ann. § 7.44(a) (stating that a reviewing court "shall" dismiss a shareholder derivative action if a majority of a board's independent directors or a SLC comprised of two or more independent directors determine "in good faith after conducting a reasonable inquiry upon which its conclusions are based, that the maintenance of the derivative proceeding is not in the best interests of the corporation").

undertaken with respect to the shareholder's allegations, and that the decision reached was reasonable.[88] This decision's validity has been nullified by New Jersey's enactment of the MBCA statute which precludes a reviewing court from assessing the reasonableness of the independent directors' or SLC's determination that the shareholder derivative action should be dismissed.[89]

The irony of these developments is that, when compared to many other states—in cases where demand on the board of directors is excused—Delaware has a more protective approach favoring shareholder-litigants in the derivative suit setting. In demand-excused situations under Delaware law, the reviewing court is to assess (among other inquiries) whether the SLC's decision has reasonable bases in determining whether to grant the subject corporation's motion to dismiss the shareholder derivative action.[90] Nonetheless, as discussed earlier in this chapter, Delaware's onerous standards for a shareholder to establish demand futility significantly reduces, in practical effect, the frequency in which demand is excused.[91]

V. The Lack of Fiduciary Standards

This chapter focuses on the lack of fiduciary standards in the derivative action setting. In the vast majority of jurisdictions, if adequately informed independent directors (with the meaning of "independent" being loosely defined) determine in good faith that a derivative action is not in the company's best interests, dismissal is thereupon granted—without judicial inquiry into the reasonableness or bases of that determination. As a consequence, judicial scrutiny of the propriety of the underlying alleged director or officer misconduct never occurs.

---

[88] *See In re PSE & G Shareholder Litigation*, 801 A.2d 295, 312 (N.J. 2002) ("Moreover, shareholders in these circumstances must be permitted access to corporate documents and other discovery limited to the narrow issue of what steps the directors took to inform themselves of the shareholder demand and the reasonableness of the decision").

[89] *See* New Jersey Rev. Stat. § 14A:3-6.5(a) (mandating dismissal of a derivative proceeding if a majority of a board's independent directors or a SLC comprised of one or more independent directors determine "in good faith, after conducting a reasonable inquiry upon which its conclusions are based, that the maintenance of the derivative proceeding is not in the best interests of the corporation").

[90] *See Zapata*, 430 A.2d at 788–89, discussed *supra* notes 40–44 and accompanying text.

[91] *See* discussion *supra* notes 45–57 and accompanying text.

The application of the expansive business judgment rule in this setting is not consonant with fiduciary duty principles. In the vast majority of jurisdictions, independent directors or a SLC comprised of independent directors, after conducting in good faith an adequate inquiry, can decide that a shareholder derivative suit should be dismissed without judicial review of the reasonableness of that determination. Moreover, with respect to the adequacy of the inquiry undertaken, business judgment rule application signifies that negligent practices may be engaged in without recourse. As an additional layer of protection, with the presence of exculpation clauses, an independent director (e.g., who serves on a SLC) must engage in intentional misconduct in order to be held monetarily liable for deficient performance in this role.

The conclusion is inescapable that fiduciary standards are lacking in this setting. To provide a more accurate portrayal, independent directors (loosely defined) act as "discretionaries" in effectuating the dismissal of derivative actions against their fellow directors and corporate officers. Being provided with broad leeway, these directors are obligated to perform their tasks consistently with specified standards in determining whether to seek the termination of shareholder derivative suits. While the successful invocation of these standards require that certain conditions must be satisfied, they lack meaningful fiduciary substance. Hence, like other contexts that are addressed herein, the "independent" corporate director acts as a "discretionary" in the derivative suit termination setting.

6
Mergers, Acquisitions, and Dispositions: A Semblance of Fiduciary Duty

I. The Presence of Differing Standards

This chapter focuses on the duties of directors and officers with respect to corporate mergers, acquisitions, and dispositions (hereinafter M&A). Situations where parent corporations engage in transactions with one or more of their subsidiaries also are addressed. In several of these types of transactions, the inveterate business judgment rule applies to assess corporate director and officer conduct. With respect to other transactions or actions undertaken by corporate boards of directors, a greater level of scrutiny is invoked by courts. Indeed, in some instances, applicable standards should be viewed as fiduciary. Hence, the legal standards invoked range from the business judgment rule to more rigorous standards depending on the type of transaction and its underlying facts and circumstances.

When plaintiff-shareholders challenge director and officer conduct in the M&A context, many of these actions are direct, rather than derivative, actions.[1] Accordingly, the intracorporate hurdles that a shareholder must satisfy before pursuing a derivative suit (such as making a demand on the board of directors) do not apply.[2] This fact, along with the prospect of the award of hefty damages, explains why there exists plentiful litigation in the M&A setting.[3]

---

[1] *See, e.g., Coster v. UIP Companies, Inc.*, 300 A.3d 656 (Del. 2023); *In re Straight Path Communications, Inc. Stockholder Litigation*, 2023 WL 6399095 (Del. Ch. 2023); *Galindo v. Stover*, 2022 WL 226848 (Del. Ch. 2022). *See also Tooley v. Donaldson, Lufkin & Jenrette, Inc.*, 845 A.2d 1031, 1035 (Del. 2004) (In determining whether a shareholder may sue directly or must institute a derivative action, "[t]he analysis must be based solely on the following questions: Who suffered the alleged harm—the corporation or the suing stockholder individually—and who would receive the benefit of the recovery or other remedy?").

[2] For discussion of the intracorporate requirements that apply in order for a shareholder to pursue a derivative action, *see* Chapter 5.

[3] *See* Matthew D. Cain, et al., *The Shifting Tides of Merger Litigation*, 71 Vand. L. Rev. 603, 604 (2018) ("In recent years, over 96% of publicly announced mergers have attracted a shareholder lawsuit, with many mergers attracting suits in multiple jurisdictions"). Nonetheless, due to that Delaware courts no longer countenance disclosure-only merger litigation settlements that provide no meaningful benefit to stockholders while awarding plaintiffs' counsel substantial fees (*Anderson*

Frequently, these direct actions seek equitable, such as injunctive, relief rather than damages.[4] Because money damages are not sought against the subject directors and officers, the lenient standards of a company's exculpation provision may not be invoked under Delaware law by defendants.[5] Rather, as addressed in this chapter, the applicable standards depend on the type of transaction and its underlying facts and circumstances. Irrespective of the legal standard applied in cases seeking solely equitable relief, the vast majority of state exculpation statutes preclude their availability to directors and officers in this situation.[6]

The identification of corporate directors and officers as "discretionaries" is fitting in the M&A setting. The predominance of the business judgment rule in many M&A transactions, with its gross negligence culpability standard, evidences the absence of fiduciary standards. On the other hand, in certain other situations, such as parent–subsidiary mergers, the standards that at times apply should be viewed as fiduciary in substance. Thus, acting as a "discretionary," the corporate director or officer must adhere to specified obligations that are diverse and have differing levels of normative conduct mandated. Utilizing this framework, this chapter focuses on a wide array of M&A transactions.

II. Business Judgment Rule Prevalence in the M&A Setting

It is commonplace for the business judgment rule to be applied in M&A transactions. The discussion that follows addresses several situations where the business judgment rule is applied to address the propriety of corporate

---

v. Magellan Health, Inc., 298 A.3d 734 (Del. Ch. 2023), *In re Trulia*, 129 A.3d 884, 899 (Del. Ch. 2016)), plaintiffs increasingly are filing their actions in other jurisdictions. *See* Cain, et al., at 615. This route has met with mixed results. *Compare In re Walgreen Co. Stockholder Litigation*, 832 F.3d 718, 724 (7th Cir. 2016) ("The type of class action illustrated by this case—the class action that yields fees for class counsel and nothing for the class—is no better than a racket"), *with Gordon v. Verizon Communications, Inc.*, 148 A.D.3d 146, 161–62, 164 (N.Y. App. Div. 2017) (approving disclosure-only settlement and awarding attorneys' fees).

[4] *See, e.g., Omnicare, Inc. v. NCS Healthcare, Inc.*, 818 A.2d 914 (Del. 2003); *Revlon, Inc. v. MacAndrews & Forbes Holdings, Inc.*, 506 A.2d 173 (Del. 1986); *Unocal Corp. v. Mesa Petroleum Co.*, 493 A.2d 946 (Del. 1985).

[5] For discussion of exculpation clauses herein, *see, e.g.*, Chapter 3 at notes 55–85 and accompanying text.

[6] A small number of states extend their exculpation statutes to encompass shareholder actions seeking equitable relief. *See, e.g.*, Ohio Rev. Code § 1701.59(D)-(E), *discussed in* Chapter 3 at notes 75–76 and accompanying text.

director and officer conduct in the M&A setting. Indeed, in the M&A transactional setting, the business judgment rule applies to a greater extent than any other standard. For example, the business judgment rule prevails in the following M&A situations:

(1) In an arm's length transaction, the determination by a board of directors to sell a valuable corporate asset (such as a highly profitable subsidiary) to an unrelated third party in a transaction that does not constitute the sale of substantially all of such corporation's assets.[7]
(2) In a post-closing damages action, the determination by a subject board of directors to sell all of the corporation's assets or stock to an unrelated third party, provided that disinterested shareholders approved the transaction in an adequately informed and uncoerced manner.[8]
(3) The determination by a corporation's board of directors to authorize the acquisition of an unrelated business enterprise, where such acquisition does not require a vote by the acquiring corporation's shareholders.[9] Applying this principle, the Delaware Chancery Court recently opined that, under Delaware law, "a board comprised of a majority of disinterested and independent directors is free to make a terrible business decision without any meaningful threat of liability, so long as the directors [are adequately informed and] approve the transaction in good faith."[10]
(4) A decision by a bidder's board of directors to launch a hostile takeover bid to purchase the shares of an unrelated business enterprise, including by means of a hostile tender offer.[11]

---

[7] *See, e.g., Gimbal v. Signal Companies, Inc.*, 316 A.2d 599 (Del. Ch.), *aff'd*, 316 A.2d 619 (Del. 1974); Samuel Arsht, *The Business Judgment Rule Revisited*, 8 Hofstra L. Rev. 93, 109–10 (1979).

[8] *See* cases cited in *Corwin v. KKR Financial Holdings LLC*, 125 A.3d 304, 309–10 n. 19, 313 n. 28 (Del. 2015); *Kihm v. Mott*, 2021 WL 3883875, at * 24 (Del. Ch. 2023) (holding informed stockholders' decision to tender their shares to nonaffiliated buyer resulted in the application of the business judgment rule); *In re General Motors Class H Shareholders Litigation*, 734 A.2d 611, 616 (Del. Ch. 1999) ("Because the shareholders were afforded the opportunity to decide for themselves on accurate disclosures and in a non-coercive atmosphere, the business judgment rule applies").

[9] *See, e.g., In re Oracle Corp. Derivative Litigation*, 2023 WL 3408772 (Del. Ch. 2023); *City of Coral Springs Police Officers' Pension Plan v. Dorsey*, 2023 WL 3316246 (Del. Ch. 2023); *In re Dow Chemical Company Derivative Litigation*, 2010 WL 66769 (Del. Ch. 2010).

[10] *City of Coral Springs*, 2023 WL 3316246, at * 1.

[11] *See Paramount Communications, Inc. v. Time, Inc.*, 571 A.2d 1140 (Del. 1990); *Smith v. Van Gorkom*, 488 A.2d 858 (Del. 1985). *See also* Afra Afsharipour and J. Travis Laster, *Enhanced Scrutiny on the Buy-Side*, 53 Ga. L. Rev. 443, 472 (2019) (in an article coauthored by Vice Chancellor Laster, stating that enhanced scrutiny "does not currently apply to stock-for-stock mergers between widely-traded companies"); Ryan Houseal, *Beyond the Business Judgment Rule: Protecting Bidder Firm Shareholders From Value-Reducing Acquisitions*, 37 U. Mich. J. L. Ref. 193, 223 (2003) ("Bidder

(5) In a post-closing damages action, the determination by a company's board of directors to engage in an arm's-length merger with an unrelated business enterprise, provided that the merger transaction was voluntarily approved by a majority of disinterested stockholders after receiving adequate disclosure.[12]

(6) In long-form mergers whereby a parent corporation undertakes a going-private transaction with its subsidiary.[13] Pursuant to this transaction, the parent corporation effectuates the cash-out of the subsidiary's minority stockholders' equity interests. In this setting, the business judgment rule applies in Delaware provided that (1) the subsidiary corporation appointed a special negotiation committee comprised of its independent directors who meaningfully bargained with the parent corporation; and (2) the merger transaction was approved by a majority of the minority shareholders in an adequately informed and uncoercive manner.[14]

(7) In a post-closing damages action involving the sale of the affected corporation even where *Revlon* principles otherwise would apply.[15]

---

company management wishing to engage in a hostile acquisition of a target company need only comply with the business judgment rule in order to fulfill its fiduciary obligation to its shareholders").

[12] *See, e.g., Corwin v. KKR Financial Holdings LLC*, 125 A.3d 304, 314 (Del. 2015) (applying business judgment as the governing standard when a merger transaction that was not subject to the entire fairness test was approved by disinterested shareholders in an uncoerced and fully informed vote); *S. Peru Copper Corp. Shareholder Derivative Litigation*, 52 A.3d 761, 793 n. 113 (Del. Ch. 2011) (stating that under Delaware law, "approval of an uncoerced, disinterested electorate of a merger . . . would have the effect of invoking the business judgment rule standard of review"). Note that provided specified conditions are met, shareholders of the surviving company have no voting rights with respect to a merger transaction whereby no more than 20 percent of such company's outstanding common stock is issued pursuant to such transaction. *See* Del. Gen. Corp. L. § 251(f). Also, an acquiror can avoid a vote of its shareholders by consummating the transaction by means of a triangular merger. Nonetheless, a shareholder vote may be mandated pursuant to stock exchange rules. *See Paramount Communications*, 571 A.2d at 1146.

The *Corwin* decision has been extended by the Delaware courts to tender offers. *See Morrison v. Berry*, 191 A.3d 268, 274 (Del. 2018) (stating that "the *Corwin* doctrine has been extended" to tender offers), citing *In re Volcano Corp. Stockholder Litigation*, 143 A.3d 727, 743–44, 747 (Del. Ch. 2016) and *Larkin v. Shah*, 2016 WL 4485447, at * 20 (Del. Ch. 2016)).

[13] A long-form merger generally involves a merger transaction with respect to which the parent corporation, prior to the transaction, owns less than 90 percent of its subsidiary's common stock. A going-private transaction refers to "a transaction or series of transactions in a publicly-held company whereby the controlling (or other) group substantially reduces or eliminates entirely the number of shares held by the public by inducing shareholders to exchange their stock for cash, thereby causing the company to attain privately-held status." Marc I. Steinberg, *Understanding Securities Law* 602 (8th ed. 2023).

[14] *See Flood v. Synutra International Inc.*, 195 A.3d 754 (Del. 2018); *Kahn v. M&F Worldwide Corp.*, 88 A.3d 634 (Del. 2014); discussion *infra* notes 62–64 and accompanying text.

[15] For discussion of the *Revlon* principles, *see infra* notes 44–56 and accompanying text.

The business judgment rule is the governing principle provided that the merger transaction is not subject to entire fairness scrutiny and was voluntarily approved by disinterested stockholders having the requisite information.[16]

Shareholders seeking to challenge several of the foregoing transactions must sue derivatively on their corporation's behalf. For example, challenges to M&A transactions involving the sale of key corporate assets where no shareholder vote is required ordinarily must be instituted as derivative actions.[17] Likewise, in a situation not requiring a shareholder vote, a stockholder alleging that a company's board of directors acted imprudently by authorizing the acquisition of another business enterprise must bring a derivative, rather than a direct, action.[18] In such situations, as addressed in Chapter 5, plaintiff-shareholders typically must make a demand on the company's board of directors.[19] Once demand has been made and has been rejected by a majority of the board's independent directors on the basis that

---

[16] *See Corwin*, 125 A.3d at 312–14. In holding that in a post-closing damages action the business judgment rule is the governing standard provided that the merger transaction was not subject to entire fairness review and was approved by disinterested shareholders pursuant to an uncoerced and fully informed vote, the Delaware Supreme Court stated: "*Unocal* and *Revlon* are primarily designed to give stockholders and the Court of Chancery the tool of injunctive relief to address important M&A decisions in real time, before closing. They were not tools designed with post-closing money damages claims in mind...." *Id.* at 312. Subsequent Delaware decisions have applied this principle to acquisitions effectuated by way of a tender offer. *See, e.g., In re Volcano Corp. Stockholder Litigation*, 143 A.3d 727, 743 (Del. Ch. 2016) (reasoning that "the policy considerations underlying the holding in *Corwin* do not provide any basis for distinguishing between a stockholder vote and tender offer"); *supra* note 12 and accompanying text; *infra* notes 52–56 and accompanying text.

Note that *Corwin's* breadth has been elaborated upon by the Delaware courts. As set forth in a Delaware Chancery Court opinion:

> The *Corwin* decision states that the cleansing effect of a stockholder vote does not apply to a transaction subject to the entire fairness standard. But despite this phrasing, *Corwin* precludes cleansing only when entire fairness applies *ab initio* because of the presence of a conflicted controlling shareholder. A transaction involves a conflicted controlling shareholder when (i) the controller stands on both sides of the deal, as in a parent–subsidiary merger, or (ii) the controller stands on only one side of the deal, as in a third-party sale but receives differential consideration for itself or another non-ratable benefit not shared by other stockholders. A transaction involving a non-conflicted controlling stockholder is subject to *Corwin* cleansing.

Firefighters' Pension System of the City of Kansas City v. Presidio, Inc., 251 A.3d 212, 254–55 (Del. Ch. 2021), *citing Larkin v. Shah*, 2016 WL 4485447, at * 13 (Del. Ch. 2016). *See In re Tesla Motors, Inc. Stockholder Litigation*, 298 A.3d 667 (Del. 2023).

[17] *See* sources cited note 7 *supra*.

[18] *See, e.g., In re Tesla Motors, Inc. Stockholder Litigation*, 298 A.3d 667 (Del. 2023); *In re Oracle Corporation Derivative Litigation*, 2023 WL 3408772 (Del. Ch. 2023); *City of Coral Springs Police Officers' Pension Plan v. Dorsey*, 2023 WL 3316246 (Del. Ch. 2023).

[19] *See* discussion in Chapter 5, notes 20–33, 58–65 and accompanying text.

the lawsuit would not be in the corporation's best interests, the business judgment rule applies to ascertaining whether the independent directors' determination is to be upheld.[20] Hence, in the M&A context as well, the omnipresent business judgment rule is invoked in the derivative suit setting to preclude judicial review of the propriety of the defendant directors' and officers' conduct with respect to the underlying M&A transaction.[21]

It thus is clear that the business judgment rule acts as an impressive shield to deflect shareholder challenges that allege director and officer misconduct with respect to M&A transactions. With its gross negligence culpability standard that mandates a showing of impropriety that is greater than that required to be proven for procuring a criminal conviction premised on criminal negligence,[22] great deference is given to director and officer conduct in this setting. Whether that deference enhances public policy objectives—including that directors rather than shareholders manage or oversee the corporation's business and affairs, courts are not business experts, business decisions are risk-taking determinations and should not be unduly restrained, and implementation of an onerous liability regime would significantly discourage independent directors from serving on corporate boards—is not the focus of this chapter.[23] Rather, identical to other situations addressed in this book, application of the business judgment rule in the M&A setting, with its broad umbrella protection from liability, evidences once again that corporate directors and officers are "discretionaries" rather than fiduciaries.

---

[20] *See* discussion in Chapter 5, notes 25–33, 66–72 and accompanying text.
[21] *See, e.g., City of Coral Springs*, 2023 WL. 3316246, at * 11 (stating that "the demand requirement is a manifestation of the business judgment rule").
[22] *In re McDonald's Corporation Stockholder Litigation*, 291 A.3d 652, 690 n. 21 (Del. Ch. 2023). Under Delaware law, criminal negligence is defined as follows:

> A person acts with criminal negligence with respect to an element of an offense when the person fails to perceive a risk that the element exists or will result from the conduct. The risk must be of such a nature and degree that failure to perceive it constitutes a gross deviation from the standard of conduct that a reasonable person would observe in the situation.

11 Del. Code § 231(a). For definitions of gross negligence under corporation law, *see* the discussion in Chapter 3, notes 40–53 and accompanying text.
[23] *See* William T. Allen, Jack B. Jacobs, and Leo E. Strine Jr. *Realigning the Standard of Review of Director Due Care With Delaware Public Policy: A Critique of Van Gorkom and its Progeny as a Standard of Review Problem*, 96 Nw. U. L. Rev. 449 (2002); discussion in Chapter 3, notes 25–26 and accompanying text.

III. Tender Offers: Differing Levels of Judicial Review

In Delaware, defensive maneuvers undertaken by a target corporation's board of directors in response to a hostile takeover bid are subject to greater judicial scrutiny than the traditional business judgment rule. As the Delaware Supreme Court stated in *Unocal*, "[b]ecause of the omnipresent specter that a board may be acting primarily in its own interests . . . there is an enhanced duty which calls for judicial examination at the threshold before the protections of the business judgment rule may be conferred."[24] Accordingly, before a court applies the broad parameters of the business judgment rule, the defendant directors and officers must show there existed "reasonable grounds for believing that a danger to corporate policy and effectiveness existed" and that the action taken was "reasonable in relation to the risk posed."[25]

A. Application of the Unocal Modified Business Judgment Rule

The *Unocal* test, which may be viewed as a modified business judgment rule standard under Delaware law,[26] is utilized to evaluate the propriety of actions undertaken by a target company's board of directors to maintain the corporation as an ongoing independent enterprise or to effectuate a long-term strategic plan.[27] Generally, a defensive measure, as stated by the Delaware Supreme Court, is deemed "an unreasonable response in relation to the threat if it is either draconian—coercive or preclusive—or falls outside a range of reasonable responses."[28] The Delaware courts' broad interpretation of this standard has prompted commentators to assert that its application resembles the "plain vanilla" business judgment rule.[29]

---

[24] *Unocal Corp. v. Mesa Petroleum Co.*, 493 A.2d 946, 954 (Del. 1985).
[25] *Id.* at 955. *See Unitrin, Inc. v. American General Corp.*, 651 A.2d 1361, 1388 (Del. 1995) ("[I]f the board of directors' defensive response is not draconian (preclusive or coercive) and is within a range of reasonableness, a court must not substitute its judgment for the board's").
[26] The *Unocal* standard also is viewed as an "intermediate" level of review. *See, e.g.,* Ronald J. Gilson and Reinier Kraakman, *Delaware's Intermediate Standard for Defensive Tactics: Is There Substance to Proportionality Review?,* 44 Bus. Law. 247 (1989).
[27] *See, e.g., Paramount Communications, Inc. v. Time, Inc.,* 571 A.2d 1140, 1153–54 (Del. 1990). *See also* Marc I. Steinberg, *Nightmare on Main Street: The Paramount Picture Horror Show,* 16 Del. J. Corp. L. 1 (1991).
[28] *Coster v. UIP Companies, Inc.,* 300 A.3d 656, 668 (Del. 2023), *citing Unitrin, Inc. v. American General Corp.,* 651 A.2d at 1367.
[29] *See, e.g.,* Theodore N. Mirvis, *Time/Warner: The Delaware Supreme Court Speaks,* 4 M&A Corp. Gov. L. Rep. No. 2 (April 1990) (stating that Delaware Supreme Court case law applying the

A myriad of defensive tactics have been upheld under the *Unocal* test, several of which materially hindered the successful undertaking of hostile takeover bids. For example, the Delaware courts have validated the following defensive measures that materially impeded hostile takeover bids as compliant under *Unocal:* (1) a target company's board of directors' adoption of an "anti-takeover" poison pill (also known as a shareholder rights plan) as an amendment to the subject company's bylaws that, if triggered, would have been severely detrimental to the corporation;[30] (2) the incurrence by a company of $10 billion of debt which substantially impaired the company's ongoing and future operations;[31] (3) target companies engaging in corporate restructurings and recapitalizations, including issuer self-tender offers to their shareholders;[32] and (4) the use of the "Just Say No" defense whereby a target corporation's board of directors declined to redeem the company's poison pill even though a reputable bidder sought to acquire control by means of an all-cash, all-share offer at a significant premium over the then current market price of such company's stock.[33]

Unocal analysis "seems to reduce rather importantly the differences between that form of heightened judicial review and the plain vanilla business judgment rule test").

[30] *See, e.g., Versata Enterprises, Inc. v. Selectica, Inc.,* 5 A.3d 586 (Del. 2010); *MacAndrews & Forbes Holdings v. Revlon, Inc.,* 506 A.2d 173 (Del. 1986).
[31] *See Paramount Communications, Inc. v. Time, Inc.,* 571 A.2d 1140 (Del. 1990).
[32] *See, e.g., Revlon,* 506 A.2d at 181; *Unocal,* 493 A.2d at 951–52.
[33] *See, e.g., Moore Corp. v. Wallace Computer Services, Inc.,* 907 F. Supp. 1545 (Del. 1995) (interpreting Delaware law, upholding the refusal by the target board of directors to redeem the subject company's poison pill when presented with the bidder's all-share, all-cash offer at a substantial premium over market price); *Air Products & Chemicals, Inc. v. Airgas,* 16 A.3d 48 (Del. Ch. 2011) (affirming the target board's decision to keep in place a poison pill that had a 15 percent trigger when faced with a hostile noncoercive takeover bid). *But see The Williams Companies Stockholder Litigation,* 2021 WL 754593, at * 1, 40 (Del. Ch. 2021) (declaring a poison pill unenforceable and permanently enjoining its operation when it had the following features—"a 5% trigger threshold, an expansive definition of 'acting in concert,' and a narrow definition of 'passive investor' "). Generally, a poison pill is "an antitakeover provision (also called a 'shareholder rights plan') whereby certain securities (such as rights or warrants) of the target company, upon consummation of an enumerated transaction or event, are convertible into the common stock or other security of the target (or of the acquiror) or into cash." Steinberg, *supra* note 13, at 610.

The validation of the poison pill to preclude shareholders from accepting a noncoercive offer from a reputable bidder was criticized by then Chancellor Allen:

> To acknowledge that directors may employ the recent innovation of 'poison pills' to deprive shareholders of the ability effectively to choose to accept a noncoercive offer, after the board has had a reasonable opportunity to explore or create alternatives, or attempt to negotiate on the shareholders' behalf, would it seems to me, be so inconsistent with widely shared notions of appropriate corporate governance as to threaten the legitimacy and authority of our corporation law.

City Capital Associates v. Interco, Inc., 551 A.2d 787, 799–800 (Del. Ch. 1988).

A target company's burden to make an adequate showing that the defensive measures that were implemented complied with *Unocal* is materially enhanced if its board of directors is comprised of a majority of independent directors.[34] Because publicly traded companies whose securities are traded on a national securities exchange ordinarily must have a majority of independent directors as a requirement of listing,[35] this condition easily is met. The end result is that, by upholding a target company's use of defensive maneuvers that materially and adversely impact the prospect of success for hostile bidders, the *Unocal* test frequently is rendered "toothless."[36] In effect, there frequently is not much differentiation between this standard and the traditional business judgment rule. Consequently, under *Unocal*, target company directors should be viewed as "discretionaries" rather than fiduciaries.

In this context, a distinct issue is presented when a target company's board of directors or management interferes with shareholder voting rights with respect to an election of directors or a corporate control contest. For decades, the Delaware courts had ruled that, even assuming good faith conduct, a board of directors' interference with the shareholder franchise required proof by defendants of a "compelling justification" in order to be upheld.[37] In *Coster v. UIP Companies, Inc.*, the Delaware Supreme Court abandoned the compelling justification standard as "unworkable in practice."[38] In its stead, the court "folded" this standard into the *Unocal* test, asserting that this approach protects "the fundamental interests at stake—the free exercise of the stockholder vote as an essential element of corporate democracy."[39]

---

[34] See *Paramount Communications v. Time, Inc.*, 571 A.2d 1140, 1152 (Del. 1990); *Moran v. Household International, Inc.*, 500 A.2d 1346, 1356 (Del. 1985).

[35] See New York Stock Exchange Listed Manual § 303A.01; Rule 5605(b)(1) of the Nasdaq Listing Rules.

[36] See Mark J. Loewenstein, *Unocal Revisited: No Tiger in the Tank*, 27 J. Corp. L. 1 (2001). Occasionally, a defensive tactic has been invalidated pursuant to the *Unocal* analysis. *See, e.g., Omnicare, Inc. v. NCS Healthcare, Inc.*, 818 A.2d 914 (Del. 2003) (holding that a merger agreement locking-up a majority of the votes needed to approve the merger with no "fiduciary-out" provision was impermissible). *But see Monty v. Leis*, 123 Cal. Rptr. 3d 641 (Cal. App 2011) (rejecting *Omnicare's* holding regarding the requirement of a fiduciary-out provision in the M&A setting).

[37] See, e.g., *Blasius Industries, Inc. v. Atlas Corp.*, 564 A.2d 651, 659–61 (Del. Ch. 1988) (opining that interference by the subject board of directors with the shareholder franchise with respect to election of directors must show a compelling justification for its conduct). See also *MM Companies, Inc. v. Liquid Audio, Inc.*, 813 A.2d 1118, 1126 (Del. 2003) (characterizing the stockholder franchise as "the ideological underpinning upon which the legitimacy of the directors' managerial power rests"); *Schnell v. Chris-Craft Industries, Inc.*, 285 A.2d 437, 439 (Del 1971) (stating that "inequitable action does not become permissible simply because it is legally possible," and that, accordingly, the board and management cannot inequitably manipulate corporate governance processes to perpetuate their positions and disenfranchise the shareholders).

[38] 300 A.3d 656, 669 (Del. 2023).

[39] *Id.* at 672 ("Experience has shown that *Schnell* and *Blasius* review, as a matter of precedent and practice, can be folded into *Unocal* review to accomplish the same ends—enhanced judicial scrutiny

Accordingly, under the *Unocal* standard applied in this setting, the board of directors has the burden of proof to show: first, that the board faced a threat to a significant corporate interest or to the attainment of an important benefit to the corporation;[40] and second, that the board's response to the threat "was reasonable in relation to the threat posed and was not preclusive or coercive to the stockholder franchise."[41] In this regard, the board's response must not deprive shareholders of their vote or coerce them to vote in a particular way. When a realistic path exists for a stockholder or insurgent group to gain control of the corporation, the board's conduct is not deemed to have a preclusive impact.[42]

Whether application of the *Unocal* test in the shareholder voting setting has substantive impact and holds directors to meaningful standards at this time is unresolved. In light of the sanctity of the shareholder voting franchise as the principal basis to legitimize the separation of ownership from control of a corporation,[43] it is reasonable to expect that the Delaware courts applying this compartmentalized aspect of the *Unocal* test (i.e., when a company's board of directors interferes with shareholder voting rights in the election of directors and in corporate control contest settings) will hold directors to standards that have fiduciary substance. This optimistic

---

of board action that interferes with a corporate election or a stockholder's voting rights in contests for control").

[40] *Id.* ("The threat must be real and not pretextual, and the board's motivations must be proper and not selfish or disloyal").

[41] *Id.* at 673 (stating that to "guard against unwarranted interference with corporate elections or stockholder votes in contests for corporate control, a board that is properly motivated and has identified a legitimate threat must tailor its response to only what is necessary to counter the threat [and that, moreover,] [t]he board's response to the threat cannot deprive the stockholders of a vote or coerce the stockholders to vote in a particular way"). *See Kellner v. AIM ImmunoTech*, 2024 WL 3370273 (Del. 2024) (applying enhanced scrutiny under *Coster* to advance notice bylaws).

[42] 300 A.3d at 672–75. One may question whether, as applied to the facts and circumstances at bar, the court's application of this standard lacked rigor. There, two stockholders, one the widow of a former shareholder, each owned 50 percent of the company's stock and were in deadlock. Subsequently, the corporation issued a one-third stock interest in the company to a long-time employee. The court held that this measure met the *Unocal* test because "the new three-way ownership of the company potentially presented a more effective way for [the widow] to exercise actual control" and that, therefore, the stock sale was not "preclusive." *Id.* at 675. What the court neglected to meaningfully address was the distinct possibility that the other 50 percent shareholder, a founding shareholder, had used his influence with fellow board members to cause the issuance of the one-third stock interest to a friendly third person, a long-time company employee who would side with the positions advanced by the founding shareholder rather than those of the widow.

[43] *See Blasius*, 564 A.2d at 659 (stating that the stockholder vote "is critical to the theory that legitimates the exercise of power by some (directors and officers) over vast aggregations of property that they do not own").

expectation is consistent with this book's focus that the corporate director or officer is a "discretionary," signifying that at times, fiduciary standards apply.[44]

B. The Revlon Sale Standard

It may be posited that the Delaware courts apply meaningful fiduciary standards in the corporate sale or auction setting. Under the Delaware Supreme Court's decision in *Revlon* and its progeny, a sale occurs and *Revlon* duties apply when (1) a corporation commences an active bidding process with the intent to sell the company or to effectuate a break-up of the company; (2) in response to a hostile takeover bid, the company abandons its long-term strategies and instead seeks an alternative transaction that would result in the break-up of the corporation; and (3) a corporation undertakes a transaction that, if consummated, would shift control of the company from the public shareholders to a controller.[45] Hence, in these situations constituting a sale of the corporation, the board of directors is obligated to seek to maximize immediate shareholder return. If the board elects to favor a particular bidder, such conduct is permissible only if this favoritism rationally relates to maximizing shareholder value.[46]

Under *Revlon*, in ascertaining which of the alternatives offered by competing bidders provides the best value for the company's shareholders, a subject company's board of directors is not confined to considering solely the amount of cash offered. Rather, the entirety of the situation should be analyzed in a disciplined manner, including the total consideration being offered by competing bidders, whether any offer is conditioned on the bidder

---

[44] *But see supra* note 42 where the Delaware Supreme Court arguably applied *Unocal* in the shareholder franchise setting with laxity. *Coster*, 300 A.3d at 672–75.

[45] *See Paramount Communications, Inc. v. QVC Network, Inc.*, 637 A.2d 34 (Del. 1993); *Revlon, Inc. v. MacAndrews & Forbes Holdings, Inc.*, 506 A.2d 173 (Del. 1986). Hence, *Revlon* duties are not ordinarily triggered in stock-for-stock mergers between widely held publicly traded stock exchange listed companies. Moreover, the adoption by a target corporation's board of directors of structural safety devices, such as certain lock-ups and no shop provisions, "alone does not trigger *Revlon*." *Paramount Communications, Inc. v. Time Inc.*, 571 A.2d 1140, 1150–51 (Del. 1990). For further discussion, *see, e.g.*, Marc I. Steinberg, *Nightmare on Main Street: The Paramount Picture Horror Show*, 16 Del. J. Corp. L. 1 (1991).

[46] *See QVC Network*, 637 A.2d at 48 (holding that, in the sale setting, the board of directors is obligated "to seek the best value reasonably available to the stockholders"); *Revlon*, 506 A.2d at 182 (stating, in the sale context, the board's duty has "changed from the preservation of... [the] corporate entity to the maximization of the company's value at a sale for the stockholder's benefit").

procuring adequate financing, and the risk of nonconsummation (perhaps due to questions of illegality).[47] When undertaking this task of seeking to maximize shareholder value in a *Revlon* sale situation, directors do not necessarily have the obligation to auction the company.[48] Rather, directors have discretion to select an appropriate route to value maximization as "there is no single blueprint that a board must follow to fulfill its duties."[49] They assume the burden of showing "the reasonableness of the decision-making process employed by the directors, including the information on which the directors based their decision [as well as] the reasonableness of the directors' action in light of the circumstances then existing."[50]

This standard better comports with the concept that directors are subject to standards that have meaningful fiduciary content. As stated by the Delaware Chancery Court: "Unlike the bare rationality standard applicable to garden-variety decisions subject to the business judgment rule, the *Revlon* standard contemplates a judicial examination of the reasonableness of the board's decision-making process."[51] Thus, it may be posited that if faithfully applied, the *Revlon* standard treats directors as fiduciaries. To adhere to their obligations when a corporate sale takes place, directors must act in good faith, be sufficiently informed, conduct a reasonable decision-making process, and demonstrate the reasonableness of their conduct, including the ultimate decision reached. Unlike the business judgment rule that requires a

---

[47] *See QVC Network*, 637 A.2d at 44, *quoting Mills Acquisition Co. v. Macmillan, Inc.*, 559 A.2d 1261, 1282 n. 29 (Del. 1989) (stating that a board of directors "may assess a variety of practical considerations relating to each alternative [from bidders], including: [an offer's] fairness and feasibility; the proposed or actual financing for the offer and the consequences of that financing; questions of illegality; the risk of non-consummation; the bidder's identity, prior background, and other business venture experiences; and the bidder's business plans for the corporation and their effects on stockholder interests").

[48] *See, e.g., C&J Energy Services, Inc. v. City of Miami General Employees' and Sanitation Employees' Retirement Trust*, 107 A.3d 1049, 1067 (Del. 2014) ("*Revlon* does not require a board to set aside its own view of what is best for the corporation's stockholders and run an auction whenever the board approves a change of control transaction"), *citing Barkan v. Amsted Industries, Inc.*, 567 A.2d 1279, 1286 (Del. 1989); *In re Columbia Pipeline Group, Inc.*, 2021 WL 772562, at *37 (Del. Ch. 2021) ("The Delaware Supreme Court has held squarely and repeatedly that *Revlon* does not create a duty to auction or require that directors adhere to judicially prescribed steps to maximize stockholder value").

[49] *C&J Energy Services, Inc.*, 107 A.3d at 1067. *See In re Mindbody, Inc. Stockholder Litigation*, 2023 WL 2518149, at *34 (Del. Ch. 2023) (stating that, under *Revlon*, "directors are generally free to select the path to value maximization, so long as they choose a reasonable route to get there").

[50] *See Unitrin, Inc. v. American General Corp.*, 651 A.2d 1361, 1361, 1386 (Del. 1995) (stating that "a court applying *Revlon's* enhanced scrutiny must decide whether the directors made a reasonable decision, not a perfect decision"); *QVC Network*, 637 A.2d at 45 (applying *Revlon*, a court is to "determine if the directors' decision was, on balance, within a range of reasonableness").

[51] *In re Network Technologies, Inc. Stockholder Litigation*, 924 A.2d 171, 192 (Del. Ch. 2007). *See Chen v. Howard-Anderson*, 87 A.3d 648, 673 (Del. Ch. 2014) (stating that "the metric for measuring fiduciary duties under the enhanced scrutiny test [of *Revlon*] is reasonableness").

complainant to prove that the subject directors and officers acted with gross negligence, the *Revlon* standards reflect a more rigorous approach that has fiduciary substance.[52]

Nonetheless, the *Revlon* standards apply only in the context of requests for equitable relief, such as injunctive relief.[53] After the subject transaction is consummated and a post-closing damages action is instituted, the "irrebuttable" business judgment rule is the governing standard provided that specified requirements are met. These conditions, as set forth by the Delaware Supreme Court, are that the transaction is "not subject to the entire fairness standard [and] is approved by a fully informed, uncoerced vote of the disinterested stockholders . . . ."[54] When these conditions are met, plaintiffs evidently are relegated to a waste claim where the possibility of success is slim.[55]

It may be posited that application of the business judgment rule rather than the *Revlon* standard in a damages action is appropriate because the

---

[52] For cases interpreting state law other than Delaware, *see, e.g., Edelman v. Fruehauf Corp.*, 798 F.2d 882 (6th Cir. 1986) (applying Michigan law and following *Revlon*); *Hanson Trust v. ML SCM Acquisition, Inc.*, 781 F.2d 264 (2d Cir. 1986) (applying New York law and adhering to flexible construction of business judgment rule); *Shenker v. Laureate Education, Inc.*, 964 A.2d 675 (Md. 2009) (holding directors have obligation to maximize shareholder value in sale of corporation setting); *Bayberry Associates v. Jones*, 783 S.W.2d 553 (Tenn. 1990) (following *Revlon*).

[53] *See Corwin v. KKR Financial Holdings LLC*, 125 A.3d 504, 512 (Del. 2015) (stating that "*Unocal* and *Revlon* are primarily designed to give stockholders and the Court of Chancery the tool of injunctive relief to address important M&A decisions in real time, before closing [but] were not tools designed with post-closing money damages claims in mind").

[54] *Id.* at 309–14. For a more recent construction of *Corwin*, *see Firefighters' Pension System of the City of Kansas City v. Presidio, Inc.*, 251 A.3d 212, 254–55 (Del. Ch. 2021), *discussed in* note 16 *supra*. Note that a number of Delaware chancery court decisions hold that the business judgment rule in this setting is "irrebuttable." *See, e.g., In re Volcano Corp. Shareholder Litigation*, 143 A.3d 727, 738 (Del. Ch. 2016) ("[R]ecent [Delaware] Supreme Court decisions confirm that the approval of a merger by a majority of a corporation's outstanding shares pursuant to a statutorily required vote of the corporation's fully informed, uncoerced, disinterested stockholders renders the business judgment rule irrebuttable"). On the other hand, as a recent Delaware court of chancery decision illustrates, *Corwin* cleansing is problematic when adequate disclosure has not been made to the shareholders voting on the subject transaction:

> In this case, the stockholders were as in the dark as the Board. Generally, when a Plaintiff proves the paradigmatic *Revlon* claim, a defendant will not be able to show that the stockholder vote was fully informed, precisely because the Board did not know about and could not disclose information about the [controller's] machinations. . . . The stockholders were not made aware of [this material information]. This is more than sufficient to defeat a *Corwin* defense.

In re Mindbody, Inc. Stockholder Litigation, 2023 WL 2518149, at * 39 (Del. Ch. 2023).

[55] *See, e.g., Larkin v. Shah*, 2016 WL 4485447, at * 7 (Del. Ch. 2016) (concluding that, "by operation of *Corwin* and related authority on the legal effects of stockholder approval, the irrebuttable business judgment rule applies, a holding that extinguishes all challenges to the merger except those predicated on waste"). The Delaware Supreme Court has made clear that plaintiffs rarely will succeed on a waste claim. *See, e.g., Singh v. Attenborough*, 137 A.3d 151, 151–52 (Del. 2016). *See also* discussion in Chapter 3, notes 10–54 and accompanying text.

subject transaction—such as a merger transaction with an unrelated third party that constituted the sale of the corporation—was not subject to entire fairness scrutiny and was voluntarily approved by disinterested shareholders having requisite information.[56] Whether this distinction is meritorious is not pertinent to the analysis contained herein. Rather, the important point is that application of a gross negligence standard is not compatible with fiduciary status. Moreover, because post-closing lawsuits may raise duty of care claims, the presence of an exculpation clause in the subject company's charter signifies that monetary liability may be incurred by these defendant directors and officers only if they acted with intentional misconduct. Hence, although meaningful fiduciary standards apply under *Revlon* when equitable relief is sought, they dissipate when a post-closing damages action is brought against defendant directors and officers. This approach is consistent with the position that corporate directors and officers are "discretionaries" whose conduct and liability exposure are measured by the applicable facts and circumstances.

IV. Parent–Subsidiary Relations: The Prospect of Fiduciary Standards

When a parent corporation engages in a transaction with its subsidiary or its subsidiary's unaffiliated shareholders, the parent may be viewed as engaged in self-dealing. In the parent–subsidiary context, the Delaware Supreme Court has held that self-dealing giving rise to the entire fairness test occurs "when the parent, by virtue of its domination of the subsidiary, causes the subsidiary to act in such a way that the parent receives something from the subsidiary to the exclusion of, and detriment to, the minority stockholders of the subsidiary."[57] More recently, the Delaware Supreme Court phrased this standard in somewhat different language, opining that "in a suit claiming that a controlling shareholder stood on both sides of the transaction with the controlled corporation and received a non-ratable benefit, entire fairness is the presumptive standard of review."[58]

---

[56] *See* discussion and sources cited *supra* notes 45–55 and accompanying text.
[57] *Sinclair Oil Corp. v. Levien*, 280 A.2d 717, 720 (Del. 1971).
[58] *In re Match Group, Inc. Derivative Litigation*, 315 A.3d 446, 451 (Del. 2024). In that opinion, the Delaware Supreme Court restated this standard as follows: (1) "[W]here a controlling stockholder transacts with the controlled corporation and receives a non-ratable benefit, the presumptive standard of review is entire fairness." *Id.* at 460. (2) "Entire fairness is the standard of review in

Frequently, the controlling stockholder is a publicly held company that has a majority ownership interest in a publicly traded subsidiary. Exercising this controlling interest, the parent company can elect all of the subsidiary's directors and vote its stock at shareholder meetings of the subsidiary to effectuate its objectives. By these means, the parent corporation may seek to satisfy its own interests to the detriment of the subsidiary and its minority shareholders. The opportunity for the parent corporation to abuse the subsidiary's minority shareholders is clear.[59]

Recognizing the leverage that a parent corporation has over its subsidiaries and their minority shareholders, the Delaware courts have placed conditions on parent corporations and their boards of directors. One key example arises in the parent–subsidiary long-form, cash-out merger context. In this setting, absent the implementation of structural safeguards that are protective of the minority shareholders' interests, the entire fairness standard applies whereby a court's focus is on fair dealing and fair price—with the defendants having the burden of proof.[60] This standard, when dutifully applied, imposes meaningful obligations upon the parent corporation and its directors and officers. Miscreant behavior in this setting may result in the levying of hefty damages.[61] On the other hand, as Delaware case law evidences, the entire

transactions between a controlled corporation and a controlling stockholder when the controlling stockholder receives a non-ratable benefit." *Id.* at 462.

[59] *See id.* at 460 (stating that, "without arm's length negotiation, controlling stockholders can exert outsized influence over the board and minority stockholders"); Marc I. Steinberg and Evalyn N. Lindahl, *The New Law of Squeeze-Out Mergers*, 62 Wash. U.L.Q. 351 (1984).

[60] *See, e.g., Weinberger v. UOP, Inc.*, 457 A.2d 701, 711–14 (Del. 1983). *See also Alpert v. 28 Williams Street Corp.*, 473 N.E.2d 19 (N.Y. 1984) (adopting entire fairness standard in a cash-out merger). *But see Weinberger*, 457 A.2d at 714 (stating that "a plaintiff's monetary remedy ordinarily should be confined to the more liberalized appraisal proceeding herein established [but the] appraisal remedy . . . may not be adequate in certain cases, particularly where fraud, misrepresentation, self-dealing, deliberate waste of corporate assets, or gross and palpable overreaching are involved"). Note that the entire fairness test may apply in any setting, such as a reverse spinoff transaction, where "a controlling stockholder [stands] on both sides of a transaction with the controlled corporation and receive[s] a non-ratable benefit. . . ." *In re Match Derivative Litigation*, 315 A.3d at 451. *See* discussion in Chapter 4 at note 86.

[61] *See, e.g., In re Dole Food Co. Stockholder Litigation*, 2015 WL 5052214 (Del. Ch. 2015) (finding that two executive officers, the CEO and the president, committed duty of loyalty breaches in connection with a cash-out merger and levying damages of more than $148 million); *In re Straight Path Communications, Inc. Consolidated Stockholder Litigation*, 2023 WL 6399095, at * 32 (Del. Ch. 2023) (finding that the controller "breached his fiduciary duty to the minority shareholders through his coercion of the Special Committee" but only nominal damages awarded due to lack of damages because the price received by the minority shareholders was fair). *See also In re Sears Hometown and Outlet Stores, Inc.*, 309 A.3d 474, 512 (Del. Ch. 2024) (applying enhanced scrutiny to controller's conduct, acting in his shareholder capacity, to change the status quo but applying a lenient liability standard—holding that in such situation, "a controlling stockholder owes a fiduciary duty of loyalty which requires that the controller not *intentionally* harm the corporation or its minority

fairness test may be met even without the implementation of structural safeguards that are protective of minority shareholder interests.[62] For our purposes here, the entire fairness test serves as an example of the application of fiduciary standards when assessing the conduct of a parent corporation and its directors and officers in certain M&A situations.

A. The Implementation of Structural Safeguards: Business Judgment Rule Application

Significantly, the parent corporation may avoid entire fairness scrutiny by adopting and adequately implementing structural safeguards that protect the subsidiary's minority shareholders. If properly effectuated, this strategy signifies that the business judgment rule becomes the governing standard. This standard applies when (1) the subsidiary corporation establishes a well-functioning special negotiation committee comprised entirely of independent directors who meaningfully bargain with the parent corporation, and (2) the negotiated transaction and its terms are approved by the subsidiary's minority shareholders pursuant to an uncoerced and adequately informed vote.[63] To elaborate, the business judgment rule is applied under

---

stockholders, plus a fiduciary duty of care that requires that the controller not harm the corporation or its minority stockholders through *grossly negligent* action") (emphasis supplied).

[62] *See, e.g., In re Tesla Motors, Inc. Stockholder Litigation*, 298 A.3d 667, 708–09 (Del. 2023), where the Delaware Supreme Court stated:

> [O]ur decisions ... have established a "best practices" pathway that, if followed, allow for conflicted transactions ... to avoid entire fairness review. Tesla's and Musk's determination not to form a special committee invited much risk.... Although the Vice Chancellor aptly observed that perhaps the Tesla Board subjected itself to "unnecessary peril," we also recognize that there may be reasons why a board decides not to employ such devices, including transaction execution risk. Also, a board may wish to maintain some flexibility in the process ... by having the ability to access the technical expertise and strategic vision of the controller. Although we continue to encourage the use of special committees as a "best practice," nothing in Delaware law requires a board to form a special committee in a conflicted transaction. Here, the price of not utilizing a special committee was being subjected to entire fairness review—an expensive, risky, and "heavy lift" in the litigation arena.

[63] *See, e.g., Sarasota Firefighters' Pension Fund v. Inovalon*, 2024 WL 1896096 (Del. 2024); *In re Match Group, Inc. Derivative Litigation*, 315 A.3d 446 (Del. 2024); *Kahn v. M & F Worldwide Corp.*, 88 A.3d 635, 644 (Del. 2014); *In re Kenneth Cole Productions, Inc., Shareholder Litigation*, 52 N.E.3d 214, 219–22 (N.Y. 2016). Note that where the subject going-private transaction is approved by a majority of the minority shareholders having adequate disclosure, the burden shifts to the plaintiffs to prove unfairness. *See, e.g., Weinberger*, 457 A.2d at 710. Similarly, where such transaction is approved by a well-functioning committee comprised solely of independent directors, the burden of persuasion likewise shifts to the plaintiffs to show that the transaction was unfair. *See, e.g., Kahn*

Delaware law in parent–subsidiary long-form merger transactions if "(i) the controller conditions the procession of the transaction on the approval of both a Special Committee and a majority of the independent stockholders; (ii) the Special Committee is independent; (iii) the Special Committee is empowered to freely select its own advisers and to say no definitively; (iv) the Special Committee meets its duty of care in negotiating a fair price; (v) the vote of the minority is informed; and (vi) there is no coercion of the minority."[64] With the satisfaction of these substantive measures, the implementation of the business judgment rule may be viewed as consistent with fiduciary standards. It nonetheless may be posited that the application of a gross negligence culpability level in any circumstance where corporate or shareholder interests may be adversely affected constitutes an unduly lenient approach that lacks meaningful fiduciary content.[65]

B. Short-Form Mergers: Minority Shareholders Relegated to Appraisal in Delaware

A short-form merger may be undertaken when a parent corporation owns 90 percent or more of its subsidiary's outstanding shares.[66] In Delaware, absent the commission of fraud or illegality by a controlling shareholder or its affiliate or agent, a minority shareholder is relegated to appraisal as the exclusive remedy in a short-form merger.[67] By eliminating the entire fairness test in this situation, this approach significantly eases the burden on controllers to cash-out minority shareholders, thereby facilitating the consummation

---

v. Lynch Communication, Inc., 638 A.2d 1110, 1117 (Del. 1994); discussion in Chapter 9, notes 37–40 and accompanying text. As stated by the Delaware Supreme Court in *In re Match, Inc. Derivative Litigation*: "The controlling stockholder can shift the burden of proof to the plaintiff by properly employing a special committee or an unaffiliated stockholder vote. But the use of just one of these procedural devices does not change the standard of review." 315 A.3d at 451.

[64] *Kahn*, 88 A.3d at 646, *quoted approvingly in, In re Tesla Motors, Inc. Stockholder Litigation*, 298 A.3d at 707–08. In *Flood v. Synutra International, Inc.*, 195 F.3d 754, 763–64 (Del. 2018), the Delaware Supreme Court elaborated on this standard, stating that "a controller is required to condition the buyout on both the approval of an independent, fully empowered Special Committee and the approval of the majority of the minority stockholders at the beginning stages of the process of considering a going-private proposal and before any negotiations commence between the Special Committee and the controller over the economic terms of the offer."

[65] *See* discussion is Chapter 3.
[66] *See, e.g.*, Del. Code Ann. tit. 8, § 253.
[67] *See Glassman v. Unocal Exploration Corp.*, 777 A.2d 242, 247–48 (Del. 2001) (stating that "§ 253 must be construed to obviate the requirement to establish entire fairness").

of merger transactions.[68] While the Delaware Supreme Court has construed the appraisal statute to provide fair value to objecting shareholders,[69] the remedy is procedurally complex and burdensome on smaller shareholders.[70] The result is that these shareholders ordinarily fail to perfect their appraisal rights, thereby having no other recourse than to accept the monetary consideration determined by the controlling shareholder.[71] Hence, under Delaware law, absent fraud or illegality, fair dealing and fair price are inapplicable in short-form mergers.[72]

This approach is not consonant with characterizing corporate directors and officers as fiduciaries. Upholding the propriety of conduct engaged in by controlling shareholders and their affiliates (e.g., directors and officers) in connection with short-form mergers unless fraud or illegality is proven contravenes fiduciary-based principles. Although aggrieved shareholders theoretically can pursue an appraisal claim, the fact remains that this remedy is an arduous obstacle for smaller shareholders.[73] Moreover, even assuming that the appraisal remedy may be successfully invoked by institutional and active individual shareholders,[74] this in no way detracts from the fact that adherence to a fraud or illegality level of culpability upon controllers and their directors and officers is not a fiduciary-based standard.[75] Nonetheless,

---

[68] See Steinberg, *Short-Form Mergers in Delaware*, 27 Del. J. Corp. L. 489, 491–92 (2002) (asserting that "the *Glassman* decision facilitates the effectuation of [short-form] mergers with an increased assurance of commercial certainty [and that,] [i]f adequate disclosure is provided to minority shareholders to enable them to ascertain whether to perfect their right to appraisal, short-form mergers will rarely be subject to successful minority shareholder challenge in breach of fiduciary duty actions").

[69] See, e.g., *Weinberger*, 457 A.2d at 713 (stating that, in an appraisal proceeding, fair value "is to be determined by taking into account all relevant factors, exclusive of the speculative effects of the merger"). Note that the appraisal remedy is not available by statute for specified merger transactions. See Del. Code Ann. tit. 8, § 262(b). Moreover, with respect to an arm's-length merger transaction between unaffiliated corporations, the Delaware Supreme Court affirmed a chancery court decision that relied exclusively on a subject company's "unaffected market price" in ascertaining "fair value" in an appraisal proceeding where the stock traded in an efficient market. See *Fir Tree Value Master Fund L.P. v. Jarden Corp.*, 236 A.3d 313 (Del. 2020).

[70] See Randall Thomas, *Revising the Delaware Appraisal Statute*, 3 Del. L. Rev. 1, 30 (2000) (asserting that the appraisal remedy is "procedurally complex" with "several strict deadlines that a shareholder must satisfy in order to perfect her appraisal right," with the consequence that these "procedural requirements seem quite burdensome on smaller shareholders"). See also Melvin Aron Eisenberg, *The Legal Roles of Shareholders and Management in Modern Corporate Decisionmaking*, 57 Calif. L. Rev. 1, 85 (1969) (stating that the appraisal remedy is one of "desperation").

[71] Note, however, that institutional and other large shareholders invoke the appraisal remedy with some frequency. See Cain, et al., *supra* note 3, at 612–13.

[72] See *Glassman*, 777 A.2d at 247–48 (construing § 253 of the Delaware Code "to obviate the requirement to establish entire fairness").

[73] See sources cited note 70 *supra*.

[74] See Cain, et al., *supra* note 3, at 612 (stating that "both the frequency and size of appraisal claims have grown dramatically in the last several years").

[75] See discussion in Chapters 3 and 4.

because of SEC regulations, fair dealing and fair price continue to be relevant criteria with respect to short-form mergers. SEC Exchange Act Rule 13e-3, and regulations implementing the rule, require that the subject company or its affiliate must disclose whether it "reasonably believes" whether the going-private transaction, such as a short-form merger, "is fair or unfair to unaffiliated security holders."[76] Accordingly, if a company or its affiliate engages in an actionable disclosure deficiency with respect to a going-private transaction, liability may be incurred under either federal or state law.[77] In this respect, an alleged fraudulent breach of the duty of disclosure under Delaware law presents a viable approach for plaintiffs to pursue.[78]

C. A Glimpse at Other States: Appraisal Sole Remedy in Merger Transactions

Although the preceding discussion focuses on Delaware law, the fact remains that several other states provide less protection for aggrieved shareholders. In these states, absent fraud or illegality, appraisal is the exclusive remedy in both long-form and short-form mergers.[79] By doing so, these states have set their priority on facilitating the consummation of merger transactions rather than minority shareholder protection. Depending on one's position, that approach may be laudable and beneficial to the economy.[80] Nonetheless, lacking fiduciary substance, this standard exemplifies that corporate directors and officers are discretionaries.

---

[76] *See* SEC Schedule 13E-3, Item 8 (Fairness of the Transaction), 17 C.F.R. § 240.13e-100, mandating the furnishing of information required by Item 1014 of Regulation M-A, 17 C.F.R. § 229.1014.

[77] *See Howing Co. v. Nationwide Corp.*, 826 F.2d 1470 (6th Cir. 1987), 927 F.2d 263 (6th Cir. 1991), 972 F.2d 700 (6th Cir. 1992); *Malone v. Brincat*, 722 A.2d 5 (Del. 1998); *Weinberger v. UOP, Inc.*, 457 A.2d 701 (Del. 1983); *In re Mindbody, Inc. Stockholder Litigation*, 2023 WL 2518149 (Del. Ch. 2023).

[78] *See* cases cited note 77 *supra*.

[79] *See, e.g., Yanow v. Teal Industries, Inc.*, 422 A.2d 311 (Conn. 1979); *Stepak v. Schey*, 533 N.E.2d 1072 (Ohio 1990); *Sound Infiniti, Inc. v. Snyder*, 237 P.3d 241 (Wash. 2010); *Sifferle v. Micom Corp.*, 384 N.W.2d 503 (Minn. App. 1986). In this regard, *see* Minn. Stat. Ann. § 302A.601 cmt. 3 (providing that "[t]he remedy for lack of 'entire fairness' in the transaction in this Act is the appraisal section").

[80] *See, e.g.*, US Chamber of Commerce, *The Business Case for Mergers and Acquisitions* (Feb. 17, 2022) ("[W]hen executed well, [mergers and acquisitions] promote competition amongst businesses, empower entrepreneurship, and protect consumers while allowing for increased freedom"). *See also* Bruce A. Blonigen and Justin R. Pierce, *Mergers May Be Profitable, But Are They Good for the Economy?*, Harv. Bus. Rev. (Nov. 15, 2016) ["W]hile much has been written to speculate whether mergers improve or harm economic welfare, there is little empirical evidence supporting either side of the argument. In recent research, [the authors] provide new evidence that while mergers may raise profits, many fail to deliver efficiency gains that could increase overall prosperity").

V. "Discretionaries" Sometimes Have Fiduciary Duties

As the preceding discussion in this chapter addresses, the business judgment rule is the prevailing standard in the M&A setting to assess director, officer, and controlling shareholder conduct when challenged as being violative of legal mandates. The rule's broad parameters insulate their actions unless a disabling conflict of interest, lack of good faith, or gross negligence is proven. Moreover, with the application of exculpation provisions in cases seeking money damages for alleged breaches of the duty of care, intentional misconduct must be established in order for plaintiffs to recover. In these situations, the conduct of directors, officers, and controllers is not subject to fiduciary scrutiny.

Viewed from a different perspective, directors, officers, and controllers must adhere to fiduciary standards in certain M&A transactional situations. For example, in long-form merger transactions in Delaware, whereby a parent corporation seeks to cash-out its subsidiary's minority shareholders, faithful application of the entire fairness test implicates meaningful fiduciary review. Likewise, pursuant to the *Revlon* prescription, fiduciary standards apply when a board of directors engages in a sale of the subject corporation.

Hence, at times, the conduct of corporate directors, officers, and controllers in certain M&A transactions are subject to fiduciary standards. By no means does this treatment in specified situations diminish the reality that these persons are "discretionaries." The legal principles that are employed regarding the propriety of their conduct vary depending on the type of M&A transaction as well as the underlying facts and circumstances. Ordinarily, as addressed in this book, directors and officers are subject to mandates that lack fiduciary substance. But, as discussed in this chapter, situations exist where meaningful fiduciary standards apply. Hence, identifying corporate directors and officers as "discretionaries" accurately reflects the legal standards to which they must adhere.

7

Close Corporations: The Presence (or Waiver) of Fiduciary Duties

I. Setting the Stage

A close corporation generally is characterized by a relatively small number of shareholders, the absence of a ready market whereby the company's securities may be traded, and substantial shareholder participation in the daily management and operations of the company.[1] Many state legislatures have enacted specialized close corporation statutes that permit eligible companies to implement substantial deviations from corporate governance standards that otherwise would apply.[2] The extent to which business enterprises use these statutes is open to question.[3] Nonetheless, a *non*statutory close corporation may achieve many of the same objectives by having all of its shareholders adopt a written agreement that modifies or eliminates certain statutory norms.[4]

Even if a company is not a statutory close corporation, Section 7.32 of the Model Business Corporation Act provides that, pursuant to a unanimous written shareholder agreement, the subject corporation's board of directors may be eliminated and specified shareholders or other persons may

---

[1] *See, e.g., Donahue v. Rodd Electrotype Co. of New England, Inc.*, 328 N.E.2d 505, 511 (Mass. 1975) ("deem[ing] a close corporation to be one typified by: (1) a small number of stockholders; (2) no ready market for the corporate stock; and (3) substantial majority stockholder participation in the management, direction, and operations of the corporation").

[2] *See, e.g.*, Ala. Code § 10A-30-2.11; Cal. Corp. Code § 300; Del. Gen. Corp. L. § 354; Ga. Code § 14-2-920; Ill. Stat. § 5/2A.40; Kan. Stat. § 17-7214; Nev. Rev. Stat. § 78A.070; So. Car. Stat. § 33-18-200; Wy. Stat. § 17-17-120.

[3] *See Nixon v. Blackwell*, 426 A.2d 1366, 1380 n. 19 (Del. 1993) ("Statutory close corporations have not found particular favor with practitioners"), *quoting* David A. Drexler, et al., *Delaware Corporation Law and Practice* § 43.01 (1993); Joan MacLeod Heminway, Mark J. Loewenstein, Marc I. Steinberg, and Manning Gilbert Warren III, *Business Enterprises: Legal Structures, Governance, and Policy* 473 (5th ed. 2024) ("Although most state legislatures [have enacted] specialized close corporation statutes authorizing broad deviations from the traditional norm of corporate governance, they have seldomly been used"); Dennis J. Karjala, *An Analysis of Close Corporation Legislation in the United States*, 21 Ariz. St. L.J. 663 (1989) (stating the case against statutory close corporations).

[4] *See* discussion *infra* notes 57, 72–74 and accompanying text.

be conferred authority to manage such corporation's business and affairs.[5] A number of these statutes expressly liken close corporations to partnerships. For example, the Tennessee statute provides that an otherwise permissible shareholder agreement that restricts the discretion of the subject company's board of directors in its management of such company's business is not invalid because the agreement treats such company "as if it were a partnership" or arranges the shareholders' "relationships in a manner that would be appropriate only between partners."[6] Hence, the recognition that a close corporation may modify or eliminate corporate governance norms pursuant to the provisions of a unanimous shareholder agreement has been widely accepted.[7]

This approach views close corporations as incorporated partnerships. Formation of a corporation rather than a partnership is elected primarily because of the benefit of limited liability protection for the company's shareholders.[8] Otherwise, the familiarity of the shareholders with one another and their participation in the enterprise resemble the status of partners in a general partnership.[9] As a consequence, fiduciary duties are owed in close corporations, according to these courts, not only by directors and officers but also by shareholders to one another, particularly when a controlling shareholder or group of shareholders join together to take action that

---

[5] Section 7.32(a) of the Model Business Corporation Act (which has been enacted by many states) provides, for example, that a unanimous shareholder agreement may eliminate the board of directors, determine the making of distributions, set forth who are the company's directors and officers, transfer to one or more stockholders or other persons the authority to manage the corporation, and "otherwise govern the exercise of the corporate powers or the management of the business and affairs of the corporation or the relationship among the shareholders, the directors and the corporation, or among any of them, and is not contrary to public policy."

[6] Tenn. Code § 48-17-302(b).

[7] *See* Wulf A. Kaal, *Shareholder Agreements—National Report of the United States of America* in *International Compendium on Shareholder Agreements* (Kristian Csach, et al. eds. 2017); Rainer Kulms, *A Shareholder's Freedom of Contract in Close Corporations—Shareholder Agreements in the USA and Germany*, Cambridge Univ. Press (online Feb. 17, 2009); Gabriel Rauterberg, *The Separation of Voting and Control: The Role of Contract in Corporate Governance*, 38 Yale J. Reg. 1124 (2021); Harwell Wells, *The Rise of the Close Corporation and the Making of Corporation Law*, 5 Berk. Bus. L.J. 263 (2008).

[8] *See, e.g., Donahue*, 328 N.E.2d at 512 (stating that "the close corporation bears striking resemblance to a partnership [and that it] is often little more than an incorporated or chartered partnership [whereby] the stockholders clothe their partnership with the benefits peculiar to a corporation [,such as] limited liability, perpetuity, and the like").

[9] *See id.* at 515 (holding that "stockholders in the close corporation owe one another substantially the same fiduciary duty in the operation of the enterprise that partners owe to one another"); *Crosby v. Beam*, 548 N.E.2d 217, 220 (Ohio 1989) (stating that the fiduciary duty owed by the majority to the minority shareholders in a close corporation "is similar to the duty that partners owe one another in a partnership because of the fundamental resemblance between the close corporation and a partnership").

causes injury to the corporation or a fellow shareholder.[10] Heightened fiduciary duties thus prevail in many jurisdictions in the close corporation setting.[11] Nonetheless, one may question whether this approach is appropriate in view of state partnership statutes that enable partners pursuant to a unanimous partnership agreement to significantly reduce their duties of care and loyalty.[12] In addition, similar to publicly traded companies, a close corporation may adopt an exculpation provision in its articles of incorporation that eliminates monetary liability for breach of the duty of care as well as, in certain jurisdictions, aspects of the duty of loyalty.[13] Moreover, in several states, corporate opportunities are authorized to be taken by directors and officers pursuant to waiver provisions contained in a subject company's articles of incorporation, bylaws, or board of director resolution.[14] And in a number of states, applying principles of the Revised Uniform Partnership Act, unanimous shareholder agreements may treat the relationship among the corporation and its shareholders as if they were partners, thereby reducing fiduciary duties that otherwise would be owed—provided that any provision adopted thereunder is not deemed contrary to public policy.[15]

From this perspective, this chapter focuses on the presence of fiduciary duties in close corporations. Nonetheless, while heightened fiduciary duties are recognized by many courts in this setting and the existence of these duties is firmly entrenched in such jurisdictions, the application of fiduciary duties may be significantly lessened by insertion of a permissible provision in the subject company's articles of incorporation or by unanimous shareholder agreement. Thus, while directors, officers, and shareholders owe fiduciary

---

[10] See, e.g., Barth v. Barth, 659 N.E.2d 559 (Ind. 1995); Crosby v. Beam, 548 N.E.2d 217 (Ohio 1989); Wilkes v. Springside Nursing Home, Inc., 353 N.E.2d 657 (Mass. 1976). Note that in certain situations, a minority shareholder may owe a fiduciary duty to the majority. See, e.g., Smith v. Atlantic Properties, Inc., 422 N.E.2d 798 (Mass. App. 1981) (minority shareholder who improperly used his veto power held to have breached his fiduciary duty).

[11] See, e.g., Crosby v. Beam, 548 N.E.2d at 220 (recognizing "a heightened fiduciary duty between majority and minority shareholders in a close corporation"); F. Hodge O'Neal, Robert B. Thompson and Douglas K. Moll, O'Neal and Thompson's Oppression of Minority Shareholders and LLC Members § 7.4 (rev. 2d ed. 2023) ("Judicial decisions and statutes reflect a trend toward recognizing enhanced fiduciary duties in a close corporation context") (and cases and statutes cited therein).

[12] See, e.g., RUPA § 105(d)(3) (permitting the partnership agreement to significantly reduce the duties of care and loyalty). Delaware permits the elimination of fiduciary duties by the terms of the partnership agreement. See, e.g., Boardwalk Pipeline Partners LP v. Bandera Master Fund LP, 288 A.3d 1083 (Del. 2022); discussion in Chapter 2, notes 34–69 and accompanying text.

[13] See, e.g., Del. Gen. Corp. L. § 102(b)(7); discussion infra notes 46–54 and accompanying text; Chapter 3, at notes 55–85 and accompanying text; Chapter 4, at notes 42–55 and accompanying text.

[14] See discussion infra notes 55–64 and accompanying text; Chapter 4 at notes 21–32, 107–114 and accompanying text.

[15] See RULPA § 105(d)(3) (permitting the partnership agreement to significantly reduce the duties of care and loyalty); discussion infra at notes 65–74 and accompanying text.

duties in the close corporation context, these duties may not be nearly as vibrant as they are portrayed.

II. Close Corporations (Fiduciary Duties) Likened to Partnerships

A number of states, such as Delaware and Texas, ordinarily do not accord special status for shareholders of *non*statutory close corporations.[16] In these states, generally, the relations among the directors, officers, and shareholders are given the same level of fiduciary treatment as in a publicly traded company.[17] Nonetheless, in a Texas nonstatutory close corporation, a shareholder may institute a derivative suit without making a demand on the board of directors. Moreover, such suit is not subject to dismissal by the corporation pursuant to the determination by independent directors that the action is not in the corporation's best interests.[18] Indeed, in Texas, for example, a court may treat a derivative action as a direct action if deemed appropriate.[19]

In many other states, the relations of the directors, officers, and shareholders of a close corporation are likened to those of partners in a general partnership. Invoking the words of Justice Cardozo in *Meinhard v. Salmon*,[20] shareholders in close corporations, like partners, owe one

---

[16] *See, e.g., Ritchie v. Rupe*, 443 S.W.3d 856, 881 (Tex. 2014); *Nixon v. Blackwell*, 626 A.2d 1366, 1380 (Del. 1993). In *Nixon*, the Delaware Supreme Court stated: "It would run counter to the spirit of the doctrine of independent legal significance, and would be inappropriate judicial legislation for this Court to fashion a special judicially-created rule for minority investors when the entity does not fall within [the close corporation] statutes, or when there are no negotiated special provisions in the certificate of incorporation, by-laws, or stockholder agreements." 626 A.2d at 1380–81. In *Rupe*, although declining generally to give special treatment to shareholders of nonstatutory close corporations, the Texas Supreme Court recognized that "the Legislature has enacted special rules to allow [a non-statutory close corporation's] shareholders to more easily bring a derivative suit on behalf of the corporation." 443 S.W.3d at 880–81.

[17] *See, e.g., Nixon*, 626 A.2d at 1380 ("One cannot read into the situation presented in the case at bar any special relief for the minority stockholders in this closely-held, but not statutory 'close corporation'"); sources cited note 16 *supra*.

[18] *See* Tex. Bus. Org. Code § 21.563(b). In *Sneed v. Webre*, 465 S.W.3d 169, 181 (Tex. 2015), the Texas Supreme Court recognized that under this statute, even in a nonstatutory close corporation, the "standing, demand, and mandatory dismissal requirements do not apply to shareholder derivative lawsuits...."

[19] *See* Tex. Bus. Org. Code § 21.563(c)(1) (stating that "a derivative proceeding brought by [a non-statutory close corporation] shareholder ... may be treated by a court as a direct action brought by the shareholder for the shareholder's own benefit"). This approach is prevalent. *See, e.g.*, O'Neal, et al., *supra* note 11, at § 7.8 ("Judicial authority for direct suits in close corporations now exists in more than half of the states").

[20] 164 N.E. 545 (N.Y. 1928).

another "undivided loyalty."[21] For example, the Ohio Supreme Court recognized "a heightened fiduciary duty" characterized by "utmost good faith and loyalty" between controlling and minority shareholders in the close corporation setting.[22] This duty, according to the court, is similar to the obligation that partners owe one another and is worthy of adoption due to the fundamental resemblance between a partnership and a close corporation. Accordingly, the court held: "Where majority or controlling shareholders in a close corporation breach their heightened fiduciary duty to minority shareholders by utilizing their majority control of the corporation to their own advantage, without providing minority shareholders with an equal opportunity to benefit, such breach, absent any legitimate business purpose, is actionable."[23] This approach, whereby rigorous standards are applied to determine the legality of controlling shareholder conduct in close corporations, has been widely embraced.[24]

In many of these situations, freeze-outs of minority shareholders have been perpetrated by controlling shareholders, resulting in the loss of a minority shareholder's employment and director and officer positions.[25] The loss of employment particularly is poignant as a minority shareholder may derive her livelihood by working in the business.[26] Moreover, after the minority shareholder's termination of employment, the controlling shareholders may significantly increase their salaries, thereby receiving de facto dividends to

---

[21] *Id.* at 546 (opining that "copartners owe to one another, while the enterprise continues, the duty of the finest loyalty [and that] many forms of conduct permissible in a workaday world for those acting at arm's length, are forbidden to those bound by fiduciary ties").
[22] *Crosby v. Beam*, 548 N.E.2d 217, 220 (Ohio 1989).
[23] *Id. See Gigax v. Repka*, 615 N.E.2d 644 (Ohio App. 1992).
[24] *See, e.g., Hollis v. Hill*, 232 F.3d 460, 470 (5th Cir. 2000) (applying Nevada law) ("That a controlling shareholder cannot, consistent with his fiduciary duty, effectively deprive a minority shareholder of his interest as a shareholder by terminating the latter's employment or salary has been widely accepted"): *Rexford Rand Corp. v. Ancel*, 58 F.3d 1215, 1218 (7th Cir. 1995) (applying Illinois law) ("Under Illinois law, a shareholder in a close corporation owes a duty of loyalty to the corporation and to the other shareholders"); *A. Teixeira & Co. v. Teixeira*, 699 A.2d 1383, 1387 (R.I. 1998) (stating that close corporation shareholders owe similar fiduciary duties as do partners to one another and to the enterprise); *Demoulas v. Demoulas Super Markets, Inc.*, 677 N.E.2d 159, 179 (Mass. 1997) (with respect to close corporations, opining that "duties of loyalty extend to shareholders, who owe one another substantially the same duty of utmost good faith and loyalty in the operation of the enterprise that partners owe to one another, a duty that is even stricter than that required of directors and shareholders in corporations generally"). *But see* Mary Siegel, *Fiduciary Myths in Close Corporation Law*, 29 Del. J. Corp. L. 377, 382 (2004) (asserting that the adoption of this expansive fiduciary duty approach being characterized as the prevailing view "has been greatly exaggerated").
[25] *See, e.g., Wilkes v. Springside Nursing Home, Inc.*, 353 N.E.2d 657 (Mass. 1976); cases cited in O'Neal, et al., *supra* note 11, at § 7.3.
[26] *See, e.g., Wilkes*, 353 N.E.2d at 662 ("The minority stockholder typically depends on his salary as the principal return on his investment, since the earnings of a close corporation... are distributed in major part in salaries, bonuses and retirement benefits").

the exclusion of the terminated minority shareholder.[27] Unlike a general partnership that allows any partner to disassociate from the partnership, either rightfully or wrongfully,[28] a shareholder in a close corporation does not have that prerogative. Unless a shareholder agreement entitles a shareholder to exit the enterprise (such as pursuant to a buy-sell provision),[29] the only practical alternative in many situations is for the minority shareholder to sue for oppression and seek dissolution of the enterprise. The end game is to procure a court order mandating that the close corporation or its remaining shareholders buy-out the minority shareholder's interest at fair value.[30]

Viewing the minority shareholder's plight as untenable, many courts adhere to a pro-minority shareholder approach when ascertaining whether to order liquidation or a buyout of the minority's shares.[31] Viewed as "perhaps the most reliable guide" to determine whether appropriate relief should be ordered in this setting, a court should assess "the reasonable expectations of the shareholders, as they exist at the inception of the enterprise, and as they develop thereafter through a course of dealing concurred in by all of [the shareholders]. . . ."[32] After all, in a close corporation, a corporation's articles of incorporation and bylaws "almost never reflect the full business bargain of the [shareholder] participants."[33] A second standard deems

---

[27] *See, e.g., In the Matter of Kemp & Beatley, Inc.*, 473 N.E.2d 1173, 1180–81 (N.Y. 1984) (holding defendants acted improperly by excluding former minority shareholders from any financial return while increasing other executive compensation for their financial benefit).

[28] *See* RUPA § 602(a) (giving a general partner "the power to disassociate as a partner at any time, rightfully or wrongfully").

[29] *See Ritchie*, 443 S.W.3d at 878 (stating that shareholders in a close corporation may enter into shareholder agreements to define such matters as "their respective management and voting powers, the apportionment of losses and profits, the payment of dividends, and their rights to buy or sell their shares from or to each other, the corporation, or an outside party").

[30] *See Wilkes*, 353 N.E.2d. at 664 ("It is an inescapable conclusion from all the evidence that the action of the majority stockholders here was a designed 'freeze-out' for which no legitimate business purpose has been suggested [with a likely objective of] pressur[ing] Wilkes into selling his shares to the corporation at a price below their value...."); O'Neil, et al., *supra* note 11 at § 7.11 (stating that the buyout remedy "has become the most common relief in oppression contexts").

[31] *See* cases cited notes 32–35 *infra*; cases cited in O'Neal, et al., *supra* note 11, at § 7.11.

[32] *Meiselman v. Meiselman*, 307 S.E.2d 551, 563 (N.C. 1983), *quoting* F. Hodge O'Neal, *Close Corporations: Existing Legislation and Recommended Reform*, 33 Bus. Law. 873, 886 (1978).

[33] *See* sources cited note 32 *supra*. The North Carolina Supreme Court opined that a minority shareholder's reasonable expectations are to be determined by examining the complete history of the relationship among the shareholders, including "the reasonable expectations created at the inception of the participants' relationship; those reasonable expectations as altered over time; . . . the reasonable expectations which develop as the participants engage in a course of dealing in conducting the affairs of the corporation; [and in order for such minority shareholder's] expectations to be reasonable, they must be known to or assumed by the other shareholders and concurred in by them." 307 S.E.2d at 563. *See In the Matter of Kemp & Beatley, Inc.*, 473 N.E.2d 1173, 1179 (N.Y. 1984) (holding that "oppression should be deemed to arise only when the majority conduct substantially defeats expectations that, objectively viewed, were both reasonable under the circumstances and were central

oppressive conduct in the close corporation context to be "burdensome, harsh, and wrongful conduct; a lack of probity and fair dealing in the affairs of a company to the prejudice of some of its members; or a visible departure from the standards of fair dealing, and a violation of fair play on which every shareholder who entrusts his money to a company is entitled to rely."[34] Applying either or both of these standards, courts have ordered a liquidation of the subject corporation's assets or, alternatively, a buyout of the minority shareholder's stock at fair value.[35]

Thus, in many jurisdictions, fiduciary duties are vibrant when assessing the obligations of controlling shareholders to the minority in close corporations.[36] Unlike general partnerships where a general partner has the power to dissociate at any time,[37] aggrieved minority shareholders in close corporations ordinarily have no exit from their enterprises absent the presence of a buy-out (or comparable) provision or the procurement of judicial relief.[38] Thus, it may well be equitable for courts flexibly to construe the meaning of oppressive conduct in order to provide appropriate

---

to the [minority shareholder's] decision to join the venture"); *In re the Application of Topper*, 433 N.Y.S.2d 359, 366 (Sup. Ct. 1980) (stating that a minority shareholder's rights and interests in a close corporation derive from the expectations of the parties and special circumstances that underlie the formation of close corporations"); O'Neal, et al., *supra* note 11, at § 7.12 ("Judicial or statutory authority to use reasonable expectations as a basis for relief under oppression statutes or fiduciary duty claims now exists in more than half of the states").

[34] *Gimpel v. Bolstein*, 477 N.Y.S.2d 1014, 1018 (Sup. Ct. 1984). *See, e.g., Skierka v. Skierka Brothers, Inc.*, 629 P.2d 214, 221 (Mont. 1981); *Fix v. Fix Material Co.*, 538 S.W.2d 351, 358 (Mo. App. 1976). In *Gimpel*, the court opined that the reasonable expectations approach and the "burdensome, harsh, and wrongful conduct" approach are "not mutually exclusive, and will frequently be found to be equivalent." Nonetheless, often "it will be found that one or the other lends itself more nearly to the facts of the case as an appropriate analytical framework." 477 N.Y.S.2d at 1019.

[35] *See, e.g., Guge v. Kassel Enterprises, Inc.*, 962 N.W.2d 764, 768 (Iowa 2021) (stating that, in lieu of defending a dissolution proceeding, the law allows a close corporation to purchase the aggrieved shareholders' stock for its fair value); *Kemp & Beatley*, 473 N.E.2d at 1181 (upholding trial court's decision that "a forced buyout of [the minority shareholders'] shares or liquidation of the corporation's assets was the only means by which [such shareholders] could be guaranteed a fair return on their investment"); Heminway, et al., *supra* note 3, at 505-06 ("Given the extreme nature of the dissolution remedy, courts have increasingly exercised their equitable authority to condition orders of dissolution on the corporation's or the majority's purchase of the minority shareholder's shares at a fair price"). *See generally* Douglas K. Moll, *Shareholder Oppression in Close Corporations: The Unanswered Question of Perspective*, 53 Vand. L. Rev. 749 (2000).

[36] *See* discussion *supra* notes 21-35 and accompanying text.

[37] *See* RUPA § 602(a) (providing that a general partner "has the power to disassociate as a partner at any time, rightfully or wrongfully").

[38] *See Wilkes*, 353 N.E.2d at 664 n. 14; *Fought v. Morris*, 543 So.2d 167, 171-72 (Miss. 1989); *Walta v. Gallegos Law Firm, P.C.*, 40 P.3d 449, 459 (N.M. App. 2001); cases and sources cited *supra* notes 21-35 and accompanying text.

relief, including a buyout of the minority's interest, when the controlling shareholders engage in draconian conduct.[39]

On the other hand, as some courts have observed, minority shareholders may protect themselves by successfully bargaining for specified protections that provide them with sufficient comfort to participate in the venture.[40] Moreover, it may be asserted that the analogy to partnership law is misguided in view of the right of general partners to enter into a partnership agreement that significantly reduces fiduciary duties that otherwise would apply.[41] Indeed, in Delaware, with respect to unincorporated enterprises (such as partnerships and limited liability companies), an agreement among the participants may eliminate fiduciary duties in their entirety.[42] Hence, the utmost good faith and loyalty principle of partnership law, although having application as a default standard,[43] becomes minimized in view of contractual agreements that substantially alter the fiduciary duties that otherwise would be owed.[44] Thus, to say that general partners must act with undivided loyalty toward the partnership and their copartners significantly overstates the actuality of present-day partnership law.[45]

III. The Diminution of Fiduciary Duties in Close Corporations

As set forth in Chapters 3 and 4 of this book, fiduciary duties may be diminished by means of several maneuvers. To serve as examples, the following discussion addresses three such vehicles: the state exculpation statutes,

---

[39] *See* Douglas K. Moll, *Shareholder Oppression and "Fair Value": Of Discounts, Dates, and Dastardly Deeds in the Close Corporation*, 54 Duke L.J. 293 (2004); O'Neal, note 32 *supra*; Robert B. Thompson, *The Shareholder's Cause of Action for Oppression*, 48 Bus. Law. 699 (1993).

[40] *See, e.g., Nixon v. Blackwell*, 626 A.2d at 1380 (stating that a minority stockholder "could bargain for definitive provisions of self-ordering permitted to a Delaware corporation through the certificate of incorporation or by-laws [and also could] enter into definitive stockholder agreements, and such agreements may provide for elaborate earnings tests, buy-out provisions, voting trusts, or other voting agreements"); note 29 *supra*.

[41] *See* UPA § 105(d)(3); discussion in Chapter 2, notes 24–61 and accompanying text.

[42] *See, e.g., Boardwalk Pipeline Partners LP v. Bandera Master Fund LP*, 288 A.3d 1083 (Del. 2022); discussion in Chapter 2, notes 52–61 and accompanying text.

[43] *See, e.g., McConnell v. Hunt Sports Enterprises*, 725 N.E.2d 1193, 1206 (Ohio App.1999). After stating that LLC members "owe one another the duty of utmost trust and loyalty," the court held that this duty must be considered in the context of the LLC's operating agreement which significantly limited the fiduciary duties that otherwise would have applied. For further discussion, *see* Chapter 2, notes 48–51 and accompanying text.

[44] *See* discussion in Chapter 2, notes 24–61 and accompanying text.

[45] *See* discussion in Chapter 2, notes 24–69 and accompanying text.

provisions enabling directors, officers, and shareholders to take corporate opportunities, and unanimous shareholder agreements that limit the application of fiduciary duties. Hence, although fiduciary duties ordinarily have meaningful substance in the close corporation setting, these duties may be diminished to a substantial degree by charter provisions and unanimous shareholder agreements.

A. Exculpation Statutes

As addressed in Chapters 3 and 4, by means of the inclusion of a provision in a subject corporation's articles of incorporation, monetary liability for breach of the duty of care may be eliminated for directors and, in some states, officers as well.[46] For example, the Delaware statute provides that director monetary liability (and senior officer monetary liability in direct actions) may be eliminated for breach of the duty of care pursuant to an effective charter provision.[47] Under the Delaware exculpation provision, however, liability may not be eliminated for breach of the duty of loyalty, intentional misconduct, knowing violation of law, knowing authorization of an illegal distribution, or receipt of an improper personal benefit.[48] A number of other states provide greater protection, insulating directors and officers from liability for certain breaches of the duty of loyalty.[49] For example, the Nevada statute is self-executing and expansive, covering both directors and officers. That statute provides that a director or officer is not liable to the corporation, its shareholders, or its creditors unless it is proven that such director or officer breached his fiduciary duties and "such breach involved intentional misconduct, fraud, or a knowing violation of law."[50] Hence, under this statute, directors and officers may usurp corporate opportunities and engage in other types of self-dealing (e.g., related party transactions) without incurring monetary liability so long as they do not intentionally or knowingly commit such breaches.[51]

---

[46] *See* discussion in Chapter 3, notes 55–85 and accompanying text; Chapter 4, notes 42–55 and accompanying text.
[47] *See* Del. Gen. Corp. L. § 102(b)(7); discussion in Chapter 3, notes 60–62 and accompanying text; Chapter 4, notes 52–55 and accompanying text.
[48] *See* sources cited note 47 *supra*.
[49] *See* discussion in Chapter 4, notes 43–51 and accompanying text.
[50] *See* Nev. Rev. Stat. § 78.138(7); discussion in Chapter 3, notes 80–83 and accompanying text; Chapter 4, note 46 and accompanying text.
[51] *See* sources cited in note 50 *supra*.

It may be posited that in a close corporation that has eliminated its board of directors by means of a valid charter provision or unanimous shareholder agreement and that has its controlling shareholders manage the corporation, these shareholders (rather than the directors and officers) are the persons to have engaged in the alleged misconduct and that, accordingly, the subject exculpation statute is inapplicable. In such event, the shareholders charged with managing the corporation may be subject to liability for engaging in misconduct in their assumed positions.[52] Whether such misconduct comes under the umbrella of an applicable state's exculpation statute is uncertain. For purposes of our discussion, the point is that shareholders who themselves manage the affairs of a close corporation and commit duty of care and loyalty breaches incur the risk that, even with the inclusion of an exculpation provision in such company's articles of incorporation, they will be subject to monetary liability in an action brought by an aggrieved minority shareholder.[53]

Thus, from a general perspective, the state exculpation statutes may have some impact on diminishing fiduciary duties in the close corporation context, particularly in those states that insulate certain director and officer duty of loyalty breaches from liability. Nonetheless, self-dealing and acts of minority shareholder oppression engaged in by controlling shareholders ordinarily are deliberate. They are usually intended to inflict injury upon the minority while benefitting those shareholders who engage in the misconduct. As a result, irrespective of whether these breaches are committed in one's director, officer, or shareholder capacity, state exculpation statutes often are unlikely to provide significant protection from liability in the close corporation setting.[54]

---

[52] By their terms, the exculpation statutes provide insulation from monetary liability for directors (and, in some states, officers as well) for specified breaches. See sources cited in notes 45–47, 50 supra. Section 7.32(e) of the Model Business Corporation Act, adopted in many states, provides: A unanimous shareholder "agreement authorized by this section that limits the discretion or powers of the board of directors shall relieve the directors of, and impose upon the person or persons in whom such discretion or powers are vested, liability for acts or omissions imposed by law on directors to the extent that the discretion or powers of the directors are limited by the agreement." Whether a court would recognize the applicability of an exculpation provision in the close corporation setting where shareholders assume the functions of directors is unresolved.

[53] Because breaches of the duty of loyalty in the close corporation setting by controlling shareholders often are committed intentionally, there is further reason to conclude that the exculpation statutes are likely to have little impact in this setting. See infra note 54 and accompanying text.

[54] See sources cited supra notes 22–39 and accompanying text.

B. Taking of Corporate Opportunities

As discussed in Chapter 4, pursuant to statute in Delaware and several other states, the fiduciary duty of loyalty with respect to directors and officers taking corporate opportunities may be waived in advance of any such opportunity arising.[55] For example, the Delaware statute authorizes a corporation to "[r]enounce, in its certificate of incorporation or by action of its board of directors, any interest or expectancy of the corporation in, or being offered an opportunity to participate in, specified business opportunities or specified classes or categories of business opportunities that are presented to the corporation or one or more of its officers, directors or stockholders."[56] Hence, a corporate opportunity waiver may be adopted not only in a subject company's certificate of incorporation but also by means of a board of director resolution or a board-promulgated bylaw amendment.[57] Accordingly, under the Delaware statute, specified business opportunities that otherwise would properly belong to the subject corporation lawfully may be taken by its directors, officers, and shareholders.

The Model Business Corporation Act likewise authorizes a corporation to adopt a provision in its articles of incorporation that limits or eliminates the obligation of "a director or any other person" to offer to such corporation "the right to have or participate in any, or one or more classes or categories of business opportunities, before the pursuit or taking of the opportunity by the director or other person...."[58] Notably, this waiver of corporate opportunity

---

[55] See discussion in Chapter 4, notes 21–32 and accompanying text.

[56] Del. Gen. Corp. L. § 122(17).

[57] As set forth in the legislative synopsis of this statute, advance corporate opportunity waivers are subject to the same level of judicial scrutiny that applies "to the renunciation of an interest or expectancy of the corporation in a business opportunity, which will be determined based on the common law of fiduciary duty, including the duty of loyalty." *Senate Bill 363, Original Synopsis, Delaware General Assembly*, 72 Del. Laws 619 (2000). See discussion in Chapter 4, notes 21–32 and accompanying text.

[58] MBCA § 2.02(b)(6). Note that with respect to an officer or a related person of such officer, the statute "(i) also requires approval of the [officer's or related person's] application by the board of directors, subsequent to the effective date of the [business opportunity waiver] provision, by action of qualified directors taken in compliance with the same procedures as set forth in [MBCA] section 8.62, and (ii) may be limited by the authorizing action of the board." The Official Comment elaborates on this approval process as follows:

> Although officers may be included in a [business opportunity waiver] provision under this subsection, the limitation or elimination of corporate opportunity obligations of officers must be addressed by the board of directors in specific cases or by the directors' authorizing provisions in employment agreements or other contractual arrangements with such officers. Accordingly, section 2.02(b)(6) requires that the application of an advance limitation or elimination of the duty to offer a business opportunity to the corporation to any person who is an officer of the corporation or a related person of an officer also

may be all-encompassing, extending to any business opportunity that a corporation otherwise would be entitled to enjoy.[59] As the Official Comment recognizes, the adoption of such a waiver provision "constitutes a curtailment of the duty of loyalty which includes the doctrine of corporate opportunity."[60] With such a waiver provision adopted, a corporate director, officer, shareholder, or any other authorized person can properly seize, for example, a business opportunity within the subject corporation's line of business or with respect to which such corporation has a valid interest or expectancy.[61] In such instances, no monetary damages or any other relief may be awarded against an authorized taker of the corporate opportunity.[62]

This provision has clear application in the close corporation setting. With the inclusion of a corporate opportunity waiver provision in its articles of incorporation to encompass directors, officers, and shareholders, these persons can take any corporate opportunity that otherwise would belong to the corporation.[63] This provision can be invoked by a controlling shareholder or group of shareholders to the minority's detriment—as the subject corporation is deprived of financially benefitting from the opportunity. Although there exist policy considerations supporting the propriety of corporate opportunity waivers,[64] these waiver provisions are incompatible with fiduciary duty principles. Accordingly, corporate opportunity waivers provide a vivid

---

requires action by the board of directors acting through qualified directors. This action must be taken subsequent to the inclusion of the provision in the articles of incorporation and may limit the application....

MBCA § 2.02 Official Comment. *See* discussion in Chapter 4, at note 22.

[59] *Id.* MBCA § 2.02 Official Comment (stating that the applicable waiver provision "may be blanket in nature and apply to any business opportunities").

[60] *Id.* MBCA § 2.02 Official Comment ("If such a [waiver of business opportunity] provision is included in the articles, taking advantage of a business opportunity covered by the provision in the articles without offering it to the corporation will not expose the director or other person to whom it is made applicable either to monetary damages or to equitable or other relief in favor of the corporation upon compliance with the requirements of section 2.02(b)(6)").

[61] *See* sources cited notes 59–60 *supra*.

[62] *Id.* Section 2.02(b)(6) of the Model Business Act, which authorizes the waiver of corporate opportunities, has been adopted in whole or in part by many states. *See, e.g.*, Ala. Code § 10A-2A-2.02(b)(6); Colo. Stat. § 7-102-102(2)(e); Conn. Gen. Stat. § 33-636(b)(6); Idaho Code § 30-29-202(b)(6); La. Stat. § 12:1-202(B)(6); Mont. Code § 35-14-202(2)(f); Neb. Rev. Stat.§ 21-220(b)(6); N.C. Gen. Stat. § 55-2-02(b)(4); Va. Code § 13.1-619(B)(5); Wash. Rev. Code § 23B.02.020(2)(g).

[63] *See* MBCA § 2.02(b)(6) and Official Comment; *supra* notes 58–62 and accompanying text.

[64] These policy considerations include, for example, that a controller who has invested in several different business enterprises having the same or similar line of business (*e.g.*, ownership of apartment buildings) should not ordinarily be obligated to offer any such opportunity to one particular enterprise and that the adoption of strict standards would dissuade financially successful independent directors from serving on corporate boards. *See* discussion in Chapter 4, notes 94–114 and accompanying text.

example in the close corporation setting where directors, officers, and controlling shareholders are not fiduciaries.

C. Unanimous Shareholder Agreements

Many states recognize that shareholders may enter into unanimous written shareholder agreements that modify corporate governance norms.[65] At least in certain states, the extent to which these agreements may lessen or eliminate fiduciary duties that are owed by directors, officers, and shareholders is unresolved. Interpreted expansively, some courts may uphold fiduciary duty waivers in unanimous shareholder agreements unless they are contrary to core principles of corporate governance public policy. For example, a waiver provision exculpating directors, officers, and controllers from monetary liability for engaging in fraud or other intentional misconduct likely would be invalid.[66] The same result follows in partnership law where, irrespective of the lax provisions of a partnership agreement, a partner's intentional misconduct is actionable.[67]

In this context, an ambiguous view is advanced by the Model Business Corporation Act. In an Official Comment, the position is taken that a provision in a unanimous shareholder agreement relieving directors from monetary liability more broadly than that allowed under the Act's exculpation provision "might" be viewed as contrary to public policy and thereby invalid.[68] Delaware law appears to take a different position. As discussed in Chapter 4, waivers of the duty of loyalty pursuant to a unanimous shareholder agreement are permissible under Delaware law provided that such waiver provision (provision) (1) must appear in a stockholder agreement; (2) must be clear and unambiguous; (3) must be narrow and targeted, thereby identifying the specific type of conduct or transaction that otherwise would be regarded as a breach of the duty of loyalty; and (4) must pass close judicial

---

[65] See MBCA § 7.32. Many states have enacted statutes that are identical or similar to Section 7.32. See, e.g., Ala. Code § 10A-30-2.11; Cal. Corp. Code § 300(b); Ga. Code § 14-2-920; Kan. Stat. § 17-7214; Mo. Stat. § 351.800; Nev. Rev. Stat. § 78A.070; Pa. Stat. § 2335; So. Car. § 33-18-200; Wy. Stat. § 17-17-120.

[66] See New Enterprise Associates 14 L.P. v. Rich, 295 A.3d 520, 593 (Del. Ch. 2023) ("To the extent the [waiver provision in a stockholder agreement] seeks to prevent the [stockholders] from asserting a claim for an intentional breach of fiduciary duty, then [such provision] is invalid...."); discussion in Chapter 4, notes 13–20 and accompanying text.

[67] See RUPA § 105(d)(3)(C); Chapter 2, notes 25–27 and accompanying text.

[68] MBCA § 7.32 Official Comment.

scrutiny for reasonableness, with relevant criteria including: "(i) a written contract formed through actual consent, (ii) a clear provision, (iii) knowledgeable stockholders who understood the provision's implications, (iv) the [affected stockholders'] ability to reject the provision, and (v) the presence of bargained-for consideration."[69] As interpreted by a Delaware Chancery Court, a valid waiver provision may foreclose specified breach of loyalty claims where directors, officers, and controllers engage in "self-dealing transactions with reckless disregard for the best interests of the company."[70] Hence, evidently under Delaware law, directors, officers, and controlling shareholders of a close corporation pursuant to a unanimous shareholder agreement that complies with the foregoing criteria may engage in "reckless" (but not "intentional") breaches of the duty of loyalty without being subject to monetary liability to the corporation or their fellow shareholders.[71] Needless to say, exonerating these individuals, who ostensibly are fiduciaries, from being held responsible for their self-dealing and reckless misconduct is irreconcilable with fiduciary duty principles. In addition, a number of state statutes seemingly authorize broad waivers of fiduciary duty in unanimous written shareholder agreements. For example, under Texas law, a unanimous shareholder agreement may govern the relationship among the corporation, the directors, and the shareholders "as if the corporation were a partnership or in a manner that would otherwise be appropriate only among partners and not contrary to public policy."[72] Taking a contractual approach similar to that prevailing in partnership law, the Texas Supreme Court has opined that "the [Texas] Legislature has granted corporate founders and owners broad freedom to dictate for themselves the rights, duties, and procedures that govern their relationship with each other and with the corporation."[73] In Texas and other states following this approach, directors, officers, and shareholders pursuant to expansive terms contained in a unanimous shareholder agreement evidently may engage in such conduct as self-dealing

---

[69] *New Enterprise Associates 14 L.P. v. Rich*, 295 A.3d at 570, *relying on Manti Holdings, LLC v. Authentix Acquisition Co.*, 261 A.3d 1199 (Del. Ch. 2021). Moreover, the applicable waiver provision must not conflict with the corporation's charter or bylaws or the Delaware corporate code. *See* discussion in Chapter 4, notes 12–20 and accompanying text.

[70] *New Enterprise Associates*, 295 A.3d at 593 (stating that a waiver provision in a stockholder agreement may validly foreclose specified breach of duty of loyalty claims where directors and officers engage in "self-dealing transactions with reckless disregard for the best interests of the company").

[71] *See* sources cited notes 69–70 *supra*; discussion in Chapter 4, notes 13–20 and accompanying text.

[72] Tex. Bus. Orgs. Code § 21.101(a)(12).

[73] *Ritchie v. Rupe*, 443 S.W.3d 856, 881 (Tex. 2014).

transactions, the taking of corporate opportunities, and competing with the corporation without the levying of liability—unless such conduct is deemed contrary to public policy.

Hence, based on partnership law waiver standards, it appears that in certain states, pursuant to a provision contained in a unanimous shareholder agreement, only the commission of highly egregious misconduct (such as authorizing a shareholder intentionally to inflict injury to the corporation) would constitute a basis for invalidating such a provision as contrary to public policy.[74] Clearly, in the close corporation setting, fiduciary duties are minimized when expansive provisions are contained in a unanimous shareholder agreement authorizing directors, officers, and controllers to engage in blatant self-dealing conduct without incurring monetary liability to the corporation or its shareholders.

IV. The Status of Fiduciary Duties in Close Corporations

Perhaps more so than in any other area of corporate law, fiduciary duties have meaningful substance in the close corporation setting. Directors, officers, and controlling shareholders in many jurisdictions frequently are held to rigorous duty of loyalty standards when they engage in self-dealing transactions or take actions that deprive a minority shareholder of her reasonable expectations. Yet as this chapter addresses, fiduciary duties in this setting may be diluted and, at times, eliminated pursuant to provisions contained in a subject company's articles of incorporation or in a unanimous shareholder agreement.[75] For the most part, however, many courts apply fairly rigorous standards to assess director, officer, and controller alleged misconduct in this setting.

---

[74] *See* discussion *supra* notes 68–73 and accompanying text; discussion in Chapter 4, notes 33–40 and accompanying text. *See generally* Jill E. Fisch, *Stealth Governance: Shareholder Agreements and Private Ordering*, 99 Wash. U. L. Rev. 913, 913–14 (2021) (asserting that the use of shareholder agreements for corporate governance objectives (which her article calls "stealth governance") "sacrifices critical corporate law values" and, in its stead, there should be adopted "a uniform structural approach to corporate law that would limit private ordering to the charter and bylaws"); Lawrence E. Mitchell, *The Death of Fiduciary Duty in Close Corporations*, 138 U. Pa. L. Rev. 1675, 1675–76 (1990) (positing that "courts, aided in part by legislatures, increasingly have moved away from applying broad prophylactic fiduciary principles to prevent or resolve intra-corporate conflicts [and have] replaced them with remedial approaches which focus on the putative fiduciary's wrongful conduct").

[75] *See* discussion *supra* notes 46–74 and accompanying text; discussion in Chapter 3, notes 55–85 and accompanying text; Chapter 4, notes 12–55 and accompanying text.

This assessment is consistent with the focus of this book. At times, as evidenced by the discussion in this chapter on close corporations, directors and officers owe meaningful fiduciary duties. Nonetheless, as examined throughout this book, when determining director and officer liability for alleged breaches of the duties of care and loyalty, far more often lenient standards are applied that lack fiduciary content. Accordingly, corporate directors and officers are "discretionaries" whose liability exposure varies depending on the underlying facts and circumstances. And, ordinarily, the liability standards that apply in these myriad situations show that, in actuality, corporate directors and officers are not fiduciaries.

8
Rhetoric versus Reality: The Federal Securities Laws

I. Introduction

As a general proposition, the federal securities laws are based on the principle of disclosure rather than substantive fairness.[1] Nonetheless, as addressed in my two recent Oxford University Press books,[2] the federalization of aspects of corporate governance is now well established.[3] This federalization includes, by way of example, the SEC's shareholder proposal rule,[4] prohibiting corporate directors and officers (among others) of engaging in short sales in their company's equity securities,[5] generally precluding publicly traded companies from making loans to their directors and officers,[6] and requiring that shareholders have an advisory say-on-pay vote with respect to executive

---

[1] *See, e.g., Santa Fe Industries, Inc. v. Green*, 430 U.S. 462, 477–79 (1977). *See generally* Ralph C. Ferrara and Marc I. Steinberg, *A Reappraisal of Santa Fe: Rule 10b-5 and the New Federalism*, 129 U. Pa. L. Rev. 263 (1980).

[2] *See* Marc I. Steinberg, *The Federalization of Corporate Governance* (2018); Marc I. Steinberg, *Rethinking Securities Law* (2021) (awarded Winner Best Law Book of 2021 in the United States by American Book Fest).

[3] *See infra* notes 4–8 and accompanying text.

[4] The SEC shareholder proposal rule was adopted in 1942. SEC Rule 14a-8, 17 C.F.R. § 240.14a-8. *See* Securities Exchange Act Release No. 3347 (1942) (adopting release); Steinberg, *Federalization of Corporate Governance*, *supra* note 2, at 157–90 (addressing SEC shareholder proposal rule in the context of federalism); Patrick J. Ryan, *Rule 14a-8, Institutional Shareholder Proposals and Corporate Democracy*, 23 Ga. L. Rev. 97, 98 (1988) ("Since 1942, the Securities and Exchange Commission (SEC) has required corporate management to include shareholder proposals in its solicitation materials when management itself seeks shareholder voting proxies").

[5] *See* § 16(c) of the Securities Exchange Act, 15 U.S.C. § 78p(c) (enacted in 1934) (prohibiting officers, directors, and security holders beneficially owning more than ten percent of a class of equity security from transacting short-sales in their company's equity securities). Short-selling generally may be defined as "the sale of a security that the seller does not own or that the seller owns but does not deliver." Ralph Janvey, *Short-Selling*, 20 Sec. Reg. L.J. 270, 271 (1992). *See generally* Peter J. Romeo and Alan J. Dye, *Section 16 Treatise* (2023).

[6] *See* § 402 of the Sarbanes Oxley Act, *adding*, § 13(k) of the Securities Exchange Act, 15 U.S.C. § 78m(k). Generally, loans to directors and executive officers are permitted by the subject company if they are made on the same market terms as those provided to the general public. This statute is an example of a federal fiduciary provision—namely, the outright prohibition of loans to company insiders in order to prevent unfair dealing.

compensation.[7] This phenomenon of the federalization of corporate governance has been a gradual process, commencing with the enactment of the federal securities laws in the 1930s and becoming more prominent by the Sarbanes Oxley Act of 2002 and the Dodd-Frank Act of 2010.[8]

Nonetheless, the bedrock of the federal securities laws is that of disclosure: the providing by subject companies of accurate and adequate information to allow investors and the securities markets to be duly informed.[9] Although the mandatory disclosure framework has been significantly dismantled by the SEC in the private offering setting (principally pursuant to Rule 506(b) of Regulation D),[10] compulsory disclosure remains rigorous for Exchange Act reporting companies and issuers seeking to go public by means of a Securities Act registered offering.[11] Relying on the overriding disclosure

---

[7] *See* § 951 of the Dodd-Frank Wall Street Reform and Consumer Protection Act of 2010, *adding*, § 14A of the Securities Exchange Act, 15 U.S.C. § 78n-1. The shareholder vote is not binding on the subject company.

[8] For discussion of this process commencing in the early part of the twentieth century and becoming prominent with the enactment of the Sarbanes Oxley and Dodd Frank Acts, *see* Steinberg, *Federalization of Corporate Governance*, note 2 *supra*.

[9] *See, e.g., Ernst & Ernst v. Hochfelder*, 425 U.S. 185, 195 (1976) (opining that the Securities Act of 1933 "was designed to provide investors with full disclosure of material information concerning public offerings of securities" and that the Securities Exchange Act of 1934 "was intended principally to protect against manipulation of stock prices ... and to impose regular reporting requirements on companies whose stock is listed on a national securities exchange").

[10] Provided that the conditions of Regulation D are met, Rule 506(b) permits an issuer to raise an unlimited amount of funds solely from accredited investors without any mandatory disclosure requirements—provided that no advertising or general solicitation takes place. *See* Rules 501–508, 17 C.F.R. § 230.501–508. More funds are raised annually pursuant to Rule 506(b) than are raised in any other type of offering, including registered offerings. During fiscal year 2023, $2.7 trillion of funds were raised pursuant to Rule 506(b). *See* Office of the Advocate for Small Business Capital Formation, *Annual Report Fiscal Year 2023*, at 14. For discussion of Rule 506(b), including the requirements for invoking this exemption, *see* Marc I. Steinberg, *Understanding Securities Law* § 3.07 (8th ed. 2023).

[11] *See, e.g., Basic, Inc. v. Levinson*, 485 U.S. 224, 230 (1988) ("This Court repeatedly has described the fundamental purpose of the [Securities Exchange] Act as implementing a philosophy of full disclosure"); Securities Act Release No. 10825 (2020) (setting forth that the SEC's "disclosure requirements ... are rooted in materiality and facilitate an understanding of a registrant's business, financial condition and prospects through the lens through which management and the board of directors manage and assess the performance of the registrant").

Note, however, that, unlike other developed markets, there is no requirement for a company affirmatively to disclose material information unless such disclosure is mandated by a SEC filing (such as the annual report Form 10-K) or the company has previously spoken on the matter. *See, e.g., J&R Marketing SEP v. General Motors Corp.*, 549 F.3d 484, 496–97 (6th Cir. 2008) ("There is no general duty on the part of a company to provide the public with all material information"). Although the US stock exchange rules generally require affirmative disclosure by listed companies of all material information (*see, e.g.,* New York Stock Exchange, Listed Company Manual §§202.01–06), these rules are rarely enforced and do not provide investors with a private remedy. *See, e.g., Harris v. TD Ameritrade, Inc.*, 805 F.2d 664 (6th Cir. 2015). *Compare* Council Regulation (EU) No. 596/2014 of the European Parliament and the Council of 16 April 2014 on Market Abuse Regulation, at art. 17 (absent the presence of a justifiable business reason, requiring prompt disclosure of all material information to investors and the securities markets); *Market Abuse Regulation—Commentary and Annotated Guide* (Marco Ventoruzzo and Sebastian Mock eds. 2018). In *Rethinking Securities Law*, I recommend

focus of the federal securities laws, the US Supreme Court has largely rejected the application of federal fiduciary principles.[12] Nonetheless, on numerous occasions in both the securities law and other contexts, the Supreme Court has deemed corporate directors and officers to be fiduciaries.[13] As addressed in this chapter, although recognized as fiduciaries to their corporations, both the US Congress and the federal courts have adopted overall lax standards in determining the liability exposure of corporate directors and officers. Accordingly, like state company law, there exists a glaring gap between the rhetoric and standards of liability in the federal securities law setting.

II. US Supreme Court Pronouncements: Directors and Officers Are Fiduciaries

The US Supreme Court's recognition of corporate directors and officers as fiduciaries dates back over a century. Of course, these older cases were decided prior to the enactment of the federal securities laws. Nonetheless, they are important for purposes of this book because they demonstrate the Court's acknowledgment that company directors and officers are fiduciaries. The Supreme Court's early decisions on this subject focused on directors. For example, in a 1862 decision, *Koehler v. The Black River Falls Iron Company*, the Court identified the company's directors as "trustees."[14] Six years later, in *Drury v. Cross*, the Court opined that the conduct of the directors "was very

---

that the United States adopt a continuous disclosure framework similar to the European Union. See Steinberg, *supra* note 2, at 43–48.

[12] See, e.g., *Santa Fe Industries, Inc. v. Green*, 430 U.S. 462 (1977). At times, the Supreme Court has recognized fiduciary principles in the securities law context. See, e.g., *Chiarella v. United States*, 445 U.S. 222 (1980) (recognizing federal fiduciary principles in the insider trading setting); *Securities and Exchange Commission v. Capital Gains Research Bureau, Inc.*, 375 U.S. 180 (1963) (applying fiduciary standards in determining the obligations of investment advisers under the Investment Advisers Act of 1940). Prior to the Supreme Court's decision in *Santa Fe*, a number of federal courts opined that fiduciary standards were within the scope of Section 10(b) of the Securities Exchange Act and Rule 10b-5 thereunder. See, e.g., *McClure v. Borne Chemical Company, Inc.*, 292 F.2d 824, 834 (3d Cir. 1961) (stating that § 10(b) "imposes broad fiduciary duties on management vis-à-vis the corporation and its individual stockholders [and] provides stockholders with a potent weapon for enforcement of many fiduciary duties").

Note that a subject director's or officer's duty of disclosure comes within the duty of care and/or the duty of loyalty, depending on the applicable facts and circumstances, under state law. See e.g., *Malone v. Brincat*, 722 A.2d 5 (Del. 1998).

[13] See US Supreme Court decisions notes 14–26 *infra*.

[14] 67 U.S. 715, 720 (1862) (stating that directors "hold a place of trust, and by accepting the trust are obliged to execute it with fidelity").

discreditable" and that they "were guilty of a plain breach of trust."[15] The term "fiduciary" was used by the Court in a decision seven years after *Drury* where the Court stated in *Twin-Lick Oil Company v. Marbury*: "That a director of a joint-stock corporation occupies one of those fiduciary relations where his dealings with the subject matter of his trust . . . and with the beneficiary or party whose interest is confided to his care, is viewed with jealousy by the courts. . . ."[16] Five years thereafter in *Wardell v. Railroad Company*, the Court opined that a corporate director is a "fiduciary" and occupies a position of "great trust."[17] Hence, in the nineteenth century, the Supreme Court decided several cases in which it categorized corporate directors as fiduciaries.

In *Southern Pac. Co. v. Bogert*, decided in 1919, Justice Brandeis, writing for the Court, noted that corporate officers as well as directors have "a fiduciary relation" to the subject corporation.[18] Similarly, in *Pepper v. Litton*, handed down in 1939, the Court focused on the conduct of a dominant and controlling stockholder, stating that, like a corporate director, he was a fiduciary.[19] In two subsequent decisions, *Manufacturers Trust Co. v. Becker*, decided in 1949, and *Wolf v. Weinstein*, decided in 1963, the Court likewise recognized the fiduciary obligations of corporate directors and officers.[20]

The Supreme Court also has addressed the fiduciary status of corporate directors and officers in the securities law setting. One such case, *Strong v. Repide*, was decided in 1909 prior to the enactment of the federal securities laws.[21] There, the Court adopted the "special facts" doctrine[22] to hold that a corporate director had a legal obligation "to make [adequate] disclosures"

---

[15] 74 U.S. 299, 302 (1868) (also stating that the directors were "[b]ound to execute the responsible duties intrusted to their management, with absolute fidelity to . . . stockholders").

[16] 91 U.S. 587, 588 (1875).

[17] 103 U.S. 651, 658 (1880).

[18] 250 U.S. 483, 487–88 (1919).

[19] 308 U.S. 295, 306 (1939) (also stating: "A director is a fiduciary"), citing *Twin-Lick Oil Company v. Marbury*, 91 U.S. 587, 588 (1875). For a subsequent decision holding that a controlling shareholder is a fiduciary, *see Superintendent of Insurance v. Bankers Life & Casualty Co.*, 404 U.S. 6, 12 (1971) ("The controlling shareholder owes the corporation a fiduciary obligation").

[20] *See Wolf v. Weinstein*, 372 U.S. 633, 644 (1963) (stating that corporate directors and officers have "the obligation of loyal and disinterested service" and that they occupy "fiduciary positions"); *Manufacturers Trust Co. v. Becker*, 338 U.S. 304, 310 (1949) ("This Court has repeatedly insisted on good faith and fair dealing on the part of corporate fiduciaries").

[21] 213 U.S. 419 (1909).

[22] "Under the special facts doctrine, also called the special circumstances doctrine, a corporate insider does not ordinarily have a fiduciary relation to corporate shareholders in stock transactions; nevertheless, in certain circumstances, a fiduciary relationship arises, and the insider must disclose material nonpublic information before trading." Marc I. Steinberg and William K. S. Wang, *Insider Trading* 1040 (3d ed. 2010).

when engaging in a purchase of stock from a current shareholder.[23] After the passage of the federal securities acts, the Court in *Securities and Exchange Commission v. Chenery Corporation* recognized the fiduciary status of officers and directors under one of those Acts, stating: "We completely agree with the Commission that officers and directors who manage a holding company in process of reorganization under the Public Utility Holding Company Act of 1935 occupy positions of trust [and we accordingly] reject a lax view of fiduciary obligations and insist upon their scrupulous observance."[24]

Over four decades ago, the Supreme Court recognized the fiduciary status of corporate directors and officers in the insider trading setting. In *Chiarella v. United States*, the Court held that, absent the presence of a fiduciary relationship or a relationship of trust and confidence, silence is not actionable under Section 10(b) of the Securities Exchange Act.[25] The Court opined that such a relationship exists between corporate directors and officers and the stockholders of the subject company, stating that "a relationship of trust and confidence [is present] between the shareholders of a corporation and those insiders who have obtained confidential information by virtue of their position with that corporation."[26] By the officer or director trading on material nonpublic information, he breaches the duty that is owed. Applying state law principles in the federal securities law setting, the Supreme Court premised insider trading liability on traditional concepts of fiduciary duty.[27]

---

[23] 213 U.S. at 434.

[24] 318 U.S. 80, 85 (1943). Justice Frankfurter, authoring the Court's decision, presented the following inquiries that have been frequently restated: "But to say that a man is a fiduciary only begins analysis; it gives direction to further inquiry. To whom is he a fiduciary? What obligations does he owe as a fiduciary? In what respect has he failed to discharge these obligations? And what are the consequences of his deviation from duty?" *Id*. at 85–86.

[25] 445 U.S. 222, 230 (1980) (interpreting insider trading liability under § 10(b) of the Securities Exchange Act, 15 U.S.C. § 78j(b), and SEC Rule 10b-5 promulgated thereunder, 17 C.F.R. § 240.10b-5).

[26] *Id*. at 228. *See* Donald C. Langevoort, *Insider Trading and the Fiduciary Principle: A Post-Chiarella Restatement*, 70 Cal. L. Rev. 1 (1982).

[27] *See* A. C. Pritchard and Robert B. Thompson, *A History of Securities Law in the Supreme Court* 147 (2023) ("In *Chiarella*, [Justice] Powell [authoring the Court's opinion] focused more on fiduciary principles in the corporate context").

With respect to the federal appellate courts, the status of directors and officers as fiduciaries under the federal securities laws has been recognized in a number of contexts. One such situation is under Section 16(b) of the Securities Exchange Act, 15 U.S.C. § 78o(b), which requires corporate directors and officers (as well as shareholders beneficially owning ten percent or more of a class of the subject issuer's equity securities) to disgorge all profit made from purchases and sales or sales and purchases within a six-month period. *See* Peter Romeo and Alan Dye, *Section 16 Treatise and Reporting Guide* (2023); Marc I. Steinberg and Daryl L. Lansdale, *The Judicial and Regulatory Constriction of Section 16(b) of the Securities Exchange Act of 1934*, 68 Notre Dame L. Rev. 33 (1992). As stated by the Second Circuit, Section 16(b), in practical effect, makes directors and officers "fiduciaries . . . at least to the extent of making all short-swing transactions by such persons in the issuer's stock breaches of trust." *Donoghue v. Bulldog Investors General Partnership*, 696 F.3d 170, 177 (2d Cir. 2012), *citing Adler*

The foregoing US Supreme Court decisions aptly demonstrate that corporate directors and officers are deemed fiduciaries. A number of these decisions involved issues arising under the federal securities laws. With this background in focus, the chapter proceeds to examine the gap between fiduciary status and standards of liability under the federal securities laws. Consistent with the disparity present in state company law, concepts of fiduciary duty lack meaningful substance when ascertaining director and officer liability under various provisions of the federal securities laws.[28]

III. The Federal Securities Laws: The Fiduciary Duty Misnomer

Thus, it is clear that the US Supreme Court on many occasions has opined that corporate directors and officers are fiduciaries. The use of this term suggests that these individuals are held to meaningful standards of responsibility. As the following discussion provides, with regularity, corporate directors and officers benefit from lax standards. In many situations, these fiduciaries only will be held liable if they engage in reckless or intentional misconduct—a culpability standard that is antithetical to fiduciary status.

This section focuses first on director and officer liability under Section 11 of the Securities Act and thereafter under Section 10(b) of the Securities Exchange Act. From this discussion, it becomes clear that the portrayal of corporate directors and officers as fiduciaries is a misnomer.

---

v. Klawans, 267 F.2d 840 (2d Cir. 1959); *Gratz v. Claughton*, 187 F.2d 46 (2d Cir. 1951). *See Donoghue*, 696 F.3d at 177, *quoting Gratz*, 187 F.2d at 49 (Judge Learned Hand) ("Drawing an analogy between trust law and the fiduciary duty created by § 16(b), Judge Hand observed that: 'Nobody is obliged to become a director [or] officer . . ., just as nobody is obliged to become the trustee of a private trust, but as soon as he does so, he accepts whatever are the limitations, obligations, and conditions attached to the position. . .'"). As recently stated in *Avalon Holdings Corp. v. Gentile*, 2023 WL 4744072, at * 3 (S.D.N.Y. 2023), "the issuer's right to the defendant's [director's or officer's] short-swing profits 'derives from breach of a fiduciary duty created by the statute [i.e., § 16(b)],'" *quoting Donoghue*, 187 F.2d at 178. And, most recently, in *Packer v. Raging Capital Management, LLC*, 105 F.4th 46, 55 (2d Cir. 2024), the Second Circuit premised constitutional standing for a shareholder to bring suit under Section 16(b) on the concrete injury caused by "the breach by a statutory insider of a fiduciary duty owed to the issuer not to engage in and profit from short-swing trading of its stock."

[28] In addition to the analysis presented in this book, *see* Marc I. Steinberg, *To Call a Donkey a Racehorse—The Fiduciary Duty Misnomer in Corporate and Securities Law*, 48 J. Corp. L. 1 (2022).

A. Section 11 of the Securities Act: The Semblance of Fiduciary Standards

Section 11 of the Securities Act grants allegedly injured purchasers a private right of action if they acquired securities pursuant to a Securities Act registration statement that contained a material misrepresentation or omission.[29] Among the persons that a plaintiff can sue under Section 11 are the subject company's directors and certain high-level officers.[30] Significantly, these individuals can avert liability by establishing their Section 11 due diligence defense.[31] If a material misrepresentation or omission is contained in the registration statement, the invocation of the due diligence defense frequently is the principal means by which a director or officer seeks to avoid liability.[32] Generally, the due diligence defense places the burden of proof

---

[29] 15 U.S.C. § 77k. To be actionable under Section 11, any such misrepresentation or omission must be material. Generally, in interpreting materiality under this statute, materiality is defined as a fact that, if accurately and sufficiently disclosed, would be important to a reasonable investor in her decision to purchase the subject securities. See *Matrix Initiatives, Inc. v. Siracusano*, 563 U.S. 27, 38 (2011). This standard does not require that the investor would have acted otherwise if he had received accurate and sufficient information. See *TSC Industries, Inc. v. Northway, Inc.*, 426 U.S. 438, 446 (1976) (stating that this standard "does not require proof of a substantial likelihood that [accurate] disclosure of the [misstated or] omitted fact would have caused the reasonable investor to change his [mind]"). This seemingly expansive terminology is narrowed by also requiring that "there must be a substantial likelihood that [such accurate] disclosure of the [applicable] fact would have been viewed by the reasonable investor as having significantly altered the total mix of information made available." *Id*. Moreover, with respect to contingent or uncertain events, courts employ the probability-magnitude test: whether a fact is material depends "at any given time upon a balancing of both the indicated probability that the event will occur and the anticipated magnitude of the event in light of the totality of the company activity." *Basic, Inc. v. Levinson*, 485 U.S. 224, 238 (1988), quoting *Securities and Exchange Commission v. Texas Gulf Sulphur Co.*, 401 F.2d 833, 849 (2d Cir. 1968) (en banc). In addition, in ascertaining the presence of materiality, both qualitative and quantitative considerations are pertinent. Hence, depending on the underlying circumstances, even a small quantitative misstatement (such as a company overstating its earnings by two percent) may be deemed material if such misstatement has substantial impact (such as the company missing analysts' projections). See *Ganino v. Citizens Utilities Co.*, 228 F.3d 154, 163 (2d Cir. 2000); SEC Staff Accounting Bulletin (SAB) 99, 64 Fed. Reg. 45,150 (1999).

To add to this complexity is the increasing length of SEC prospectuses and periodic filings, resulting in information overload. See James A. Deeken, *More Is Better? Concerns on the Growing Amount of Securities Disclosure in Offering Documents and Public Filings*, 50 Sec. Reg. L.J. 107 (2022); Andrew J. Jennings, *Disclosure Procedure*, 82 Md. L. Rev. 920 (2023); Troy A. Paredes, *Blinded by the Light: Information Overload and Its Consequences for Securities Regulation*, 81 Wash. U. L.Q. 417 (2003).

[30] Officers subject to suit under Section 11 include the corporation's chief executive officer, controller, and chief financial officer. These individuals come within Section 11's reach because they must sign the registration statement, and, hence, are signatories. See § 6(a) of the Securities Act, 15 U.S.C. § 77f(a). Other persons subject to Section 11 liability exposure are the issuer, the company's directors, the underwriters, and the experts (including, the auditor by certifying the corporation's financial statements). See § 11(a), 15 U.S.C. § 77k(a).

[31] § 11(b) of the Securities Act, 15 U.S.C. § 77k(b).

[32] The statute does not require the conducting of due diligence. However, if the registration statement contains a material misstatement or omission, the exercise of adequate due diligence by a

on the defendant fiduciary to prove that she had conducted a reasonable investigation and that, after such investigation, had no reasonable ground to believe and did not believe that the registration statement contained a material misrepresentation or omission.[33] In determining whether a director or officer conducted a reasonable investigation and had a reasonable belief, Section 11 applies a rigorous standard: namely, that "required of a prudent man in the management of his own property."[34] Derived from trust law, this standard was embraced by the Massachusetts high court almost 200 years ago. It mandates that a trustee act "faithfully and exercise a sound discretion ... observ[ing] how men of prudence, discretion, and intelligence manage their own affairs, not in regard to speculation but in regard to the permanent disposition of their funds, considering the probable income, as well as the probable safety of the capital to be invested."[35]

In the seminal case of *Escott v. Bar Chris Construction Corp.*, this fiduciary or fiduciary-like standard was faithfully applied.[36] Decided over fifty years ago, that decision's interpretation of Section 11 has been instrumental in the development of federal case law, SEC regulatory oversight, and customary

---

defendant is a key defense. As a consequence, due diligence may be viewed as a practical necessity. Note, however, that the issuer has no due diligence defense.

The other key Section 11 defense is the loss causation defense—that the material misstatement or omission in the registration statement did not cause the plaintiffs' financial loss. *See* § 11(e) of the Securities Act, 15 U.S.C. § 77k(e); *Akerman v. Oryx Communications, Inc.*, [1984 Transfer Binder] Fed. Sec. L. Rep. (CCH) ¶ 91,680 (S.D.N.Y. 1984), *aff'd*, 810 F.2d 336 (2d Cir. 1987). The statute of limitations for Section 11 claims is one year after the plaintiff discovered or should have discovered the facts constituting the violation and, in no event, more than three years after the securities were offered for sale. *See* § 13 of the Securities Act, 15 U.S.C. § 77m; *Calpers v. ANZ Securities, Inc.*, 137 S. Ct. 2042 (2017).

[33] *See* § 11(b)(3) of the Securities Act, 15 U.S.C. § 77k(b)(3). To establish a meritorious due diligence defense, reasonable investigation is required with respect to the contents of the registration statement—except for those statements made by experts. However, with respect to statements made by experts (the "expertise" portion), nonexperts are not required to make a reasonable investigation; rather such persons (including defendant directors and officers) must prove that they reasonably believed that the statements made in the expertise portion of the registration statement were accurate. In regard to the expertise portion of the registration statement, a defendant expert who made the allegedly deficient statement must prove that it conducted a reasonable investigation and, after such investigation, reasonably believed that the statement made by such expert was accurate.

[34] *See* § 11(c) of the Securities Act, 15 U.S.C. § 77k(c) (stating that, in determining whether a defendant has satisfied the due diligence defense, "what constitutes reasonable investigation and reasonable ground for belief, the standard of reasonableness shall be that required of a prudent man in the management of his own property").

[35] *Harvard Coll. v. Amory*, 26 Mass. (9 Pick.) 446, 461 (1830). *See* Mayo Adams Shattuck, *The Development of the Prudent Man Rule for Fiduciary Investment in the United States in the Twentieth Century*, 12 Ohio St. L.J. 491 (1951). In this regard, Section 11's legislative history refers to this principle. *See* H.R. Rep. No. 73-1838, at 28, 41 (1934); James M. Landis, *The Legislative History of the Securities Act of 1933*, 28 Geo. Wash. L. Rev. 29, 47–48 (1959).

[36] 283 F. Supp. 643 (S.D.N.Y. 1968).

practice.[37] In that case, Judge McLean addressed the Section 11 liability exposure of all the defendants, including the issuer, directors, officers, underwriters, and auditors.[38] With respect to the inside directors and the officers who did not serve as directors, the court employed a rigorous due diligence standard.[39] Indeed, the court's analysis arguably treated these persons as guarantors in regard to the veracity of the registration statement.[40] But as Ernest Folk astutely commented shortly after this decision, *Bar Chris* "does not deny the [due diligence] defense [for these persons], but recognizes the obvious difficulty of establishing it."[41] This approach continues to be followed by the federal courts.[42]

Accordingly, it may be posited that with respect to inside directors and officers who are signatories of the registration statement (irrespective of whether they are directors), a fiduciary duty-like standard applies for determining whether they have satisfied their due diligence defense.[43] As will be shortly addressed, however, this standard has been significantly weakened due to US Supreme Court and federal statutory developments.[44]

In regard to outside directors, the due diligence defense standard is relaxed. An outside (or independent) director may be defined to include an individual who is not an immediate family member of an inside director, does not currently have (or in the past had) an employment relationship (such as being an officer) with the company, and does not have a significant business relationship with the company (such as being a partner of an investment

---

[37] See discussion *infra* notes 38–61 and accompanying text.
[38] 283 F. Supp. at 683–703. Note that the issuer has no due diligence defense.
[39] *Id.* at 684–92.
[40] Congress, however, rejected a guarantor standard. See H.R. Rep. No. 85, 73d Cong. 1st Sess. 5 (1933); Landis, *supra* note 35, at 48.
[41] Ernest L. Folk, III, *Civil Liabilities Under the Federal Securities Acts: The BarChris Case*, 55 Va. L. Rev. 1, 22 (1969).
[42] *See, e.g., In re Software Toolworks, Inc. Securities Litigation*, 38 F.3d 1078 (9th Cir. 1994); *In re Livent, Inc. Noteholders Securities Litigation*, 355 F. Supp. 2d 722 (S.D.N.Y. 2005); *In re Worldcom, Inc. Securities Litigation*, 346 F. Supp. 2d 628 (S.D.N.Y. 2004).
[43] *See In re Livent, Inc. Noteholders Securities Litigation*, 355 F. Supp. 2d 722, 733 (S.D.N.Y. 2005) (stating that the defendants' due diligence burden with respect to the nonexpertise portion of the registration statement "is a heavy one"); *In re Worldcom, Inc. Securities Litigation*, 2005 WL 638268, at *9 (S.D.N.Y. 2005) (reviewing case law with respect to heavy burden placed upon inside directors to show that they exercised due diligence); *Feit v. Leasco Data Processing Equipment Corp.*, 322 F. Supp. 544, 578 (E.D.N.Y. 1971) (stating that the due diligence defense for inside directors is so stringent that "liability will lie in practically all cases of misrepresentation"); William K. Sjostrom Jr., *The Due Diligence Defense Under Section 11 of the Securities Act of 1933*, 44 Brandeis L.J. 549, 578 (2006) (stating that, while the due diligence defense may be invoked, "it will be a rare case that an inside director or management defendant will meet it with respect to defects in the non-expertized portions of a registration statement").
[44] See discussion *infra* notes 65–84 and accompanying text.

banking firm that serves as the lead underwriter in the subject company's financings).[45] The rationale underlying this more relaxed standard is that outside directors do not have the same degree of familiarity with the company as compared to executive officers, may lack access to receiving material information as they may largely depend on executive management to provide such information, and that an unduly strict liability standard would dissuade qualified individuals from serving as outside directors.[46] Nonetheless, in order to satisfy their due diligence defense, outside directors must undertake affirmative measures in an effort to independently verify the accuracy and sufficiency of the information contained in a registration statement. As stated by the *Worldcom* court, "directors are not excused from performing a meaningful due diligence investigation due to the involvement of professionals, such as underwriters and auditors."[47] Taking prevailing case law and practitioner commentary into account, an outside director who takes the following actions—and after taking these actions reasonably believes that the registration statement does not contain a material misrepresentation or omission—may well meet her due diligence defense. Depending on the facts and circumstances of the particular registered offering,[48] an outside director generally should undertake the following measures for such securities offerings as initial public offerings (IPOs), important primary offerings, and offerings in connection with a major acquisition or merger: "attend board of director meetings regarding the offering and the registration statement; review with due care a draft (or drafts) of the registration statement at a board of director meeting or meetings (probing relevant corporate personnel, counsel, and

---

[45] This definition generally is consistent with the approach adopted by the New York Stock Exchange and the Nasdaq Stock Exchange. *See* NYSE Manual § 303A.02; Nasdaq, Inc. Stock Market Rule § 5605. Unfortunately, the SEC has declined to adopt rules defining the term independent director or outside director. *See In re Worldcom, Inc. Securities Litigation*, 2005 WL 638268, at *10 (S.D.N.Y. 2005) ("The lack of a uniform understanding of who is an outside director within the case law is exacerbated by the SEC's failure to promulgate its own definition of inside and outside directors for purposes of Section 11, despite Congress's explicit instruction within the PSLRA [Private Securities Litigation Reform Act] that it define the term 'outside director'").

[46] *See, e.g., In re Worldcom*, 2005 WL 638268, at * 9; *Goldstein v. Alodex Corp.*, 409 F. Supp. 1201, 1203 n. 1 (E.D. Pa. 1976); *Feit v. Leasco Data Processing Equipment Corp.*, 332 F. Supp. 544, 577–78 (E.D.N.Y. 1972). *See also* 1 Thomas Lee Hazen, *Treatise on the Law of Securities Regulation* § 7.4[2][A] (8th ed. 2023) (stating that *BarChris* recognized "a sliding scale of liability [and drew] a distinction between insiders and outsiders").

[47] 2005 WL 638268, at * 6.

[48] In view of the different facts and circumstances of a subject registered offering, the type of person, and the nature of such person's relationship with the issuer, the SEC adopted Rule 176, 17 C.F.R. § 230.176. The rule lists several factors that should be considered as "circumstances affecting the determination of what constitutes reasonable investigation and reasonable grounds for belief under Section 11 of the Securities Act." Securities Act Release No. 6335 (1981) (adopting release).

other appropriate sources on the factual contents and representations made therein); review with due care the Exchange Act filed documents that are incorporated by reference into the registration statement; with the aid of competent advisers, assess the abilities of management as well as the company's reputation; ask questions and follow up if necessary."[49] Provided that an outside director undertakes the preceding measures and absent circumstances that otherwise should alert such director of a material disclosure deficiency, it may be posited that his actions are compliant with the fiduciary-like "prudent man" standard set forth in Section 11.[50] Nonetheless, two important yet implicit deficiencies exist that outside directors have the wherewithal to remedy yet decline to do so. One of the greatest obstacles for outside directors is their access to internal company information which normally is within the control of management. The consequence is that all too frequently corporate executives embargo adverse material information that they decline to share with the company's board of directors.[51] Although aware of this potential risk and the detrimental consequences that may ensue to the corporation and to themselves personally if such risk should eventuate,[52] outside directors have refused to implement two readily available measures that would ameliorate the corporation's and their individual liability exposure.

The first measure is to appoint an outside director to serve as chair of the company's board of directors. As I stated in my award-winning Oxford University Press book *Rethinking Securities Law*, the benefits are clear: "The CEO no longer is monitoring herself but is subject to greater independent

---

[49] Marc I. Steinberg, *Understanding Securities Law* 291 (8th ed. 2023). *See* American Bar Association, Corporate Laws Committee, *Corporate Director's Guidebook* 110 (7th ed. 2020):

> Although all registration statements should be prepared with appropriate care, certain registered offerings may have a higher potential for liability, such as an initial public offering, a follow-on equity offering, a large acquisition using the corporation's equity, or a financing or reorganization of a public corporation that has experienced problems. Accordingly, a board meeting or meetings with counsel, accountants, and management present at which there is discussion and analysis of the disclosures in the registration statement should precede the filing of registration statements for such offerings.

See Weinberger v. Jackson, 1990 U.S. Dist. LEXIS 18394 (N.D. Cal. 1990) (applying numerous criteria in holding that outside director met his § 11 due diligence defense).

[50] The prudent man standard is set forth in Section 11(c) of the Securities Act, 15 U.S.C. § 77k(c).

[51] With respect to the composition and tasks of a publicly held company's audit committee comprised entirely of independent directors, *see* § 301 of the Sarbanes Oxley Act; SEC Rule 10A-3, 17 C.F.R. § 240.10A-3; *In the Matter of Self-Regulatory Organizations*, Securities Exchange Act Release No. 48745 (2003).

[52] *See* cases cited *supra* notes 43–46. With respect to underwriter liability under Section 11, the court in *In re Worldcom, Inc. Securities Litigation*, 348 F. Supp. 2d 628, 670 (S.D.N.Y. 2004), observed that "academics and practitioners alike have asserted that the current regime for underwriter liability under Section 11 no longer makes sense."

oversight; the distinct prospect of CEO dominance is lessened with respect to his role with the board and with other internal as well as outside constituents; control of the agenda for board of director meetings is better allocated between the CEO and board chair; the flow of internal corporate information to the outside directors, including adverse developments, is improved; significant decisions are more likely to be subject to greater scrutiny and, if deemed appropriate, challenged; and, even with the presence of committees comprised solely of independent directors (such as the audit, compensation, and nominating/corporate governance committees), independent director empowerment is reasonably likely to be enhanced."[53] In view that, with certain exceptions, a publicly held company must have a majority of independent directors on its board of directors as a condition of having its securities listed on a national exchange,[54] appointing an independent chair should not ordinarily pose an onerous burden.[55] Yet as of November 2023, only thirty-seven percent of S&P 500 companies have opted for independent board chairs.[56] By failing to implement this readily available measure that improves corporate governance processes, including enhancing the flow of information from executive management to the board of directors, a legitimate question arises whether this abstention is compliant with a director's fiduciary-like prudent man obligation under Section 11.

The second measure is the refusal by independent directors to cause their respective board of directors to form a corporate disclosure committee comprised solely of independent directors. Currently, disclosure committees of publicly held corporations consist of corporate officers and other high-level internal personnel.[57] Although beneficial to some degree, the current composition of disclosure committees signifies that outside directors unduly rely on inside personnel and thereby may fail to adequately assess the

---

[53] Marc I. Steinberg, *Rethinking Securities Law* 141 (2021) (awarded winner best law book for 2021 in the United States by American Book Fest).

[54] *See* NYSE Listed Company Manual § 303A.01; Nasdaq, Inc. Stock Market Rules § 5605(b).

[55] It may be challenging for a number of smaller publicly held companies to recruit a qualified outside director who is willing to serve as chair of the board of directors. Serving as board chair entails greater responsibility and liability exposure than serving solely as an outside (or independent) director. If this challenge in fact proves unduly problematic, then a possible alternative is to provide an exception for specified smaller Exchange Act reporting companies.

[56] *See* The Conference Board, *Board Leadership and Structure* (Nov. 21, 2023). Independent board chairs appear to be somewhat more prevalent for companies outside the S&P 500. *See* Matteo Tonello, *Corporate Board Practices in the Russell 3000, S&P 500, and S&P Mid-Cap 400*, Harv. Law School Forum on Corp. Gov. (Nov. 6, 2021) (stating that "44.5 percent of Russell 3000 companies and 46.1 percent of S&P Mid-Cap 400 companies have an independent board chair").

[57] *See* KPMG, *Transparency and Management Disclosure Committee* (2018).

accuracy and sufficiency of the subject company's SEC filings. Nearly thirty years ago, the SEC's Advisory Committee on the Capital Formation and Regulatory Processes recognized this shortcoming and recommended the formation by publicly held companies of a disclosure committee comprised entirely of independent directors.[58] The effective operation of such a committee would enable the independent directors to exert greater input with respect to the disclosure function and, in the registered offering context, provide these directors with greater assurance that the disclosures contained in the registration statement are legally compliant. As stated by the SEC Advisory Committee, the effective formation by a subject company of a disclosure committee of independent directors would provide greater focus "for due diligence in the context of primary offerings by issuers, thereby ensuring greater involvement by outside directors as one set of monitors."[59]

Accordingly, by being informed of disclosure matters on a continuous basis, the independent directors serving on the disclosure committee would be in a significantly better position to undertake meaningful due diligence. In addition, by meeting with the other independent directors who do not serve on this committee (along with the company's or committee's legal counsel and other appropriate personnel), a more meaningful analysis and verification of the applicable disclosures are more likely to occur.[60] The implementation of this approach would be particularly beneficial in the integrated disclosure and shelf registration settings as it would significantly facilitate the conducting of ongoing due diligence. Accordingly, "the functioning of a sound disclosure committee [comprised entirely of independent directors] should instill greater discipline in the disclosure process, enhance the quality of disclosures made, and (with respect to conducting a reasonable investigation under case law and Rule 176) serve as a valuable source for outside directors to satisfy their due diligence defense."[61]

---

[58] See Report of the Advisory Committee on the Capital Formation and Regulatory Processes, Securities and Exchange Commission, [1996–1997 Transfer Binder] Fed. Sec. L. Rep. (CCH) ¶ 85,834, at 88,427–28 (1996).

[59] Id. at 88,428.

[60] It may be posited that the preferred approach is that the disclosure committee retain its own independent legal counsel. The approach recommended is similar for that of the audit committee which has the authority to have its own legal counsel. See Steinberg, supra note 53, at 113.

[61] Id. at 114. The existence of a disclosure committee should be particularly beneficial in shelf registered offerings. In such offerings, by means of the integrated disclosure framework, Exchange Act reports are incorporated by reference into a Securities Act registration statement. Shelf registration enables qualified companies to raise funds in an expedited manner while benefitting from significant cost savings due to reduced accounting, legal, and other fees. These offerings, particularly in the case of automatic shelf registration, often are completed in a matter of hours. See SEC Rules 415, 430B, 17 C.F.R. §§ 230.415, .430B; Securities Act Release No. 8591 (2005). As a consequence, in order to satisfy

Hence, although recommended by an SEC advisory committee decades ago, companies have declined to form disclosure committees consisting of independent directors. As outside (or independent) directors today comprise a majority of an exchange listed company's board of directors, these individuals clearly have the authority and leverage to require their respective company to establish such a disclosure committee. Their failure to do so is questionable in light of the meaningful benefits that would be provided by a diligent and effective disclosure committee composed solely of outside directors. In the face of this refusal, the question is asked whether a prudent man or woman in the management of his or her own property would decline to form such a disclosure committee.[62]

This section now turns to two other developments that have diluted the prudent man standard under Section 11: (1) statements of belief as interpreted by the US Supreme Court's decision in *Omnicare*;[63] and (2) forward-looking statements as enacted pursuant to the Private Securities Litigation Reform Act of 1995 (PSLRA).[64]

1. Statements of Belief: The Slighting of Section 11's Prudent Man Standard

The US Supreme Court and Congress have penetrated substantial gaps in the prudent man or woman standard under Section 11. One such gap was effected by the Supreme Court in the *Omnicare* decision.[65] Frequently, in SEC filed documents and other company statements (such as press releases), the subject corporation accompanies the disclosure made with the language "in our opinion" or "we believe." For example, in a registration statement for an offering of common stock, assume that the statement is made that "we believe that the corporation is in compliance with all environmental laws and

---

Section 11's due diligence defense, outside directors (and other Section 11 potential defendants, such as underwriters) must conduct ongoing due diligence. The formation and effective functioning of an independent disclosure committee would substantially enhance this process and serve as a valuable source for outside directors to raise as a key component of their due diligence defense.

[62] *See* Steinberg, *supra* note 53, at 114 (stating that an effective independent disclosure committee "would enable outside directors to perform ongoing due diligence in a proactive manner").

[63] *Omnicare, Inc. v. Laborers District Council Construction Industry Pension Fund*, 135 S. Ct. 1318 (2015), discussed *infra* notes 65–76 and accompanying text.

[64] Pub. L. No. 104-67, 109 Stat. 737 (1995). *See* discussion *infra* notes 77–84 and accompanying text. For a discussion of other topical Section 11 issues, *see* Marc I. Steinberg and Brent A. Kirby, *The Assault on Section 11 of the Securities Act: A Study in Judicial Activism*, 63 Rutgers L. Rev. 1 (2010).

[65] *Omnicare, Inc. v. Laborers District Council Construction Industry Pension Fund*, 135 S. Ct. 1318 (2015).

regulations." Assume that subsequently the US Environmental Protection Agency (EPA) brings a successful enforcement action against the company for serious violations of the federal environmental laws, with hefty money penalties imposed. Hence, in fact, the company was not compliant with the environmental laws. In *Omnicare*, the question presented was under what circumstances are "we believe" statements actionable under Section 11.

In its decision, the Court distinguished between statements of fact and statements of belief or opinion. Differentiating statements of fact from statements of belief or opinion, the Court opined that a belief or opinion is not certain and not premised on grounds sufficient for "complete demonstration."[66] By contrast, a fact is an actual or existing happening.[67] Section 11, the Court reasoned, makes actionable the latter—a materially false or misleading statement of fact.[68]

Applying this rationale, among other holdings, the Court ruled that a statement of belief or opinion may be actionable when the person making such statement (for example, a company in its registration statement) does not hold the stated belief or opinion and the statement in actuality is false.[69] Phrased similarly, a statement of belief or opinion is subject to Section 11 liability exposure when "the speaker did not hold the belief [or opinion] she professed and the belief [or opinion] is objectively untrue."[70] The consequence is that in Section 11 cases premised on misrepresentation, a plaintiff must prove that the defendant directors and officers knew that the statement of belief or opinion was false. In other words, proof of knowing misconduct must be established.[71]

The Supreme Court's rationale is misplaced as it obliterates the prudent man standard. Consistent with this standard, the Court should have held

---

[66] *Id.* at 1325, *quoting and citing Oxford English Dictionary* (1933) and *Webster's New International Dictionary* (1927).
[67] 135 S. Ct. at 1325, *quoting and citing Webster's New International Dictionary* (1927).
[68] 135 S. Ct. at 1326.
[69] *Id.* In *Omnicare*, the Supreme Court also held:

[W]hen a plaintiff relies on a theory that a statement of fact contained within an opinion statement is materially misleading, the plaintiff must allege that "the supporting fact [the issuer] supplied [is] untrue." [Moreover,] when a plaintiff relies on a theory of omission, the plaintiff must allege "facts going to the basis for the issuer's opinion ... whose omission makes the opinion statement at issue misleading to a reasonable person reading the statement fairly and in context."

City of Dearborn Heights v. Align Technology, Inc., 856 F.3d 605, 616 (9th Cir. 2017), *quoting Omnicare*, 135 S. Ct. at 1327, 1332.
[70] 856 F.3d at 616, *quoting* 135 S. Ct. at 1327.
[71] *See* 135 S. Ct. at 1325–26.

that a statement of belief or opinion must have a reasonable basis. The reasonable basis approach has been adopted by the SEC for forward-looking statements made in a registration statement by a company undertaking its initial public offering (IPO).[72] For example, a company conducting its IPO may make projections of future earnings under SEC Rule 175 so long as such projections are made with a reasonable basis.[73] The type of information coming within Rule 175 is identical or similar to statements of belief or opinion—constituting "soft" information that is not capable of factual verification.[74] Thus, the Court's decision in *Omnicare* contravenes Section 11's prudent man standard.

For our purposes here, the *Omnicare* decision reflects an attitude that belies the status of corporate directors and officers as fiduciaries. The prudent man standard recognizes the fiduciary responsibilities of corporate directors and officers with respect to the disclosures contained in a registration statement. Yet the Supreme Court swept away these fiduciary obligations for statements of belief or opinion. After *Omnicare*, directors and officers are absolved of Section 11 liability if the registration statement for which they are responsible contains materially false statements of belief or opinion so long as such statements are made with "mere" carelessness or gross negligence rather than with knowledge of the falsity.[75] While this approach arguably makes sound public policy,[76] it is inconsistent with the fiduciary-like standards to which Section 11 defendants must adhere to in order to establish

---

[72] *See* Rule 175, 17 C.F.R. § 230.175. Under Rule 175, "a safe harbor [is provided] from the applicable liability provisions of the federal securities laws for statements [made by or on behalf of an issuer] relating to or containing: (1) projections of reserves, income (loss), earnings (loss) per share or other financial items, such as capital expenditures, dividends or capital structure, (2) management plans and objectives for future company operations, and (3) future economic performance included in management's statement." Securities Act Release No. 6084 (1979). The plaintiff has the burden to prove that such forward-looking statement was made lacking good faith or a reasonable basis. Moreover, Rule 175 is available to enterprises conducting Regulation A offerings. *See* Rule 175(a), (b) (1)(i).

[73] *See* Rule 175(b)(1)(i), (c).

[74] Generally, soft information relates to forward-looking statements, including forecasts and projections. Viewed broadly, soft information encompasses any statement that cannot be factually verified, including "statements of subjective analysis or extrapolation, such as opinions, motives and intentions...." *In re Craftmatic Securities Litigation*, 890 F.2d 628, 642 (3d Cir. 1989).

[75] *See* 135 S. Ct. at 1327–32; *In re Sanofi Securities Litigation*, 816 F.3d 199, 209 (2d Cir. 2016).

[76] Arguably, holding Section 11 defendants, including directors and officers, liable for alleged negligent expressions of belief or opinion would exacerbate the specter of litigation exposing these persons to substantial monetary damages and would deter the disclosure of such soft information to investors and the securities markets. *See generally* James D. Cox, *"We're Cool" Statements After Omnicare: Securities Fraud Suits for Failure to Comply with the Law*, 68 SMU L. Rev. 715 (2015). Note that the federal courts have applied *Omnicare* to other causes of action, including Section 10(b) claims. *See, e.g., City of Dearborn Heights v. Align Technology, Inc.*, 85 F.3d 605 (9th Cir. 2017).

their due diligence defense. Thus, *Omnicare* significantly dilutes Section 11's prudent man standard, thereby diverging from the principle that officers and directors owe fiduciary duties to the subject corporation and its shareholders in this setting. In its stead is a duty to refrain from committing fraud—an approach that clearly does not resemble the prudent man standard.

A similar dilution of Section 11's prudent man standard is evidenced by the expansive safe harbor enacted by Congress with respect to forward-looking statements made by Exchange Act reporting companies in their Securities Act registration statements. The discussion on this broad statutory protection provided to corporate directors and officers follows.

2. Forward-Looking Statements: Abandoning the Prudent Man Standard
Pursuant to the Private Securities Litigation Reform Act (PSLRA), Congress created an expansive safe harbor for forward-looking statements made by Exchange Act reporting companies.[77] This safe harbor not only applies to SEC periodic reports (such as the annual report on Form 10-K); it also encompasses Securities Act registration statements by these companies.[78] As applied to Section 11, the PSLRA's safe harbor insulates directors and officers from liability.[79]

The safe harbor is broad. First, assume that a forward-looking statement is made in a registration statement without adequate cautionary language being provided. In this situation, the safe harbor protects such forward-looking statement unless a plaintiff proves that it was made by the subject defendant(s) with actual knowledge of the falsity. "Mere recklessness" is insufficient to impose liability.[80] Second, assume that a forward-looking statement is made in a registration statement and is "accompanied by meaningful cautionary language identifying important factors that could cause actual results to differ materially from those projected in the statement."[81] In this

---

[77] *See* § 27A of the Securities Act, 15 U.S.C. § 77z-2. Likewise, the Securities Exchange Act has this safe harbor for forward looking statements. *See* § 21E of the Exchange Act, 15 U.S.C. § 78u-5. Certain exceptions apply. *See, e.g.,* § 27A(b) of the Securities Act.

[78] *See* sources cited note 77 *supra*. The safe harbor also encompasses oral forward-looking statements if the conditions of the applicable statute are met. *See, e.g.,* § 27A(c)(2) of the Securities Act.

[79] *See* § 27A(a), (c) of the Securities Act.

[80] *Id.* § 27A(c)(1)(B). *See Asher v. Baxter International, Inc.*, 377 F.3d 727 (7th Cir. 2004).

[81] Joint Explanatory Statement of the Conference Committee, Private Securities Litigation Reform Act of 1995 (stating that under this prong of the safe harbor, "boilerplate warnings will not suffice as meaningful cautionary statements" and that the "cautionary statements must convey substantive information about factors that realistically could cause results to differ materially from those projected in the forward-looking statement" although "[f]ailure to include the particular factor that ultimately causes the forward-looking statement not to come true will not mean that the statement is not protected by the safe harbor"). *See Harris v. Ivax Corporation*, 182 F.3d 799 (11th Cir. 1999).

situation, the forward-looking statement is not actionable under Section 11 as a matter of law. The officer's or director's state of mind, even if she acted fraudulently, is irrelevant.[82]

Clearly, this safe harbor cannot be reconciled with the prudent man standard contained in Section 11. Although the PSLRA retains the prudent man standard in Section 11, the Act's broad safe harbor eviscerates this standard in the context of forward-looking statements. Indeed, under the PSLRA, with no cautionary disclosure provided, directors and officers can recklessly make rosy projections of future company performance without incurring Section 11 liability. And, if meaningful cautionary language is provided, then corporate miscreants, including rogue directors and officers, can knowingly engage in outright lies yet avoid private liability under the federal securities laws, including under Section 11.[83]

A prudent person does not act in this manner. The PSLRA's expansive safe harbor makes a mockery of fiduciary principles in the Section 11 setting. To say that directors and officers act as prudent persons in their quest to perform a reasonable investigation and have a reasonable belief by engaging in reckless and even intentional misconduct with respect to forward-looking statements in their company's registration statement is nonsensical. Nonetheless, that is the law as illogical as it currently stands.[84]

3. Would a Prudent Man or Woman Act in This Manner?

From the foregoing discussion, the prudent man standard is a core principle of Section 11. The fiduciary or fiduciary-like principle contained in the statute has been applied for over fifty years.[85] Yet this standard has been significantly eroded by means of inaction and the adoption of lenient liability parameters. It thus may be asked whether a prudent man or woman would:

---

[82] See § 27A(c)(1)(A)(i) of the Securities Act; *Wochos v. Tesla, Inc.*, 985 F.3d 1180 (9th Cir. 2021).

[83] Note that the PSLRA does not preclude the SEC and the Department of Justice from instituting prosecutorial actions. The Act applies solely to private litigants. *See* Joint Explanatory Statement, note 81 *supra* ("This safe harbor applies only to private actions and not to SEC enforcement actions"). This safe harbor for forward-looking statements also applies to Securities Exchange Act claims, including Section 10(b) claims. *See infra* notes 115–116 and accompanying text.

[84] Relying on the US Supreme Court's decision in *Omnicare*, it may be posited that forward-looking statements constitute statements of belief or opinion and are not statements of fact. Therefore, based on this rationale, a forward-looking statement that is set forth as a statement of belief or opinion should be actionable only if the subject defendant knew that such statement was untrue. *See* discussion *supra* notes 65–76 and accompanying text. Even assuming the validity of this position, the focus of this chapter and book is that, although identified as fiduciaries, the lenient liability standards that frequently apply to directors and officers belie fiduciary status.

[85] *See* sources cited notes 36–43 *supra*.

(1) As an outside director, recognizing that he or she is largely dependent on executive management for receiving important company-related information and that executive management may have reason to exaggerate positive developments while minimizing adverse events, decline to appoint an independent director as chair of the board of directors?[86]

(2) As an outside director, decline to create an independent disclosure committee comprised entirely of independent directors when the formation of such a committee was recommended by a prestigious SEC advisory committee[87]—with the clear upsides of enhancing access to internal company information, conducting continuous due diligence, and providing significantly greater protection from Section 11 liability exposure?[88]

(3) As a director or a member of executive management, approve the inclusion of "we believe" language in the company's registration statement if such person is ignorant whether there exists a sound basis for such statement's accuracy?[89]

(4) As a director or a member of executive management, approve the inclusion of projections of future earnings in the company's registration statement when such person has substantial doubts as to the accuracy and rationality of these projections?[90]

The answers to the above questions clearly are that a prudent man or woman in the management of his or her own property would not act in such a cavalier manner. Yet such persons acting in this fashion today are insulated from Section 11 liability. This consequence signifies that with frequency, Section 11's prudent man fiduciary or fiduciary-like standard is illusory and lacks meaningful substance. Hence, even when a securities statute identifies directors and officers as fiduciaries, there exists a glaring gap between the language of the statute and liability exposure. Thus, like other situations that are addressed in this book, rhetoric prevails over reality.[91]

---

[86] See discussion *supra* notes 51–56 and accompanying text.
[87] See SEC Advisory Committee, note 58 *supra*. The Committee Chair was SEC Commissioner Steven Wallman and its members included prominent practitioners and a distinguished academician, John C. Coffee Jr.
[88] See discussion *supra* notes 57–62 and accompanying text.
[89] See discussion *supra* notes 65–76 and accompanying text.
[90] See discussion *supra* notes 77–84 and accompanying text.
[91] Provided that the requirements of the applicable statute are met, Section 12(a)(2) of the Securities Act, 15 U.S.C. § 77l(a)(2), and Section 14(a) of the Securities Exchange Act, 15 U.S.C. § 78n(a), impose liability against directors and officers based on their negligent conduct. Moreover,

B. Section 10(b) of the Securities Exchange Act: Abandoning Fiduciary Standards

Pursuant to Section 10(b) of the Securities Exchange Act (Exchange Act)[92] and SEC Rule 10b-5 promulgated thereunder,[93] deceptive and manipulative conduct (which may include the making of material misrepresentations and omissions), in connection with the purchase or sale of a security, is prohibited.[94] The statute and rule constitute the principal antifraud provisions of the federal securities laws in both government and private litigation.[95] They

---

Section 17(a)(2) and 17(a)(3) of the Securities Act, 15 U.S.C. § 77q(a)(2), (a)(3), in SEC enforcement actions levies liability premised on negligence. *See Aaron v. Securities and Exchange Commission*, 446 U.S. 680 (1980); *Gould v. American-Hawaiian Steamship Company*, 535 F.2d 761 (3d Cir. 1976). Like Section 11, the broad safe harbor for forward-looking statements and the *Omnicare* protection given to statements of belief extend to Section 12(a)(2) of the Securities Act and Section 14(a) of the Exchange Act. Moreover, Section 12(a)(2) applies solely to prospectuses (and oral statements related thereto) in public offerings and limits liability to "sellers" of the subject securities. *See Gustafson v. Alloyd Company*, 513 U.S. 561 (1995); *Pinter v. Dahl*, 486 U.S. 622 (1988). Under *Pinter*, a seller is: a person who is the vendor, the vendor's agent, or one who solicits the purchase intending to personally benefit thereby or solicits the purchase seeking to serve the vendor's financial interests. Depending on the facts and circumstances, a director or officer may be deemed a "seller" of securities but frequently does not have that status—particularly with respect to outside directors. *See, e.g., Wildes v. Bitconnect International PLC*, 25 F.4th 1341, 1345–47 (11th Cir. 2022); *In re Craftmatic Securities Litigation*, 890 F.2d 628, 636 (3d Cir. 1990); *Capri v. Murphy*, 856 F.2d 473, 478 (2d Cir. 1988).

With respect to Section 14(a), that statute applies solely in the proxy setting. The statute and SEC Rule 14a-9, 17 C.F.R. § 240.14a-9, prohibit the use of a proxy statement by an Exchange Act company that contains a materially false or misleading fact "or which omits to state any material fact necessary in order to make the statements therein not false or misleading. . . ." Rule 14a-9(a). Generally, the same points that were made with respect to Section 11 apply here, namely: the refusal by the vast majority of publicly held companies to have an independent director serve as chair of the board of directors; the rejection by publicly held companies to form an independent disclosure committee comprised solely of outside directors; the broad safe harbor for forward-looking statements; and the lenient liability standards applied to statements of belief or opinion.

[92] 15 U.S.C. § 78j(b).
[93] 17 C.F.R. § 240.10b-5. Rule 10b-5 provides:

It shall be unlawful for any person, directly or indirectly, by the use of any means or instrumentality of interstate commerce, or of the mails or of any facility of any national securities exchange,
(a) To employ any device, scheme, or artifice to defraud,
(b) To make any untrue statement of a material fact or to omit to state a material fact necessary in order to make the statements made, in the light of the circumstances under which they were made, not misleading, or
(c) To engage in any act, practice, or course of business which operates or would operate as a fraud or deceit upon any person,

in connection with the purchase or sale of any security.

[94] *See* notes 92–93 *supra*.
[95] For example, in *Blue Chip Stamps v. Manor Drug Stores*, 421 U.S. 723, 737 (1975), Justice Rehnquist stated: "When we deal with private actions under Rule 10b-5, we deal with a judicial oak

apply to any manipulative or deceptive conduct in connection with the purchase of sale of a security, irrespective whether such transaction occurs on a national securities exchange or is privately negotiated between two individuals.[96]

At an earlier time, these provisions were viewed by a number of courts as a federal corporation law encompassing standards of fairness and fiduciary duty.[97] After numerous US Supreme Court decisions confining the reach of the statute and rule, the law is clear that only deficient disclosure or manipulation involving knowing or intentional misconduct is proscribed under Section 10(b) and Rule 10b-5.[98] Hence, although identified as fiduciaries by the Supreme Court,[99] the legal standards that apply to directors and officers in this setting are lax. The following discussion provides several examples supporting this assertion.

1. Rejection of a Federal Fairness Standard

An important issue presented was whether Section 10(b) and Rule 10b-5 reached substantive misconduct by corporate fiduciaries. A number of courts held that these provisions encompassed constructive fraud—even if full disclosure was provided to shareholders.[100] In the *Santa Fe* decision,

---

which has grown from little more than a legislative acorn." *See, e.g., Halliburton Co. v. Erica P. John Fund, Inc.,* 573 U.S. 258 (2014); *Herman & MacLean v. Huddleston,* 459 U.S. 375 (1983); *Aaron v. Securities and Exchange Commission,* 446 U.S. 680 (1980); Alan R. Bromberg, et al., *Bromberg and Lowenfels on Securities Fraud* (2023).

[96] *See Herman & MacLean v. Huddleston,* 459 U.S. at 382 (emphasis in original) (stating that "a § 10(b) action can be brought by a purchaser or seller of "*any* security" against "*any* person" who has used "*any* manipulative or deceptive device or contrivance" in connection with the purchase or sale of a security").

[97] *See, e.g., McClure v. Borne Chemical Company, Inc.,* 292 F.2d 824, 831 (3d Cir. 1961) ("Section 10(b) imposes broad fiduciary duties on management vis-à-vis the corporation and its individual stockholders. As implemented by Rule 10b-5, . . . Section 10(b) provides stockholders with a potent weapon for enforcement of many fiduciary duties. It can be said fairly that the Exchange Act . . . constitutes far reaching substantive corporation law").

[98] *See* cases cited *infra* notes 101–105 *infra.*

[99] See discussion *supra* notes 14–28 and accompanying text.

[100] *See, e.g., Green v. Santa Fe Industries, Inc.,* 533 F.2d 1283 (2d Cir. 1976), *rev'd,* 430 U.S. 462 (1977). *See generally* Marc I. Steinberg, *The Federalization of Corporate Governance* 136–40 (OUP 2018); Arthur Fleischer Jr., *"Federal Corporation Law": An Assessment,* 78 Harv. L. Rev. 1165 (1965); Richard W. Jennings, *Federalization of Corporate Law: Part Way or All the Way,* 31 Bus. Law. 991 (1976); Donald E. Schwartz, *Federal Chartering of Corporations: An Introduction,* 61 Geo. L.J. 71 (1972).

the US Supreme Court rejected this approach, holding that deceptive or manipulative conduct is a necessary requirement. Premising its decision on Section 10(b)'s legislative history and its statutory language, the Court found "no indication that Congress meant to prohibit any conduct not involving manipulation or deception."[101] The Court further supported its decision by recognizing the Exchange Act's "fundamental purpose" of implementing "a philosophy of full disclosure," and that once such disclosure has been made, "the fairness of the transaction is at most a tangential concern of the statute [namely, Section 10(b)]."[102] The Court's decision thus stands for the general principle that breach of fiduciary duty, unaccompanied by a material disclosure deficiency, is beyond the parameters of the federal securities laws.[103]

In light of the disclosure primacy of the federal securities laws, the Supreme Court's holding was to be expected, particularly in view of its restrictive decisions handed down shortly before *Santa Fe*.[104] Viewed from a federal securities law disclosure primacy perspective, *Santa Fe* did not pose an insurmountable barrier for the application of fiduciary standards for corporate directors and officers with respect to their disclosure obligations. However, several Supreme Court decisions as well as statutory developments signify that fiduciary standards are minimal with respect to director and officer conduct under Section 10(b), Rule 10b-5, and generally under other federal securities law provisions.[105]

2. Requiring Pleading and Proof of Knowing Misconduct
As corporate fiduciaries, it stands to reason that directors and officers would be held to a standard of reasonableness under Section 10(b) and Rule 10b-5.

---

[101] 430 U.S. at 473.

[102] *Id.* at 477–80. Note that by requiring a subject company or its affiliate to disclose whether it "reasonably believes" that a going-private transaction (such as a short-form merger) "is fair or unfair to unaffiliated security holders," SEC Rule 13e-3 may be said to indirectly impact fairness. *See* discussion in Chapter 6, notes 75–77 and accompanying text.

[103] 430 U.S. at 479 ("Absent a clear indication of congressional intent, we are reluctant to federalize the substantial portion of the law of corporations that deals with transactions in securities, particularly where established state policies of corporate regulation would be overwritten"). *Accord, Schreiber v. Burlington Northern, Inc.*, 472 U.S. 1 (1985) (holding that a claim under the tender offer antifraud statute, § 14(e) of the Securities Exchange Act, 15 U.S.C. § 78n(e), must be based on a disclosure deficiency).

[104] *See, e.g., Ernst & Ernst v. Hochfelder*, 425 U.S. 185 (1976) (holding scienter required to be proven in § 10(b) private actions); *Blue Chip Stamps v. Manor Drug Stores*, 421 U.S. 723 (1975) (holding plaintiff must be a purchaser or seller of the subject securities in § 10(b) private actions for damages); *Cort v. Ash*, 422 U.S. 66 (1975) (declining to imply a private cause of action for damages brought by a shareholder against corporate directors under 18 U.S.C. § 610).

[105] The exception is Section 11 of the Securities Act even though its fiduciary standards have been eroded as discussed *supra* notes 51–91 and accompanying text.

This is not the law. In *Ernst & Ernst v. Hochfelder*, the US Supreme Court held that scienter—intentional or knowing misconduct—must be proven.[106] Subsequently, the Supreme Court held that scienter must also be shown in SEC enforcement actions alleging a violation of these provisions.[107] The Court's rationale largely was based on Section 10(b)'s statutory language that prohibits deceptive or manipulative practices, thereby rejecting arguments relying on the statute's remedial purposes.[108]

The impact of these decisions is evident: corporate directors and officers are not liable under the principal remedial statute of the federal securities laws unless they act with knowing misconduct. However consistent that the Court's decision may be (or may not be) with the applicable statutory language and legislative history, fiduciary standards are nonexistent under Section 10(b) and Rule 10b-5. Although identified as fiduciaries by the Supreme Court in numerous decisions,[109] corporate directors and officers enjoy immunity from liability under these provisions unless they engage in fraud.[110]

---

[106] 425 U.S. 185, 214 (1976) ("When a statute speaks so specifically in terms of manipulation and deception, and of implementing devices and contrivances—the common understood terminology of intentional misconduct—and when its history reflects no more expansive intent, we are quite unwilling to expand the scope of the statute to negligent conduct"). The Supreme Court left unresolved whether reckless conduct constitutes scienter under Section 10(b). *See id.* at 193 n. 12. As currently interpreted, with specified exceptions (such as with respect to forward-looking statements by Exchange Act reporting companies as set forth in the PSLRA), reckless conduct has been deemed actionable under Section 10(b). *See e.g.*, § 20(e) of the Securities Exchange Act, 15 U.S.C. § 78t(e) (SEC enforcement actions against aiders and abettors); *In re Ikon Office Solutions, Inc.*, 277 F.3d 658, 667 (3d Cir. 2002); *Hollinger v. Titan Capital Corporation*, 914 F.2d 1564, 1569 (9th Cir. 1990) (en banc); *Sanders v. John Nuveen & Co., Inc.* 554 F.2d 790, 793 (7th Cir. 1977).

[107] *See Aaron v. Securities and Exchange Commission*, 446 U.S. 680 (1980).

[108] *See* 425 U.S. at 199–210. The Supreme Court also rejected the argument that the language of Rule 10b-5 encompasses negligent conduct, reasoning that an administrative rule cannot exceed the scope of the statute on which the rule is based. *See id.* at 213–14.

[109] *See* discussion *supra* notes 14–28 and accompanying text.

[110] *See supra* notes 104–108 and accompanying text. See 425 U.S. at 216 (Blackmun, J., dissenting) (stating that "an investor can be victimized just as much by negligent conduct as by positive deception, and that it is not logical to drive a wedge between the two").

Significantly, in view of restrictive US Supreme Court decisions, it may be problematic for plaintiffs to sue directors and officers under Section 10(b). This is particularly the situation with respect to outside directors. In 1994, the Supreme Court held that aiding and abetting liability is foreclosed under Section 10(b). *See Central Bank of Denver v. First Interstate Bank of Denver*, 511 U.S. 164 (1994). Therefore, primary liability must be alleged which in many circumstances may be an insurmountable obstacle. *See, e.g., Janus Capital Group, Inc. v. First Derivative Traders*, 564 U.S. 135 (2011) (limiting liability under Rule 10b-5(b) to makers of a statement and narrowly defining "maker" as a person who has authority over the content of such statement and whether and how to communicate such statement); *Stoneridge Investment Partners, LLC v. Scientific-Atlanta, Inc.*, 552 U.S. 148 (2008) (rejecting flexible "scheme to defraud" approach under Rule 10b-5(a) and (c)). *But see Lorenzo v. Securities and Exchange Commission*, 139 S. Ct. 1094 (2019) (holding that the knowing dissemination of materially misleading statements is actionable in government enforcement actions under Rule 10b-5(a) and (c)).

168 CORPORATE DIRECTOR AND OFFICER LIABILITY

This protection from liability is enhanced by the onerous pleading requirements that a private litigant must satisfy in order to proceed. Once a motion to dismiss is filed, discovery is stayed until and unless a plaintiff fends off the motion to dismiss.[111] In order to do so, under the Private Securities Litigation Reform Act (as construed by the US Supreme Court), a complaint must set forth facts that create an inference of scienter which a reasonable person would deem "cogent and at least as compelling as any opposing inference one could draw from the facts alleged."[112] The consequence of this standard is that a substantial percentage of federal securities law cases (e.g., in some years, 40 percent to 50 percent) are disposed of at the motion to dismiss stage.[113] Placing this hefty pleading burden upon plaintiff-shareholders when they seek redress for allegedly violative conduct from corporate directors and officers further demonstrates the absence of fiduciary standards under Section 10(b) and Rule 10b-5.[114]

3. Statements of Belief and Projections: Lacking Fiduciary Content

As discussed earlier in this chapter, the prudent man standard of Section 11 has been eroded by several developments, including the broad protection from liability provided to corporate directors and officers with respect to statements of belief and forward-looking statements.[115] These measures apply with equal vigor in private litigation alleging violations of Section 10(b) and Rule 10b-5.[116] Their impact is to provide further support that, although called fiduciaries, standards of liability under these provisions for

---

[111] *See* § 21D(b)(3)(B) of the Securities Exchange Act, 15 U.S.C. § 78u-4(b)(3)(B).

[112] *See Tellabs, Inc. v. Makor Issues & Rights, Ltd.*, 127 S. Ct. 2499, 2510 (2007), *interpreting* § 21D(b)(2) of the Securities Exchange Act, 15 U.S.C. § 78u-4(b)(2).

[113] *See* Alexander "Sasha" Aganin, *Securities Class Action Filings—2019 Year in Review*, Harvard Law School Forum on Corporate Governance (Feb. 14, 2020) (stating that "from 1997 to 2018, 49 percent of core federal filings were settled, 43 percent were dismissed, less than 1 percent were remanded, and 7 percent are continuing [with] less than 1 percent of core federal filings have reached a trial verdict"); Renzo Comolli, et al., *Class Action Litigation: 2012 Full-Year Review* 16 (2013) (stating that in 2012, 47 percent of motions to dismiss were granted).

[114] *See* Marc I. Steinberg, *Pleading Securities Fraud Claims—Only Part of the Story*, 45 Loy. U. Chi. L.J. 603, 613 (2014) ("When evaluated in conjunction with one another—the staying of discovery until and unless the motion to dismiss is fended off, the unavailability of the section 10(b) private remedy against aiders and abettors, and the narrow construction of the requisite conduct that subjects a collateral actor [e.g., depending on the facts and circumstances, directors and officers] to section 10(b) liability exposure—the conclusion emerges that these developments adversely impact the quest of investors to hold those collateral actors perceived responsible for their financial losses to answer for the alleged misconduct"); notes 112–114 *supra*.

[115] *See* discussion *supra* notes 77–84 and accompanying text.

[116] *See* § 21E of the Securities Exchange Act, 15 U.S.C. § 78u-5.

corporate directors and officers do not reflect the responsibilities of persons having fiduciary status.

4. Puffery: Corporate Fiduciaries as Used Car Salespersons

A question may be asked what corporate directors and officers have in common with used car salespersons in the performance of their respective occupations.[117] The answer is the nonactionable use of puffery that each liberally may employ.[118] Today, federal courts give expansive protection to generalized statements of optimism involving core aspects of a subject company's business, including its compliance with rigorous diligence practices, its sound culture and reputation, its commitment to adherence to regulatory mandates, and its disciplined pricing policies. Such statements, courts hold, are not actionable under the federal securities laws because they lack materiality and are not relied upon by a reasonable investor. Thus, even when corporate fiduciaries allegedly lie when they engage in puffery, this disingenuous conduct is not actionable.[119]

Engaging in exaggerated or false lofty generalized statements (namely, puffery) is not the way that fiduciaries should act. To state that corporate directors and officers are fiduciaries yet can engage in this type of aberrant conduct reflects poorly on their status. For these individuals to engage in this type of conduct and not be held accountable is incompatible with fiduciary duty principles.[120] Accordingly, the puffery doctrine provides another

---

[117] See Sarah Lee, *The Puffery Defense: From Used-Car Salesman to CEO*, 30 Sec. Reg. L.J. 440 (2002). For a case applying the puffery doctrine over a century ago, *see Harrison v. United States*, 200 U.S. 662, 665–66 (6th Cir. 1912).

[118] For example, the broker says to a prospective client: "I'm the best broker in Manhattan. You'd be making a big mistake not to use me." The CEO of a New York Stock Exchange listed company says at the company's annual meeting: "Our company is poised to earn impressive earnings this coming year. We have the best personnel and products in our industry." Further assume that both the broker and the CEO know that their respective statement is untrue. Nonetheless, as held by many courts, both of these statements constitute nonactionable puffery. *See e.g.*, cases cited note 119 *infra*.

[119] *See, e.g., Plumbers & Steamfitters Local 773 v. Danske Bank*, 11 F.4th 90 (2d Cir. 2021) (statements that bank engages in business practices consistent with internationally recognized anti-corruption standards deemed puffery); *Indiana Public Retirement System v. SAIC, Inc.*, 818 F.3d 85 (2d Cir. 2016) (boastful statements regarding the company's reputation and culture deemed puffery); *Lloyd v. CVB Financial Corp.*, 811 F.3d 1200 (9th Cir. 2016) (laudatory statement of the company's "sound credit culture" deemed puffery); *City of Edinburgh Council v. Pfizer, Inc.*, 754 F.3d 159 (3d Cir. 2014) (optimistic statements made by a corporation concerning its clinical trial data deemed puffery); *In re Aetna, Inc. Securities Litigation*, 617 F.3d 272 (3d Cir. 2010) (statements regarding the company's disciplined pricing of insurance policies deemed puffery).

On the other hand, when the statements at issue are sufficiently specific, courts may reject that they constitute mere puffery and hold that they are actionable. *See, e.g., In re Level 3 Communications, Inc. Securities Litigation*, 667 F.3d 1331, 1340–41 (10th Cir. 2012) (holding that company's statement that its integration was "85%, 90% done" actionable).

[120] See discussion *supra* notes 14–28 and accompanying text. *See generally* Jennifer O'Hare, *The Resurrection of the Dodo: The Unfortunate Re-Emergence of the Puffery Defense in Private Securities*

pointed example of the divergence between the rhetoric used and the liability standards applied in the federal securities law context.

5. Insider Trading: Misapplication of Fiduciary Standards

When addressing insider trading liability under Section 10(b) and Rule 10b-5, the US Supreme Court has opted for an approach based on a fiduciary relationship or a relationship of trust and confidence.[121] Hence, in *Chiarella v. United States*, the Court, applying state law concepts, held that silence gives rise to liability under these provisions if there exists a duty to disclose premised on a fiduciary relationship or a relationship of trust and confidence.[122]

The inconsistent application of this fiduciary standard subsequently was evidenced in *Dirks v. Securities and Exchange Commission*.[123] There, the issue presented was whether the defendant (the tipper), who was a securities analyst, was subject to liability for communicating (tipping) material nonpublic information to his employer and to its clients (the tippees) that had been conveyed to him by corporate insiders.[124] Applying fiduciary principles, the Court held a Section 10(b) violation occurs in this context when a tipper provides material and nonpublic information to the tippee(s) for the tipper's personal gain or to convey a gift to the tippee(s).[125] Hence, the Court looked to state law concepts of the fiduciary duty of loyalty when adopting this federal liability standard.

In rejecting the parity of information and access to information approaches embraced by the lower federal courts,[126] the Supreme Court has

---

Fraud Actions, 59 Ohio St. L.J. 1697 (1998); Stefan Padfield, *Is Puffery Material to Investors: Maybe We Should Ask Them*, 10 U. Pa. Bus. & Emp. L. 339 (2008).

[121] *See, e.g., United States v. O'Hagan*, 521 U.S. 642 (1997); *Dirks v. Securities and Exchange Commission*, 463 U.S. 646 (1983); *United States v. Chiarella*, 445 U.S. 222 (1980).

[122] 445 U.S. at 230 (stating that § 10(b) liability based on a defendant's silence "is premised upon a duty to disclose arising from a relationship of trust and confidence between parties to a transaction"). For criticism of this decision, *see* sources cited note 127 *infra*.

[123] 463 U.S. 646 (1983).

[124] *Id.* at 655–59.

[125] *Id.* at 662. Accordingly, the Court held that Dirks was not liable under Section 10(b) because he conveyed the information to expose a massive fraud. With respect to a gift being sufficient for Section 10(b) liability in this context, the Court stated that "the tip and trade resemble trading by the insider himself followed by a gift of the profits to the recipient." *Id.* The Supreme Court subsequently has reaffirmed the *Dirks* rationale in *Salman v. United States*, 137 S. Ct. 420 (1916).

[126] These principles were adopted in the landmark case of *Securities and Exchange Commission v. Texas Gulf Sulphur Co.*, 401 F.2d 833 (2d Cir. 1968) (en banc). In its opinion, the Second Circuit

been criticized.[127] For purposes of this chapter, the focus is on the consistency of the Court's application of fiduciary standards under Section 10(b) with respect to directors and officers allegedly engaging in illegal insider trading. Clearly, if the officer or director trades the subject company's securities while aware of material nonpublic information, she would have breached a fiduciary duty to the corporation and collectively its shareholders.[128] This result follows logically from the Court's adherence to a fiduciary rationale. The inconsistency occurs in the context of tipping. There, improper tipping under Section 10(b) occurs only when the corporate insider, such as a director, conveys the information to his tippee for such director's personal benefit or as a gift.[129]

Hence, in determining corporate insider-tipper liability under Section 10(b), the Supreme Court looks solely to the duty of loyalty—and confines that inquiry to the insider's motive to personally benefit or convey a gift.[130] In doing so, the Court ignores application of the duty of care. Clearly, a careless "loose lip" corporate officer who indiscriminately informs financial analysts

espoused both the parity and equal access rationales, including the broad assertion that "anyone in possession of material inside information must either disclose it to the investing public, or ... [if] he chooses not to do so, must abstain from trading in or recommending the securities concerned while such information remains undisclosed." *Id.* at 848. The access theory posits that "[a]nyone—corporate insider or not—who regularly receives material nonpublic information may not use this information to trade in securities without incurring an affirmative duty to disclose." *United States v. Chiarella*, 588 F.2d 1358, 1365 (2d Cir. 1978), *rev'd*, 445 U.S. 222 (1980). *See generally Texas Gulf Sulphur 50th Anniversary Symposium*, 71 SMU L. Rev. No. 3 (2018).

The parity and access theories have been widely adopted in developed markets. *See, e.g.*, Corporations Act 2001 (Cth) § 1043A (Australia) (possession standard); EU Regulation No. 596/2014 of the European Parliament and of the Council of 16 April 2014 on Market Abuse Regulation, art. 8 (possession standard); Province of Ontario Securities Act, R.S.O. c. S. 5, § 76 (Canada) (access standard).

[127] *See, e.g., Chiarella* 445 U.S. at 246–52 (Blackmun, J. dissenting) (criticizing the majority's unduly narrow approach); Steinberg, *supra* note 53, at 235 (asserting that "the fiduciary duty rationale has been problematic" and "the law of insider trading currently existing in this country is unacceptable"). Alison Anderson, *Fraud, Fiduciaries, and Insider Trading*, 10 Hofstra L. Rev. 341, 376–77 (1982) ("This is not a Supreme Court construing a complicated federal statutory scheme with wisdom, craft, and candor; this is a first-year Torts class on a bad day").

[128] *See Chiarella*, 445 U.S. at 230.

[129] *See Dirks*, 463 U.S. at 662. The *Dirks* decision reversed lower court case law. Generally, prior to *Dirks*, if the insider-tipper could not trade on the material nonpublic information, neither could her tippee(s) who knowingly received such information. *See, e.g., Elkind v. Liggett & Myers, Inc.*, 635 F.2d 156 (2d Cir. 1980).

[130] *See* 463 U.S. at 668 (Blackmun, J., dissenting) (stating that the Court's decision "excuses a knowing and intentional violation of an insider's duty to shareholders if the insider does not act from a motive of personal gain").

and institutional shareholders of material nonpublic information should be held to breach that duty.[131] Moreover, the duty of loyalty may be breached irrespective of the corporate fiduciary's personal or financial gain. For example, an outside director with minimal financial interest in the company may knowingly and indiscriminately convey material nonpublic information regarding the company's ongoing merger negotiations seeking to scuttle the prospective deal. He does so because, as the sole dissenter on the company's board, he believes that the prospective deal would harm the city in which he resides due to the likely loss of thousands of jobs that would be incurred as a consequence of the contemplated transaction. Such conduct would violate the duty of good faith under Delaware law and constitute a breach of the duty of loyalty.[132] Yet under the US Supreme Court's holding, this misconduct would not constitute an actionable breach for purposes of Section 10(b) application.

Thus, although corporate directors and officers are deemed fiduciaries, as recognized by the US Supreme Court,[133] and the law of Section 10(b) insider trading is premised on fiduciary duty,[134] the Court ignores the duty of care and misconstrues the breadth of the duty of loyalty in the tipper-tippee setting. The Court's rationale is illogical. It also illustrates the substantial gap between fiduciary duty rhetoric and the applicable legal standards by which corporate directors and officers are held accountable under Section 10(b) for conveying material nonpublic information to their tippees.[135]

---

[131] For a case prior to *Dirks* so holding in similar circumstances, *see Elkind v. Liggett & Myers, Inc.*, 635 F.2d 156 (2d Cir. 1980). Today, an insider that engages in such selective disclosure of material nonpublic information violates Regulation FD. However, Regulation FD is not an antifraud provision and does not provide for a private right of action. *See* 17 C.F.R. § 243.101 et seq.; Securities Exchange Act Release No. 43154 (2000) (adopting release).

[132] *See Stone v. Ritter*, 911 A.2d 362, 369 (Del. 2006) (stating that "a failure to act in good faith may be shown, for instance, where the fiduciary intentionally acts with a purpose other than that of advancing the best interests of the corporation"). Even under a stakeholder analysis, the outside director's conduct evidently would be a breach of the duty of loyalty. Note that the subject director likely violated SEC Regulation FD by engaging in selective disclosure of material nonpublic information. *See* note 131 *supra*.

[133] *See* discussion *supra* notes 14–28 and accompanying text.

[134] *See* discussion *supra* notes 121–132 and accompanying text.

[135] Note, moreover, that, as held by a number of courts, the US Department of Justice may criminally prosecute in the tipper-tippee setting under the Title 18 U.S.C. criminal statutes without proof of personal benefit. *See, e.g., United States v. Blaszczak*, 947 F.3d 19, 36 (2d Cir. 2019), *vacated and remanded on other grounds*, 141 S. Ct. 1040 (2021), *dismissal granted on other grounds*, 56 F.4th 230 (2d Cir. 2022) (stating that "the government may avoid the personal benefit test altogether by prosecuting insider trading with less difficulty under the Title 18 [criminal] statutes"); *United States v. Ramsey*, 565 F. Supp. 3d 641 (E.D. Pa. 2021); *United States v. Melvin*, 143 F. Supp. 3d 1354 (N.D. Ga. 2015).

C. Analogous Example: Investment Adviser Fees

For purposes of comparison, the substantial gap between rhetoric and application of fiduciary standards exists in a number of other contexts under the federal securities laws. Investment adviser fees serve as an example of this gap between rhetoric and the levying of liability. Section 36(b) of the Investment Company Act provides that "the investment adviser of a registered investment company shall be deemed to have a fiduciary duty with respect to the receipt of compensation for services...."[136] In *Jones v. Harris Associates L.P.*, the US Supreme Court referred to this statute and its fiduciary standard.[137]

With the recognition of this statutory fiduciary duty, it logically follows that this standard should have meaningful substance. However, this is not the case. The standard adopted by the US Supreme Court embraces the *Gartenberg* formulation adhered to by the US Court of Appeals for the Second Circuit.[138] In adopting this lax standard, the Supreme Court held that "to face liability under § 36(b), an investment adviser must charge a fee so disproportionately large that it bears no reasonable relationship to the services rendered and could not have been the product of arm's length bargaining."[139] It is difficult to comprehend how this standard is consistent with the implementation of meaningful fiduciary standards. Not surprisingly, challenges by mutual fund shareholders to allegedly excessive investment adviser fees have faced difficulties.[140] This is supported by the fact that since this lax standard was adopted, investors have lost every case that has gone to trial, amounting to a fifty-year losing streak.[141] Thus, the investment adviser fee setting provides an example that is similar to director and officer

---

[136] 15 U.S.C. § 80a-35(b).

[137] 559 U.S. 335, 346 (2010). The US Supreme Court has recognized that investment advisers are fiduciaries. *See Securities and Exchange Commission v. Capital Gains Research Bureau*, 375 U.S. 180, 194 (1963).

[138] *See* 559 U.S. at 346 ("The *Gartenberg* approach fully incorporates this understanding of the fiduciary duty...."); *Gartenberg v. Merrill Lynch Asset Management, Inc.*, 694 F.2d 923 (2d Cir. 1982).

[139] 559 U.S. at 346. In making this determination, all pertinent facts must be considered. These facts include "the adviser-manager's cost in providing the service, ... the extent to which the adviser-manager realizes economies of scale as the fund grows larger, ... the volume of orders which must be processed by the manager, ... and the independence, expertise, care, and conscientiousness of the board in evaluating adviser compensation...." *Id.* at 345–46, *quoting Gartenberg*, 694 F.2d at 930.

[140] *See* Daniel J. Morrissey, *Are Mutual Funds Robbing Retirement Savings?*, 14 N.Y.U. J. Law & Bus. 143 (2017).

[141] *See Fifty-Year Losing Streak Continues for Excessive Fund Fee Claims*, Fed. Sec. L. Rep. (CCH) No. 2984, at 1 (Aug. 12, 2021).

fiduciary rhetoric where there exists a glaring gap between the supposed rigorous obligations that purportedly apply and, in actuality, the existence of permissive liability standards.

IV. Summation: "Discretionaries," Not Fiduciaries

Like state corporation law, the federal securities laws recognize the fiduciary status of corporate directors and officers yet frequently adhere to lenient standards of liability. The distinction between rhetoric and substance prevails. This disparity provides further support for the position that corporate directors and officers—in actuality—should not be identified as fiduciaries. The federal securities laws thus provide an important illustration—outside the purview of state company law—of the misdirected perception that corporate directors and officers are fiduciaries. These individuals, in fact, are not fiduciaries and their status should be redefined to accurately reflect reality.

Reality is that, like state company law, corporate directors and officers are "discretionaries." Depending on the underlying facts and circumstances as well as the applicable statutory and regulatory mandates, differing standards apply. For example, in the registration statement setting, but for the exceptions discussed earlier in this chapter,[142] Section 11 imposes fiduciary-like standards of liability for inside directors and executive management. In the integrated disclosure and shelf registration framework, fiduciary standards under Section 11 are diluted for outside directors. By contrast, pursuant to the principal antifraud provisions of the federal securities laws—Section 10(b) and Rule 10b-5—laxity prevails. The fiduciary duty is transformed into a duty not to perpetrate fraud against those persons with whom the subject director or officer has a relationship of trust and confidence. Going further, in the setting of forward-looking statements, a director or officer can engage in intentional misconduct yet not be held liable in private litigation if such statements are accompanied by adequate cautionary language.

---

[142] *See supra* notes 51–91 and accompanying text.

In view of these differing standards of liability, the corporate director or officer acts with discretion. Depending on the statute and SEC rule implicated, this discretion may be strictly evaluated (such as for inside directors under Section 11) or may be broad (such as for corporate insiders under Section 10(b) and Rule 10b-5). Thus, although company directors and officers may have fiduciary-like obligations in certain registered offerings, their activities overall lack meaningful fiduciary content (such as with respect to Section 10(b) liability standards). The result is that corporate directors and officers are not fiduciaries; in actuality, they are "discretionaries."

9
Corporate Directors and Officers Are "Discretionaries": Proposed Standards of Liability

I. Setting the Stage

This chapter focuses on the standards that should apply with respect to director and officer liability in their role as "discretionaries."[1] Although maintaining that they are not fiduciaries, the framework proposed in this chapter must recognize the standards that are firmly established in ascertaining director and officer liability exposure. Accordingly, proposals that are advanced in this chapter must be deemed reconcilable with current liability standards—at least to the extent that they are capable of practical implementation. Hence, rather than writing on a blank slate, the following discussion seeks to formulate an improved corporate governance liability structure that can be accommodated to currently prevailing standards.

From this perspective, the chapter focuses on significant concepts that impact corporate director and officer liability. It expands upon subjects addressed earlier in this book, including such concepts as the business judgment rule, exculpation statutes, the lack of good faith, related party transactions, derivative litigation, independent directors, and the application of legal standards to the facts at issue in a myriad of contexts. Because of their vast number, not all pertinent issues are discussed herein. Rather, this chapter's objectives are to "rethink" the current framework, address the deficiencies of the standards that currently apply, and propose practical guidelines that would enhance corporate governance accountability.[2] In this

---

[1] Accordingly, this chapter focuses on corporate directors and officers as "discretionaries," there by recognizing that these individuals, in reality, are not fiduciaries.

[2] This approach was adopted in this author's Oxford University Press book *Rethinking Securities Law*, which was awarded Winner best law book of 2021 by American Book Fest. The book contains approximately 125 recommendations to improve the US securities law framework and may be consulted for in-depth coverage of this subject matter.

manner, corporate directors and officers will be recognized for what, in actuality, they are: "discretionaries" rather than fiduciaries.

II. The Business Judgment Rule

The inveterate business judgment rule is a fundamental principle of corporate law. Because judges are not business experts,[3] boards of directors are provided broad discretion when making business decisions. Provided that the directors involved are independent, do not have a disabling conflict of interest, and are adequately informed, their decisions are to be respected unless a complainant establishes that they acted with gross negligence[4]— a culpability level that is defined by *Black's Law Dictionary* as "[a] conscious, voluntary act or omission in reckless disregard of a legal duty and of the consequences to another party, who may typically recover exemplary damages."[5] Clearly, this is not a standard by which fiduciary conduct should be measured. Fiduciaries should be held to a higher standard than to abstain from engaging in gross negligence. The business judgment rule therefore evidences that directors in fact are "discretionaries" rather than fiduciaries.[6]

---

[3] This approach has been embraced for at least a century. *See, e.g., Dodge v. Ford Motor Co.*, 170 N.W. 668, 684 (Mich. 1919) ("The judges are not business experts").

[4] With respect to Delaware incorporated companies, the decision reached by a subject board of directors must have a rational basis for the business judgment rule to be successfully invoked. *See, e.g., Smith v. Van Gorkom*, 488 A.2d 858 (Del. 1985). In their recognition of the business judgment rule, a number of courts, however, do not require that the decision reached by the board of directors or other qualified decisionmaker be rational. *See, e.g., WLR Foods, Inc. v. Tyson Foods Inc.*, 65 F.3d 1172, 1182–83 (4th Cir. 1995) (interpreting Virginia law); discussion in Chapter 3, notes 25–54 and accompanying text.

Whether the business judgment rule applies to corporate officers is subject to different views. *Compare Federal Deposit Insurance Corporation v. Perry*, 2012 WL 589569, at * 4 (C.D. Cal. 2012) (applying California law and holding that the business judgment rule does not apply to decisions made by corporate officers), *with Rosenfeld v. Metals Selling Corp.*, 643 A.2d 1253, 1261 n. 16 (Conn. 1994) ("Although the business judgment rule is usually defined in terms of the role of corporate directors, it is equally applicable to corporate officers exercising their authority"). See discussion in Chapter 3, notes 36–39 and accompanying text.

[5] *Black's Law Dictionary* 1246 (11th ed. 2019) (also stating that "Gross negligence is traditionally said to be the omission of even such diligence as habitually careless and inattentive people do actually exercise in avoiding danger to their own person or property"). As discussed frequently in this book, the Delaware Supreme Court distinguishes between standards of conduct and standards of liability. In *United Food and Commercial Workers Union v. Zuckerberg*, 262 A.3d 1034, 1049–50 (Del. 2021), the court conflated these two standards in a single sentence: "Predicated upon concepts of *gross negligence*, the *duty of care* requires that [corporate] fiduciaries *inform themselves of material information* before making a business decision and act *prudently* in carrying out their duties" (emphasis supplied).

[6] *See* discussion in Chapter 3, notes 25–54 and accompanying text.

Nonetheless, sound arguments can be made in support of the business judgment rule. Many business decisions carry a high degree of uncertainty. To permit challenges based on alleged ordinary negligence, asserted with the benefit of hindsight, would expose corporate directors to an onslaught of vexatious litigation. With the attendant risks of significant monetary liability, reputational harm, lack of adequate indemnification and insurance coverage, and impeding the making of good faith entrepreneurial decisions, the inordinate costs of serving in a director role—particularly for outside directors—frequently would be unacceptable.[7] Indeed, the successful recruitment and retention of competent outside directors to serve on the boards of publicly held companies could well pose insurmountable challenges if the business judgment rule were to be discarded.[8] When applied in an appropriate setting, the business judgment rule may be viewed as a commendable legal principle that promotes entrepreneurship, limits undue liability exposure for corporate directors, and deters meritless shareholder litigation. Thus, as a generalization, with respect to entrepreneurial and operational decisions, the business judgment rule correctly balances the role of the corporate director acting as a "discretionary" within the corporate governance framework.

The business judgment rule's application today, however, reaches decisions that should not be within its parameters. As now construed, the rule extends beyond what may be viewed as traditional entrepreneurial or operational decisions,[9] thereby encompassing such matters as the approval of interested director transactions and the dismissal of shareholder derivative litigation.[10] As discussed herein, the extension of the business judgment rule to these types of matters is inappropriate and should be replaced with a more evenly balanced approach which would still provide these director "discretionaries" with ample room to make sensible decisions without undue fear of liability.

---

[7] *See* William T. Allen, Jack B. Jacobs, and Leo E. Strine Jr., *Realigning the Standard of Review of Director Due Care with Delaware Public Policy: A Critique of Van Gorkom and Its Progeny as a Standard of Review Problem*, 96 Nw. U. L. Rev. 449, 449 (2002); discussion in Chapter 3, notes 25–26 and accompanying text.

[8] *See* Dennis J. Block, et al., *Advising Directors on the D&O Insurance Crisis*, 14 Sec. Reg. L.J. 130 (1986); Bayless Manning, *Reflections and Practical Tips on Life in the Boardroom After Van Gorkom*, 41 Bus. Law. 1 (1985); Symposium, *Van Gorkom and the Corporate Board: Problem, Solution, or Placebo?*, 96 Nw. U. L. Rev. 447 (2002).

[9] The business judgment rule, for example, extends to independent and disinterested director approval of interested director transactions and determinations made by these directors to terminate shareholder derivative litigation. *See* discussion *infra* notes 28–59 and accompanying text.

[10] *See* discussion *infra* notes 28–59 and accompanying text.

180 CORPORATE DIRECTOR AND OFFICER LIABILITY

III. Exculpation Statutes

Perceiving that the business judgment rule does not adequately protect directors (and, in some states, also officers) from monetary liability, states have enacted exculpation statutes. As discussed in Chapters 3 and 4, the Delaware version, enacted in many states, insulates directors (and officers in direct actions) from money damages for breach of the duty of care if a suitable provision is contained in the subject company's certificate of formation.[11] Other state statutes provide greater protection, extending monetary liability for certain breaches of the duty of loyalty as well as the duty of care.[12] A number of these statutes are self-enabling[13] while others mandate that the subject corporation adopt the exculpation provision in its articles of incorporation.[14]

Even with a director's or officer's "discretionary" (rather than fiduciary) status, these statutes are objectionable. Why directors and officers should be insulated from monetary liability for breach of the duty of care unless they engage in intentional misconduct is hard to fathom.[15] To extend this protection from monetary liability to certain duty of loyalty breaches slights the gravity of these improprieties.[16] By comparison, under the federal securities laws, the requisite mental culpability that ordinarily applies to hold corporate directors and officers monetarily liable if they engage in fraud is

---

[11] See § 102(b)(7) of the Delaware General Corporation Law; Stephen A. Radin, *The Director's Duty of Care Three Years after Smith v. Van Gorkom*, 39 Hastings L.J. 707, 747-48 (1988) ("As of the end of 1987, legislation modeled upon the Delaware statute has been enacted in Arizona, Arkansas, California, Colorado, Georgia, Idaho, Iowa, Kansas, Louisiana, Massachusetts, Michigan, Minnesota, Montana, New Jersey, New Mexico, New York, North Carolina, Oklahoma, Oregon, Pennsylvania, Rhode Island, South Dakota, Texas, Utah, Washington, and Wyoming"); discussion in Chapter 3, notes 59-70 and accompanying text; Chapter 4, notes 52-55 and accompanying text.

[12] For example, under the Nevada statute, a director or officer is not liable to the corporation, its stockholders, or its creditors unless it is shown that such director or officer breached a fiduciary duty and "such breach involved intentional misconduct, fraud, or a knowing violation of law." Nev. Rev. Stat.§ 78.138(7). See Theo Francis and Erin Mulvaney, *Frustrated Executives Look Past Delaware*, Wall St. J., Feb. 12, 2024, at A1, A2 ("Nevada . . . has broad protections for directors and officers in many cases that Delaware wouldn't, including involving improper personal gain"); discussion in Chapter 3, notes 71-84 and accompanying text; discussion in Chapter 4, notes 43-51 and accompanying text. A number of these state exculpation statutes extend to corporate officers. See, e.g., state statutes cited in Chapter 3, at note 72.

[13] See, e.g., state statutes cited in Chapter 3, at note 71.

[14] See sources cited note 11 *supra*.

[15] See discussion in Chapter 4, notes 52-55 and accompanying text.

[16] As discussed in Chapters 3 and 4, these duty of loyalty breaches, depending on the facts and circumstances, include self-dealing transactions, usurpation of corporate opportunities, and failure to act in good faith. See discussion in Chapter 3, notes 73-84 and accompanying text; Chapter 4, notes 43-51 and accompanying text.

recklessness.[17] There is no sound basis to apply a more lenient monetary culpability standard for breaches of the duties of care and loyalty under state company law than for knowing misconduct under the federal securities laws.[18] By doing so, expansive exculpation statutes, in practical effect, convert every breach of duty case seeking monetary damages into an action based on fraud. This approach is nonsensical and contravenes the application of anything approaching meaningful corporate governance standards.

Although exculpation statutes evidently are here to stay, they should be modified to provide at least a scintilla of scrutiny. Because the presumption of the business judgment rule may be rebutted by showing a disabling conflict of loyalty or grossly negligent conduct,[19] exculpation statutes should exclude duty of loyalty breaches and reckless misconduct from their umbrella of protection. Pursuant to this proposed approach, reckless misconduct engaged in by directors and officers would subject them to monetary liability exposure. Utilizing the standard for recklessness under the federal securities laws, this proposed standard would impose monetary liability if a director's or officer's conduct was "highly unreasonable" and constituted such an "extreme departure from the standards of ordinary care that the danger was either known to [such director or officer] or [was] so obvious that [he or she] must have been

---

[17] Although not definitively resolved by the US Supreme Court, reckless misconduct is customarily applied for the requisite intent under the federal securities laws' principal antifraud provision, Section 10(b) of the Securities Exchange Act (and SEC Rule 10b-5 promulgated thereunder). *See, e.g., In re Ikon Office Solutions, Inc. Securities Litigation*, 277 F.3d 658, 667 (3d Cir. 2002); *Hollinger v. Titan Capital Corporation*, 914 F.2d 1564, 1569 (9th Cir. 1990) (en banc); *Sanders v. John Nuveen & Co. Inc.*, 554 F.2d 790, 793 (7th Cir. 1977). Note, however, that with respect to Section 10(b) monetary liability being imposed for materially false forward-looking statements made by Exchange Act companies, a showing of reckless misconduct is not sufficient. *See* § 27A of the Securities Act; § 21E of the Securities Exchange Act. As stated by this author in *Understanding Securities Law* 446–47 (8th ed. 2023): "The safe harbor [from monetary liability for Exchange Act reporting companies] applies to both forward-looking written and oral statements, so long as: (1) the statement is identified as a forward-looking statement and is accompanied by meaningful cautionary statements . . . ; (2) the state lacks materiality; or (3) the plaintiff fails to prove that the statement was made with actual knowledge of its falsity. . . ." *See* discussion in Chapter 8, notes 77–91 and accompanying text.

[18] By analogy, under Section 11 of the Securities Act, which provides a damages remedy for plaintiffs who purchased their securities pursuant to a registration statement that contained a material misstatement or omission, a subject defendant (other than an issuer which is subject to strict liability) can avoid liability by proving that it exercised due diligence. *See, e.g., Escott v. Bar Chris Construction Corp.*, 283 F. Supp. 643 (S.D.N.Y. 1968). Similarly, with respect to materially false and misleading statements contained in a proxy statement, Section 14(a) requires a plaintiff to prove only negligence, rather than scienter, against a defendant director or officer. *See, e.g., Gould v. Hawaiian American S.S. Co.* 535 F.2d 561 (3d Cir. 1976). These rights of action that are not premised on fraudulent misconduct do not require proof that a defendant director or officer engaged in knowing or intentional misconduct while Section 10(b), which is an antifraud provision, mandates such a showing. *See Aaron v. Securities and Exchange Commission*, 446 U.S. 680 (1980); *Ernst & Ernst v. Hochfelder*, 425 U.S. 185 (1976); discussion in Chapter 8.

[19] *See supra* note 4 and accompanying text; discussion in Chapter 3, notes 25–53 and accompanying text.

aware of it."[20] In sum, even though corporate directors and officers enjoy broad protection with respect to their actions—as "discretionaries"—they should not be financially absolved of responsibility for reckless misconduct.

IV. Lack of Good Faith

The disconnect between standards of conduct and standards of review is vividly illustrated when the lack of good faith is at issue. In a Delaware Supreme Court decision, two very different statements are made. Espousing aspirational standards of conduct, the court opined that "it is important that the board exercise its good faith judgment that the corporation's information and reporting system is in concept and design adequate to assure the board that appropriate information will come to its attention in a timely manner as a matter of ordinary operations, so that it may satisfy its responsibility."[21] Yet shortly thereafter in that same decision, applying the standard of review in determining whether to hold directors liable for failure to act in good faith with respect to their oversight obligations, the court embraced a far more permissive standard, namely that "(a) the directors utterly failed to implement any reporting or information system or controls; or (b) having implemented such a system or controls, consciously failed to monitor or oversee its operations, thus disabling themselves from being informed of risks or problems requiring their attention."[22] The deviation between the rhetoric of aspirational good director conduct and the levying of liability is crystal clear.[23]

Why actual knowledge is required to establish that directors and officers breached their duty of loyalty with respect to their oversight responsibilities is mystifying.[24] Moreover, with a subject corporation having an exculpation provision, Delaware law enables directors (and officers in direct actions) to avert monetary liability if they cavalierly and recklessly ignore their

---

[20] *See* cases cited note 17 *supra*; discussion in Chapter 8, notes 106–114 and accompanying text.

[21] *Stone v. Ritter*, 911 A.2d 362, 368, *quoting In re Caremark Int'l Derivative Litigation*, 698 A.2d 959, 970 (Del. Ch. 1996).

[22] *Stone*, 911 A.2d at 970 (*see id.*—also stating that either of these failures requires "a showing that the directors knew that they were not discharging their fiduciary obligations").

[23] *See* discussion in Chapter 1, notes 33–41 and accompanying text.

[24] Under Delaware law, the *Caremark* standard also applies to corporate officers. *See In re McDonald's Corporation Stockholder Derivative Litigation*, 289 A.3d 343 (Del. Ch. 2023). *See also Segway Inc. v. Hong*, 2023 WL 8643017, at * 1 (Del. Ch. 2023) (rejecting the contention that "the high bar to plead a *Caremark* claim is lowered when the claim is brought against an officer").

oversight obligations.[25] To state that such directors are fiduciaries and nonetheless shield them from monetary liability—in view of such unacceptable behavior—is incompatible with corporate governance principles. Rather, directors and officers are "discretionaries." As discretionaries, they should be held financially accountable for their reckless misconduct when performing their law compliance and other oversight functions. A director or officer should not be given carte blanche to minimize or slight the corporation's adherence to law compliance and other core areas involving substantial risk. Accordingly, a discretionary's avoidance of monetary liability under state corporation law should have some nexus to sensible boundaries. At a minimum, reckless misconduct should be adopted as the logical monetary liability standard for directors and officers in this context.[26] This proposed lenient standard would insulate directors and officers from monetary liability unless they acted far beyond norms of conduct expected of individuals having these weighty responsibilities.[27]

V. Interested Director and Officer Transactions

With respect to related party transactions, this section focuses on interested director and officer transactions.[28] These transactions exemplify the need for devising revised standards that would provide a more balanced perspective. From a general perspective, as discussed in Chapter 4, where there is neither disinterested director nor shareholder approval, the interested director or officer must establish the transaction's fairness.[29] This long-established

---

[25] *See, e.g., In re Walt Disney Company Derivative Litigation*, 906 A.2d 27, 67 (Del. 2006) (stating that a director breaches the duty of good faith "where the fiduciary intentionally acts with a purpose other than that of advancing the best interests of the corporation"); discussion and cases cited in Chapter 4, notes 58–78 and accompanying text.

[26] Note that under Delaware law, reckless conduct is within the scope of a suitably drafted exculpation provision, thereby insulating defendant directors (and officers in direct actions) from monetary liability for engaging in this misconduct. *See, e.g., New Enterprise Associates 14 L.P. v. Rich*, 295 A.3d 520, 551 (Del. Ch. 2023). Nonetheless, corporate directors and officers may incur liability under federal and state law for the failure by their corporations to comply with regulatory directives. *See* American Bar Association, Section of Business Law (Committee on Corporate Laws), *Corporate Director's Guidebook* 37–43 (7th ed. 2020); discussion in Chapter 4, note 78 and accompanying text.

[27] For further analysis herein with respect to the duty of good faith, *see* Chapter 4, notes 56–78 and accompanying text.

[28] This book addresses several types of related party transactions. For purposes of providing a key example with respect to the need for formulating a revised framework, this discussion addresses interested director and officer transactions.

[29] *See, e.g.*, Del. Gen. Corp. L. § 144(a); *Fliegler v. Lawrence*, 361 A.2d 218 (Del. 1976); discussion in Chapter 4, notes 79–84 and accompanying text.

principle remains vibrant.[30] Such scrutiny, however, frequently is avoided by having disinterested directors approve the subject transaction. In such event, laxity prevails.

In Delaware, approval of an interested director or officer transaction by independent, disinterested, and adequately informed directors often means that such transaction's propriety is reviewed under the business judgment rule.[31] As discussed earlier, to rebut the presumption of the business rule, a plaintiff must prove that the defendant directors who approved the transaction were themselves conflicted or acted with gross negligence.[32] When these directors do not have a disabling conflict of interest and are deemed independent and disinterested, the alleged breach would be that of the duty of care. With the customary inclusion of an exculpation provision in a subject company's charter, monetary liability could be levied against such directors only if they engaged in intentional misconduct when approving the interested director or officer transaction.[33] This lenient standard provides an arduous hurdle to successfully challenge these transactions.[34] The Model Business Corporation Act provision, enacted by several states, has an even more lenient standard.[35] Pursuant to this standard, provided that disinterested and independent directors who are adequately informed approve the interested director transaction, judicial review of such transaction's propriety is foreclosed. As the Official MBCA Comment provides, if such director approval is obtained, "then a director's conflicting interest transaction is immune from attack by a shareholder or the corporation on the ground of an

---

[30] See sources cited in Chapter 4, notes 79–84 and accompanying text.
[31] See, e.g., Marciano v. Nakash, 535 A.2d 400, 405 n. 3 (Del. 1987) (stating that "approval by fully informed disinterested directors... permits invocation of the business judgment rule"). Significantly, in conflicted-controller transactions, including in the interested director setting, approval by informed disinterested directors shifts the burden of proof to the plaintiff-shareholder to proof unfairness. See In re Match Group, Inc. Derivative Litigation, 315 A.3d 446, 451 (Del. 2024) (stating that a "controlling stockholder can shift the burden of proof to the plaintiff by properly employing a special committee [comprised of independent directors] or an unaffiliated stockholder vote"). In order to invoke the business judgment rule with respect to a controller-conflicted transaction, both the employment of a well-functioning special committee comprised of independent directors and the procurement of an unaffiliated stockholder vote are required. See Match, 315 A.3d at 462–63; discussion in Chapter 4, notes 85–88 and accompanying text.
[32] See, e.g., Smith v. Van Gorkom, 488 A.2d 858 (Del. 1985); discussion supra notes 3–9 and accompanying text; Chapter 3, notes 36–39 and accompanying text.
[33] See, e.g., Del. Gen. Corp. L. § 102(b)(7); New Enterprise Associates 14 L.P. v. Rich, 295 A.3d 520, 551 (Del. Ch. 2023); discussion in Chapter 3, notes 85–88 and accompanying text
[34] See discussion in Chapter 4, notes 85–88 and accompanying text.
[35] See MBCA §§ 8.60–8.63. For states that have adopted the MBCA approach, see Chapter 3, at note 90.

interest of the director."[36] This approach is even more expansive than business judgment rule application to these transactions (at least as applied in Delaware) as determinations made by subject directors are beyond judicial purview—even if such directors were grossly negligent (and perhaps even more culpable).[37] These approaches slight the structural bias concerns that prevail on corporate boards as well as minimizing the personal relationships that develop through years of board service.[38] Their effect, therefore, is to facilitate rather than to restrain these self-dealing actions. A more balanced position is appropriate. Certainly, the fact that disinterested and independent directors reviewed and approved the subject interested director transaction merits deference. The degree of deference, however, must take into account that these transactions financially benefit corporate insiders, frequently those who are controlling shareholders or chief executive officers. Moreover, a persuasive business need for subject companies to enter into these transactions often is lacking.[39]

The application of the "plain vanilla" business judgment rule or more lenient standard in this context thus is incompatible with appropriate norms of corporate governance. Accordingly, the standard proposed is to shift the burden of persuasion: Approval of an interested director or officer transaction by adequately informed disinterested and independent directors is enforceable unless the complainant establishes that such transaction is unfair.[40]

---

[36] MBCA § 8.61 Official Comment. The same result occurs if there is informed disinterested shareholder approval of the interested director transaction. See MBCA § 8.63.

[37] Pursuant to the MBCA, in order for this lenient standard to apply, the decision must be made by "qualified directors." For the definition of qualified director, see MBCA § 1.43(a)(4). As explained in the Official Comment to Section 8.62: "The definition of 'qualified director' in section 1.43(a)(4) excludes not only a director who is conflicted directly or because of a person specified in the categories of the 'related person' definition in section 8.60, but also any director with a familial, financial, employment, professional or other relationship with another director for whom the transaction is a director's conflicting interest transaction that would be likely to impair the objectivity of the first director's judgment when participating in a vote on the transaction."

[38] See, e.g., James D. Cox and Harry L. Munsinger, Bias in the Boardroom: Psychological Foundations and Legal Implications of Corporate Cohesion, 48 Law & Contemp. Probs. 79 (1985) (focusing on bias among directors on corporate boards); Note, The Propriety of Judicial Deference to Corporate Boards of Directors, 96 Harv. L. Rev. 1894, 1901 (1983) ("Given cohesiveness and informational dependence in the boardroom, directors are likely to conform to the expectations of both management and of their fellow board members"); discussion in Chapter 3, notes 92–93 and accompanying text; Chapter 5, notes 73–88 and accompanying text.

[39] See MBCA § 8.60 (Official Comment): "[I]f a manufacturing company that lacks sufficient working capital allocates some of its scarce funds to purchase at a market price a sailing yacht owned by one of its directors, it will not be easy to persuade the court that the transaction was 'fair' in the sense that it was reasonably made to further the business interests of the corporation."

[40] Delaware applies this standard in conflicted-controller transactions, including in situations outside of the M&A setting. See, e.g., In re Match Group, Inc. Derivative Litigation, 315 A.3d 446 (Del. 2024) (making clear that this standard applies in all conflicted-controller transactions); Tornetta v. Musk, 310 A.3d 430 (Del. Ch. 2024) (adhering to this standard with respect to compensation

Delaware law recognizes this standard when a self-dealing transaction engaged in by a controlling shareholder is challenged (a conflicted-controller transaction), such as in the context of a cash-out merger or other M&A transaction where the entire fairness test applies.[41] In such instances, where the self-dealing transaction was approved by a well-functioning committee comprised of independent directors, the burden of persuasion is shifted to the plaintiffs to show that the transaction was unfair.[42] This standard, comporting with their status as "discretionaries," gives considerable latitude but not undue deference to independent director approval of self-dealing transactions desired by and beneficial to their board peers.

VI. Derivative Litigation

Chapter 5 addresses derivative litigation, focusing on the lax nonfiduciary standards that are applied by courts and legislatures in the dismissal of shareholder derivative actions based on determinations by independent directors.[43] The following discussion addresses appropriate modifications

---

plan awarded to Tesla's controlling shareholder, Elon Musk). Moreover, in a few jurisdictions, this standard applies to all interested director transactions. *See, e.g., Cohen v. Ayers*, 596 F.2d 733, 740–41 (7th Cir. 1979) (interpreting New York law) (stating that the approval of an interested director transaction by informed disinterested directors shifts the burden of proving the unfairness of the transaction to the challenging shareholder); Stuart R. Cohn, *The Shifting Sands of Conflict of Interest Standards: The Duty of Loyalty Meets the Real World with Questions of Process and Fairness*, 74 Bus. Law. 1077, 1085 (2019) (identifying Maryland, New York, and South Carolina as states where the burden is placed on the plaintiff-shareholder if there is informed approval of the transaction by disinterested and independent directors). *See also* Harold Marsh Jr., *Are Directors Trustees?*, 22 Bus. Law. 35, 39–43 (1966) (and cases cited therein). Note that in cash-out mergers under Delaware law whereby the parent corporation takes the publicly held subsidiary private, informed approval of the merger by disinterested shareholders shifts the burden to the plaintiffs to prove unfairness. *See, e.g., Weinberger v. UOP, Inc.*, 457 A.2d 701, 710 (Del. 1983); Marc I. Steinberg and Evalyn N. Lindahl, *The New Law of Squeeze-Out Mergers*, 62 Wash. U. L.Q. 351, 371–73 (1984).

[41] *See, e.g., American Mining Corporation v. Theriault*, 51 A.3d 1213, 1239–40 (Del. 2012); *Emerald Partners v. Berlin*, 726 A.2d 1215, 1222–23 (Del. 1999); *Kahn v. Lynch Communication, Inc.*, 638 A.2d 1110, 1117 (Del. 1994); discussion in Chapter 6, notes 60–65 and accompanying text.

[42] *See, e.g., American Mining Corporation*, 51 A.3d at 1240 (also stating: "Regardless of where the burden lies, when a controlling shareholder stands on both sides of the transaction, the conduct of the parties will be viewed under the more exacting standard of entire fairness as opposed to the more deferential business judgment standard"); cases cited note 41 *supra*.

[43] For purposes of this discussion, the term "independent" encompasses both the terms "independent" and "disinterested." *See, e.g.,* Georgia Code Ann. § 14-2-744 Comment (Although "decisions that have examined the qualifications of special litigation committees have required that they be both 'disinterested' in the sense of not having a personal interest in the transaction being challenged as opposed to a benefit that devolves upon the corporation or all shareholders generally and 'independent' in the sense of not being influenced in favor of the defendants by reason of personal or other

that should be made in the derivative suit setting while being mindful of the status of independent directors as "discretionaries."

With respect to shareholder demand on the board of directors, the universal demand rule is the appropriate standard: unless irreparable harm will occur, a stockholder seeking to institute a derivative action must make a demand on the corporation's board of directors. Hence, the demand requirement is a necessary condition to be satisfied prior to a plaintiff-shareholder's filing of a derivative suit. This position comports with the universal demand statutes enacted by many states.[44]

Requiring that demand must be made on a subject company's board of directors is good policy. Like other significant corporate decisions, litigation decisions normally are made by the board of directors. With some frequency, derivative actions are sought to be brought for their perceived settlement value.[45] In certain situations, the benefits that may accrue from a potential recovery are substantially outweighed by the costs to the company that would be incurred.[46] Moreover, even in situations where a prospective derivative action pursues creditable claims, the corporation may well be better served by utilizing its internal processes to inquire into and, if appropriate, implement corrective measures to remediate the situation presented.[47] Accordingly, universal demand on the board of directors ordinarily serves the best interests of the subject corporation and its shareholders.[48]

After conducting their assessment, the independent directors (or special litigation committee (SLC) comprised solely of independent directors)

---

relationships, [this statute uses] only the word 'independent' . . . because this word necessarily also includes the requirement that a person have no interest in the transaction").

[44] *See, e.g.*, MBCA § 7.42. Approximately 20 states require universal demand based on the Model Business Corporation Act. For a listing of several of these states, *see* Chapter 5, at note 58.

[45] *See, e.g.*, American Law Institute, *Principles of Corporate Governance: Analysis and Recommendations* vol. 2, at 6 (stating that "in both class and derivative litigation, incentives exists for a private enforcer to bring a non-meritorious action for its nuisance or settlement value").

[46] *See Joy v. North*, 692 F.2d 880, 892 (2d Cir. 1982) (applying Connecticut law) (stating that "judicial scrutiny of special litigation committee recommendations should be limited to a comparison of the direct costs imposed upon the corporation by the litigation with the potential benefits"); ALI, *Principles of Corporate Governance*, *supra* note 45, vol. 2, at 6 ("Experience suggests that the social costs associated with intracorporate litigation can sometimes outweigh the benefits").

[47] *See Spiegel v. Buntrock*, 571 A.2d 767, 773 (Del. 1990) ("The purpose of pre-suit demand is to assure that the stockholder affords the corporation the opportunity to address an alleged wrong without litigation, to decide whether to invest the resources of the corporation in litigation, and to control any litigation which does occur").

[48] *See* discussion in Chapter 5, notes 60–63 and accompanying text. Note, however, that in the close corporation setting, the shareholder should be able to pursue the derivative action without making a demand on the board of directors. *See* discussion in Chapter 7, notes 16–19 and accompanying text.

typically determine that the derivative action is not in the company's best interests.[49] The governing principle that courts and statutes ordinarily apply to that determination is the business judgment rule.[50] Unlike the traditional invocation of the business judgment rule where it shields entrepreneurial or operational decisions made by boards of directors, the rule is used as a sword in this setting to preclude the bringing of shareholder derivative actions alleging breaches of fiduciary duty.[51] By granting dismissal of these actions, judicial review of the propriety of the underlying alleged director or officer misconduct never occurs.[52]

In view of this severe impact—that shareholders are unable to seek recompense on their corporation's behalf and substantive judicial review of the underlying alleged director or officer misconduct (e.g., an interested director transaction) is precluded—it stands to reason that meaningful standards would exist. For the most part, however, as addressed in Chapter 5, the precise opposite is frequently the case: An expansive version of the business judgment rule applies where the only criteria are the independence of the directors that recommend dismissal, their good faith, and that they conducted a reasonable inquiry upon which their conclusions are based.[53]

---

[49] *See, e.g.*, Ralph C. Ferrara, et al., *Shareholder Derivative Litigation: Besieging the Board* § 8.06 (1995 and supp.) (stating that "it is well established that special litigation committees have sided with the defendants in an overwhelming number of cases in which they have been employed"); Jonathan R. Macey, *Corporate Governance: Promises Kept, Promises Broken* 65 (2008) (commenting that "SLCs uniformly recommend that derivative actions ... be dismissed"); Daniel J. Morrissey, *The Path of Corporate Law: Of Options Backdating, Derivative Suits, and the Business Judgment Rule*, 86 Or. L. Rev. 973, 1003 (2007) (asserting that SLCs "almost always recommend dismissal"); Charles W. Murdock, *Corporate Governance—The Role of Special Litigation Committees*, 68 Wash. L. Rev. 79, 84 (1993) (opining that "invariably the [special litigation] committee moves to dismiss the litigation"); James D. Cox, *Searching for the Corporation's Voice in Derivative Suit Litigation: A Critique of Zapata and the ALI Project*, 1982 Duke L.J. 959, 963 (stating that "in all but one [case] the [special litigation] committee concluded that the suit in question was not in the corporation's best interests"). *But see* Minor Myers, *The Decision of the Corporate Special Litigation Committees: An Empirical Investigation*, 84 Ind. L.J. 1309, 1311 (2009) (based on original data, finding that SLCs "sought some form of formal relief much more frequently than heretofore recognized: approximately forty percent of the time, SLCs pursued or settled claims against one or more defendants").

[50] *See, e.g.*, MBCA § 7.44 (as adopted in approximately 20 states) (*see* Chapter 5, at note 58); *Boland v. Boland*, 31 A.3d 529 (Md. 2011); *Auerbach v. Bennett*, 393 N.E.2d 994 (N.Y. 1979); *Desigoudar v. Meyercord*, 108 Cal. App. 4th 173 (2003); discussion in Chapter 5, notes 34–39 and accompanying text. As discussed in Chapter 6, with respect to Delaware incorporated companies, the business judgment rule does not apply in demand-excused cases. *See Zapata Corp. v. Maldonado*, 430 A.2d 779, 788–89 (Del. 1981); note 58 *infra*; discussion in Chapter 5, notes 40–57 and accompanying text.

[51] *See Maldonado v. Flynn*, 413 A.2d 1251, 1257 (Del. Ch. 1980), *rev'd and remanded sub nom., Zapata Corp. v. Maldonado*, 430 A.2d 779 (Del. 1981) (stating that the business judgment rule "provides a shield with which directors may oppose stockholders' attacks on the decisions made by them but nothing in it grants any independent power to a corporate board of directors to terminate a derivative suit").

[52] *See* discussion in Chapter 5, notes 25–33, 55–80 and accompanying text.

[53] *See, e.g.*, MBCA § 7.44(a) (as adopted in approximately 20 states) (*see* Chapter 5, at note 58) (requiring dismissal of a derivative action if a majority of the independent directors or a

The reasonableness of the special litigation committee's determination that the derivative action is not in the corporation's best interests and accordingly should be dismissed is beyond judicial review.[54]

This standard slights board dynamics of structural bias and other relationship factors that impede impartial assessment.[55] With directors having similar backgrounds and work experiences as well as sharing a common bond of being colleagues on the same board of directors, it is not surprising that independent directors nearly always determine that the subject derivative action is contrary to the company's best interests.[56] In this manner, derivative actions that strike at the heart of corporate governance practices are foreclosed, thereby precluding adjudication of the underlying alleged director or officer misconduct. A more balanced approach should be adopted. The more balanced view advanced herein comes from decisions handed down by the Delaware and North Carolina courts,[57] with modifications proffered. First, absent irreparable harm, universal demand on the board of directors is required in all situations. Second, the special litigation committee must establish that its members were independent. Third, the SLC must show that it acted in good faith and conducted a reasonable inquiry concerning the alleged misconduct. Fourth, the members of the SLC must be privy to all material information when making their assessment. Fifth, the determination by the special litigation committee that the derivative action should be dismissed must have a reasonable basis.[58] With respect to this last

committee thereof "has determined in good faith, after conducting a reasonable inquiry upon which its conclusions are based, that the maintenance of the derivative suit is not in the best interests of the corporation"); *Auerbach v. Bennett*, 393 N.E.2d 994, 1000-03 (N.Y. 1979).

[54] *See, e.g.*, MBCA § 7.44 Official Comment ("Section 7.44(a) does not authorize the court to review the reasonableness of the determination to reject a demand or seek a dismissal").
[55] *See* discussion in Chapter 5, notes 73–77 and accompanying text.
[56] *See, e.g., Hasen v. Clevetrust Realty Investors*, 729 F.3d 372, 376 (6th Cir. 1982) ("The delegation of corporate power to a special committee, the members of which are hand-picked by defendant directors, carries with it inherent structural biases"); *Joy v. North*, 619 F.2d 880, 888 (2d Cir. 1982) ("It is not cynical to expect that such committee will tend to view derivative actions against the other directors with skepticism"); sources cited note 49 *supra;* sources cited in Chapter 5, at notes 75–76.
[57] *See Zapata Corporation v. Maldonado*, 430 A.2d 779 (Del. 1981) (demand-excused situations); *Alford v. Shaw*, 358 S.E.2d 323 (N.C. 1987). Note that *Alford* no longer is good law in North Carolina in view of that state's enactment of the MBCA statute. *See* discussion in Chapter 5, notes 82–83 and accompanying text.
[58] This proposed approach is similar to that adopted by a number of courts. *See, e.g., Zapata*, 430 A.2d at 788–89 (In situations where demand on the board of directors is excused: "If the Court determines either that the [special litigation] committee is not independent or has not shown reasonable bases for its conclusions, or, if the Court is not satisfied for other reasons relating to the process, including but not limited to the good faith of the committee, the Court shall deny the corporation's motion"); *Alford*, 358 S.E.2d at 326 (in all derivative actions, the court is to examine the SLC's independence, good faith, adequacy of its inquiry, and the merits of the SLC's recommendations); *In re*

criterion, the complainant has the burden of persuasion that the SLC's determination lacks a reasonable basis. In this regard, the shareholder-plaintiff must be afforded adequate discovery, including the taking of deposition testimony and document production as ordered within the sound discretion of the court.[59]

This approach is consistent with the status of corporate directors and officers as discretionaries. Generally, so long as these dismissal determinations are made by adequately informed independent directors in good faith and have a reasonable basis, they should be validated. With the complainant bearing the burden of persuasion in regard to whether there exists a reasonable basis for the independent directors' determination, deference is accorded to the independent directors' ultimate decision. In this manner, independent directors in their assessment whether shareholder derivative litigation should proceed act as "discretionaries" pursuant to the criteria set forth herein.

VII. "Independent" Director: Misapplication of Standards

Even when seemingly strict standards are enunciated to apply to director and officer conduct in their perceived role as fiduciaries, a marked difference is seen between rhetoric and application. This contrast is illustrated throughout this book, particularly with respect to standards of conduct as compared to standards of review (namely, standards of liability).[60] At this point, one last vivid example is provided which addresses the deference

---

PSE & G Shareholder Litigation, 801 A.2d 295, 312 (N.J. 2002) (in all derivative actions, the court is to assess the SLC's independence, good faith, adequacy of its inquiry, and the reasonableness of its decision); discussion in Chapter 5, notes 82–90 and accompanying text.

[59] Without procuring such discovery, a derivative plaintiff's task of successfully disputing the directors' independence, their good faith, adequacy of their inquiry, and the reasonableness of their recommendation that the derivative suit should be dismissed would be too arduous. Moreover, unlike several of the decisions adopted by courts, the proposal advanced herein places the burden of persuasion that the SLC's determination lacks a reasonable basis on the derivative plaintiffs. *See* discussion in Chapter 5, notes 82–90 and accompanying text.

[60] The contrast between standards of conduct and standards of review is addressed in several chapters herein. *See, e.g.*, discussion in Chapter 1, notes 33–41 and accompanying text.

given by statutes and courts to decisions made by independent directors.[61] While this deference may well be warranted if the determinations were in fact made by directors who truly were independent, with frequency, courts deem directors independent when, in actuality, they are biased in favor of their colleagues.

Decisions made by independent directors are given substantial deference under state corporation law. As discussed in this book, examples where legislatures and courts confer such deference include interested director transactions, M&A conflicted transactions, the termination of shareholder derivative actions, and defensive tactics utilized by target companies to fend off hostile takeover bids. Such deference is warranted provided that these directors in fact are independent. All too often, however, directors who are defined as independent in fact are not, thereby rendering such deference unwarranted.[62]

---

[61] Stated generally, pursuant to stock exchange rules, provided that a director does not have a material relationship with the subject company (other than serving as a director), such director is deemed independent. The rules enumerate specific situations where a director is not independent. See NYSE Manual § 303A.02; Nasdaq, Inc. Stock Market Rule § 5605(a). For example, the NYSE rules set forth five situations where a director is deemed to be not independent. These rules also apply to such director's immediate family members. Stated succinctly, these five situations are as follows:

(1) Being an employee or executive officer of the listed company within the last three years;
(2) Having been directly compensated (other than receipt of director and committee fees or payment of deferred compensation based on prior service) more than $120,000 by the listed company within any twelve-month period during the last three years;
(3) Being a current employee or partner of the listed company's internal or external auditor;
(4) Being or having been an executive officer within the past three years of another company where any of the listed company's current executive officers "serves or served" on such other company's compensation committee;
(5) Being a current employee of an enterprise that within any of the past three fiscal years "has made payments to, or received payments from, the listed company for property or services," provided such amount "exceeds the greater of $1 million, or 2% of such other [enterprise's] consolidated gross revenues."

Marc I. Steinberg, *The Federalization of Corporate Governance* 235 (2018), *quoting and summarizing*, NYSE Manual § 303A.02(b).

[62] Indeed, in many of these decisions, the Delaware courts held that the plaintiffs failed to even allege a reasonable doubt that the subject directors lacked independence. Or, stated differently, that the plaintiffs failed to show even a five percent possibility that the subject directors were not independent. The myth of Delaware's reasonable doubt standard with respect to alleging a director's lack of independence is addressed in Chapter 5, notes 53–57 and accompanying text.

Pursuant to statute and case law, directors have been deemed independent in situations where, for example: (1) the outside directors were dependent on the defendant who owned 47 percent of the corporation's common stock for their continued positions and were subject to removal from their director positions at such defendant's behest;[63] (2) an outside director was the mentor of the defendant founder and CEO of the subject corporation;[64] (3) an outside director was a friend of the defendant director;[65] (4) an outside director and defendant director were social acquaintances;[66] (5) an outside director who was the sole member of the SLC belonged to the same golf club as the former chairman of the company's board of directors;[67] (6) an outside director's employer had a business relationship with the subject company whose CEO, chair of its board of directors, and majority shareholder was the principal defendant;[68] (7) an outside director approved the conduct or transaction that was the subject of a derivative action;[69] (8) due to his approval of a challenged transaction that was the subject of the lawsuit, an

---

[63] See, e.g., Aronson v. Lewis, 473 A.2d 805, 815 (Del. 1984) (There, the plaintiff-shareholder alleged that the defendant Fink dominated and controlled the company's board of directors because he owned 47 percent of the corporation's outstanding shares and personally selected each incumbent director. Rejecting that assertion, the Delaware Supreme Court stated: "Such contentions do not support any claim under Delaware law that these directors lack independence"). Note that Delaware courts have opined that shareholders who owned less than 50 percent of the subject company's outstanding stock may be controlling shareholders because of their "ability to exert influence as a stockholder, in the boardroom, and outside of the boardroom through managerial roles." *Tornetta v. Musk*, 310 A.3d 430, 497–520 (holding that Elon Musk is a controlling shareholder of Tesla with ownership of 21 percent of the outstanding stock); *id.* at 498 n. 556 (citing several Delaware decisions declining to grant motions to dismiss where it was "reasonably conceivable" that shareholders owning far less than 50 percent of the outstanding shares were controllers).

[64] See, e.g., United Food and Commercial Workers Union v. Zuckerberg, 262 A.3d 1034, 1063 (Del. 2021) (There, the plaintiff-shareholder alleged that defendant director Peter Thiel was not independent because, among other reasons, he "is Zuckerberg's close friend and mentor." In reply, the court held that "[t]hese allegations do not raise a reasonable doubt that Thiel is beholden to Zuckerberg" or that he "lacks independence" from Zuckerberg.).

[65] See id. ("alleging that Thiel is a personal friend of Zuckerberg is insufficient to establish a lack of independence").

[66] See, e.g., Marchand v. Barnhill, 212 A.3d 805, 820 (Del. 2019) (stating that "the fact that fellow directors are social acquaintances who occasionally have dinner or go to common events does not, in itself, raise a fair inference of non-independence").

[67] See, e.g., Teamsters Local 443 Health Services & Insurance Plan v. Chou, 2023 WL 7986729, at * 31 (Del. Ch. 2021) (finding that this relationship was "not disabling or suspicious").

[68] See, e.g., Beam ex rel. Martha Stewart Living Omnimedia v. Stewart, 845 A.2d 1040, 1051–52 (Del. 2004) (allegations of "mere personal friendship or a mere outside business relationship, standing alone are insufficient" to show lack of independence and thereby excuse demand on the board of directors).

[69] See, e.g., Lewis v. Graves, 701 F.2d 245, 248 (2d Cir. 1983) ("The fact that a corporation's directors have previously approved transactions subsequently challenged in a derivative suit does not inevitably lead to the conclusion that those directors, bound by their fiduciary obligations to the

outside director was a named defendant in a derivative action;[70] and (9) an outside director was nominated to the board of directors by a defendant director who engaged in a self-dealing transaction that was the subject of the derivative action.[71]

To expect that a director who is a mentor, a friend, or has another significant personal or business relationship with another director (or officer) to act impartially when her colleague's conduct is at issue belies reality. The same holds true when an outside director herself is alleged to have engaged in actionable misconduct when approving a challenged transaction or other matter. A more sensible definition of independence should be embraced.[72] A director should be precluded from being considered independent if there is either the presence of a friendship, social, or business relationship between such director (or such director's family or employer) and a defendant director or officer. Moreover, if an outside director himself is being sued as a consequence of his alleged misconduct, that predicament also should preclude such director from independent director status for purposes of that litigation. Clearly, the standard for defining an independent director, as implemented in practice, should be improved in order to help ensure

---

corporation, will refuse to take up the suit [and that] excusing demand on the mere basis of prior board acquiescence, therefore, would obviate the need for demand in practically every case").

[70] See, e.g., MBCA § 1.43(c)(3) ("The presence of one or more of the following circumstances shall not automatically prevent a director from being a qualified director: ... (3) With respect to action to be taken [in a derivative action] under section 7.44, status as a named defendant...."); id. Official Comment ("Subsection (c)(3) confirms a number of decisions, involving dismissal of derivative proceedings, in which the court rejected a disqualification claim predicated on the mere fact that a director had been named as a defendant, was an individual against whom action has been demanded, or had approved the action being challenged").

[71] See, e.g., MBCA § 1.43(c)(1); id. Official Comment ("Special litigation committees acting with regard to derivative litigation often consist of directors nominated or elected (after the alleged wrongful acts) by directors named as defendants in the action").

[72] In its decisions, the Delaware courts at times have espoused standards that may be viewed as more favorable to shareholder-plaintiffs in ascertaining whether a subject director is independent. See, e.g., Zuckerberg, 262 A.3d at 1061 (emphasis supplied) ("The plaintiff must allege that the director in question had ties to the person whose proposal or actions he or she is evaluating that are sufficiently substantial that he or she could not objectively discharge his or her fiduciary duties. In other words, the question is whether ... the alleged ties *could* have affected the impartiality of the individual director." Yet when applying these standards, unless a director has financially benefitted from the challenged transaction or is clearly under the domination or control of a subject defendant (such as being an employee of a corporation with respect to which a challenged transaction financially benefits the CEO), shareholder-plaintiffs have a hefty burden to show lack of independence. For example, in *Zuckerberg*, the Delaware Supreme Court held that a reasonable doubt was not raised with respect to director Thiel's independence even though Thiel was alleged to be Zuckerberg's "close friend and mentor." *Id.* at 1063.

that decisions made by boards of directors and committees thereof are as impartial and free from bias as practicable. This assertion holds true irrespective of whether independent directors are identified as fiduciaries or discretionaries. A decisionmaker deemed independent in fact should be so. Currently, this is not the case. Accordingly, corrective measures should be implemented to ameliorate the illusory applications of director independent status that currently exist.

VIII. Conclusion

This chapter addresses the appropriate standards that should apply with respect to the monetary liability of corporate directors and officers as discretionaries. As the law relating to director and officer liability is well-developed, proposing alternative standards without adequate focus on ensconced legal principles likely would be a futile effort. With this backdrop in mind, the chapter examines several but by no means all of the situations where director and officer liability exposure arises and seeks to espouse standards that are adaptable to implementation. Although directors and officers are not fiduciaries, they nonetheless should be held accountable to their companies and shareholders pursuant to norms of corporate governance that are reconcilable with current liability standards and aptly serve corporate, shareholder, and public policy interests. From this perspective, the chapter seeks to formulate an improved and practical corporate governance liability framework that, at least to some degree, comports with currently prevailing standards. Corporate directors and officers are "discretionaries" and should be subject to realistic and meaningful corporate governance standards.

10
The Clear Reality: "Discretionaries" Not Fiduciaries

I. Corporate Directors and Officers Are "Discretionaries"

The principal theme of this book focuses on the fact that corporate directors and officers are "discretionaries" rather than fiduciaries. Although at times fiduciary duties of substance apply to director and officer conduct, the liability standards that ordinarily exist are far too lenient to be characterized as fiduciary. In view of this reality, to identify corporate directors and officers as fiduciaries perpetuates a fiction that should be remedied. This book creates a new term that accurately portrays the status of corporate directors and officers: They are "discretionaries" who are held to varying standards of liability depending on the applicable facts and circumstances. As this book shows, with frequency, the liability standards to which directors and officers are subject lack fiduciary substance. By way of example, the following ten situations addressed in preceding chapters illustrate the laxity that prevails:

(1) In Delaware, breach of the duty of care requires proof that the defendant director or officer acted with *gross negligence*.[1] As stated by the Delaware courts: "In the corporate context, gross negligence means *reckless indifference* to or a *deliberate disregard* of the whole body of stockholders or actions which are *without the bounds of reason*."[2] In other contexts, a defendant who acts with this degree of culpability may incur punitive damages.[3]

---

[1] *See, e.g., United Food and Commercial Workers Union v. Zuckerberg*, 262 A.3d 1034, 1049 (Del. 2021) (stating that the duty of care is "predicated upon concepts of gross negligence"); cases cited in Chapter 3, at notes 20, 22.

[2] *In re DSI Renal Holdings, LLC*, 574 B.R. 446, 470 (D. Del. 2017) (emphasis supplied), *quoting Benihana of Tokyo, Inc. v. Benihana, Inc.*, 891 A.2d 150, 192 (Del. Ch. 2005) (emphasis supplied).

[3] *See, e.g.,* Gross Negligence, *Black's Law Dictionary* 1246 (11th ed. 2019) (defining gross negligence as "a conscious, voluntary act or omission in reckless disregard of a legal duty and of the consequences to another party, who may typically recover exemplary damages"); discussion in Chapter 3, notes 43–54 and accompanying text.

Corporate Director and Officer Liability. Marc I. Steinberg, Oxford University Press.
© Marc I. Steinberg 2025. DOI: 10.1093/9780197751534.003.0010

(2) To rebut the presumption of the business judgment rule, the subject directors must have a disabling conflict of interest or act with *gross negligence*.[4] In the words of Delaware Vice Chancellor Laster: *"To hold a director liable for gross negligence requires conduct more serious than what is necessary to secure a conviction for criminal negligence."*[5]

(3) The enactment by Delaware (and many other states) of *exculpation statutes* signify that absent a breach of the duty of loyalty or other improper self-dealing conduct, directors and (in certain situations) officers are monetarily liable only if they act with *intentional misconduct*.[6]

(4) Providing an even more lenient standard, several states have enacted statutes that *exculpate directors and officers for breaches of the duty of loyalty*. For example, the Nevada statute is self-executing, providing that an officer or director is not liable to the corporation, shareholders, or creditors unless it is proven that such officer or director breached a fiduciary duty *and* "such breach involved *intentional misconduct, fraud, or a knowing violation of law.*"[7]

(5) In Delaware, directors breach their duty of good faith with respect to their oversight functions only if they "*utterly failed* to implement *any* reporting or information system or controls; or having implemented such a system or controls, *consciously failed* to monitor or oversee its operations...."[8]

(6) With respect to self-dealing interested director transactions, as provided by the Model Business Corporation Act and as enacted

---

[4] *See, e.g., Aronson v. Lewis*, 473 A.2d 805, 812 (Del. 1985) (stating that "under the business judgment rule director liability is predicated upon concepts of gross negligence"); discussion in Chapter 3, notes 25–52 and accompanying text.

[5] *In re McDonald's Corporation Stockholder Derivative Litigation*, 291 A.3d 652, 690 n. 21 (Del. Ch. (2023) (emphasis supplied). Under Delaware law, criminal negligence is defined as follows:

> A person acts with criminal negligence with respect to an element of an offense when the person fails to perceive a risk that the element exists or will result from the conduct. The risk must be of such a nature and degree that failure to perceive it constitutes a gross deviation from the standard of conduct that a reasonable person would observe in the situation.

11 Del. Code § 231(a).

[6] *See, e.g., New Enterprise Associates 14 L.P. v. Rich*, 295 A.3d 520, 551 (Del. 2023) (stating that § 102(b)(7) "permits exculpation for recklessness"); discussion in Chapter 3, notes 64–66 and accompanying text.

[7] Nev. Rev. Stat. § 78.138(7) (emphasis supplied). For other state statutes that authorize exculpation for directors and officers with respect to certain breaches of the duty of loyalty, *see* Chapter 4, notes 43–51 and accompanying text.

[8] *Stone v. Ritter*, 911 A.2d 362, 370 (Del. 2006) (emphasis supplied). *See* discussion in Chapter 4, notes 58–78 and accompanying text.

by many states, *a broad business judgment rule standard* applies, foreclosing judicial scrutiny of the propriety of such transactions upon the approval of adequately informed disinterested and independent directors.[9]

(7) With respect to the seizing of *corporate opportunities*, under Delaware law as well as many other state statutes, a corporation by means of a provision contained in its articles of incorporation or by a board-promulgated bylaw amendment or a board resolution may allow its *directors and officers to take "specified business opportunities or specified classes or categories of business opportunities...."*[10]

(8) Under the American Law Institute's standard, enacted by several states, an outside director under certain circumstances properly may take for her own benefit a *corporate opportunity* that is in such *corporation's line of business (or closely related thereto).*[11]

(9) If specified conditions are met, pursuant to a shareholder agreement, the affected shareholders *may waive breaches of the duty of loyalty*, including with respect to *"self-dealing transactions [engaged in by defendant directors and officers who act] with reckless disregard for the best interests of the company."*[12]

(10) Pursuant to the Model Business Corporation Act's *derivative suit* provisions, enacted by many states, as well as Delaware law in cases where demand on the subject corporation's board of directors is required, *the business judgment rule* applies to a determination made by independent directors that a derivative action should be dismissed—*including in cases involving alleged self-dealing and breaches of the duty of loyalty by defendant corporate directors and*

---

[9] *See* MBCA § 8.61 Official Comment (providing that, if the requisite procedures are complied with and disinterested director is approved, "then a director's conflicting interest transaction is immune from attack by a shareholder or the corporation on the ground of an interest of the director"). For a listing of several states that have adopted the MBCA approach, *see* Chapter 4, note 90. For further discussion, *see* Chapter 4, notes 86–93 and accompanying text.

[10] Del. Gen. Corp. L. § 122(17) (emphasis supplied). For a listing of other states that have enacted similar statutes, *see* Chapter 4, note 21. For further discussion, *see* Chapter 4, notes 21–33 and accompanying text.

[11] These circumstances are that, in connection with the opportunity, the outside director was not: carrying out her functions as a director; employing corporate resources to avail herself of the opportunity; or offered the opportunity with the understanding that such opportunity was to be offered to the corporation. *See* American Law Institute, *Principles of Corporate Governance: Analysis and Recommendations* § 5.05(b) (1994); discussion in Chapter 4, notes 110–114 and accompanying text.

[12] *New Enterprise Associates 14, LP v. Rich*, 295 A.3d 520, 593 (Del. Ch. 2023) (emphasis supplied). *See* discussion in Chapter 4, notes 12–20 and accompanying text; Chapter 7, notes 65–74 and accompanying text.

officers.[13] With these examples in focus, the next section of this chapter reviews the book's scope, concepts, and objectives.

II. A Review of the Book's Scope, Concepts, and Objectives

The first chapter of the book provides an overview of the book's contents, including its purposes, themes, and public policy objectives. Chapter 2 addresses fiduciary duties in unincorporated business enterprises, including partnerships and limited liability companies (LLCs). To some extent, these duties, primarily from a historical perspective, also are examined in the corporate law setting. The chapter's objective is to highlight that the existence of fiduciary principles in partnerships and LLCs have been substantially diminished. The diminution largely is due to the presence of enabling statutes that authorize partners and LLC members pursuant to contractual agreement to decrease and, at times, eliminate fiduciary duties that otherwise would apply.[14] Because of this drastic reduction of the duties owed, general partners and LLC members, like corporate directors and officers, no longer should be deemed fiduciaries. Rather, these persons should be recognized as "discretionaries." Accordingly, the duties that these persons owe are dependent on the terms of the applicable governing agreement as well as the underlying facts and circumstances of the situation at issue.

Chapter 3 focuses on the liability exposure of directors and officers in situations where the duty of loyalty is *not* implicated. As the chapter addresses, directors and officers are rarely held liable for breach of the duty of care in either direct or derivative actions brought by shareholders.[15] To support this assertion, the chapter examines case and statutory law with respect to the duty of care, the business judgment rule, and director and officer exculpation statutes. The analysis evidences that liability premised on breach of the duty of care by a director or officer in a number of jurisdictions, including Delaware, requires proof of gross negligence.[16] With respect to the business judgment rule, as Vice Chancellor Laster opined, it is more difficult

---

[13] *See* MBCA § 7.44(a) (for a listing of many states that have enacted this provision, *see* Chapter 5, note 58); *United Food and Commercial Workers Union v. Zuckerberg*, 262 A.3d 1034 (Del. 2021); *Zapata Corp. v. Maldonado*, 430 A.2d 779 (Del. 1981); discussion in Chapter 5, notes 25–72 and accompanying text.

[14] *See* discussion in Chapter 2, notes 23–61 and accompanying text.

[15] *See* discussion in Chapter 3, notes 10–85 and accompanying text.

[16] *See, e.g.,* cases cited in Chapter 3, notes 20, 22.

for a plaintiff-stockholder to rebut the presumption of the rule than it is for a prosecutor to obtain a conviction for criminal negligence.[17] In regard to state exculpation statutes, directors (and officers in several states) can avoid monetary liability for duty of care breaches unless they engage in intentional misconduct.[18] Accordingly, corporate directors and officers are not fiduciaries. Rather than fiduciary principles being applied, legislatures and courts consider legal concepts and public policy to determine appropriate standards of liability for implementation. By establishing this framework in the duty of care context, corporate directors and officers are treated as "discretionaries"—being held accountable for specified obligations and frequently being subject to varying degrees of lax liability exposure.

Chapter 4 provides a broad-ranging treatment of this obligation. Although the duty of loyalty is implemented with vigor in certain situations, the overall enforcement of this duty has become far less demanding. From this perspective, the chapter focuses on the duty of loyalty with the objective of establishing that, with undue frequency, the strict standards enunciated are not applied with rigor when director and officer liability exposure is at issue. Like the subjects addressed elsewhere in this book, rhetoric often prevails over substantive application. To support this assertion, the chapter examines several situations where the duty of loyalty has been significantly diluted. First, the chapter discusses principles of waiver that diminish the application of the duty of loyalty.[19] Second, state statutes that exculpate certain director and officer breaches of the duty of loyalty are examined.[20] Third, the chapter focuses on the duty of good faith, deemed a component of the duty of loyalty by the Delaware Supreme Court, showing that laxity often prevails.[21] Fourth, self-dealing transactions, which historically were (but frequently no longer are) rigorously scrutinized for fairness,[22] are examined in the context principally of interested director transactions.[23] Fifth, the chapter addresses corporate directors and officers taking corporate opportunities with lenient standards all too often being applied.[24] The last section of the chapter provides insights into the dilution of the duty of loyalty with respect

---

[17] *In re McDonald's Corporation Stockholder Litigation*, 291 A.2d 652, 690 n. 21 (Del. Ch. 2023). *See* cases discussed and cited in Chapter 3, notes 45–53 and accompanying text.
[18] *See* discussion in Chapter 3, notes 59–85 and accompanying text.
[19] *See* discussion in Chapter 4, notes 10–41 and accompanying text.
[20] *See* discussion in Chapter 4, notes 42–55 and accompanying text.
[21] *See* discussion in Chapter 4, notes 56–78 and accompanying text.
[22] *See* discussion in Chapter 4, notes 79–84 and accompanying text.
[23] *See* discussion in Chapter 4, notes 79–93 and accompanying text.
[24] *See* discussion in Chapter 4, notes 94–114 and accompanying text.

to director and officer liability.[25] As evidenced by the materials covered in this chapter, the duty of loyalty has been diminished to such a degree that no longer should corporate directors and officers be deemed fiduciaries. More fittingly, they should be viewed as "discretionaries" whose obligations are defined by applicable facts and circumstances.

Chapter 5 focuses on derivative litigation, positing that the statutory and judicial standards that apply in this setting lack fiduciary substance. As a generality, much of the litigation that ensues as a consequence of alleged director and officer misconduct must be brought derivatively on the corporation's behalf rather than as direct actions.[26] Unlike a direct action, a shareholder instituting a derivative action ordinarily must make a demand on the company's board of directors.[27] In some jurisdictions, such as Delaware, demand may be excused if deemed futile.[28] In many states, a derivative action must be dismissed if adequately informed independent directors determine in good faith that the lawsuit is not in the corporation's best interests.[29] The singular inquiry is whether the decision by such independent directors to seek termination of the derivative suit is within the parameters of the business judgment rule.[30] If dismissal is granted, the legality of the alleged director or officer misconduct never is adjudicated. In making this determination whether to grant dismissal, lax standards frequently apply.[31] Pursuant to the adoption and implementation of these lenient standards, fiduciary standards are lacking. To provide a more accurate portrayal—independent directors (loosely defined) act as "discretionaries"—rather than fiduciaries—in effectuating the dismissal of derivative actions against their fellow directors and corporate officers.

Chapter 6 focuses on the duties of corporate directors and officers with respect to corporate mergers, acquisitions, and dispositions (M&A). Situations where parent corporations engage in transactions with one or

---

[25] *See* discussion in Chapter 4, notes 115–122 and accompanying text.
[26] *See* discussion in Chapter 5, notes 5–7 and accompanying text.
[27] *See* discussion in Chapter 5, notes 20–33, 58–65 and accompanying text.
[28] *See, e.g., United Food and Commercial Workers Union v. Zuckerberg*, 262 A.3d 1034 (Del. 2021); discussion in Chapter 5, notes 45–57 and accompanying text.
[29] *See* MBCA § 7.44(a) (requiring a court to dismiss the derivative action if it finds that the SLC comprised solely of independent directors "has determined in good faith, after conducting a reasonable inquiry, upon which its conclusions are based, that the maintenance of the derivative proceeding is not in the best interests of the corporation"). Many states have enacted this MBCA provision. For a listing of several of these states, *see* Chapter 5, note 58. For further discussion, *see* Chapter 5, notes 20–39, 66–72 and accompanying text.
[30] *See* discussion in Chapter 5, notes 20–39, 66–72 and accompanying text.
[31] *See, e.g.,* discussion in Chapter 5, notes 73–91 and accompanying text.

"DISCRETIONARIES" NOT FIDUCIARIES 201

more of their subsidiaries also are addressed.[32] The identification of corporate directors and officers as "discretionaries" is appropriate in the M&A setting. As discussed in this chapter, the presence of the business judgment rule in many M&A transactions, with its gross negligence culpability standard, evidences the absence of fiduciary standards.[33] Nonetheless, in certain other M&A situations, such as parent–subsidiary mergers, the standards that apply often have fiduciary substance.[34] Thus, acting as a "discretionary," a corporate director or officer must adhere to specified obligations that are diverse and have different levels of normative conduct. Pursuant to this framework, the chapter focuses on a wide array of M&A transactions. The conclusion reached is that identifying corporate directors and officers as "discretionaries" accurately reflects the legal standards to which these persons must adhere.

Chapter 7 focuses on the presence or waiver of fiduciary duties in close corporations. Generally, a close corporation is characterized by a relatively small number of shareholders, the absence of a ready-market where the company's securities may be traded, and substantial shareholder participation in the daily management and operations of the company.[35] Likened to partnerships, many courts apply heightened fiduciary duties in the close corporation setting.[36] This position is supported by the fact that unlike a general partner, a minority shareholder (absent valid shareholder consent or court order) generally cannot disassociate from and exit the corporation.[37] Nonetheless, it may be questioned whether this approach is appropriate in view of state partnership statutes that enable partners pursuant to a unanimous partnership agreement to significantly reduce their duties of care and loyalty.[38] Moreover, fiduciary duties in close corporations may be diluted pursuant to provisions contained in a subject company's articles of incorporation or in a unanimous shareholder agreement.[39] Hence, although many courts apply rigorous standards of fiduciary duty in the close corporation setting, it should be recognized that these standards may be minimized. This

---

[32] *See* discussion in Chapter 6, notes 58–80 and accompanying text.
[33] *See* discussion in Chapter 6, notes 7–23 and accompanying text.
[34] *See, e.g., Kahn v. M & F Worldwide Corp.*, 88 A.3d 635 (Del. 2014); *Weinberger v. UOP, Inc.*, 457 A.2d 701 (Del. 1983); discussion in Chapter 6, notes 58–65 and accompanying text.
[35] *See, e.g., Donahue v. Rodd Electrotype Co. of New England, Inc.*, 328 N.E.2d 505, 511 (Mass. 1975); discussion in Chapter 7, notes 1–4 and accompanying text.
[36] *See* discussion in Chapter 6, notes 20–35 and accompanying text.
[37] *See* discussion in Chapter 6, notes 28–30 and accompanying text.
[38] *See* discussion in Chapter 6, notes 40–45 and accompanying text.
[39] *See* discussion in Chapter 6, notes 46–74 and accompanying text.

assessment is consistent with the focus of this book—namely, that corporate directors and officers are "discretionaries" whose liability exposure varies depending on the underlying facts and circumstances.

Chapter 8 addresses concepts of fiduciary duty under the federal securities laws. Although the federal securities laws are premised principally on disclosure rather than substantive fairness,[40] fiduciary duty concepts arise in several contexts. On numerous occasions, the US Supreme Court has recognized that corporate directors and officers are fiduciaries.[41] For example, under Supreme Court precedent, the law of insider trading under the key antifraud provision, Section 10(b) of the Securities Exchange Act,[42] is premised on fiduciary duty analysis.[43] Moreover, fiduciary-like standards apply in the Securities Act registration statement setting by means of the invocation by directors and officers of the due diligence defense.[44] Nonetheless, although viewed as fiduciaries, lax liability standards often prevail. This laxity is evidenced, for example, by the scienter requirement mandated in Section 10(b) actions[45] as well as the permissive approach to forward-looking statements, statements of belief, and puffery whereby liability is imposed, if at all, only if a director or officer acts with intentional misconduct.[46] The propriety of these lax liability standards has been embraced by both the US Congress and the federal courts.[47] The consequence is that a glaring gap exists between the rhetoric and standards of liability in the federal securities law setting. As evidenced by this approach, in actuality, corporate directors and officers are not fiduciaries and their status should be redefined to accurately reflect reality. Hence, like company law, it is appropriate to define

---

[40] *See, e.g., Santa Fe Industries, Inc. v. Green*, 430 U.S. 462, 477–79 (1977).
[41] *See, e.g., Southern Pac. Co. v. Bogert*, 250 U.S. 483, 487–88 (1919) (Brandeis, J.); cases cited and discussed in Chapter 8, notes 14–28 and accompanying text.
[42] 15 U.S.C. § 78j(b).
[43] *See, e.g., Chiarella v. United States*, 445 U.S. 222, 230 (1980); discussion in Chapter 8, notes 25–27 and accompanying text.
[44] *See* § 11(c), 15 U.S.C. § 77k(c) (providing that, in determining whether a defendant, including a defendant director or officer, has satisfied the due diligence test, "what constitutes reasonable investigation and reasonable ground for belief, the standard of reasonableness shall be that required of a prudent man in the management of his own property"); *Escott v. BarChris Construction Corp.* 283 F. Supp. 643 (S.D.N.Y. 1968); discussion in Chapter 8, notes 29–50 and accompanying text.
[45] *See, e.g., Aaron v. Securities and Exchange Commission*, 446 U.S. 680 (1980); *Ernst & Ernst v. Hochfelder*, 425 U.S. 185 (1976); discussion in Chapter 8, notes 106–114 and accompanying text.
[46] *See* discussion in Chapter 8, notes 65–91, 115–120 and accompanying text.
[47] *See, e.g.,* § 21E of the Securities Exchange Act, 15 U.S.C. § 78u-5 (providing an expansive safe harbor for forward-looking statements made by Exchange Act reporting companies); *Omnicare, Inc. v. Laborers District Council Construction Industry Pension Fund*, 135 S. Ct. 1318 (2015) (requiring knowledge of the falsity with respect to statements of belief or opinion); discussion in Chapter 8, notes 65–91, 115–120 and accompanying text.

corporate directors and officers as "discretionaries" rather than cling to the fiduciary illusion.

Chapter 9 addresses the standards that should apply with respect to director and officer liability in their role as "discretionaries." While maintaining that directors and officers are not fiduciaries, the framework proposed in this chapter nonetheless must recognize the standards that are firmly established in determining director and officer liability exposure. Accordingly, the proposals advanced in this chapter must be reconcilable with current liability standards—at least to the extent that they are capable of practical implementation. From this perspective, the chapter focuses on significant concepts that impact director and officer liability. It expands upon subjects that are addressed earlier in this book, including the business judgment rule, exculpation statutes, the lack of good faith, related party transactions, derivative litigation, and independent directors.[48] The chapter seeks to formulate an improved and practical corporate governance framework that, at least to a meaningful degree, comports with currently prevailing standards. In sum, corporate directors and officers are "discretionaries" and should be subject to realistic and substantive corporate governance standards.

As set forth in this chapter and throughout the book, it is a misnomer to characterize corporate directors and officers as fiduciaries. While fiduciary standards exist in certain situations, more lenient criteria apply with far greater frequency. While the business judgment rule, exculpation statutes, and other director and officer protective measures may be perceived as consistent with corporate governance norms, their recognition is antithetical to fiduciary standards. Succinctly put, fiduciaries are held to higher standards than refraining from engaging in grossly negligent or more culpable misconduct. An accurate portrayal is that corporate directors and officers are "discretionaries" who are required to adhere to specified minimum standards of conduct to avoid monetary liability. In certain situations, meaningful fiduciary standards apply while in many other situations far more lax standards exist that are devoid of fiduciary substance. Accordingly, corporate directors and officers are "discretionaries" whereby their liability exposure is dependent upon the applicable facts and circumstances.

---

[48] *See* discussion in Chapter 9, notes 3–72 and accompanying text.

III. The Importance of This Book

Although admittedly viewed from the author's perspective, this book is important. Insofar as I am aware, this work is the first source that calls for the removal of fiduciary status for corporate directors and officers in favor of the adoption of a new term that provides an accurate description—corporate directors and officers are "discretionaries."

The continued mischaracterization of corporate directors and officers as fiduciaries is unacceptable. Clearly, legal principles and terms related thereto should be truthfully interpreted and should be applied to accurately implement these principles and terms. In other words, the law should be truthful. Identifying corporate directors and officers as fiduciaries while embracing lax liability standards presents a false portrayal. As explained in Chapter 1 of this book, this false portrayal is detrimental to the rule of law, contravenes reasonable investor expectations, and impairs the integrity of the financial markets.[49] No longer should the term fiduciary be used to characterize the status of corporate directors and officers. Fittingly, an accurate and neutral substantive term should be recognized—corporate directors and officers are "discretionaries."

---

[49] *See* discussion in Chapter 1, notes 8–14, 70–71 and accompanying text.

Index

For the benefit of digital users, indexed terms that span two pages (e.g., 52–53) may, on occasion, appear on only one of those pages.

actual knowledge, 64n.49, 161–62, 181n.17, 182–83
American Law Institute (ALI), 75–77, 78–79, 197
appraisal, 125–27

bad faith, 23–24, 37
board of directors, 44, 59, 111–12, 113–14, 115–20, 128, 129–30, 138. *See also* derivative litigation
   CEO and, 155–56
   chair, 155–56, 163, 192–93
   compliance system, 68–69
   corporate opportunity waiver, 58–59, 139
   Dodge v. Ford Motor Co., 20
   management and, 163
   power, 20, 57
   risk (report), 68–69
business, 19–20, 33–34, 129–30, 133–34, 169
   decision, 36–37, 40–41, 83–84, 92, 111, 178–79
   enterprise, 10–11, 77–78, 111–12, 113–14, 129
   ethics, 75
   executive (person), 31, 75, 78–79, 153–55
   need, 184–85
   opportunity, 57–58, 77–79, 139–40, 197
   purpose, 132–33
   relationship, 192–94
business judgment rule, 14, 20, 32, 34, 36–37, 39, 41, 81–82
   discretionary and, 1–2, 6–7, 102–3, 110, 114, 198–99, 200–1, 203
   fiduciary and, 5–6, 11, 32–33, 38–39, 41–42, 48, 72–73, 74
   presumption of, 37, 40–41, 48, 87–88, 181–82, 184–85, 196, 198–99
   scope of, 37–38
Business Roundtable ("Statement on the Purpose of a Corporation" 2019), 7

buy-out, 12–13, 112, 125n.64, 126–27, 134n.30, 134–36, 136n.40, 166n.102

care and loyalty, 10, 13, 22, 23–24, 30, 83–84, 201–2
   breach of, 11, 130–31, 138, 144, 180–81
Chiarella v. United States. See insider trading
chief executive officer (CEO), 7, 95, 192–93. *See also* board of directors
close corporation, 61, 129–35, 138
   fiduciary duty in, 10, 13, 59, 135–37, 138, 140–44
   management participation, 129, 201–2
   minority shareholder, 134–35, 136
   nonstatutory, 129, 132
   partnership status, 130–31
competing with the corporation, 19, 22–23, 83–84, 141–43
contractual waivers, 141–43
conflict of interest, 1–2, 12, 37, 41–42, 87–88, 128, 178, 184–85
controlling
   interest, 25, 123
   shareholder, 10, 12–13, 63, 122, 125–27, 128, 132–34, 135–36
corporate
   directors and officers, deference to, 36–37, 97–98, 114, 184–86, 190–91
   opportunity doctrine, 57–58, 77–79, 136–37, 139–40, 197
corporate governance, 3, 12, 47–48, 129, 155–56, 177–78, 179, 180–81. *See also* policy
   federalization, 145–46
   norms, 129–30, 141, 185–86, 194, 203
   participation in, 3
   principles, 58–59, 182–83
   sound practice, 10, 14, 97–98, 189–90
criminal liability, 41, 46, 59–60, 62, 63, 88, 114, 196

INDEX

damages, 1–2, 12–13, 43–44, 45–46, 47, 62, 63, 66–67
  exemplary, 39, 48
  post-closing, 111, 112, 121–22
Del. Gen. Corp. L. § 102(b)(7), 3n.10, 6n.23, 6n.26, 11n.47, 29n.68, 42–44, 56n.19, 57n.23
  Delaware Chancery Court, 27–28, 57–58, 88, 111, 120–21, 141–43
  intentional misconduct, 198–99
Delaware statute (corp. opportunity), 57, 78, 139
Delaware Supreme Court, 31, 44, 66–68, 87, 93–95, 117–18, 119, 121
  business judgment rule and, 115
  fiduciary duty and, 27–28, 39, 42, 51–52, 53–54, 56, 72–73, 103
  good faith and, 182, 199–200
  intentional misconduct and, 184–85
  mergers and, 125–26
  reckless misconduct and, 182–83
  self-dealing and, 122
  Smith v. Van Gorkom, 42
  Stone v. Ritter, 67–68
  target company, 115–18
  Unocal test, 115–19
demand excusal, 84, 89–90, 91–94, 95–96, 104, 106
demand on directors, 87, 89–90, 93, 97, 99, 103, 187
derivative litigation, 10, 12, 68–69, 98–99, 177–78, 186–87, 190, 200
  board of directors and, 84, 86–88, 92–94, 96–97, 98–99, 100–2
  corporate interests and, 92, 104
  demand excusal, 84, 89–90, 91–94, 95–96, 104, 106
  demand requirement, 87, 89–90, 93, 97, 99, 103, 187
  jurisdiction, 17–18, 48–49, 53, 74
  principles, 83, 85–86, 97n.61
  purpose (pre-suit demand), 187n.47
  self-dealing and, 192–93
  SLC, 84, 97–98, 106, 107, 187–88
  universal demand, 86, 95–96, 98–99, 102–3, 187, 189–90
director, 89–91, 107
  conflicted, 72–73, 74, 184–85
  independent, 12, 89, 98, 100, 106, 117, 186–87, 190
  inside, 98–99, 152–55, 174–75
  misconduct, 187–90
  outside, 5–6, 78–79, 82, 95–96, 98–99, 153–58, 174, 179

disclosure, 4, 24, 27–28, 112, 126–27, 163, 165, 174. *See also* federal securities law
  public policy and, 160–61
discovery, 91–92n.40, 93n.45, 106n.88, 168, 189–90
discretionaries, 100, 144, 174–75, 177–78, 181–82, 193–94, 195, 198–204
  business judgment rule and, 117, 121–22, 179, 185–86
  corporate, 4, 15, 16, 30, 53, 82, 83, 107
  liability of, 2, 6–7, 9–10, 15, 48–49, 86, 102–3
  mergers and, 110, 114, 127, 128
Dodd-Frank Act, 145–46
Drury v. Cross. *See* US Supreme Court
due diligence, 151–55, 156–57, 160–61, 163, 202–3
duty of
  care, 4, 31, 32, 35–36, 39, 42, 62, 137
  fiduciary, 51–52, 57–58, 59–60, 78–79, 80, 81
  good faith, 66–67, 81
  loyalty, 3, 51–52, 53, 58–59, 61–62, 65–66, 137, 182–83

entire fairness standard, 37n.27, 71n.83, 113n.16, 121, 123–24
equitable relief, 110, 121
Ernst & Ernst v. Hochfelder. *See* scienter
Escott v. Bar Chris Construction Corp. *See* registration statement
exculpation
  clause (provision), 42–45, 47–48, 62, 107, 121–22
  statute, 32–33, 41–42, 47–48, 141–43, 177–78, 180–82, 184–85, 196
exemplary damages, 39, 48
expectancy or interest test, 18–19, 57–58, 75–77, 78, 82, 139–40

fairness test, 75–77, 112n.12, 122, 123–24, 125–26, 128, 185–86
federal securities law, 13–14, 148–49, 153–55, 156–59, 160–61
  disclosure and, 13–14, 145–47, 148–49, 162, 165–66
  fiduciary identification and, 3
  intentional (knowing) misconduct, 180–81
  liability (exposure) under, 10, 146–47, 149–50, 162, 167–68, 173, 174, 202–3
  litigation, 164–65, 168–69, 174
  reckless (conduct) and, 65, 181–82
  SEC Rule 506(b) of Regulation D, 146–47
  shareholder proposal rule, 145–46
short sales, 145
Strong v. Repide, 148–49

fiduciary, 2–3, 20–21, 150, 153, 155–56, 166–67, 169–70, 172
  breach of duty, 53–54, 60–62, 63–67, 71–72, 80, 81, 149
  duty, 8, 13–14, 22–23, 26, 32–33, 36–37, 38–39, 47
  liability, 149–50, 162, 163, 167, 168–69, 170, 171–72, 173–75
forward-looking information, 14n.68

good faith, lack of, 62, 63, 128, 177–78, 182, 203
gross negligence, 1–2, 11, 14, 20, 22, 32–33, 34–37, 110

hostile takeover, 111, 115, 116, 119, 191

indemnification, 79–80n.114, 83n.2, 179
independent directors, 12, 89, 98, 100, 106, 117, 186–87, 190
information, 39, 44, 74, 91, 112, 119–20, 121–22, 153–55
  access, 153–55, 163, 170–71
  material nonpublic, 149
  parity, 170–71
  system, 67–69, 81
initial public offering (IPO), 153–55
  registration statement, 159–60
  SEC Rule 175 (future earnings), 159–60
injunction, 12–13, 32, 43n.60, 45–46, 110, 113n.16, 121
In re Brazilian Rubber Plantations and Estates. *See* management
inside directors, 98–99, 152–55, 174–75
insider trading, 13–14, 149, 170, 172, 202–3
  Chiarella v. United States, 149, 170
intent, 119
interested director transactions, 72–74, 81–82
Investment Company Act
  Gartenberg formulation, 173–74
  investment adviser, 173
  Jones v. Harris Associates L.P., 173
  section 36(b), 173–74

Jones v. Harris Associates L.P.. See Investment Company Act

knowledge, 5–6, 47, 160–62
Koehler v. The Black River Falls Iron Company. *See* US Supreme Court

liability, 47, 111, 130–31, 143, 161–62, 168, 190–91. *See also* federal securities law
  Delaware and, 39, 40–41, 42–47, 51, 52, 56–57, 64–65, 66–68

limitations on, 46
  monetary, 32–33, 41–46, 47, 48–49, 181–83, 184–85
  standards, 15–16, 173–74, 175, 177, 194, 195, 202–3, 204
limitations on liability, 46
limited liability companies (LLCs), 10–11, 17, 22–24, 25–29, 30, 198
  agreements, 23–24, 26–28, 29, 44, 136
line of business test, 82
litigation, 3. *See also* derivative litigation; federal securities law; mergers, acquisitions, and dispositions (M&A)
  corporate (business) decision, 87, 92, 187
loyalty, fiduciary duty of, 51–52, 57–58, 59–60, 78–79, 80, 81

majority, 40–41, 70–71, 73–74, 98–99, 111, 112, 113–14, 117
  independent director, 155–56
  independent stockholder, 124–25
  stockholder, 77–78, 123, 132–33, 192–93
  vote, 25
management, 19–20, 47–48, 117–18, 129–30, 151–52, 153–56, 158
  excessive compensation, 83–84
  In re Brazilian Rubber Plantations and Estates, 19–20
mergers, acquisitions, and dispositions (M&A)
  appraisal (short-form), 125–27
  business judgment rule and fiduciary standard in, 109, 110–11, 112–15, 120–22, 123–25, 128, 185–86, 191
  cash-out, 123–24, 185–86
  litigation, 109
  target company, 191
misconduct, 193–94, 200. *See also* Delaware Chancery Court; Delaware Supreme Court; officer
  Delaware statute, 196
  intentional, 22, 23–24, 42–43, 47, 63, 64–65, 137, 165
  Nevada statute, 196
  reckless, 181–82
Model Business Corporation Act (MBCA), 9, 32, 63, 73–74, 98–99, 100–1, 103–4, 184–85
  Alford v. Shaw, 103
  section 2.02(b)(4) (exculpatory provision), 59–60
  section 7.32(a)(8), 59–60
  universal demand statute, 102–3, 187

negligence, 31, 33–34
  gross, 1–2, 11, 14, 20, 22, 32–33, 34–37, 110

officer, 5–7, 11n.47, 38–39, 42–43, 66, 67–69, 198–99
 misconduct, 187–90, 200
Omnicare, Inc. v. Laborers District Council Construction Industry Pension Fund. See US Supreme Court
oppression, 133–34, 138
outside directors, 5–6, 78–79, 82, 95–96, 98–99, 153–58, 174, 179

partnership
 agreement, 23–25, 27–28, 60–61, 130–31, 136, 141, 201–2
 disclosure and, 24, 27–28, 29
Pepper v. Litton. See US Supreme Court
policy, 9–10, 79, 82, 89, 102–3, 115, 140–41, 187
 corporate charter provisions, 47–48
 corporate governance, 141, 194
 justifications for, 14
 liability exposure and, 198–99
 objectives, 198
 public, 12, 14, 44, 48–49, 59–61, 114, 130–31
Private Securities Litigation Reform Act (PSLRA), 13–14, 158, 161, 162, 168
projections, 159–60, 162, 163
proximate cause requirement, 33–34

reasonable doubt standard, 93–94, 95
recklessness, 40, 43–44, 46, 47, 65, 161–62, 180–82
registration statement, 151–55, 156–57, 158–59, 161–62, 163, 174, 202–3. *See also* initial public offering (IPO)
 Escott v. Bar Chris Construction Corp., 152–53
Revised Uniform Partnership Act, 130–31

sale of substantially all assets, 25, 111, 113–14
Santa Fe Industries, Inc. v. Green. See US Supreme Court
Sarbanes Oxley Act, 145–46, 155n.51
scienter, 166–67, 202–3
 Ernst & Ernst v. Hochfelder, 166–67
scrutiny
 corporate, 5–6, 38–39, 55–56, 70–71, 73–74, 81–82, 106, 109
 judicial, 55–56, 57–58, 70–71, 73–74, 81–82, 98, 99, 106
 officers and, 115, 121–22, 128, 141–43, 181–82, 183–84
SEC Rule 10b-5, 164–69, 174–75
Securities Act, 146–47, 150–52, 161, 202–3
 prudent man (standard), 151–52, 153–56, 158–61, 162, 163
 section 11 of, 151–53, 160–61, 174

Securities Exchange Act (Exchange Act), 13–14, 164–66, 202–3
 insider trading, 170–71
 purpose of, 165–67, 171–72
 section 10(b), 13–14, 149, 150
 section 10(b)-5, 164–69, 174–75
Securities Exchange Commission (SEC), 145–47, 161, 164–65, 166–67, 175
self-dealing transactions, 71–73, 74, 137
shareholder, 3. *See also* controlling; federal securities law
 primacy, 7–8
Smith v. Van Gorkom. See Delaware Supreme Court
Southern Pac. Co. v. Bogert. See US Supreme Court
special litigation committee (SLC), 192–93. *See also* derivative litigation
 independence and good faith of, 85, 89–91, 103, 104, 189–90
 misconduct and, 189–90
standard
 entire fairness, 37n.27, 71n.83, 113n.16, 121, 123–24
 fiduciary, 1, 3, 10–11, 15, 21, 107, 126–27, 153
 prudent man, 158
 reasonable doubt, 93–94, 95
state statutes
 Alabama, 59n.35, 63n.47
 Arizona, 59n.35, 96n.58, 180n.11
 Arkansas, 180n.11
 California, 180n.11
 Colorado, 180n.11
 Connecticut, 96n.58
 Delaware, 6n.23, 41n.53, 42–44, 47, 71n.82, 72n.85, 180n.11, 197n.10
 Florida, 6n.23, 59n.35, 96n.58
 Georgia, 59n.35, 180n.11, 186–87n.43
 Idaho, 180n.11
 Indiana, 6n.23, 45n.71, 46, 64
 Iowa, 180n.11
 Kansas, 57n.21, 180n.11
 Louisiana, 180n.11
 Maryland, 6n.26, 45n.72, 45, 57n.21, 62, 63
 Massachusetts, 6n.23, 180n.11
 Michigan, 180n.11
 Minnesota, 180n.11
 Missouri, 57n.21
 Montana, 180n.11
 Nebraska, 96n.58
 Nevada, 6n.26, 40–41, 45nn.71–72, 47, 63, 180n.12, 196

INDEX   209

New Jersey, 57n.21, 180n.11
New Mexico, 180n.11
New York, 180n.11
North Carolina, 96n.58, 180n.11
Ohio, 6n.23, 45n.71, 45–46, 62, 110n.6
Oklahoma, 57n.21, 180n.11
Oregon, 180n.11
Pennsylvania, 6n.23, 180n.11
Rhode Island, 180n.11
South Dakota, 180n.11
Texas, 57n.21, 74, 96n.58, 180n.11
Utah, 59n.35, 180n.11
Virginia, 6n.26, 45n.72, 46, 62, 96n.58
Washington, 57n.21, 180n.11
Wisconsin, 6n.23
Wyoming, 180n.11
statement of belief or opinion, 159–60
stockholder agreement, 54–56, 141–43
Stone v. Ritter. See Delaware Supreme Court
Strong v. Repide. See federal securities law

tender offer, 12–13, 112n.12, 113n.16, 166n.103
   hostile, 111
   issuer self-, 116
   judicial scrutiny of, 115
transactions
   buyout (going-private), 12–13, 112, 125n.64, 126–27, 134n.30, 134–36, 136n.40, 166n.102
   conflicted, 72–73, 74, 191
   conflicted-controller, 185–86
   interested director, 72–74, 81–82
   judicial scrutiny of, 196
   self-dealing, 71–73, 74, 137
Twin-Lick Oil Company v. Marbury. See US Supreme Court

Uniform Limited Liability Company Act (ULLCA), 22–24

Uniform Limited Partnership Act (ULPA), 22–24
unincorporated enterprise, 10–11, 27–30, 136, 198
Unocal test. *See* Delaware Supreme Court
US Supreme Court, 4, 18, 87–88, 146–50, 153, 165–66, 168, 170
   controlling stockholder conduct, 148
   deceptive/manipulative conduct, 165–66
   director conduct, 147–48
   Drury v. Cross, 147–48
   "fiduciary" corporate officer, 148, 172, 202–3
   "fiduciary" director, 147–48, 172, 202–3
   Koehler v. The Black River Falls Iron Company, 147–48
   Omnicare, Inc. v. Laborers District Council Construction Industry Pension Fund (Omnicare), 158–59
   outside director misconduct, 171–72
   Pepper v. Litton, 148
   precedent, 13–14
   Santa Fe Industries, Inc. v. Green (Santa Fe), 165–66
   scienter, 168
   Southern Pac. Co. v. Bogert, 148
   "trustee" director, 147–48
   Twin-Lick Oil Company v. Marbury, 147–48
   Wardell v. Railroad Company, 147–48
utmost good faith and loyalty, 13n.60, 76n.99, 132–33, 136

waiver
   contractual, 141–43
   corporate opportunity, 139–41
   fiduciary duties, 26–27, 53, 55–56, 57–58, 78, 80, 130–31
   public policy and, 55–56, 141–43
Wardell v. Railroad Company. See US Supreme Court
waste, 41n.53, 121, 123n.60

www.ingramcontent.com/pod-product-compliance
Lightning Source LLC
Chambersburg PA
CBHW070153020925
31867CB00043B/408